FORTRAN 77:
A Structured, Disciplined Style

FORTRAN 77: A Structured, Disciplined Style

1234567890WEBWEB89321098

ISBN 0-07-015905-x

This book was set in Clearface by Better Graphics, Inc.
The editors were David Shapiro and Sheila Gillams;
the cover was designed by Caliber Design Planning, Inc.;
the production supervisor was Denise L. Puryear.
New drawings were done by Caliber Design Planning, Inc.
Webcrafters, Inc. was printer and binder.

Library of Congress Cataloging-in-Publication Data

Davis, Gordon Bitter.
  FORTRAN 77: a structured, disciplined style.

  Includes index.
  1. FORTRAN (Computer program language)
  2. Structures programming.   I. Hoffmann,
Thomas Russell, (date)   II. Title.
QA76.73.F25D385 1988   005.13'3   88-2993
ISBN 0-07-015905-X

THIRD EDITION

FORTRAN 77: A *Structured,* Disciplined *Style*

Gordon B. Davis

Thomas R. Hoffmann
University of Minnesota

McGraw-Hill Book Company

New York   St. Louis   San Francisco   Auckland   Bogotá   Caracas
Colorado Springs   Hamburg   Lisbon   London   Madrid   Mexico   Milan
Montreal   New Delhi   Oklahoma City   Panama   Paris   San Juan
São Paulo   Singapore   Sydney   Tokyo   Toronto

Contents

Preface   vii

Introduction: Preparing to Program in FORTRAN   1

1

a Programming Discipline, the FORTRAN Language, and FORTRAN Statements to Write a Simple Program   19

b Example Programs and Programming Exercises to Read, Compute, and Print   46

2

a Intrinsic Functions, Integer-Type Data, Type Statement, IF Selection, Data Validation, and Introduction to Program Testing   64

b Example Programs and Programming Exercises Using Intrinsic Functions, IF Selection, and Data Validation   109

3

a Format-Directed Input and Output   136

b Example Programs and Programming Exercises Using Format-Directed Input and Output   171

v

4

a Repetition Program Structure, Subscripted Variables, and DO Loops 200

b Example Programs and Programming Exercises Using Subscripted Variables and DO Loops 229

5

a FORTRAN Subprograms and Case Program Structure 261

b Example Programs and Programming Exercises Using Subprograms and Case Structure 287

6

a Use of Files on External Storage 320

b Example Programs and Programming Exercises Using External Files 336

7

a Additional Features 362

b Example Programs and Programming Exercises Using Additional Features 390

Appendix A Differences between Versions of FORTRAN 411

Appendix B ASCII Standard Character Codes 419

Index 423

List of 1977 American National Standard FORTRAN Statements and Specifications 429

Preface

The FORTRAN language is over 30 years old. It was first released to customers of IBM 704 computers in April 1957. At that time, it was a powerful innovation. Because of the introduction of other languages, many have predicted that FORTRAN would fade and die. It is a testament to its basic value that it continues to flourish. It is the language of choice for supercomputers (Cray released CFT 77, full FORTRAN 77 implementation for its supercomputers in 1986). The FORTRAN implementations for microcomputers continue to improve; in 1987, Microsoft released a full FORTRAN 77 for IBM PC–compatible microcomputers. There are competitor languages that are superior to FORTRAN for some types of problems, but FORTRAN continues to be an excellent language for a wide variety of mathematical problems. For other areas such as robotics and engineering design, it is the major language.

The third edition maintains the direction of the second edition but with several changes to reflect the current environment for programming in FORTRAN. FORTRAN has not changed; FORTRAN 77 is still the current standard for all FORTRAN compilers. However, the environment for programming has changed significantly.

This revision retains the innovative pedagogical approach of the first two editions in which the programming concepts and statements are described in part *a* of each chapter and the concepts are illustrated in part *b* of each chapter by two complete program examples. There is an emphasis in both the general explanation and the example notes on a disciplined, structured style for programming in FORTRAN. Students learn and use the disciplined style from their very first small program. Experience has shown that students who learn with this pedagogical approach write disciplined programs and never develop bad habits which they must unlearn later.

The use of the complete program examples, plus frequent self-testing quizzes with answers at the end of the chapter, allows the text to be used for self instruction or for a course that emphasizes student initiative in learning the language. It is excellent for a traditional lecture course because it describes and illustrates features in good program design. This allows the instructor to focus on general programming concepts, algorithm development, purposes and uses of FORTRAN statements, and reinforcement of both theoretical and practical principles of FORTRAN program design.

The major change in the third edition is in the explanation of how programs are entered into the computer and how data items and records are provided for program execution. Changes in the programming and execution environment for FORTRAN programs are reflected in the following changes in the text:

1. The Introduction, "Preparing to Program in FORTRAN," explains the various alternatives for preparing and entering a FORTRAN program into the computer and the alternatives for providing data for program execution. The introduction explains the differences between programming in FORTRAN with a microcomputer and using a mainframe computer. There are some very simple program examples that readers can use to explore the capabilities of the FORTRAN compiler and the computer available to them.
2. All references to use of punched cards for input and output have been removed because punched cards are no longer used.
3. The text explanations describe the two major methods for entering a program into the computer: using a text editor or using a terminal or workstation in interactive programming mode. The introduction explains the use of a text editor and interactive programming.
4. Explanations include FORTRAN on both mainframe and personal computers. Appendix A describes differences in implementations of FORTRAN and includes a section on FORTRAN for a personal computer.
5. The two example programs in part *b* of each chapter have been redone to illustrate the two alternatives for execution of the program: batch execution using a previously prepared data file or interactive execution in which data items are entered at a keyboard when requested by the program. In most cases, one program is designed for batch execution and the other is designed for interactive execution. The notes describing the example explain the reason for the differences in program design.
6. Additional scientific and engineering problems have been added to each chapter that specify interactive execution.

The text adheres to the 1977 American National Standard (ANS) FORTRAN. Most of the current FORTRAN compilers follow this standard, but many small computers will have compilers that implement only a subset version of the 1977 standard FORTRAN. The full 1977 FORTRAN is presented in the text, but features in the full version not included in the 1977 subset FORTRAN are noted in the chapters and summarized in Appendix A.

Color is used to highlight key explanations and reference boxes in the text.

Key features of the second edition that are continued in the third edition are:

1. Easily accessible reference material, such as a list of intrinsic functions on the inside front cover and a reference list of features, each with an example statement showing its use, following the index as the last pages in the text.
2. Use of the inside back cover for recording and easily referencing specifications for the FORTRAN compiler being used.
3. A large number of problems suited to different disciplines. These are tested problems; a solution has been written for each one to check for completeness of the problem statement.
4. The use of list-directed input and output for the first two chapters. This allows students to write a program without learning the FORMAT statement. The

emphasis is on writing complete, well-structured programs starting with the first program.

5. The emphasis on using features that reduce the possibility of programming errors.

6. Material on debugging presented in each chapter as the level of difficulty of programs increases.

There is an Instructor's Manual that contains a sample solution for each of the over 120 programming problems. There are also suggestions for using the text.

We would like to express our thanks for the many useful comments and suggestions provided by colleagues who reviewed this text during the course of its development, especially to, Joyce Brennan, University of Texas at Austin; Henry Etlinger, Rochester Institute of Technology; David Franklin, Southern Technical Institute; George Main, Bellvue Community College; Robert Dourson, California Polytechnic State University; and Rebecca Rutherford, Southern Technical Institute.

The revision has been aided by Janice DeGross who did manuscript typing and preparation of figures and by Timothy Hoffmann who provided assistance in reviewing the manuscript and added his insight as a commercial FORTRAN user.

Gordon B. Davis
Thomas R. Hoffmann

FORTRAN 77:
A Structured,
Disciplined Style

Introduction: Preparing to Program in FORTRAN

The FORTRAN Language
Development of FORTRAN
How to Study FORTRAN Using This Text

Instructing a Computer
Hardware, Software, and Files
Machine-Level Languages
High-Level Languages

A Structured, Disciplined Style in FORTRAN Programming
Objectives of a Disciplined Approach to Programming
Modular Design of Programs
Structured Programming

Entering and Executing Computer Programs
Computer Codes for Representing and Storing Programs and Data
Methods for Entering Programs and Data
Execution of a FORTRAN Program

Getting Necessary Information about Your FORTRAN
Your FORTRAN Compiler Specifications
Logging on Your Computer
Submission Procedures for FORTRAN Compilation and Execution
Input of Data and Output of Program Listings and Results

Learning to Use the Text Editor to Enter Programs and Data
Building a Program or Data File
Correcting a Program or Data File
Sending and Receiving Files Using Your Personal Computer

A Simple FORTRAN Program to Test Your Procedures

Summary

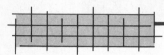

The purpose of this introductory chapter is to prepare for programming in FORTRAN. There is a short background section on the FORTRAN language. This is followed by a survey of hardware, software, files, and programming languages as background for programming. The text emphasizes the value of a structured, disciplined approach to programming, and the next section explains the objectives and features underlying it. The different methods for entering and executing computer programs are then explained in order to assist the beginner in understanding the characteristics of the computer system and the FORTRAN system being used.

There are two sections describing information needed by a programmer in order to enter FORTRAN programs and execute them. Finally, a simple seven-statement FORTRAN program is given to aid in testing your understanding of the FORTRAN system you are using.

The FORTRAN Language

FORTRAN (an acronym for FORmula TRANslator) is the most widely used of a class of high-level languages called scientific or algebraic languages. (The meaning of *high-level language* will be explained in the chapter.) It is available for use on almost all computers. Although not limited to mathematical problems, it is especially useful for problems that can be stated in terms of formulas or arithmetic procedures. This covers a wide range of problems. For example, FORTRAN is suitable for such diverse problems as analysis of sales statistics in a business and analysis of structural stress for designing a building.

Development of FORTRAN

FORTRAN was developed in 1957 by IBM in conjunction with some major users, but it is now used by all computer vendors. FORTRAN has changed and evolved. This evolutionary process resulted, during the development period, in several FORTRANs of increasing complexity. Major versions were called FORTRAN, FORTRAN II, and FORTRAN IV. Each new version made a few changes in the basic instructions and included additional features. In 1966, a voluntary FORTRAN standard, American National Standard (ANS) FORTRAN, was adopted. The International Standards Organization (ISO) also defined standard FORTRAN.

A revised American National Standard (ANS) FORTRAN was adopted in 1977. This 1977 standard adds features to the previous 1966 standard FORTRAN, clarifies some ambiguities, and makes a few minor changes. The standard also defines two different levels for FORTRAN implementation: subset FORTRAN and full FORTRAN. Subset FORTRAN is a compatible subset of the comprehensive full FORTRAN. This text is based on the 1977 standard adhered to by almost all implementations of

2

FORTRAN in use today. The text concentrates on the most-used features of FORTRAN; some advanced or little-used features will be summarized in less detail in Chapter 7.

Concurrent with the development of standard FORTRAN has been the development of special teaching-oriented FORTRAN compilers. The best known of these, developed at the University of Waterloo (Waterloo, Canada), are termed WATFOR and WATFIV. There are similar teaching FORTRANs for many other large computers. The teaching-oriented systems were designed to provide excellent error-diagnostic messages for students and to do fast execution of small student programs. For production applications, FORTRAN is available on all large-scale systems by IBM, Control Data Corporation, Unisys, Digital Equipment Corporation, etc. For supercomputers, such as those from Cray Research, FORTRAN is a primary language.

Although almost all versions of FORTRAN adhere to the 1977 standard, they frequently provide extra nonstandard statements and features. This text takes the view that programmers should generally avoid use of nonstandard features so that their programming knowledge is not limited to a particular FORTRAN implementation.

FORTRAN is available for personal computers. The most common is by the Microsoft Corporation (often termed Microsoft FORTRAN). It is also based on 1977 standard FORTRAN but contains a few extra features to deal with the limitations or take advantage of a personal computer. Although early versions did not implement all the features of standard FORTRAN, Microsoft Version 4.0 does so. Other fully standard micro-based FORTRANs include IBM's Professional FORTRAN, F77L by Lahey Computer Systems, and FORTRAN by Ryan-McFarland Corporation. The 1977 American National Standard FORTRAN is therefore recommended as the basis for all FORTRAN programming, by students as well as by professional programmers.

How to Study FORTRAN Using This Text

FORTRAN is a machine-independent language for instructing a computer. In other words, the programmer writing FORTRAN does not need to know any machine-level details for the computer being used. The language is procedure-oriented—designed for instructing the computer in a problem-solving procedure. The language consists of a vocabulary of symbols and words and a grammar of rules for writing procedural instructions. The symbols, words, and rules utilize many common mathematical and English-language conventions so that the language is fairly easy to learn and to understand. The rules are, however, precise and must be followed with care. In other words, learning FORTRAN is like learning a special-purpose language. There are rules of construction and vocabulary to learn, and one becomes proficient by doing rather than by much reading.

The objective of the text is to assist you in learning to write clear, understandable, error-free FORTRAN programs. To achieve this objective, you need to do each of the following:

1. Learn the instructions and other elements of the language.
2. Learn how to apply the language rules and to use the FORTRAN instructions to compose a clear, understandable program.
3. Learn how to enter a FORTRAN program (at a terminal or PC) and how to specify that your program be translated (compiled) and executed (using the computer that is available to you).

The first objective is met by part A of each of the chapters that follow this introduction. There is a description of instructions or rules, and illustrations of their use are provided. To assist in learning, there are self-testing exercises after every major unit in each chapter. At each self-testing exercise, answer the questions and check your responses against the answers at the end of the chapter.

The second objective is achieved by part B of each chapter, which contains complete programs. You should study the example programs, noting the style, the error-control features included in the program, and the documentation describing the programs. These examples of good programming style provide a pattern to follow in writing your programs.

The third objective requires the programming of a problem, carrying out the procedures for entering the program, instructing the computer to compile and execute, and removing errors. A variety of different programming problems is provided with each chapter. In carrying out the writing, coding, running, etc., of a program, the text provides the following aids:

1. A reference list of all FORTRAN language features. (List of 1977 American National Standard FORTRAN Statements and Specifications follows the Index.)
2. A place to record specifications and features you need to know about the FOR- TRAN system for the computer you will use (including how to enter a program and how to instruct the system to compile and execute it). The form to record these is on the inside of the back cover. The specifications should be filled in from material furnished by your instructor or obtained by consulting the FORTRAN reference manual for your computer.
3. A reference list of all FORTRAN intrinsic functions on the inside of the front cover (to be explained in Chapter 2). Check off those functions that are available to you (you can wait to do this until after completing Chapter 2).

The text is based on the generally accepted 1977 American National Standard FORTRAN, but because the fundamental features of all versions of FORTRAN are the same or nearly the same, it is possible to understand and modify programs written using the older 1966 FORTRAN standard. Appendix A assists in understanding differences in these versions of FORTRAN. Implementations of FORTRAN in a personal computer generally include all the features of standard subset FORTRAN and a few additional features. Differences between standard FORTRAN and some microcomputer versions are also described in Appendix A. Before proceeding, scan the front and back endpapers, the two appendixes, and the list of 1977 American National Standard FORTRAN Statements and Specifications (follows the Index).

Instructing a Computer

Before starting the detailed explanation of the FORTRAN language, it may be helpful to review how a computer is instructed. A computer system requires both hardware and software. The *hardware* consists of all the equipment; the *software* includes the programs of instructions that direct the operations of the computer equipment. The computer hardware and software make use of files that contain programs and data.

Hardware, Software, and Files

A computer system can range in size from a large one serving hundreds of users concurrently to a personal computer with one user. A large computer system, shown in Figure 1, has input terminals connected to it over communication lines, a central processing unit (CPU), internal storage (memory), and output units (such as a

Figure 1 Large computer hardware system.

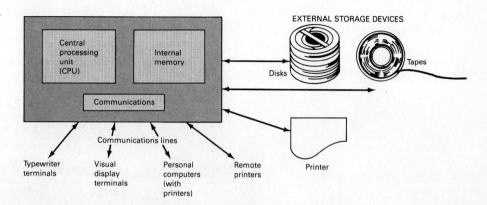

printer). It also has external storage devices, such as magnetic disks or magnetic-tape units (also called secondary or auxiliary storage). In a typical processing job, data comes from the input unit (and perhaps from external storage) into the central processor where computation and other processing is performed. After processing, the results are sent to the output device (say, a printer or terminal) or to a secondary storage device to be held for later output or further processing. Note that a terminal may be used for both input and output. The terminal may be a typewriterlike device, a visual display device with a televisionlike output display and a keyboard for input, or a personal computer equipped with communications capability. The visual display terminal will tend to be used for small amounts of output; larger volumes of output will generally be printed.

A personal computer (often called a PC or desktop computer) has the same basic parts as a large computer, but it is smaller and more compact (Figure 2). The cabinet contains the central processing unit, internal storage, and, usually, secondary or auxiliary storage (devices for "floppy" diskette and/or "hard" disk storage). There is a display device with keyboard for input and output and a separate printer for hard-copy (printed) output. For FORTRAN, the PC may be used by itself or as a terminal to a larger computer.

The CPU can perform operations such as read, write, add, etc., but the sequence in which these operations are to be performed and the specific input and output units to be used are specified by a set of instructions stored in the computer memory. The general term applied to these computer processing instructions is *software*. The instructions are organized into sets called routines and programs. A *routine* refers to a set of instructions that directs the performance of a specific task, such as calculating the square root of a quantity or producing an error message when an error is encountered in input data. A *program* consists of one or more routines that direct the solution of a complete problem.

There are several major types of software. Three types especially relevant to the study of FORTRAN are application programs, compilers, and operating systems.

1. *Application programs* Programs that direct the processing for an application of computers, such as preparing payroll, preparing checks, calculating a rate of return for a proposed project, calculating stress factors for a building structure, etc. The FORTRAN examples in this text are application programs. Application programs may be written by personnel in organizations needing them, or they may be purchased from software vendors who prepare and sell programs for frequently encountered applications.

2. *Compilers* Programs that translate instructions written in a high-level, general-

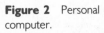

Figure 2 Personal computer.

DISPLAY WITH KEYBOARD

purpose language, such as FORTRAN, into a set of machine instructions specific to the computer being used.

3. *Operating system* A set of routines that directs and manages the operations of the computer. The operating system supports and directs the running of application programs. For example, if an application program has an instruction to print output on the printer but the printer is not operable, the operating system sends a suitable message to the operator.

Operating systems and compilers are generally obtained from either the hardware vendor or independent software vendors. Programs being executed are stored in the internal (main or primary) storage or memory, which is part of the central processing unit. Programs not currently being executed but which need to be available are stored as files in external storage. Some parts of the operating system remain in main storage all the time. Based on job control instructions to be described later, these operating system routines bring into internal memory the routines and programs to be executed and direct their execution. The programs to be run may be compilers, application programs, or other software.

A computer file is a set of stored data. The set of data can be text, such as a report or the lines of a computer program, or the data can be numeric. Files will be explained in detail later; the feature of a file that is important for this chapter is its use as a way of storing a program or saving a set of data to be used by a program. Each file is assigned a name by the person who creates it. The program file is retrieved by referring to its name.

Machine-Level Languages

A program in main memory must be in machine language to be executed. A machine-language instruction is represented as a string of binary digits called *bits* (represented by 1s and 0s), which identify the operations to be performed and the data, etc., to be used. The machine-level instructions differ for different series of computers and different manufacturers. As an example, a typical instruction for a large IBM computer has the following form (with 1 standing for a 1-bit and 0 for a 0-bit in storage):

0101101000110000101110100100000

Even though the internal machine representation is in this form, it would be very difficult and could lead to error if a programmer were required to deal with such instructions.

Because binary notation is difficult to use, a programmer who codes programs in machine-level instructions generally uses a symbolic assembly language. Symbolic assembly languages as a class are often referred to as *low-level languages*. These languages are machine-oriented because each symbolic assembly instruction is converted into one machine-language instruction. The preceding machine-language instruction coded in symbolic assembly language might be: A   3,PAY where, for example, A means "add." The computer cannot directly execute the symbolic instructions, so these must be translated into machine-language instructions. This is done by a program called a *symbolic assembly system* which converts each symbolic instruction into an equivalent machine-level code instruction. Machine-oriented programming is very useful for some applications because instruction coding can be very machine-sensitive and thus obtain very efficient use of the computer. However, an assembly language program is relatively difficult to code, and logic errors are difficult to find. It is also difficult and time-consuming to change. A program in a low-level, machine-oriented language also has limited transferability (portability) from one computer to another.

High-Level Languages

A *high-level language* is oriented to problem solution or processing procedures rather than to the machine-level instructions of a particular computer. The instruction statements use words, phrases, and symbols that are similar to those commonly used to describe solution or processing procedures. Another major difference between a high-level instruction and a symbolic assembly instruction is that one high-level instruction is translated into many machine-language instructions.

There are a number of different high-level languages for different types of problems. Each of these languages consists of a grammar (set of rules) and predefined words for writing instructions. A program called a *compiler* is used to translate the program written in the high-level language (the source program) into machine-level instructions (the object program) for the computer on which the program is to be run. Since machine-level instructions differ among computer series, there must be a unique compiler program for each computer series. For example, there are FORTRAN compilers written for each series of the IBM computers, others written for the series of VAX computers, and yet others written for personal computers.

There are two important advantages of high-level languages over symbolic assembly languages: They are machine-independent in the sense that programs written in a high-level language can be compiled and run on any computer (for which there is a compiler) with few or no changes, and they are relatively easy to learn. Today, these languages are generally so powerful and efficient that they have virtually eliminated the need for symbolic assembly language coding except for a few specialized applications. It is also relatively easy to standardize methods of programming with high-level languages. Organizations having a concern with program accuracy and a desire for programming discipline have strongly influenced the trend toward use of high-level languages.

The two most common high-level languages are FORTRAN and COBOL: FORTRAN is best suited for formula-type mathematical problems, while COBOL is the dominant language in business data processing. Other high-level languages having significant use are BASIC, Pascal, PL/1, Ada, and APL.

A Structured, Disciplined Style in FORTRAN Programming

The title of this text indicates that there can be a structured, disciplined style in writing FORTRAN programs. Since the text follows this approach, it will be useful to understand the reasons for the approach and the basic methods to implement it.

Computer programs frequently do not meet user requirements, are not produced on time, cost considerably more than estimated, contain errors, and are difficult to maintain (to correct or change to meet new requirements). These difficulties have been observed with such frequency that many organizations have attempted to change the practice of programming in order to improve performance. The revised approach can be termed a *programming discipline*—well-defined practices, procedures, and development control processes. A student should not merely learn to code FORTRAN statements. It is equally important to learn how these statements are combined into a high-quality program—one which is easy to understand (and change, if necessary) and which uses computer resources efficiently.

Objectives of a Disciplined Approach to Programming

Because programming discipline is an underlying philosophy for this text and because of the importance of programming discipline to industry, it will be useful to summarize the major objectives of this approach to programming:

1. *Meet user needs*   A program has a purpose, such as to produce an analysis or to compute a set of statistics. An assignment to prepare a program is a failure if the program is not used because the potential users of the application find it too complex or too difficult. A disciplined approach to program design includes a careful analysis of requirements before programming.
2. *Development on time within budget*   Estimates of time and cost for writing computer programs have frequently been substantially in error. By the use of a more structured, disciplined approach, installations have achieved dramatic improvements in productivity and have improved their ability to estimate time to complete.
3. *Error-free set of instructions*   It is generally considered that all large-scale computer programs contain errors, and it may be impossible to remove every single error from a large set of programs. However, using a disciplined, structured approach, programs may be designed and developed in a manner that minimizes the likelihood of errors and that facilitates detection and correction of errors in testing. The result can be virtually error-free programming.
4. *Error-resistant operation*   A program may produce erroneous results, due either to program errors or to incorrect input. The program should be designed so that errors will, whenever possible, be detected by the program itself during execution. The design features to assist in programmed detection of errors are:
   (*a*) Input validation. This is a process of testing all input data items to determine whether or not they meet the criteria set for them. For example, data input may be tested for:

Existence of necessary input data items

Data item values within acceptable range

Incorrect class of data (for example, alphabetic characters in a data item that should be numeric)

(b) Tests of correctness during processing. These generally take the form of tests for reasonableness of results and checks of logical relationships among different results. The program should also assist users to detect errors during input and output. Input data items can be restated with descriptive labels, and output can be clearly labeled.

5. *Maintainable programs* Computer programs change, especially when first placed into use. Programs should be written with the change (maintenance) activity in mind. The program documentation and the style in which a program is written should allow a programmer who did not write it to understand the logic of the program and to make a change in one part of the program without unknowingly introducing an error into another part of the same program.

6. *Portable programs* A tested program, written in FORTRAN, should be transferable without substantial change to another computer having a FORTRAN compiler. This means that all nonstandard FORTRAN instructions should be avoided. Straightforward, well-documented instructions that follow a disciplined, structured approach are portable with little difficulty; programs with intricate or poorly documented logic are not.

Modular Design of Programs

One of the key concepts in the application of programming discipline is the design of a program as a set of units referred to as *blocks* or *modules*. A program module is defined as the part of a program that performs a separate function, such as input, input validation, processing of one type of input, etc. A program module may be quite large (in terms of logic and instructions required), so that it may be further divided into logical submodules. The process of subdivision continues until all modules are of manageable size in terms of complexity of logic and numbers of instructions. In practice, a FORTRAN module with more than 50 statements (takes more than one page to list) is too large.

Although computer programs differ greatly in purpose and processing, it is possible to identify types of functions that are commonly needed in programs. Programs can be logically separated into the following functional modules:

Functional module	Description
Initialization	Establishes initial values for some variables, prints headings, messages, etc. May not always be necessary.
Input	Performs input of data required by the program.
Input data validation	Performs validation of input data to detect errors or omissions.
Processing	Performs computation or data manipulation.
Output	Performs output of data to be provided by the program.
Error handling	Performs analysis of error condition and outputs error messages. For small programs, error handling may be included in other modules.
Closing procedure	Performs procedures to end the execution of the program.

These modules reflect a logical flow for a computer program. After initialization, processing proceeds logically with input, input validation, various processing modules, and output. Error handling may be required during execution of any of the modules. At the conclusion of processing, the closing procedures to complete the program are performed. Although all the functions of these logical modules are normally found in well-written programs, they are not always defined as separate program modules; they may be combined or rearranged to suit the flow of a particular program.

Structured Programming

One method of achieving the objective of accurate, error-resistant, maintainable programs is to code (write) each module in a simple, easily understood format.

A useful starting point for understanding how to code the modules in a computer program in a clear, easily understood format is the fact that all computer program processing can be coded by using only three logic structures (patterns) or combinations of these structures:

1. Simple sequence
2. Selection
3. Repetition

The three basic patterns should be understood, since these structures have general applicability to computer programming.

The simple sequence structure consists of one action followed by another. In other words, perform operation A (Figure 3), and then perform operation B.

The selection structure consists of a test for a condition followed by two alternative paths for the program to follow. The program selects one of the program-control paths depending on the test of the condition. After performing one of the two paths, the program control returns to a single point. This pattern can be termed IF . . . ELSE because the logic can be stated (for condition P and operations C and D): IF P (is true) perform C ELSE (otherwise) perform D (Figure 3).

The repetition structure can also be called a *loop*. In a loop, an operation (or set of operations) is repeated while (as long as) some condition is satisfied. The basic form of repetition is termed DO WHILE (Figure 4) in the literature of structured programming. Using FORTRAN terminology to be explained in Chapter 4, it might be termed a DO loop. In the DO WHILE pattern, the program logic tests a condition governing the continued operation of the loop; if it is true, the program executes the operation (called E in Figure 4) and loops back for another test. If the condition is not true, the repetition ceases. In other words, DO the loop WHILE (as long as) the loop repetition

Figure 3 Simple sequence and selection program structures.

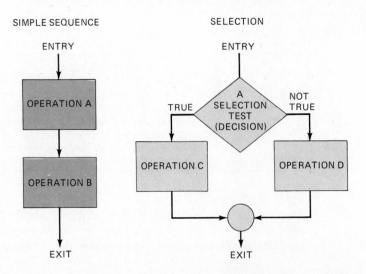

Figure 4 The DO WHILE repetition structure.

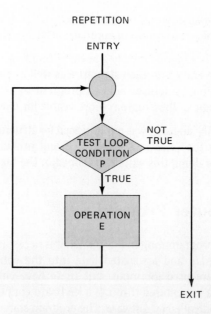

condition is true. Other loop control flows are possible, but the DO WHILE pattern is the one used by the standard FORTRAN loop instruction.

One of the objectives in using the three basic structures is to make programs more understandable to those concerned with design, review, and maintenance. It is possible to combine the three simple structures to produce more complex coding while maintaining the simplicity inherent in the three patterns. For example, the logic of the program may involve a selection between two program paths. If one path is chosen, there should be a repetition loop; if the other is selected, there is a simple sequence. The combination of the structures is illustrated in Figure 5. Note that there is still a single entry/single exit for the entire structure.

Figure 5 Nesting of coding structures.

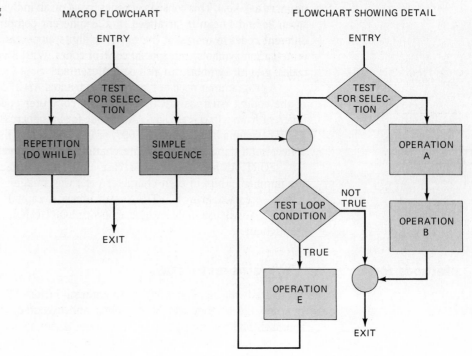

This short explanation of the three structures provides some insight into their value in a disciplined programming approach. The structures are useful because:

1. The program is simplified. Only the three building blocks are used. There is a single point of entry into each structure as well as a single point of exit.
2. The three coding structures allow a program to be read from top to bottom, making the logic of the program more visible for checking and maintenance.

The FORTRAN language was not designed for structured programming, but it is possible to follow the ideas reasonably well and produce a structured FORTRAN program. Rules for doing this will be explained in the text as they become relevant.

Entering and Executing Computer Programs

As preparation to programming in FORTRAN, it is necessary to understand how to get a FORTRAN program and associated data into the computer. In earlier periods, punched cards were used for input, but these have virtually disappeared. Today, programs and data are entered through a keyboard connected to the computer. The entry process is controlled by software. The program statements and data are encoded in the computer in a special computer code. Once entered and stored by the computer, the program can be executed. Two main approaches to execution, batch and interactive, will be explained in this section.

Computer Codes for Representing and Storing Programs and Data

The computer does not represent alphabetic text or numeric digits as individual characters; instead, characters are represented by a code consisting of a set of binary digits (0s and 1s). There are several common binary coding schemes, but the most common is the American Standard Code for Information Interchange (ASCII, pronounced ask-key). This consists of codes based on an individual set of 7 or 8 bits. Since seven 0s and 1s can be arranged in 128 different combinations, there are enough different codes to represent the numeric digits, uppercase letters, lowercase letters, punctuation symbols, and special control codes. With 8 bits providing 256 different codes, graphic symbols can also be represented.

A programmer need not know the individual ASCII codes; the main implication of the coding (such as ASCII) is that the computer code for an uppercase "A" is different from a lowercase "a." ASCII code for an uppercase "A" is 065, or 01000001. ASCII code for a lowercase "a" is 097, or 01100001. It is also useful to understand the concept of a standard code for interchange of files between systems.

FORTRAN began as an uppercase-only language because it was designed when the number of bits in each character code was smaller than today, so only capital letters were used. Many FORTRANs still adhere to capitals only; others allow both. In this text, we will use some lowercase; if your FORTRAN doesn't allow it, use uppercase throughout.

Methods for Entering Programs and Data

There are two general approaches to entering FORTRAN program statements into a program file so they can be compiled and executed: the separate or text editor approach and the integrated or interactive entry approach. In the separate (most common) approach using a text editor, the programmer employs a separate software system called a *text editor* to enter program statements at a terminal (or microcomputer keyboard) and build a FORTRAN program file. Standard word processing packages can frequently be used for this purpose as well. The program file is a text file, and there is no connection at this point with the FORTRAN compiler. The use of a text editor will be explained in more detail later in the chapter.

The integrated or interactive approach to entry of statements is controlled by the FORTRAN compiler, and the completed program is immediately available for compilation and execution. It need not be executed immediately; it can be stored by the interactive system as a FORTRAN program file. The interactive approach to entering statements may require that the programmer (or the system) place an identifying number in front of each line of the FORTRAN program. To make a correction in the program, the line number and a corrected line are entered. This line of instruction replaces the old line which had that same identifying number. These line numbers are distinct and different from the statement labels to be described in Chapter 2.

Execution of a FORTRAN Program

The compilation (translation) and execution of a FORTRAN program may use either batch processing or immediate processing. The essential difference between these is scheduled (delayed) action versus immediate action.

Batch compilation and execution   The program is stored until a scheduled time for compilation and execution. This may be after only a short delay, or it may be scheduled in the evening or other times when the computer is available. Using job control instructions, the programmer specifies the name of the program file containing the FORTRAN program to be compiled and executed. Because the program will be executed at a later time, perhaps when the programmer is not available, a data file containing the data required by the program is also prepared and specified as part of the compilation and execution instructions.

Immediate compilation and interactive execution   The programmer requests compilation and execution, which is done immediately or after only a few seconds delay. The FORTRAN system provides job messages and error messages to the programmer at the terminal. When all errors have been corrected by the programmer, immediate execution may be specified. Because the programmer is online to the computer, there may be interaction between the programmer and the program. The program may request input of data from the terminal and wait until the data items are entered before proceeding with the execution. The program may also display output at the programmer's printer or video display. The program is not limited to input and output using the terminal; data files previously prepared may be specified, and output may be printed on a high-speed printer or saved on a file.

Getting Necessary Information about Your FORTRAN

Even though FORTRAN is a standard language, there are unique commands to compile and execute FORTRAN programs on a specific computer. Most computer centers have a simple write-up to explain these commands for the system you are using, or the computer instruction manual may have a section on FORTRAN. This part of the chapter will alert you to specifications you should look for.

Your FORTRAN Compiler Specifications

Your FORTRAN is probably standard 1977 FORTRAN. However, it may implement only the subset of the full standard or the subset plus a few extensions. Also, there may be a few unique features or special considerations. There is normally a FORTRAN manual for your system that explains its adherence to the standard and any special features or considerations. You may wish to scan the reference material in the manual (perhaps an appendix) and start recording features on the FORTRAN specification sheet on the inside of the back cover of this text, where they will be readily available to you.

Logging on Your Computer

Entry of computer programs and instructing execution require that the programmer be connected to the computer (logged on if the connection is with a shared computer) and provide job control instructions to the computer about the kind of work to be done. These log-on instructions are simple, but they are unique to each computer system. There is a place in the sheet facing the back cover of this text for recording log-on instructions.

Submission Procedures for FORTRAN Compilation and Execution

Every compilation and execution of a FORTRAN program requires job control instructions to specify what is to be done and the computer resources to be used. In the case of interactive FORTRAN, in which the program was entered under the control of the FORTRAN system, the instructions to compile and execute are quite simple. For a compile and execute using a program file prepared previously, one or more job control instructions will be required. For example, the job control instruction will specify that the job is a FORTRAN program to be compiled and give the name of the program file. The operating system will interpret the job control instructions and bring the FORTRAN compiler into the main storage of the computer. The operating system then instructs the compiler program to read and translate the FORTRAN program statements, etc.

Since the job control instructions are different for each computer, a job control manual for the computer being used provides the programmer with the necessary specifications and instructions. As mentioned, computer centers running student jobs normally prepare a short description of the job control instructions required for these programs. The inside back cover of this text provides a space for you to summarize these submission job control statements.

Input of Data and Output of Program Listings and Results

The entering of programs and input data and storing of them for compilation and execution have been explained. It is also necessary to specify where the program can find input data and what is to be done with the output. There are three methods for input/output source specification. These may be used singly or in combination in a program.

1. Standard input and output device specified in FORTRAN program. Each computer installation can specify the output device that is the standard device. The standard

device can be changed by job control instructions. Examples for output might be a terminal display for a personal computer or a line printer for a larger computer.

2. Standard FORTRAN numbers for input or output devices in FORTRAN programs. The computer installation will assign standard device numbers to a few devices such as keyboard, printer, or display.

3. File for input or storage. A file name for input or output can be defined in the FORTRAN program, or the file can be specified by job control instructions.

As part of preparing to program in FORTRAN, you should obtain the following information:

Standard input and output devices (where no device number is specified)
Standard FORTRAN numbers assigned to input and output devices
How to name and specify a file for input or output using job control instructions

On the form on the inside back cover, note these specifications for your system.

Learning to Use the Text Editor to Enter Programs and Data

A text editor is a software system (a set of programs) that manages the computer in order for a user to input either text or numeric data. For all practical purposes, a text editor and a word processing software package are identical. The two terms have historical differences. Text editors were developed on large computers for users entering and manipulating data from terminals. Word processing software was developed for clerical employees preparing text and entering data on standalone word processing machines. Over time, the word processing machines have become small computers. In many respects, the word processing packages have become easier to use than text editors, and many programmers prefer to write their programs and prepare their data files on word processors.

Building a Program or Data File

Since the text processor software consists of a set of programs, it must be accessed by one or more computer instructions. The access instructions usually specify the name of the text editor and the name or label assigned to the file being created. These access and naming instructions may be quite simple. For example, the following represent the access and naming instructions using three different text processors:

```
xedit myprog fortran
edit myprog.f
edlin myprog.for
```

In the preceding three instructions, xedit, edit, and edlin tell the operating system of the computer that the text processor with that name is to be brought into use to create a new file called myprog. Note that the file label assigned has two parts: the name, myprog, plus a second part of the label (often called a file type) which provides additional specification. Some systems use a period between the two parts; others use a space. In this particular case, the second part specifies that it is a FORTRAN program that is being created. If it were a data file, the second part of the label would be additional characters that would make the file easier to locate. In some cases there may be a third part which specifies that the file is text, numeric, binary, etc. For our purposes, a program file is text.

Entering program statements or entering data that is to be put into specified columns is simpler if tab stops are set. For FORTRAN programs using fairly well accepted style, the tab stops should be set at 7, 11, 15, 19, 23, and 27. If items for a data file are to be entered starting in specific columns, then the tabs should be set for those columns. As an example, one text processor uses the following command to set tabs for FORTRAN:

```
set tabs 7 11 15 19 23 27
```

Other text processors will have similar commands.

There are text processing commands to add lines, insert lines, and delete lines. A feature of text processors (but not word processors) is that they usually make use of a line number as an identifier for working with the text. The line number is for software use and is not usually part of the resulting file. There are normally text editor commands to copy statements from one part of the file to another or from another file and to move statements within the file.

When the program statements or lines of data have all been entered, there is a command to store the file under the label (name) assigned to it when the file creation began.

Correcting a Program or Data File

When a program file has been completed and it is submitted for compilation, errors are usually detected. In order to correct these, the text editor software is reloaded and the program file is read and corrected. The text editor will have commands to find the incorrect portions of a statement and replace with correct text. For example, in one text editor, the following commands would be used to find a misspelled FORTRAN word (REED instead of READ) and change it to the correct spelling:

L/REED/	This locates the line with the misspelled word. The line can be displayed by another command.
c/REED/READ/	This command changes (replaces) the characters between the first and second slashes with those between the second and third slashes.

Global changes can be made without searching for every instance of the error. For example, if there were many occurrences of the misspelling for READ, a command would be given to start at the beginning of the file (top) and make all changes. In one text editor, this command is:

top	Moves to the beginning (top) of the file.
c/REED/READ/	Tells the editor to search every line of the file and change every occurrence of REED to READ.

After changes are made, the revised file must be stored. It is usually written over the original file, replacing it. In some systems, the original file is retained but given an identifying name alteration or suffix.

Sending and Receiving Files Using Your Personal Computer

A microcomputer or personal computer can be used as a terminal to interact with a mainframe computer. It can also be used to prepare files that are then sent to the main computer or to receive files from the main computer for printing or further editing on the microcomputer. The exact procedures for sending and receiving files between the personal computer and the mainframe depend upon the communications software being used. Frequently, the files created on a microcomputer must be stored using a standard code, such as ASCII. The files received from the mainframe are also coded in ASCII. The microcomputer software that is used to print or otherwise process the files either works with ASCII or converts from ASCII to the codes used in that software. If you are planning to create program or data files on your microcomputer for transfer to the mainframe, the commands for this will need to be learned and conditions such as conversion to or from ASCII understood.

A Simple FORTRAN Program to Test Your Procedures

There are a number of things to learn and test in order to be ready to program in FORTRAN. To assist you in this process, there is a simple, seven-statement FORTRAN program in Figure 6. At this point, no explanation will be given for the way the program is written or for the individual statements. The purpose is to give you experience in creating and storing a program file using your text editor, making corrections if necessary, and submitting the program file for compilation and execution. One input is required from the standard input device (probably your terminal keyboard). The output will be printed or displayed on the standard output device.

When creating the file, enter each line exactly as it appears, including all spaces. Look at the program in Figure 6 and note the following:

The asterisk in the first line is in column 1, the first column for the lines created with your text editor.

Set the tabs so that the first column to tab to is column 7, where the words "Sample Program" should begin. All other lines also begin at column 7.

Note that both uppercase and lowercase are used in this simple program. Uppercase is used for all FORTRAN words and names (to be explained in the next chapter). Lowercase is used for descriptive comments and instructions that are displayed or printed. As explained earlier, capital letters may be required for everything in some FORTRAN systems.

The program displays a message, "Read one value & print two results." The computer expects an input of a numeric value. On the screen or terminal printer, the

Figure 6 Sample program for testing your program building, program submission, and program execution procedure.

```
*       Sample Program
        PRINT *, 'Read one value & print two results. '
        READ *, A
        B = A/2.0
        PRINT *, 'A = ',A,' B = ',B
        STOP
        END
```

computer may display a prompt character (such as colon [:] or question mark [?]) to indicate that an input is required, but many do not. Key in a number, such as 10.5 or 19.3, and press the ENTER key. The program should then print or display a line with the results labeled with "A = " and "B = ". The number of digits printed out may be few or may be a large number. This will be explained in Chapter 1a. Some early versions of Microsoft FORTRAN use WRITE(*,*) instead of PRINT * and READ(*,*) instead of READ *. If your microcomputer FORTRAN does not accept PRINT * and READ *, try these substitutions. This will be described in more detail in Chapter 1a.

Summary

FORTRAN is a standard language to program mathematical and quantitative analysis procedures. The standard version of FORTRAN adhered to by almost all FORTRAN compilers is termed FORTRAN 77. This is the version used in this text. We recommend that a programmer use only standard FORTRAN statements in writing programs.

FORTRAN is a high-level language so that a programmer need not have detailed understanding of the computer being used. It is important for the programmer to follow a structured, disciplined approach to program design and program coding. This approach emphasizes modularity and simplicity in program design. Objectives and principles for a disciplined approach were explained. The text will illustrate these principles in the remaining chapters.

One feature of computers which may cause a beginning programmer some difficulty is the computer coding of alphabetic, numeric, and special characters. One lesson to be learned from this explanation is that the computer codes for uppercase and lowercase characters are different. There is also a standard code, called ASCII (pronounced ask-key), used for interchange of data among computers.

Programs are usually entered into computer storage using a text editor and subsequently submitted to the FORTRAN system for compilation and execution, but some FORTRAN compilers allow interactive entry of the program statements. Execution of a FORTRAN program can either be in interactive mode or batch mode. In the interactive mode, the input of data and display of results occur immediately from a keyboard and display device connected to the computer. In the batch mode, a data file is created and the program is executed using the data file without direct interaction from the user terminal. In the text, one of the two sample programs at the end of each succeeding chapter is designed for batch execution; the other is designed for interactive execution.

Although FORTRAN is a standard language, the operating system environment in which programs are created, compiled, and executed is not standardized. Text editors used in creating and storing FORTRAN programs are not standardized, although they all have essentially the same features. This introduction explained the information about the operating system and text editor that a programmer needs to begin programming in FORTRAN. There are sheets at the back of the text to record essential specifications and instructions for using your text editor and your FORTRAN system.

Programming Discipline, the FORTRAN Language, and FORTRAN Statements to Write a Simple Program

Planning a FORTRAN Program
Planning Overall Program Structure
Program Design Language in Program Planning
Program Flowchart in Program Planning
  and Documentation
Self-Testing Exercise 1-1

Coding and Keyboard Entry of a FORTRAN Program

Compiling, Correcting, and Executing a FORTRAN Program
Self-Testing Exercise 1-2

Five FORTRAN Statements for Writing a Simple Program

Variables and Constants
Self-Testing Exercise 1-3
List-Directed Input Statement
List-Directed Output Statement
Interactive Prompting of Input
Arithmetic Assignment Statements
STOP and END Statements
Blank Spaces in FORTRAN Statements and Data
Self-Testing Exercise 1-4

Summary

Answers to Self-Testing Exercises

Questions and Problems

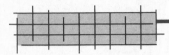

This chapter explains how to plan a FORTRAN program and how to use a program design language and a program flowchart in planning and documentation. The specifications to be followed when entering a line of FORTRAN are presented. Five FORTRAN statements needed to code a simple FORTRAN program are explained. Two complete FORTRAN programs are contained in Chapter 1b. Using these example programs as guides, you will be able to code and prepare a simple FORTRAN program for processing. Chapter 1a thus provides concepts necessary for understanding the nature of FORTRAN programming, and Chapter 1b provides an introductory experience in preparing a FORTRAN program. The program written as the assignment for Chapter 1b is also used to provide more experience in following the procedures by which a FORTRAN program is provided to the computer and processed.

Planning a FORTRAN Program

A FORTRAN program should be planned before the program instructions are written. Before planning the program, there will have been a recognition of the need for the program and some definition of what the program aims to accomplish (the requirements). The program-planning process designs a program to meet the requirements. It is usually desirable to first design the overall structures of the program and then to work on the detailed logic. Tools and techniques that assist in planning the program and the program logic include program design language (pseudocode), flowcharts, and layouts. Program design language and flowcharts are explained in this chapter; layouts are explained in Chapter 3.

Planning Overall Program Structure

Planning a program is similar to planning a building such as a home. First, there is an overall layout showing the different rooms (different functions to be performed) and their relationship to other rooms. Detailed design of each room follows. Likewise, there needs to be an overall structure for a computer program. This consists of the modules for the different program functions. When the modules are defined and relationships among modules specified, the individual modules can be designed and coded. The need for a systematic approach to design is more apparent with large programs, but the basic skill can be developed by applying planning techniques to small programs. An orderly approach to overall planning can follow a sequence such as the following:

1. Define requirements in terms of outputs:
   (a) Define fundamental requirements in terms of outputs to users of the application. The output desired can be:
   (1) A single number, such as the rate of interest for a finance proposal

(2) A set of numbers, such as a set of descriptive statistics

(3) A report, such as a financial statement

(*b*) Define additional outputs required so that recipients of the output understand it and have assurance it is correct and complete. These requirements include:

(1) Dates, versions, numbers, etc., that distinguish variations of the output.

(2) Headings, titles, and labels on the data items in the output.

(3) Identification of (or list of) data used as input, the factors used in computations, and totals (where these can be compared to related totals to demonstrate completeness). These are included as needed to assure users that the results are correct and complete.

(*c*) Define error message outputs to explain errors in input or processing and to explain what recipients of the output can (should) do to correct the errors.

2. Based on the outputs, define inputs required for the application.

3. Define the validation procedure to check that data items being input are correct and complete. Define procedures for handling data items identified as having errors.

4. Define procedures for transforming input data into output:

(*a*) Transforming valid input data into the desired output

(*b*) Converting invalid data into error outputs

If the transformation procedure has many steps, it may need to be factored into several component procedures.

5. Define the program structure in terms of major modules. The planning analysis should help to clarify why, as explained earlier, a program is likely to contain one or more modules for:

(*a*) Input

(*b*) Input data validation

(*c*) Processing

(*d*) Output

(*e*) Error handling (and error outputs)

Two other modules, initialization and closing procedures, are frequently needed to set up processing and ensure correct and complete termination.

Program Design Language in Program Planning

A *program design language* (PDL) consists of abbreviated statements in English (or other natural language) that specify the procedures the program is to perform. These program design language statements are also termed *pseudocode,* and the terms will be used interchangeably in the text. The statements are independent of the FORTRAN language but tend to recognize the features of the language. For example, a program to read information from a file of input data, compute the sum of the two input values, and print the input values and their sum might read as follows:

```
READ values for x and y from input file
Compute sum = x + y
PRINT x,y, and sum
STOP
```

In this simple case, each line of program design language results in one line of FORTRAN, but in other cases, a single line of PDL may require many lines of FORTRAN. PDL tends to be quite useful in planning the general flow of a program.

There are no standard rules for program design language; the main objective is an understandable description of the program logic. A useful approach to PDL will be illustrated in the descriptions of sample programs in part b of each chapter.

FORTRAN is well suited to the use of flowcharts in planning and documenting programs because the language is oriented toward procedural logic. Some programmers find flowcharts very useful; others do not use them. We find flowcharts are less useful than PDL for planning the general flow of a program but are more useful in planning and documenting detailed program logic. In any case, flowcharts are found frequently enough that a FORTRAN programmer should be familiar with them. Therefore, we recommend their use in the problems in this text.

Flowcharts are a means of symbolically depicting the (1) logic and procedures of programs and (2) the elements and flows of systems. The American National Standards Institute has defined standard flowcharting symbols and their use in data processing.[1] The following are the most common symbols used in flowcharting FORTRAN programs:

FLOWCHART SYMBOLS

Symbols	Represents
INPUT/OUTPUT	The input or output of data to or from the computer. The input or output medium is unspecified.
DOCUMENT	Input or output using a document such as a printed output.
DISPLAY	Output on a display device.
MANUAL INPUT	Manual input (from a terminal or other keyboard).
PROCESS	Any manipulation or processing of data within the computer.
PROCESS USING SUBPROGRAM	Perform processing using a separate subprogram unit.
TERMINAL	The beginning or end of a program module.

[1] American National Standards Institute, X3.5-1970, "Flowchart Symbols and Their Usage in Information Processing."

FLOWCHART SYMBOLS

Symbols	Represents
DECISION	The taking of alternative actions based upon presence or absence of some condition. Often called a decision symbol.
ANNOTATION	Annotation. Used for added comments. Connected to flowchart where helpful to provide additional information.
(circle)	Connector. Used to connect flowlines and to identify flowlines going to or coming from another place on the same page or another page.

Additional, supplementary symbols not included here may also be used.

Note that in the 10 symbols given, there is a general input/output symbol that can be used without regard to type of device and three specific input/output device symbols (printer, display, and keyboard). The symbols are connected with flowlines in order to indicate the direction or sequence of processing. Flowcharts are written to be read from top to bottom and from left to right. If the flow is right to left or bottom to top, arrowheads must be used on the flowlines to indicate direction of flow. Otherwise, arrowheads are optional but recommended. The flowchart symbols were used in Figures 2, 3, and 4 to describe basic program structures. Review these figures as examples of how the symbols are put together. The design of flowcharts for FORTRAN programs will be explained in the text by example and by explanations associated with programming exercises.

Self-Testing Exercise 1-1

There will be frequent self-testing exercises to help you test your comprehension of the material just explained. The answers are at the end of the chapter.

1. Distinguish between hardware and software.

2. What is the difference between machine language and symbolic assembly language?

3. What are the advantages of high-level languages over symbolic assembly languages?

4. FORTRAN stands for _____.

5. What has been the role of the American National Standards Institute (ANSI) in the development of FORTRAN?

6. Name six objectives of a disciplined approach to program design.

7. Name the functional modules in a program.

8. Name and describe the three basic program structures.

9. Match the flowchart symbol with its definition.

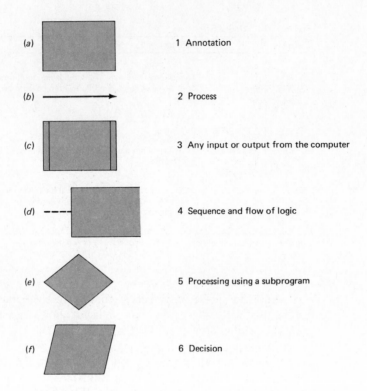

(a)　　　　　　　　　　　　1 Annotation

(b)　　　　　　　　　　　　2 Process

(c)　　　　　　　　　　　　3 Any input or output from the computer

(d)　　　　　　　　　　　　4 Sequence and flow of logic

(e)　　　　　　　　　　　　5 Processing using a subprogram

(f)　　　　　　　　　　　　6 Decision

10. If a program is transferable to another computer having a compiler for that language, without substantial change, the program is _____.

11. The most common tools for planning the logic for a FORTRAN program are _____ and/or _____.

12. Explain an orderly set of steps for planning overall program structure.

Coding and Keyboard Entry of a FORTRAN Program

When FORTRAN program design is completed, the next step is to code the program by writing FORTRAN instruction statements. As explained in the opening chapter, the statements are prepared in machine-readable form for FORTRAN compilation and execution, either by a separate process in which a FORTRAN program file is created by keyboard entry using a text editor or by an integrated process using an interactive FORTRAN compiler and keying each statement into the computer under control of the system.

FORTRAN has specific rules for the positions on the line in which different parts of a program statement are to be written. Some implementations of FORTRAN do not enforce all these rules, but it is desirable to learn and use them in order to write code in the standard FORTRAN format. The format for a FORTRAN instruction line is most easily explained by means of FORTRAN coding paper (Figure 1-1). The columns of the coding paper are marked to aid placement of the instruction on the line. Coding paper is not required, but it is helpful in layout and correct positioning of the statements and formatting input/output messages.

Figure 1-1 FORTRAN coding form.

The format of FORTRAN statements entered at a keyboard follow the same spacing as the coding paper. As described in the previous chapter, setting tabs aids in positioning the parts of the statement lines. Some rules are presented below. Review them now, and then return to them when you start coding your first program. There are 72 columns that are used as follows:

Column	How used
1	Comments and special options. An asterisk (*) or the letter C in column 1 (or C only in older versions) indicates that what follows on the line is not an instruction translated by the FORTRAN compiler. The line is printed as part of the program listing and is therefore used for explanatory comments in the program listing.
1–5	Statement label. Used as an identifier for referencing the statement. Can be written anywhere in the five columns (spaces are ignored).
6	If a FORTRAN statement is too long for one line, it may be continued on succeeding lines by putting a nonzero character (say, 1, 2, etc.) in column 6 of each continuation line. The initial line to be continued may have a blank or a 0 in column 6. Clarity of coding is enhanced if the FORTRAN statements on the continuation lines are indented to, for example, column 11.
7–72	FORTRAN statement. The statement can begin anywhere from 7 to 72. Indentation and spacing may be used to improve readability.

In coding FORTRAN statements on coding sheets, certain conventions reduce the possibility of error when the lines of coding are subsequently entered at a keyboard:

1. Code only in printed capital letters because the printed capitals are easier to read.
2. Clearly differentiate between numbers and letters that are similar. The letter O and the zero are the biggest problems, but S and 5, Z and 2, and I and 1 are often confused. Various methods are used for differentiating, such as underlining or slashing either the letter or the number. The American National Standard coding convention (shown below) is to put a line through the letter Z and to add a loop to O, leaving the related numbers as they are usually written.

Letter	Number
Ơ	0
Ƶ	2
I	1
S	5

In reading printer or terminal output, it is also possible to make a mistake between the letter O and the zero. Many new typestyles emphasize the difference. Another approach to differentiation used with many printers is to slash the zeros.

3. Set tabs of text editor to columns 7, 11, 15, 19, 23, and 27 to start indented coding at column 7 and for further indenting. Coding in lines 1 through 6 (not usually required) can be entered prior to using tabs.

Compiling, Correcting, and Executing a FORTRAN Program

After the coding (writing) and entering of a FORTRAN program (called the *source program*), the next steps are to instruct the compiler to take the program from storage and to compile it. If errors are detected during compilation, the programmer can make corrections as needed and resubmit the program for compilation. If compilation is successful and there are no errors, the compiled program may be executed. As explained in the introduction, the compilation and execution of a program may use either batch processing or immediate processing. The essential difference between these is scheduled (delayed) action versus immediate action.

Compilation and execution of a FORTRAN program require job control instructions to specify what is to be done and the computer resources to be used. One or more job control instructions may be required. For example, a job control instruction will specify that the job is a FORTRAN program to be compiled and give the name of the program file. The operating system will interpret the job control instructions and bring the FORTRAN compiler into the main storage of the computer. The operating system then turns control over to the compiler program, which reads the FORTRAN program statements from the file and translates them. The result of the translation process is an *object* program in a machine-level language for the computer. The FORTRAN object program also uses prewritten program modules from the FORTRAN library of routines. In other words, the FORTRAN compiler not only translates but also puts together (compiles) the FORTRAN routines required to make an operational program.

The terms *compile* and *execute* are often used as if they occur together. This may often appear to be true. However, the compilation process, or translation, of the FORTRAN statements into machine-level, executable instructions is performed first, and the executable program is stored for execution. Execution may be performed immediately after compilation or later. The job instructions to the computer operating system may specify compilation and immediate execution so that they appear to be one operation.

The output from compilation of a FORTRAN program (the object program) will vary depending on (1) whether or not the job ran successfully to completion or was aborted because of an error and (2) what output options have been selected by the job control instructions. The output from compilation may have a first or top sheet or screen with identification (job number and name of programmer) as well as summary job statistics and an end-of-job message. There is a listing of error messages, if any. The error messages generally refer to the line number of the FORTRAN program statement in error, but other methods may be used, such as displaying the erroneous statement. The job instructions may specify a listing of the program, but this is not usually automatic. The last output will be the results from the execution of the program, if any. There are optional outputs used by advanced programmers as aids in debugging program errors that may not have been detected by the compiler. Since most errors made by beginning programmers are detectable by the compiler, the beginning programmer can generally rely on messages generated during attempted compilation and can ignore the optional debugging output.

It is important to distinguish between errors detected during compilation and errors detected during execution. Errors detected during compilation are either nonfatal or fatal. A nonfatal error is one that does not prevent correct compilation. The compiler may be able to ignore the possible error or make corrections (but issues a message indicating a possible error). For example, a variable may be defined in a FORTRAN statement but never used in any computation or output. This may be an error but does not prevent a complete compilation. Fatal errors are mistakes that prevent compilation or would obviously lead to execution errors. For example, there may be a statement to transfer control of program execution to a labeled statement which does not exist in the program.

Compilers will detect most errors made by student programmers because most new programmer errors are made in program statement syntax—errors in punctuation, spelling, spacing, and required statement syntax. It is important to keep in mind that the error messages may not indicate the real cause but only the effect of an error. Therefore, an error early in the program may cause a large number of error messages associated with subsequent statements.

Execution errors may be due to incorrect coding. Some incorrect coding is not detected during compilation and will only be detected when execution is attempted. For example, a FORTRAN program may call (use) a subprogram that is prepared and compiled separately. If the subprogram does not exist, the error is detected at execution.

A program may be compiled and executed without error diagnostics and yet not be correct; it may still have incomplete or incorrect program logic. Completion of the program requires testing of program logic and removing logic errors. Documentation of the program also needs to be finished. Testing and documentation will be explained in subsequent chapters.

Self-Testing Exercise 1-2

1. What is the purpose of coding a C or * in column 1 of a line of FORTRAN?

2. Every batch job run on the computer must have job control instructions that provide specifications for the _____.

3. Explain the difference between entering program statements and submitting the program for compilation and execution.

4. Explain the difference between batch submission of a program for compilation and execution and immediate compilation and execution.

5. Explain the difference between compilation and execution.

6. Compilers will detect errors made by student programmers because most errors they make are _____ (punctuation, spelling, etc.) rather than program logic errors.

Five FORTRAN Statements for Writing a Simple Program

In order to get started, five FORTRAN statements will be explained. These are sufficient to write a simple but complete FORTRAN program.

1. List-directed input (free format READ)
2. List-directed output (PRINT in preset format)
3. Arithmetic assignment statement
4. STOP
5. END

In using these instructions, it will be necessary to refer to data items. Data items can be constants, which have the same value throughout the program, or variables, which can assume different values. Therefore, before explaining the five statements, the FORTRAN rules for writing and referencing data items will be discussed.

Variables and Constants

In simple formulas and computations, there are two classes of data—constants and variables. These terms are used in FORTRAN in the same sense as in mathematical notation.

1. A *constant* is a quantity that does not change; thus, the value itself is written. Examples are 3.1416, 5, and 0.06.
2. A *variable* is a representation for a quantity which is not known or can vary in different problems. In mathematics, a variable is represented by a one-character name, such as a, α, χ. In FORTRAN, a variable quantity is represented by a symbolic variable name from one to six characters, such as A, ALPHA, X1.

There is a direct correspondence between constants and variables in a mathematical formula and in the coding of a computation in FORTRAN.

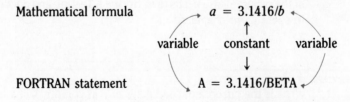

Thus, in general, if a variable is used in the mathematical formula, a variable name is used in FORTRAN; if a constant is used in the mathematical formulation, a constant is written in the FORTRAN statement. In some cases, a constant is given a name (such as k) in a mathematical formula to make the formula more general. In FORTRAN, such a constant can be represented by the constant value itself, or a variable name can be used and the constant value assigned to it.

In a mathematical formula, the variable represents an abstract number. In FORTRAN, the variable name identifies the contents of a storage location. The storage location can be thought of as a box or pigeon hole in which data may be placed. When the variable is specified in a FORTRAN statement, the contents of the box are used (but not altered by the use). When a new value for the variable is computed, it replaces the previous contents. This distinction between the abstract mathematical variable and the FORTRAN variable name as identifier for the contents of a storage location is not important at this point. It will, however, be useful in understanding some FORTRAN programming practices to be presented in later chapters.

In solving problems, there is frequently a need to distinguish between data having only integer values and data which may have a fractional part. In FORTRAN, the distinction between integer-type and real-type data is important.

1. *Integer-type data* Data having only integer (whole number) values (sometimes called fixed point data). Examples are 3, 719, and 64; note that no decimal point is used because no fractional part is to be represented.
2. *Real-type data* Data having a fractional part (sometimes called floating point data). Examples are 3.17, 46.5, 15.0, 11., and .091. Note that a decimal point is used even if the fractional portion is zero and not shown (such as 11. above). It is good practice to use the explicit zero in writing real quantities; for example, use 11.0 instead of 11. for values without a fractional part and 0.2 instead of .2. It is also good practice to code zero as 0.0 instead of 0 alone to reduce misperception by readers of the program.

There are both mathematical and practical reasons for the distinction between integer values and real values. An integer value is given an exact representation in the computer; a real value is an approximation because the computer binary coding of decimal values in some cases does not give an exact representation. This will be discussed in more detail later. For most problems, the distinction is simply whole numbers only for integer-type data and fractional part allowed for real data. A practical reason for integer data is that many procedures require integer values. Repeating a computation is done an integer number of times, such as 3 or 4, but not a fractional number of times, such as 3.1. Another practical FORTRAN language consideration for distinguishing between integer and real types is that the program uses each computer location in such a way that it can hold only a designated type of data (integer, real, or other types to be described in subsequent chapters).

There are two ways to specify that a symbolic variable name refers to storage locations for either integer or real data—implicit or explicit. The implicit method relies upon the first letter of the variable name; that is, a variable name beginning with I, J, K, L, M, or N refers to integer data. The explicit method (favored by many programmers) employs a special instruction described in Chapter 2 to specify the data type. The implicit method is used so frequently in FORTRAN programs that it is a good idea to learn and use it first. The rules for symbolic variable names and implicit type designation are summarized in the table Rules for Symbolic Variable Names.

There are specific rules for integer and real constants. Before describing the rules for writing constants, the use of exponent notation in FORTRAN will be explained. The use of exponent notation is common in mathematics. For example, 315 billion (315,000,000,000) can be written as 315×10^9. The exponent notation is used

Rules for Symbolic Variable Names

Purpose of variable name
To associate a symbolic name with an unknown or variable value.

Rules for forming
1. First character must be alphabetic.
2. No special characters are allowed (that is, the names can contain only letters and numbers, not &, $, #, etc.). Blank spaces in a name are ignored.
3. The number of characters in the name must not exceed six.

Implicit type for variables
The first letter of a variable name identifies the type of numeric data to be associated with the variable name. This implicit typing can be altered by such statements as the explicit type declaration to be defined later.

Integer variable names
Start with one of the letters I, J, K, L, M, or N. (*Hint:* The first two letters in the word INTEGER are the bounds for the integer variable names, which are from I through N.)

Real variable names
Start with one of the letters other than I, J, K, L, M, or N. In other words, names starting with A through H and O through Z are real variable names.

Examples

Variable name	Valid or not valid	If valid, integer or real	If not valid, why
X	Valid	Real	
X123	Valid	Real	
XY	Valid	Real	
ALPHA	Valid	Real	
BETA−3	Not valid		(-) is special character
$134	Not valid		$ is special character
X19.1	Not valid		(.) is special character
NUTS	Valid	Integer	
MOTHERS	Not valid		Too many characters
MOM	Valid	Integer	
RATE	Valid	Real	
1455A	Not valid		Does not start with alphabetic character
PAY DAY	Valid (equivalent to PAYDAY since blanks are ignored)	Real	

whenever very large or very small numbers are to be written but not all digits need be represented. In FORTRAN, the letter E as a separator between the number and the exponent ($\pm nn$) is used instead of 10. In other words, 315 billion may be written in FORTRAN as 315.0E + 09. The zero following the decimal, the plus sign in front of the exponent, and the zero in front of the 9 are optional; for example, 315.E + 9 is also correct. A decimal point is not required in the value; for example, 315.E + 9 and 315E + 9 are both correct forms of a real constant. (Integer constants cannot use this notation.) In writing a quantity in E format, the significant digits of the number (sometimes referred to as the fraction or characteristic) can have any scaling desired, but the exponent ($\pm nn$) must reflect the scaling. For example, the following are identical in value:

```
31.5E + 10
3.15E + 11
.315E + 12
```

A negative 315 billion would have the sign in front ($-315.0E + 9$). Note that E does not mean exponentiation of the constant by the value following E, but means to scale the constant by powers of 10. Thus, 3.0E2 does not mean 3^2; it means 3.0×10^2 or 3.0×100, which is equal to 300. To interpret any E form, multiply the fraction by the power of 10 ($\pm nn$) following E. This is the same as moving the decimal point nn places to the right for a positive exponent and nn places to the left for a negative exponent. The exponent is for scaling purposes only; it cannot be a fraction. The plus sign on the positive exponent is optional, but we recommend it be used for clarity.

Number in E format	Stated in mathematical form	Quantity being represented
1.31756E + 10	1.31756×10^{10}	13175600000.
1.31756E − 5	1.31756×10^{-5}	.0000131756

As indicated by the rules for constants and variables, different FORTRAN implementations may have different limits for the number of characters in a constant, the

Rules for Constants

Purpose of constant
 To write a specific number in the program. Two types are used—integer (fixed point) and real (floating point).

General rules for forming constants
1. The decimal digits 0 and 9 are used to form a constant.
2. The minus sign must be used for a negative constant; an unsigned constant is considered positive; a plus sign is optional.
3. The size of a constant is limited to either a maximum number of digits or a maximum magnitude. There is a considerable range in allowable sizes for different implementations of FORTRAN. Where limits are fairly small, as in microcomputer FORTRAN, there are compiler-specific commands to increase the sizes.
4. Spaces within a constant are allowed, but their use is discouraged because it can be error-prone.

Rules for forming an integer constant
1. A constant *without* a decimal point.
2. Size limits range from 5 to about 10 digits. Most implementations of FORTRAN accept at least six digits and most allow more. The size limit for microcomputer FORTRAN may be as low as the range from $-32,767$ to $32,767$ but can be set higher by the programmer.

Rules for forming a real constant
1. A constant *with* a decimal point.
2. Most implementations allow real constants with up to eight digits and many accept more digits. Microcomputer FORTRAN has a precision of six decimal digits.

Rules for exponent form of real constant
 If the quantity to be represented is larger or smaller than the allowed number of digits can represent, a special exponent form is used. The form consists of a number with or without a decimal point in it followed by the letter E and an optionally signed integer exponent. A positive exponent means the actual decimal point should be moved the number of places to the right specified by the integer. A minus exponent moves the decimal point to the left. This corresponds to scientific exponent notation. The limits of the exponent value vary with different implementations of FORTRAN, but all accept E forms with a two-digit exponent ranging from -38 to 38, and most allow much larger exponents.

Rules for Constants (continued)

Examples

Constant	Valid or not valid	If valid, integer (I) or real (R); if not valid, why
123	Valid	I
123.	Valid	R
123.0	Valid	R
12 3	Valid, but blank not recommended (and may be invalid in older versions of FORTRAN)	I
123.E + 13	Valid	R (exponent form)
123.E − 13	Valid	R (exponent form)
3.141769984376432	Uncertain	May have too many digits
987.4E + 299	Uncertain	Exponent perhaps too large

size of the exponent in the exponent form, etc. These limits reflect the limits imposed by storage and execution speed considerations. For small computers, the limits are frequently stated in terms of bytes of storage. A *byte* is a small unit of storage usually defined as 8 bits. Two bytes of storage can store an integer from $-32,767$ to $32,767$. If the computer assigns 4 bytes for storage of an integer quantity instead of 2 bytes, the limits are $\pm 2,147,483,647$. For a specific implementation, there may be job control instructions to change these limits.

Self-Testing Exercise 1-3

1. What is the purpose of the variable name in FORTRAN, and what is the difference between a variable and a constant?

2. What are the rules for naming a real variable?

3. What is the purpose of the E format for expressing quantities in FORTRAN?

4. In mathematical notation, *ab* means $a \times b$. What does AB stand for in FORTRAN?

5. Fill in the following table for constants and variables. If a form is invalid for most implementations but may be valid for some, note this difference.

	Valid or not valid	If valid, constant or variable	Integer or real type	If not valid, why
(*a*) FATHERS				
(*b*) DAD−0				
(*c*) FICA				
(*d*) INTR				
(*e*) F145				
(*f*) ABLE				
(*g*) X−14				
(*h*) 19E25				
(*i*) 18.47				
(*j*) 19876.45110				
(*k*) 98				
(*l*) 19875694315				

List-Directed Input Statement

The FORTRAN program, if it needs data not included in the program statements, must read data. The data to be read may be entered from a terminal, be in a data file, or part of a data file previously prepared and stored by the computer. The data items are not provided automatically to the program; the program must read them as needed. There are a number of instructions for use in reading data; the simplest is the list-directed input statement.

List-directed input instructions will be used in Chapters 1 and 2. A list-directed READ statement will read data items from the standard input device. For many computers, this will be a terminal keyboard, and input will be entered during interactive execution of the program. On other computers, the installation may specify that the execution be in batch mode. Data items are coded exactly the same as for interactive input but stored on a data file for use by the program. Additional input features will be explained in Chapters 3 and 6. The basic format of the list-directed input statement (also called free format READ) is shown in the box.

LIST-DIRECTED INPUT STATEMENT

READ $*, v_1, v_2, \ldots, v_n$

reads input data from standard input device (such as terminal keyboard), where v_1 = variable name that references first input data item, v_2 the second input data item, etc. The input data items must be separated by a comma or spaces. Integer values should have no decimal point; real values without a fractional part may have a decimal point, but it is not required (although we recommend it). Large values or very small values of real numbers may be input in E exponent form.

A general form of the input statement, READ (*, *), may be required by some versions of microcomputer FORTRAN. In some limited versions of FORTRAN, such as subset FORTRAN, list-directed input may not be implemented. (If list-directed input is not available to you or is restricted, read the first pages of Chapter 3a in order to write simple formatted input statements.)

In order to understand how the list-directed READ works, assume three data items are to be obtained from input at a terminal or PC keyboard. The programmer assigns each data item a symbolic variable name, say, A, B, and I. A program statement to read (accept) the three values from terminal or PC keyboard is written as follows:

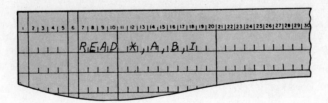

This statement reads the three values when they are received from the keyboard entry and places them in the storage locations reserved by the program for values of A, B, and I. Note that the first two values are real (with decimal points) and that the third is integer type. The space between the word READ and the asterisk is optional; we favor it

Figure 1-2 Input of three data items from a keyboard as specified by list-directed READ.

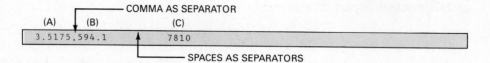

for the sake of clarity. Additional spaces could be added between items in this list, but this is not usually done.

The order of the variable names in the READ statement must correspond to the order in which the data items are to be entered at the keyboard. The data items are entered with either a comma or one or more spaces between them (Figure 1-2). Decimal points are also entered for real quantities, as are minus signs in front of negative quantities. Leading zeros and/or plus signs may be used in front of the first digit (but are not required). Large or very small real numbers may be input in exponent form.

List-Directed Output Statement

The results of a FORTRAN program are not automatically displayed or printed. The program must include statements to specify the data items to be output, the order in which these are to be displayed or printed, and labels, headings, etc., to identify output. The simplest instruction for outputs is the list-directed output statement. Other, more flexible output statements will be explained in Chapter 3.

The list-directed output statements specify the variables whose values are to be displayed or printed by listing the symbolic names for the variables. The values are output in a standard preformatted way—generally in preset positions on the printer paper or display screen. Decimal points and minus signs will be displayed where necessary. The basic form of the list-directed output is shown in the box.

LIST-DIRECTED OUTPUT

PRINT $*, v_1, v_2, \ldots, v_n$

outputs on the standard output device (probably user terminal, printer, or display) where v equals a variable name associated with a stored quantity or is a set of characters enclosed in apostrophes. The values are printed in preset areas on the output line. A preset maximum number of digits is printed. Trailing zeros may be printed with real data to make the preset number of digits. Exponent E form is used to represent values too large or too small for the output area. The first column on each print line is left blank.

A general form of the list-directed output statement, WRITE (*, *), may be required by some versions of microcomputer FORTRAN. In some limited versions of FORTRAN, such as subset FORTRAN, list-directed output may not be included. (If list-directed output is not available to you, read pages 137 to 148 in Chapter 3a in order to write simple formatted output statements.)

Since the output positions available for output of a quantity are preset, a large number requiring more digits than are available for output is represented by the E format, in which the symbol E is used to indicate powers of 10 exponential notation. As explained earlier, the digits following E, if positive, mean the decimal should be moved to the right that many places; if negative, to the left.

In the list-directed output instruction, a heading or label is output by including it in the list of variables to be printed, preceded, and followed by an apostrophe. For example, PRINT *, A, B will print as follows if A = 13.17 and B = 1.09.

13.1700   1.09000

The statement PRINT *, A, 'SUM', B will print:

13.1700   SUM   1.09000

To understand the typical operation of the list-directed output statement PRINT *, imagine that each line of output consists of a blank space in the first position as well as a set of areas or print fields for the rest of the line. All fields for the same type are of the same size. Each of the numeric data items being output is printed within the area of a fixed-size field. The computer automatically positions the value being printed in the field. Unused spaces in the field are left blank.

Spaces in the field are left blank.

Blank

Output line with fixed-size fields for use in printing numeric data items.

The size of the field places a limit on the number of digits that can be printed for a value. The maximum number of digits, the field size, and positioning within fields are not standardized. These may differ among implementations of FORTRAN. Observe the results from your compiler. As an example of a reasonable specification, assume a field size of 13 and a maximum of six significant digits that are printed for each numeric data item. Positioning within a field may be performed using rules such as the following (for a 13-position field):

1. *Integer data*   Right-justify and leave six extra spaces at the left side of field.
2. *Real data*   Start at the left of field with a blank divider space plus one space for a sign. The real value being printed takes seven spaces (six digits and a decimal point), leaving four blank spaces to the right of the field.
3. *Exponent form*   Leave one blank divider space to the left, a position for sign, six digits with a decimal, one space for letter E to indicate exponent, sign of exponent (+ or −), and a two-digit exponent.

As an example of a preset maximum of six significant digits and a preset field size of 13 spaces, the following statements cause printing in columns as shown (assuming IX = 57, X = −19.7764, and Y = 6.87580E + 06):

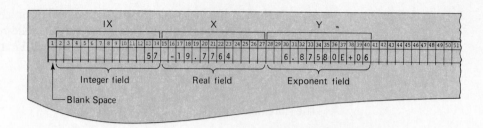

The preceding explanation for numeric data items did not include character output for labels, headings, etc. Characters are specified for printout by their inclusion in the output list before or after the variable they are to precede or follow. As noted, characters are enclosed in apostrophes, which are not printed. As with numeric data, there are no standards for positioning list-directed character output. But, in general, character data will use only the number of spaces required for the characters to be printed. If character data is printed before any numeric data, it will start in the second position on the line (because the first position is left blank in list-directed output). If character data follows numeric data, the characters are printed after the end of the numeric field. For example, using ƀ to indicate a space,

```
PRINT *, 'HOW NOW'
ƀHOW NOW
PRINT *, X, 'PROFIT'
[if X = 1317.05]
ƀƀƀ1317.05ƀƀƀƀPROFIT
PRINT *, IDATE, 'PROFIT', X
[if IDATE = 1982]
ƀƀƀƀƀƀƀƀƀ1982PROFITƀƀ1317.05
PRINT *, IDATE, 'ƀPROFIT', X
ƀƀƀƀƀƀƀƀƀ1982ƀPROFITƀƀ1317.05
```

The third example illustrates the effect of right justification of integer output with no space before (or after) character data output. In the fourth example, a space is inserted between the integer data and the character output by including the space as a character output.

Interactive Prompting of Input

When a program is executed interactively from a terminal or a personal computer, input data must also be entered from the keyboard. But how does the operator know when and in what form to enter data? In general, a READ statement is interpreted in interactive operation as accepting an input from the keyboard. The computer may prompt the operator to input the data by printing a prompt character, such as a question mark. The computer then waits for the operator to enter the data and hit the RETURN or ENTER key to indicate that the inputs are sent. The program accepts and processes the input data. The difficulty is that the operator may not know or may have forgotten the specifications for the inputs. Or there may be more than one input, and the general prompt character does not specify the one that is required. In many implementations no prompt character is displayed by the system. Therefore, as a general practice, it is desirable to print a message before the READ statement in order to prompt and describe to the operator the input to be entered. For example, if the operator is to enter the date and the latest interest rate being paid by the government for Treasury bills, the program might contain PRINT and READ statements as follows:

```
PRINT *, 'ENTER TODAY'S DATE IN FORM YYMMDD.'
PRINT *, 'ENTER MOST RECENT T-BILL RATE IN FORM XX.XX.'
PRINT *, 'SEPARATE INPUTS BY SPACES OR BY A COMMA.'
READ *, IDATE, TRATE
```

When the program executes, it prints the message and then gives the prompt character (such as a ?):

```
ENTER TODAY'S DATE IN FORM YYMMDD.
ENTER MOST RECENT T-BILL RATE IN FORM XX.XX.
SEPARATE INPUTS BY SPACES OR BY A COMMA.
?
```

The terminal operator then enters the data:

```
880118 13.05     (Hit ENTER or RETURN key to send data to computer.)
```

An issue when programming for interactive input in response to an input message is whether the input will be on the same line as the message requesting it or will be entered on the next line. Some FORTRAN implementations automatically accept input on the same line; others move to the next line for the input. For those implementations that move to the next line, there is usually a special character that can be used to suppress the move so that the input appears at the end of the message requesting the data.

Arithmetic Assignment Statements

Having described how to use a list-directed READ statement to input data items and a list-directed PRINT to output values, the next requirement is to process the input data to produce values for output. The basic statement for describing arithmetic operations is the assignment statement. Such a statement is of the general form

$$v = e$$

where v stands for a variable name and e stands for an arithmetic expression. The expression consists of one or more variable names and/or constants connected by operation symbols.

Examples

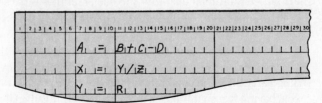

The form $v = e$ does not necessarily mean that v is equal to e. It directs the computer to replace the previous value of the variable on the left side of the equals sign with the

Operation Symbols

Symbol	Stands for	Example
+	Addition	A + B
−	Subtraction	A − B
	or negation	− A
/	Division	A/B
*	Multiplication	A * B
**	Exponentiation	A**B

results of the expression on the right. Or, in other words, it assigns the value of the expression on the right to the variable name on the left of the equals sign. Thus a statement X = X + 1.0 means that the value of X is increased by the constant 1.0 and that this new value is assigned to (stored at) X. If X is referred to later in the program, the new value is the one made available. Because the computer executes the expression on the right side of the equals sign and then stores the result at the location of the variable on the left, having anything but a variable name to the left of the equals sign is illegal.

The operation symbols used in an assignment statement are those normally used in mathematics, except for multiplication and exponentiation, which make use of the asterisk.

The compiler ignores spaces before or after operation symbols and before or after the variable names and other operands. Thus, K=A+B+C is equivalent to K = A + B + C. The use of spaces may add clarity for the reader. The multiplication operator must be used; it cannot be implied as is often done in mathematical notation; for example, ab meaning $a \times b$ must be written in FORTRAN as A * B.

In a mathematical expression, there is an accepted notational form that specifies the order in which the operations are to be performed. For example, $X + (Y/Z)$ is not the same as $(X + Y)/Z$. In the first instance, Y is divided by Z, and the result is added to X; in the second, X is added to Y, and the result is divided by Z. In some cases, the order of operation is not important because operations are commutative. Thus, $X = A + B + C − D$ can be performed in any order, and the results will be identical. The most common mathematical notation uses parentheses to specify the order of computation.

FORTRAN uses both a precedence rule and a parentheses rule to specify the way an arithmetic expression is to be handled. The *precedence rule* states that all exponentiation will be performed first, all multiplication and division next, and all addition and subtraction last. Where the precedence of operations is the same, such as in multiplication and division, the operations will be performed in order from left to right.

The *parentheses rule* states that operations will be performed in the innermost set of parentheses first (using the precedence rule where appropriate) and then in the next set, etc., until all operations inside parentheses have been performed. Then the remaining operations in the expression are carried out according to the precedence rule.

Parentheses should be used freely. If redundant, they do no harm, and they improve the readability and maintainability of the program. It is better to be explicit by using parentheses than to rely on the precedence rule. Parentheses are also used to avoid having two operations symbols together. It is illegal to write A* − B, where the minus sign is a sign relating to B. Using parentheses to separate the two operation symbols makes the expression valid: A*(− B). Parentheses are always used in pairs. A common error in writing FORTRAN is to forget the closing parenthesis.

Examples

FORTRAN	Formula
X = A + B/C − D**2	$x = a + \dfrac{b}{c} - d^2$
X = (A + B)/(C + D)	$x = \dfrac{a + b}{c + d}$
X = (A + B)/C + D	$x = \dfrac{a + b}{c} + d$
X = A * B * C + 1.5	$x = abc + 1.5$
X = (A * B * C) + 1.5	$x = abc + 1.5$
X = (A * B) * (C + 1.5)	$x = (ab)(c + 1.5)$
X = A**Z + 1.0	$x = a^z + 1.0$
X = A**(Z + 1.0)	$x = a^{z+1}$

The rules for forming arithmetic expressions and statements are summarized below. The student should pay particular attention to the precedence rules.

As explained earlier, real-type variables or constants may have a fractional part; an integer variable or integer constant cannot have a fractional part. In arithmetic operations involving integer data, the result cannot have a fractional part. This will receive further explanation in Chapter 2, but it suggests that mixing data of different types must be done with caution. For this chapter, the student should avoid possible problems in writing the assigned program by not using any integer variables or integer constants in arithmetic assignment statements. Make all variables and all constants real. An exception may be made in the case of exponents that are whole numbers. In other words, X**2 or X**N can be used, but write X**0.2 instead of X**(1/5) for a fractional exponent. There are no restrictions on integer data used for identification purposes and not included in an arithmetic expression.

STOP and END Statements

The STOP statement is used to specify that the program execution is to be terminated. The END statement is the last statement in the program. It signals the end of the program unit and consists only of the word END.

Rules for Forming Arithmetic Statements

1. The general form of an arithmetic statement is $v = e$, where v stands for any variable name and e stands for an arithmetic expression.
2. The portion of the arithmetic statement to the left of the equals sign is a variable name. It must not be a constant or contain arithmetic operations.
3. The equals sign means "assign as the value of the variable on the left the result of the expression on the right." It is not an equality sign in the mathematical sense.
4. Two operation symbols may not be used next to each other (except for two asterisks, which mean exponentiation).
5. Spaces may be used whenever desired to improve readability. The compiler ignores them.
6. Parentheses are used to specify order of operation and to avoid the two-operation symbol restriction. Operations inside parentheses are performed first. Parentheses must always be used in pairs.
7. In the absence of parentheses, the precedence rule for performing arithmetic operations specifies the order. Within one of the precedence levels, the operations are performed from left to right. The precedence rule is exponentiation first, multiplication and division second, and addition, subtraction, or negation third.

The difference between STOP and END is that STOP is an instruction to stop the program when it is being executed, whereas END is an instruction to the compiler that there are no more statements in the program unit.

In a simple program the next-to-last statement will be STOP, the last statement END.

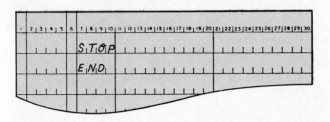

> **STOP and END STATEMENTS**
>
> STOP   Stops execution of the program
> END   The last statement in a program

Blank Spaces in FORTRAN Statements and Data

The use of blanks or spaces in writing FORTRAN is sometimes confusing to beginning programmers. Rules and recommended practices are therefore summarized for review.

Blanks in FORTRAN

Blanks are ignored in the following situations:

1. Blanks embedded in a constant

    X = 3.1751   and   X = 3.1   751

    are interpreted the same. However, for clarity of programming, do not embed blanks.
2. Blanks in a statement number field (columns 1–5).

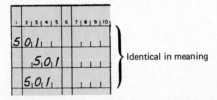

} Identical in meaning

    Recommended form is right-justified (blanks to left) as in the second example.
3. Blanks before or after FORTRAN words, parentheses, and symbols. Use or omit blanks to improve readability. The following pairs are identical to FORTRAN:

Blanks	No blanks
X = Y/Z	X=Y/Z
PRINT *, X, Y	PRINT*,X,Y

4. Blanks embedded in a variable name are ignored, but we recommend they not be used.

Blanks are important in the following cases:

1. For list-directed input, one or more blanks or a comma is used to separate data items. The following are identical input data:

```
93.17, 45
93.17  45
```

2. For input, blanks cannot be embedded in a data item. The value 93.176 cannot be input as 93.1   76.
3. For character input or output, blanks are treated the same as other characters. For example, in the following statements, the blanks inside the apostrophes are characters the same as N, O, etc.

```
PRINT *, 'NOW IS THE TIME'
```

Self-Testing Exercise 1-4

1. Write FORTRAN statements for each of the following formulas, using sufficient parentheses to make the statement execution procedure very clear.

    (a) $x = \dfrac{a}{b} + c$

    (b) $x = \dfrac{3y^2}{z^2}$

    (c) $x = a^b + \dfrac{d}{e}$

    (d) $x = \left(\dfrac{a}{b}\right) cd$

    (e) $x = \dfrac{a + b}{c + d}$

2. Rewrite the following FORTRAN statements, eliminating the redundant parentheses used for clarity:

Formula	FORTRAN
(a) $x = \dfrac{a + b}{ef}$	X = (A + B)/(E * F)
(b) $x = abc + 1$	X = (A * B * C) + 1.0
(c) $x = \left(\dfrac{ab}{c}\right) d$	X = ((A * B)/C) * D

3. Write FORTRAN statements to perform the following:
    (a) Read the values for A, B, and D interactively.
    (b) Print the values for A, B, and D but in the order B, A, D.
    (c) Print the value for A plus the words IS ALL.
    (d) Stop the program.
    (e) Identify the end of the program statements.
    (f) Read values for C and D from a terminal. Print the inputs for visual inspection along with a label C before the value of C and a label D before the value of D.

Summary

Overall FORTRAN program structure can be planned by considering the outputs to be prepared, the inputs needed to produce the outputs, and the processes to produce outputs from inputs. The design of a FORTRAN program logic can usually make effective use of a program flowchart and/or program design language. Special coding paper is useful in writing FORTRAN statements.

After the FORTRAN program is coded and entered into the computer, it can be compiled immediately or stored for later use. Fatal and nonfatal program-coding errors are detected during both compilation and execution. Logic errors are detected by program testing. In order to compile and execute a FORTRAN program, it is necessary to provide job control instructions with the program.

Five FORTRAN statements were explained in the chapter: list-directed input, list-directed output, arithmetic assignment, STOP, and END. These five statements are sufficient for writing simple but complete FORTRAN programs.

Answers to Self-Testing Exercises

Exercise 1-1

1. Hardware is the computer equipment; software consists of the operating system, compilers, application programs, and other sets of computer routines to direct the operation of the equipment.

2. A program exists in primary storage in machine language. This is the language the computer actually uses. A symbolic assembly language is a language for symbolically describing the parts of a machine-language instruction. The symbolic assembly language is easier to code and read than machine language and is directly translatable into machine-language instructions by the symbolic assembly system. (Generally, one symbolic assembly instruction is translated into one machine-language instruction.)

3. Compared to symbolic assembly languages, high-level languages such as FORTRAN are machine-independent (in the sense that they can be compiled and run with little or no changes on any computer having a compiler for the language); they are relatively easy to learn because they use formula-like instructions, require fewer instructions, provide more understandable documentation, and are easier to test and debug.

4. FORmula TRANslator

5. ANSI has established a standard language set for FORTRAN, divided into two different levels of implementation.

6. (a) Meet user needs
   (b) Development on time within budget
   (c) Error-free set of instructions
   (d) Error-resistant operation
   (e) Maintainable programs
   (f) Portable programs

7. (a) Initialization
   (b) Input
   (c) Input data validation
   (d) Processing
   (e) Output
   (f) Error handling
   (g) Closing procedure

8. (a) Sequence. One action followed by another.
   (b) Selection. Test for a condition followed by two alternative program paths.
   (c) Repetition. A set of operations is repeated while some condition continues to be true.

9. (a) 2   (b) 4   (c) 5   (d) 1   (e) 6   (f) 3

10. Portable

11. Flowcharts and/or program design language (pseudocode)

12. An orderly sequence of steps can consist of the following:
    (a) Define requirements in terms of outputs.
    (b) Based on the outputs, define inputs.
    (c) Define input validation and input error handling.
    (d) Define procedures for transforming input data into output.
    (e) Define the program structure in terms of major modules.

Exercise 1-2

1. The character C or * in column 1 means that the line is a comment line in the program and not an instruction to be translated.

2. Operating system

3. A program is stored in a program file by entering program statements a line at a time from a keyboard until the program is complete. The process of entry may be controlled by a text editor or by an interactive FORTRAN compiler. The program may be compiled and executed immediately or be stored by the computer for later compilation and execution.

4. In batch submission for compilation and execution, the process is scheduled for a later time; in the interactive mode, compilation and execution are performed immediately after entering commands by the programmer.

5. Compilation is the translation of FORTRAN statements to machine-level instructions that can be executed. The executable program from compilation (object program) can be stored for later execution or run at once.

6. Syntactical (or syntax)

Exercise 1-3

1. The variable name is used to specify a value that can change with each execution of the program. The variable name identifies the location where the value is stored. Whereas a variable represents a quantity that is unknown or may change in value during the program, a constant is used to write a specific, unchanging value in the program.

2. The name begins with the letter A to H or O to Z and may contain up to six alphabetic characters and numeric digits. No special characters are allowed.

3. The E format is used to represent very large and very small numbers.

4. AB is a FORTRAN variable name for a real variable.

5.

Valid or not valid	If valid, constant or variable	Integer or real type	If not valid, why
(a) Not valid	—	—	Too many characters
(b) Not valid	—	—	Special character not allowed
(c) Valid	Variable	Real	
(d) Valid	Variable	Integer	

Valid or not valid	If valid, constant or variable	Integer or real type	If not valid, why
(e) Valid	Variable	Real	
(f) Valid	Variable	Real	
(g) Not valid			Special character (-) not allowed
(h) Valid (decimal point and sign optional with exponent form of real constant)	Constant	Real	
(i) Valid	Constant	Real	
(j) Not valid (for most implementations)			Too large
(k) Valid	Constant	Integer	
(l) Not valid (for most implementations)			Too large

Exercise 1-4

1. (a) X = A/B + C
    (b) X = 3.0 * Y**2/Z**2 but better as X = (3.0 * (Y**2))/(Z**2)
    (c) X = A**B + D/E or X = A**B + (D/E)
    (d) X = A/B * C * D but better as X = (A/B) * C * D
    (e) X = (A + B)/(C + D)

2. (a) All are necessary.
    (b) A * B * C + 1.0
    (c) A * B/C * D

3. (a) PRINT *, 'INPUT VALUES FOR A, B, AND D SEPARATED BY COMMAS.'
        READ *, A, B, D
    (b) PRINT *, B, A, D
    (c) PRINT *, A, 'IS ALL'
    (d) STOP
    (e) END
    (f) PRINT *, 'INPUT VALUES FOR C AND D SEPARATED BY A COMMA.'
        READ *, C, D
        PRINT *, 'C', C, 'D', D

    If C has a value of 12.1 and D has a value of 98.13, the output will be:

    C 12.1000 D 98.1300

Questions and Problems

1. Define the following terms:
    (a) application program
    (b) compiler
    (c) flowchart
    (d) hardware
    (e) high-level language

  (f) job control instructions
  (g) machine-oriented language
  (h) object program
  (i) program design language
  (j) program module
  (k) routine
  (l) software
  (m) source program
  (n) structured program
  (o) symbolic assembly system

2. What are the hardware elements of a computer system?

3. What is the main difference between a machine-oriented language and a high-level language?

4. List and describe the main steps in developing a FORTRAN program.

5. Fill in the following table:

	Valid or not valid	Constant or variable	Integer or real type	If not valid, why
(a) MAN				
(b) WOMAN				
(c) X − 19				
(d) RATE				
(e) I				
(f) OUTPUT				
(g) 9FOUR				
(h) DOLL				
(i) 18.97				
(j) BETA				
(k) J19				
(l) 134.1E19				
(m) 1.9E − 20				

6. Assume three variables A, B, C. Indicate whether each of the following statements is valid. If not valid, explain.
  (a) READ *, A, B, C
  (b) PRINT ABC
  (c) READ A, B, C
  (d) PRINT *, A, TOTAL IS, B
  (e) PRINT 'THE SUM IS' , A

7. Rewite the following as FORTRAN statements. Use sufficient parentheses to make the order of operations clear.
  (a) $x = \dfrac{a + b}{c}$
  (b) $x = \dfrac{c + d}{f + g}$
  (c) $x = (a^c)(d + f)$
  (d) $x = (a^c)(b^d)$
  (e) $x = a + b - c$

Example Programs and Programming Exercises to Read, Compute, and Print

General Comments on the Example Programs
Example Program Structure
Use of Uppercase and Lowercase in Program Examples
Pseudocode and Program Flowcharts for Example Programs

General Program Example 1— Compute Employee Pay
Problem Description for General Example 1
Program Documentation for General Example 1
Planning Program Logic Using a Program Design Language
Planning Program Logic Using a Flowchart
Notes on General Example 1

Mathematical Program Example 1— Compute the Volume of a Square Pyramid
Problem Description for Mathematical Example 1

Program Documentation for Mathematical Example 1
Notes on Mathematical Example 1

Summary of Suggestions for Programming Style

Programming Exercises
Description of Assignment
Mathematics and Statistics
Business and Economics
Science and Engineering
Humanities and Social Sciences
General
Interactive Scientific and Engineering

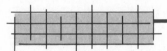

Chapter 1a contained a descriptive and conceptual introduction to programming, programming discipline, and the FORTRAN language. Five FORTRAN instructions were explained. These instructions are sufficient to write simple programs using the sequence programming structure.

Chapter 1b consists of two complete examples of programs (using the features and the five statements explained in Chapter 1a) as well as programming exercises. In subsequent chapters, the two programming examples will illustrate design of programs for the two types of execution. The general program (payroll) will be designed for batch execution with a data file, and the mathematical program will be designed for interactive execution with data input from a computer terminal or personal computer keyboard. In this chapter, both programs are written to be executed with interactive input and immediate output. The programming exercises provide a learning experience in following the procedures for writing a FORTRAN program and getting it to run on a specific computer. The student assignment is to:

1. Design a program using both a program design language and a flowchart. Both techniques are assigned to provide experience in these two alternatives.
2. Code the instructions on FORTRAN coding paper. Also code a set of input data.
3. Enter the program statements from the keyboard either using a text editor that creates a program file or an interactive FORTRAN compiler. Enter job control instructions to compile and execute the FORTRAN program.
4. Remove all errors detected during compilation, and resubmit the corrected program for compilation and execution.
5. Provide data required for program execution by entering from the keyboard as requested by the program in interactive execution mode, or, in batch mode, provide a data file to be read by the program.

The emphasis of Chapter 1b is on learning by examining complete example programs and by doing a complete program. The first programming problem not only provides experience with coding a simple FORTRAN program but also assists the student in learning the specific job control instructions and FORTRAN job submission procedures. Because the program is a simple one, the student can concentrate on the structure of a well-written program, on the keyboard entry, submission procedures, and interpretation of the output.

General Comments on the Example Programs

There are two example programs for two somewhat different types of problems:

1. *General program 1*   Compute an employee paycheck.
2. *Mathematical program 1*   Calculate volume of a square pyramid.

47

Figure 1-3 Differences between line numbers and statement labels.

```
                        Line number
                        |                  Statement label (on some statements)
                        |                  |
                        v                  v
1  *SEGMENT TO SHOW LINE NUMBERS AND STATEMENT LABELS
2  (100) READ *, X,Y
3        A = X + Y
4        PRINT *, X,Y,A
5        STOP
6        END

          |<---------- FORTRAN coding sheet ---------->|
```

The two programs provide insight into the use of FORTRAN for two different types of problems. Also, some students may be more familiar with one problem area than the other; the two examples allow the student to concentrate on the example in which the problem context is best understood.

Before examining the example programs, the use of line numbers needs to be understood. Two types of line numbers may be encountered:

1. *Statement labels to identify certain statements during execution of the program*   When needed, the statement label is coded in columns 1–5 of the line. The statement label will be explained in Chapter 2. For now, it is sufficient to understand that statement labels, when used, are an integral part of the program.
2. *Line number for identification purposes*   These are not required by the FORTRAN language but are used for convenience or because of operational needs (see Figure 1-3). Three examples of the use of line numbers are:
   (a) In entry of program statements with an interactive FORTRAN compiler, each statement is given a line number (separate from statement labels). The line identifiers are used for interactive correction of lines.
   (b) Printed listings of the FORTRAN program from the compilation process frequently have line identification numbers added to the printout as a convenience in referring to statements.
   (c) Listings displayed on a screen use line identification numbers to aid in finding lines.

The program listings in the text illustrate the practice of printed listings with line identification numbers added by the compiler. They will be useful in the text when referring to lines in the program.

Example Program Structure

Note the structure of the example programs. The structure makes extensive use of comment lines. As explained, a comment line has an asterisk or letter C in column 1.

The structure used in the example programs is recommended for the programs you are to write. This structure is not required by the FORTRAN language; it is recommended as a matter of style in writing clear, understandable, well-documented programs. The style issue becomes more significant as programs become larger and more complex; we recommend the style should be followed even in small programs as a learning experience and as a matter of programming discipline. The programs consist of the following blocks of coding:

1. *Program identification*   This block of comments describes the program and identifies the author and the date written. Any special comments regarding the program can be placed here.
2. *Variable identification*   Variable names in FORTRAN are short, and thus have limited capability to describe the variables. In order to fully document the

program, there needs to be additional description of the data associated with each variable name. The names themselves should be as descriptive as possible to help the reader of the program remember the purpose of the variable. In addition, every variable name used in the program should be described in a comment statement. When coding a program, a description is written and placed in the variable identification block each time a new variable is used. This will result in the variable identification list being arranged in order by the first use of a variable. It is also a relatively simple matter to rearrange these statements so as to have the list in alphabetical order. Alphabetical arrangement is optional but useful, especially with long lists. For readability, we have chosen to start names in column 11 and to start the definitions in column 21. The variable identification block is for clear program documentation; it does not affect program execution. In large programs, note that the concept of variable identification may be altered slightly. Global variables may be described in a variable identification block for the program; variables applying only within a block may be described in the block description itself.

3. *Constant identification*   It is frequently useful to name constants rather than to employ them directly in the program. It sometimes makes the program easier to understand. Also, changeable constants (such as tax rates) are more easily changed if the constant value is named. This block may be omitted if no constants are named. The block is for documentation purposes.

4. *Initialization*   If constants are named, the values are set by arithmetic assignment statements before any processing. There will be additional instances where initial values need to be set, such as setting variables to zero. This block may be omitted if no initialization is performed.

5. *Processing blocks*   In the simple program, a single processing block may be sufficient. In later programs there will be several separate blocks, such as to read data, validate input data, process, output normal values, output error messages, and terminate the program.

As a matter of style to achieve a readable program, each block is identified by a name, set off by asterisks.

```
**********
*                     INITIALIZATION BLOCK
**********
```

We have chosen to have the title for each block begin in column 23 so that it is somewhat centered and stands out. Blank comment lines to visually separate parts of the program begin in column 1 with an asterisk (or C). Other conventions could be used; these are recommended and will be followed in this text.

Comments should be used freely within the processing modules. In order to differentiate comment lines from executable statements, we have chosen to have each set of one or more comment lines preceded and followed by a blank comment line having only an asterisk (or C) in column 1. The comment line or lines have asterisks in column 1 and the comment begins in column 11 or after. Additional program style conventions will be given in subsequent chapters.

Use of Uppercase and Lowercase in Program Examples

Inside the computer, a capital letter is coded differently than the equivalent lowercase letter. The standard is to code FORTRAN statements in capital letters. However, some language processors do not enforce the capital letter convention. We recommend that all FORTRAN statements be coded in capital letters. The capital letter convention does not apply in two cases:

1. Documentation lines which start with an asterisk in column 1 can use both uppercase and lowercase letters. In the example program, the block identification is written in capital letters for emphasis, variable names in the variable identification block are coded in capital letters because they are FORTRAN names, and FORTRAN statements are written in capital letters. Lowercase is used for description of variables.
2. Output specified by PRINT instructions can use either uppercase or lowercase. We have chosen to use a natural English-like format with both uppercase and lowercase for messages and other output labels.

Pseudocode and Program Flowcharts for Example Programs

The documentation for each program includes a program design language (pseudocode) description of the program and a program flowchart. Since these programs use only the sequence program structure, the pseudocode description and flowchart are simple and perhaps unnecessary. However, preparation of these forms of documentation in simple situations will provide practice in understanding them and in applying them in more complex programming situations. A programmer would probably not use both a pseudocode description and a program flowchart, but both are included to provide experience in using these alternatives. For this chapter, it is important to read all material for General Program Example 1 because it contains explanations having general applicability.

General Program Example 1—Compute Employee Pay

Problem Description for General Example 1

The program is to compute an employee's gross pay, taxes, net pay, and average net pay per hour based upon the following factors:

Total hours worked
Wage rate in dollars per hour
Taxes at the rate of 15 percent of gross pay
Pension contribution at the rate of 5 percent of gross pay
Miscellaneous deductions (an input given in dollars)

Input will be from a keyboard during interactive execution. The input will consist of the employee identification number, hours worked, wage rate, and amount of miscellaneous deductions. The output (at the terminal printer) should show gross pay, taxes, net pay (paycheck), and average rate of net pay per hour. The basic arithmetic operators and list-directed input and output are to be used in this program. Appropriate labels are to be used to identify the outputs. The program is to follow good programming practice for control of input errors. The input is to be checked (validated) by printing out (echoing) the input data for visual inspection.

Program Documentation for General Example 1

Both forms of program planning documentation are given here—a pseudocode program description (Figure 1-5) and a program flowchart (Figure 1-6). Figure 1-7 gives a program listing, a sample input, and a sample output. Remember that the line numbers are not part of the program as written by the programmer; these were added by the FORTRAN compiler as line references. Students learning to program frequently find it hard to visualize the steps that produce the results shown in Figure 1-7. Figure 1-4 summarizes the flow of inputs, processes, and outputs for solving a problem using FORTRAN.

Planning Program Logic Using a Program Design Language

The pseudocode for general example 1 will be used to illustrate the use of a program design language as part of program planning and design. The resulting pseudocode is also useful as documentation of the program. Program planning and design using a program design language is an iterative process starting with a few general statements and expanding these statements as more program details are planned. When program planning and design are completed, program coding is begun. The process is illustrated for general example 1.

1. The major steps in the normal flow of processing by the program are described by general pseudocode statements. In other words, the programmer first plans for normal output with processing of normal, required inputs with no erroneous data or exceptions. Four statements are sufficient to describe the general flow of processing for general example 1:

Figure 1-4 Flow of inputs, processes, and outputs for a FORTRAN program.

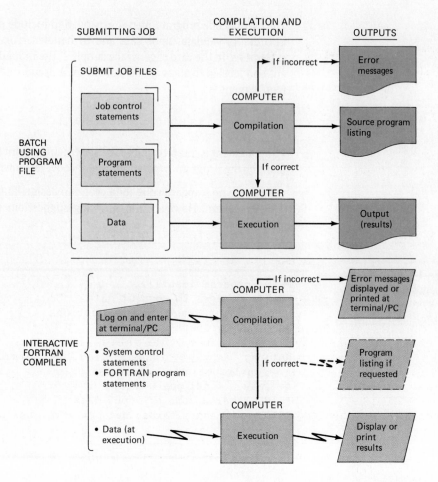

Read input data
Calculate pay amounts
Print pay amounts
Stop

More detail can be added in the pseudocode if desired. For example, the general pseudocode statements describing the flow of processing can be replaced by statements showing more detail or by sets of statements. The relationship between the pseudocode statements and planned FORTRAN coding may be made explicit by using capital letters for pseudocode words that correspond to actual FORTRAN instruction words.

General pseudocode statement	Detailed pseudocode
Read input data	PRINT program identification
	PRINT messages to request data
	READ id, hours, wage rate, deductions
Calculate pay amounts	Gross pay = hours × rate
	Taxes = gross pay × tax rate of 15%
	Net pay = gross pay − taxes − deductions − (pension contribution of 5% of pay)
	Av. net pay per hour = net pay ÷ hours
Print pay amounts	PRINT gross pay, taxes, net pay, ave. net pay per hour
Stop	STOP

2. The pseudocode program plan is expanded to include processing that is required in order to validate input data and to handle errors in input data and other exceptions. In the case of general example 1, the input data items are to be printed out and labeled to allow visual validation. A pseudocode statement to reflect this requirement is:

PRINT labeled echo of input data

The statement is inserted before the statement to print the results. The completed plan for the program, written in pseudocode, is shown in Figure 1-5.

There are no standard rules for a program design language for use in planning a FORTRAN program. However, the following suggestions may be useful and will be followed in the text:

Figure 1-5 Pseudocode description for planning general program 1— compute employee pay.

```
PRINT program identification
PRINT messages to request data
READ, id, hours, wage rate, deductions
Gross pay = hours × rate
Taxes     = pay × tax rate of 15%
Net pay   = pay − taxes − misc. deductions − pension
    contribution of 5% of pay
Av. pay   = net pay ÷ hours
PRINT labeled echo of input data
PRINT gross pay, taxes, net pay, ave. net pay rate per hour
    with labels
STOP
```

1. Each pseudocode statement describes one or more processing steps to be performed. The line is written in a condensed English-like form that also reflects the FORTRAN coding to be done.
2. Pseudocode statements referring to a specific FORTRAN instruction word (such as READ or PRINT) can include the FORTRAN word, which is then written in all capital letters.
3. A reference to a variable can describe it in words (such as sum or sum of pay amounts) or can use a descriptive name that is to be a program variable name (such as SUM or SUMPAY). The variable name in such cases is written in all capital letters. All other words in the pseudocode statement line are lowercase.

Additional pseudocode notation will be explained in later chapters.

Planning Program Logic Using a Flowchart

The process of planning and designing a program using a flowchart is similar to the process with a program design language. The major steps and logic of processing can be defined and then expanded. A major difference in using a flowchart compared to pseudocode is that the flow of processing is visually defined by symbols and lines. The

Figure 1-6 Flowchart for planning general program 1—compute employee pay.

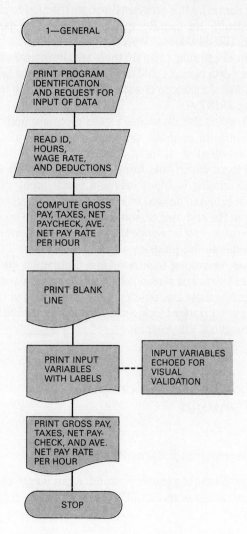

symbols may indicate the media or equipment to be used. For the simple processing flow of general example 1, there is little difference between the flowchart and the pseudocode.

The steps in planning a program using a program flowchart are:

1. Define the general flow of the program for achieving desired output from normally expected input data. Use general processing symbols for input, processing, and output. Expand the description to a suitable level of detail.
2. Add processing boxes and processing flow to perform validation of input data and to handle exceptions.

Figure 1-6 shows the flowchart at the end of step 2. The amount of detail to be shown in the boxes should be enough to clearly define what is to be done. The flowchart boxes for reading and printing contain the words READ and PRINT. These words are not necessary because the symbols imply reading from the input device or printing on paper; we include them to improve the readability of the flowcharts.

Notes on General Example 1

The variable names for this program illustrate the need to choose names that as clearly as possible identify the quantity they represent. Other names might have been used (for example, GROSPY for GRSPAY or IDNUM for ID).

Even in a beginning program there are alternative ways to code statements. For example, each data output could have been printed on a separate line. Note in Figure 1-7 the printing of a space to create a blank line between inputs/outputs (lines 40 and 47 written as PRINT *).

The program also illustrates a good programming practice. There is a line of output to identify the program, and simple input data validation is provided by having a printout (echoing) of all input data. The reader of the output can then visually validate the input data. Other forms of input validation will be explained in a later chapter; but echoing of input data and visual input validation should always be considered in program design. In interactive execution, variables are requested and are input from the keyboard, so some visual validation takes place at input. However, additional error control is provided by labeling and separately printing the input items as shown in this simple program.

Another interesting feature of this program is the naming of the two constants—rates for tax and pension. These are constants and need not be named except that rates such as these are subject to change. By our naming them and assigning the values in the initialization block, a single change in the initialization block will change the rate throughout the program.

Mathematical Program Example 1—Compute the Volume of a Square Pyramid

Problem Description for Mathematical Example 1

Calculate the volume of a square pyramid. Input length of one side of the base and its height (in either feet or meters). Print the volume in cubic feet or cubic meters.

Figure I-7 Program listing, sample input, and resulting output for general program I—compute employee pay.

```
 1  ***********
 2  *
 3  ***********
 4  *
 5  *                PROGRAM IDENTIFICATION
 6  *
 7  *      This program computes an employee's paycheck based upon
 8  *      hours worked, wage rate and various deductions.
 9  *      Designed for keyboard input and interactive execution.
10  *      Written 8/25/86 by T. Hoffmann
11  ***********
12  *
13  *                VARIABLES IDENTIFICATION
14  *
15  *      ID     = Employee Identification Number
16  *      HRSWRK = Hours worked by each employee
17  *      GRSPAY = Gross pay: $
18  *      WGRATE = Wage rate: $/hour
19  *      PAYCHK = Net paycheck amount: $
20  *      TAXES  = Taxes due: $
21  *      DEDUC  = Miscellaneous deductions
22  *      PAYRTN = Net pay per hour
23  ***********
24  *
25  *                IDENTIFICATION OF CONSTANTS
26  *
27  *      PNRATE = Pension contribution rate = 0.05
28  *      TAXRT  = Tax rate = 0.15
29  ***********
30  *
31  *                INITIALIZATION BLOCK
32  *
33        PNRATE = 0.05
34        TAXRT  = 0.15
35  ***********
36  *
37  *                READ - COMPUTE - PRINT BLOCK
38  *
39  *
40        PRINT *, 'Pay Computation Program'
41        PRINT *
42        PRINT *, 'Input Employee ID, Hours, Rate, and Deductions '
43        READ *, ID,HRSWRK,WGRATE,DEDUC
44        GRSPAY = HRSWRK*WGRATE
45        TAXES = GRSPAY*TAXRT
46        PAYCHK = GRSPAY - TAXES - DEDUC - PNRATE*GRSPAY
47        PAYRTN = PAYCHK/HRSWRK
48        PRINT *
49        PRINT *, 'For Employee ',ID
50        PRINT *, 'With ',HRSWRK,'Hours Worked at a Rate of ',WGRATE
51        PRINT *, 'and Deductions of ',DEDUC
52        PRINT *, 'The Gross Pay is ',GRSPAY,'and the taxes are ',TAXES
53        PRINT *, 'The check amount should be ',PAYCHK
54        PRINT *, 'Yielding a net pay rate per hour of ',PAYRTN
55        STOP
          END
```

INTERACTIVE INPUT AND OUTPUT

```
Pay Computation Program

Input Employee ID, Hours, Rate, and Deductions 15748,35,2.75,12.83

For Employee      15748
With   35.00000000 Hours Worked at a Rate of    2.75000000
and Deductions of   12.82999992
The Gross Pay is    96.25000000 and the taxes are   14.43750095
The check amount should be   64.16999817
Yielding a net pay rate per hour of   1.83342850
```

ID
HRSWRK
WGRATE
DEDUC

Program Documentation for Mathematical Example 1

There are a pseudocode description (Figure 1-8), a program flowchart (Figure 1-9), and a program listing (Figure 1-10) with sample input and output. Input data items are displayed as part of the output of the results.

Figure 1-8 Pseudocode description for planning mathematical program 1— compute the volume of a square pyramid.

```
PRINT program identification
Request input data for length of side and height
READ length of side and height
Compute volume of pyramid
PRINT space
PRINT echo of input items
PRINT pyramid volume
STOP
```

Figure 1-9 Program flowchart for planning mathematical program 1— compute the volume of a square pyramid.

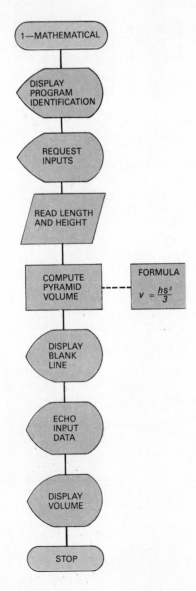

Figure 1-10 Program listing, sample input, and resulting outputs for mathematical program 1—compute the volume of a square pyramid.

```
 1  **********
 2  *        *
 3  **********
 4  *        *          PROGRAM IDENTIFICATION
 5  *        *    Compute the volume of a square pyramid.
 6  *        *    Programmed for keyboard input and interactive execution
 7  *        *    Written by T. Hoffmann 10/02/86
 8  *        *
 9  **********
10  *        *          VARIABLES IDENTIFICATION
11  **********
12  *        *
13  *        *    SIDE   = Length of a side of the pyramid's base
14  *        *    HEIGHT = Height of the pyramid
15  *        *    VOLUME = Volume of the Pyramid
16  *        *
17  **********
18  *        *          PRINT - READ - COMPUTE BLOCK
19  **********
20  *        *
21        PRINT *, 'Volume of a Square Pyramid'
22        PRINT *,
23        PRINT *, 'What is the length of one side of the base in'
24        PRINT *, 'feet or meters?'
25        READ *, SIDE
26        PRINT *, 'How high is the pyramid in feet or meters? '
27        READ *, HEIGHT
28        VOLUME = (HEIGHT*SIDE**2)/3
29        PRINT *,
30        PRINT *, 'For a side of ',SIDE,' and a height of ',HEIGHT
31        PRINT *, 'The pyramid volume is',VOLUME,' cubic feet or meters.'
32        STOP
33        END
```

INPUTS AND OUTPUTS WITH 6-DIGIT PRECISION

```
Volume of a Square Pyramid

What is the length of one side of the base in
feet or meters? 75
How high is the pyramid in feet or meters? 50

For a side of   75.0000  and a height of   50.0000
The pyramid volume is   93750.0   cubic feet or meters.
```

INPUTS AND OUTPUTS WITH 13-DIGIT PRECISION

```
Volume of a Square Pyramid

What is the length of one side of the base in
feet or meters? 75
How high is the pyramid in feet or meters? 50

For a side of   75.00000000 and a height of   50.00000000
The pyramid volume is  93750.00000000 cubic feet or meters.
```

Two outputs from running the program using two different compilers are shown. These illustrate that the format and precision (number of digits in output) of the result printed by list-directed output will vary among compilers. Precision will be explained further in Chapter 2; the methods for program control of precision in the output will be described in Chapter 3.

Notes on Mathematical Example 1

Even a simple program such as this one is illustrative of some of the problems of programming. For example, inputs are requested in either feet or meters, but what if the side measurement is 50 feet and 3 inches? The program message requesting input does not indicate what should be done in this case. An examination of the program indicates that decimal input is required rather than feet and inches. In other words, input can be 50.25, but not 50 feet and 3 inches. In a well-controlled program, this issue should be clarified by the message to the person providing input. The message indicates input can be in either feet or meters and output is in cubic feet or meters. A more complex program might ask the person doing the input whether he or she would prefer to input in feet, yards, or meters. The output would then be labeled appropriately.

It requires only one FORTRAN statement to compute the volume of a square pyramid at the base. A minimum FORTRAN program would require four or five statements. This very small program has 31 statements; 18 of these statements are for program documentation, and there are 8 print statements to give good output. The ratio of executable FORTRAN statements to documentation statements and output is quite high in this example, but a pattern of program design is being taught that will provide excellent documentation as programs get larger.

In the flowchart for the mathematical example, Figure 1-9, display symbols are used instead of printer symbols. The general input/output symbol could have been used or the printer symbol could have been used for terminal output including a visual display. To illustrate the specific use of a visual display, the flowchart is written with the assumption that a visual display is the output device.

Summary of Suggestions for Programming Style

After having reviewed the two example programs, we may summarize a set of guidelines for programming style. Additional guidelines will be added in later chapters.

Guidelines for Programming Style

1. Analyze the problem before beginning to code instructions. If you do not understand the problem and the solution procedure, you cannot tell the computer what to do. Useful design and planning methods are a program design language and program flowcharts. In planning the program logic, follow a systematic approach:
   (a) Plan the general logic of processing for producing normally expected output from normally required inputs. Expand to the desired level of detail.
   (b) Add processing logic for input validation instructions and error handling.
2. Use FORTRAN coding paper to aid in writing instructions in proper format.
3. Use a block structure to divide the program into logical segments. Include an identification block and a list of variables block. The style selected for this text to identify a block is to use a set of three lines, the first and third consisting of 10 asterisks and the second containing an asterisk in column 1 and the block name starting in column 23.

4. Use explanatory comments. Use comments freely inside the blocks. Set off each group of one or more comments by a blank comment line before the comment lines. In the text style, the comment is indented to column 11.
5. Use parentheses to avoid ambiguity. Do not rely upon unfamiliar precedence rules.
6. Consider printout (echo) of input data as a visual check against incorrect input.
7. Print headings or labels to clearly identify all output values.

Programming Exercises

Description of Assignment

Select one or more problems (or take the problems assigned to you by the instructor). Use only the five statements presented in Chapter 1a. Write the program so that either input value specified in the problem can be used (even though only one input value is to be read and processed). Follow the style guidelines in Chapter 1a and 1b in doing the assignment.

1. Write a pseudocode description of the program you design. Plan for only one set of input data; provide for validation by printing (echoing) the input data.
2. Draw a program flowchart.
3. Code the program. Use only real variables and real constants in assignment statements. Do not use any integer variables or integer constants in computations.
4. Debug and execute with a set of data.
   Hint: If a problem requires a value of e (the base for natural logarithms) or π (the ratio of the circumference of a circle to its diameter), use an approximate value of 2.7183 for e and 3.1416 for π. If a square root is required, exponentiate to the 0.5 power (that is, 1.0/2.0 power). Use only real constants for exponents requiring computations (for example, 1.0/3.0 instead of 1/3). Feel free to label variables with real names even when the formula gives letters such as n.

Mathematics and Statistics

1. For an input value of r compute the volume of the corresponding sphere.

$$v = \tfrac{4}{3}\,\pi r^3$$

Use input values for r of 10 or 26.5 inches.

2. A geometric progression is of the following form:

$$a \quad ar \quad ar^2 \quad ar^3 \ldots ar^n$$

The sum of the terms of such a progression is:

$$s = a\,\frac{r^n - 1}{r - 1}$$

Use one of the following two sets of data as input values for a, r, and n, and compute the sum.

a	r	n
1	3	6
1	0.5	7

3. The pythagorean formula can be stated as follows:

$$h = (a^2 + b^2)^{0.5}$$

where h is the hypotenuse and a and b are the sides of a right triangle. Compute h using one of the following two sets of input values a and b:

a	b
5.0	5.0
3.0	4.0

Business and Economics

4. When interest compounds q times per year at an annual rate of i percent for n years, the principal p compounds to an amount a as follows:

$$a = p\left(1 + \frac{i}{q}\right)^{nq}$$

Write a program to compute the compound amount. Use either of the following two sets of input data:

p	i	q	n
1000	0.07	4	7
18.75	0.045	12	5.25

5. Various methods are used in depreciating capital goods; one of these is the declining balance method. At the end of year n the value of the item (v_n) is given by the following relationship:

$$v_n = v_0(1 - r)^n$$

where v_0 is the initial value and r is the depreciation rate. Compare v_n using either set of input data.

n	r	v_0
5	.02	10,000.00
4	0.275	5,000.00

6. The economic order quantity (EOQ) is a function of annual usage a, interest rate i, the costs of setup s, and the cost of the item itself e. These are related as follows:

$$EOQ = \left(\frac{2as}{ci}\right)^{1/2}$$

Compute the EOQ using either of the following sets of values as input data:

a	s	c	i
8750	1.75	0.55	0.15
4000	1.55	0.45	0.25

Science and Engineering

7. The earth is not a sphere; it is slightly flattened at the poles and is therefore more of an oblate spheroid. The formula for its volume is

$$v = \tfrac{4}{3}\pi a^2 b$$

Compute the volume of the earth for input values of $a = 7927$ and $b = 7900$ miles or input values of $a = 3963$ and $b = 3950$.

8. An eraser falling out of a window is timed in its fall. Use an input for time to fall of either 5 or 6.4 seconds. Calculate and print the height of the window in feet and in meters as well as the floor from which the eraser fell (18 feet = 1 floor). The relationship between free-fall distance d in feet and time t in seconds is

$$d = 16t^2$$

(Hint: 1 foot = 0.3048 meter)

9. An empirical study has shown that the relationship between pressure and volume for superheated steam is

$$p = 1000v^{-1.4}$$

where v = volume.
   For an input for v of 1.6 or 2.0, compute the pressure.

Humanities and Social Sciences

10. Empirical studies have shown a relationship between the time to perform a task and its frequency of repetition:

$$t_x = px^{-l}$$

where x = number of repetitions
t_x = cumulative average task time for xth repetition
p = time to perform task first time
l = a learning factor

Compute the cumulative average time. Use one of the following sets of data as input:

x	p	l
100	3.4	0.465
50	3.4	0.93

11. A study was made of different groups of people to determine the number of males, females, orientals, and nonorientals. Use either set of input data. Compute the percentage of each category.

Study number	Male	Female	Oriental
1	256	244	302
2	108	492	413

12. Assuming towns are approximately circular and area equals πr^2, compute the population density of a town. Use either set of input data.

Town	Radius (miles)	Population
1	0.6	65
2	1.7	395

General

13. Students are awarded points toward their grades based upon a weighted average of their quizzes, midterm exam, and final exam. The weighting is the average of three quizzes (Q_1, Q_2, Q_3), the midterm grade (MT), and twice their final exam grade (F). Compute total weighted points using as input either set of data.

Student ID	Q_1	Q_2	Q_3	MT	F
64358	45	95	87	74	83
17651	50	89	76	71	85

14. Cars can be rented on either a daily or weekly basis. The cost for daily rental is number of days N_d times daily rate R_d plus miles driven m times rate per mile R_m. The weekly cost is a weekly charge w plus cost of buying your own gas. The latter is a function of miles driven m, gas consumption mpg, and cost of gasoline per gallon C_g. Compute both the daily and weekly costs for a rental. Use one of the sets of data as input.

Situation	N_d	R_d	m	R_m	w	mpg	C_g
1	5	$25	200	$.18	$110	20	$1.37
2	4	$37	150	$.24	$140	16	$1.43

15. The relationship between Celsius and Fahrenheit temperatures is given by

$$c = \tfrac{5}{9}(f - 32)$$

Convert a Fahrenheit temperature to Celsius. Use either 50° or 92° as input data.

Interactive Scientific and Engineering

16. The relations between temperature, pressure, and volume in the adiabatic compression of an ideal gas are as follows:

$$p_2 = p_1 \left(\frac{v_1}{v_2}\right)^r$$

$$t_2 = t_1 \left(\frac{v_1}{v_2}\right)^{r-1}$$

where r is a property dependent upon which gas is being compressed. For a diesel engine assume r is 1.4 and that the initial absolute temperature t_1 and pressure p_1 are 520°F and 15 lb/in². Compute the final temperature t_2 and pressure p_2 for any compression ratio v_1/v_2 using 13, 15, or 17 as example values.

17. When a simple threaded bolt is tightened, the pressure w it exerts at its tip is related to the pressure p applied against the tightening wrench as follows:

    $$w = 2\pi prt(1 - f)$$

    where $r =$ the length of the wrench
    $ t =$ the number of threads per inch on the bolt
    $ f =$ the fraction of the power lost to friction

    Write a program to compute w for various values of the other parameters. As a test assume $f = 0.4$, $r = 10$, $t = 6$, and p equals either 30 or 50 pounds.

18. The resistance r of a light bulb filament in ohms is related to the voltage e applied and the energy expended in watts w by

    $$r = \frac{e^2}{w}$$

    Compute the resistance of either 55- or 75-watt bulbs operating at 110 volts.

2a

Intrinsic Functions, Integer-Type Data, Type Statement, IF Selection, Data Validation, and Introduction to Program Testing

Basic Intrinsic Functions
Self-Testing Exercise 2-1

Use of Integer-Type Data and Mixed-Type Arithmetic
Internal Representation Differences for Real and Integer Data
Conversion of Data between Real and Integer Types
Self-Testing Exercise 2-2

Explicit Type Statements
Real and Integer Type Statements
Character Type Statement
Logical Type Statement
Self-Testing Exercise 2-3

Selection among Alternative Processing Paths Using the Block IF Statement
Selection Structure
Block IF Statement
Logical Expressions
Nested Block IFs
Self-Testing Exercise 2-4

Transferring Control within a Program
Statement Labels in FORTRAN
GOTO Statement

Selection of Alternative Processing Paths Using the IF Statement
Logical IF Statement
Program Switch and Delayed Selection
Arithmetic IF Statement

Validating Input Data
Self-Testing Exercise 2-5

Processing More than One Set of Input Data
A Simple IF Loop
First- and Last-Time-Through Logic

Using a File for Input Data

Planning and Design of a Program with Multiple Cases and Exceptions

Introduction to Testing and Quality Assurance for a Program
Testing and Quality-Assurance Process
Development and Use of Test Data
Debugging Programs during Compilation
Self-Testing Exercise 2-6

Precision and Accuracy in Computing
Self-Testing Exercise 2-7

Suggestions for the FORTRAN Programmer

Summary

Answers to Self-Testing Exercises

Questions and Problems

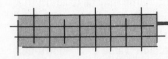

This chapter will explain a convenient method of programming common operations using a FORTRAN feature called *intrinsic functions*. It will explain the use of integer data and how the characteristics of integer data affect the execution of FORTRAN statements. Using variable names to refer to character data and logical data is explained. Type statements to explicitly declare variables to be integer, real, character, or logical are introduced. Three basic program-coding patterns were presented earlier; statements for programming selection are explained in this chapter. The chapter continues the description of good programming practices with a survey of input validation, simple repetition loops, and program testing. It concludes with some suggestions for program testing and quality assurance and a discussion of precision and accuracy in computing.

Basic Intrinsic Functions

The five operation symbols for addition ($+$), subtraction ($-$), multiplication ($*$), division ($/$), and exponentiation ($**$) were presented in Chapter 1a. In addition to these five operation symbols, FORTRAN provides prewritten program modules that perform common mathematical functions. These built-in functions are termed *intrinsic functions*. The use of an intrinsic function is specified by writing the function name followed by the expression to be operated upon (the argument) inside a set of parentheses. This is illustrated by four commonly used intrinsic functions:

SQRT   Take the square root of the expression.
ABS   Take the absolute value of the expression.
EXP   Exponentiate e to the power represented by the expression.
AMAX1   Take the largest value from the list of real values in the argument.

Examples

Problem	FORTRAN expression
$x = \sqrt{y}$	X = SQRT (Y)
$x = \sqrt{y + b}$	X = SQRT (Y + B)
$x = |y - b|$	X = ABS (Y − B)
$x = e^{y+b}$	X = EXP (Y + B)
$x = \max(a,b,c)$	X = AMAX1 (A, B, C)

The expression for a function can include another function. As an example, X = SQRT(ABS(Y − 7.0)) takes the square root of the absolute value of (Y − 7.0) and assigns it to X.

The FORTRAN standard specifies a generic name for each intrinsic function as well as specific names for use with different data types (integer, real, etc.) in the

65

arguments and results. (The implications of the distinction between the real and integer functions will be made clear in the next section.) If the generic name is used, the compiler examines the type of the arguments and selects the correct function type. In other words, either the generic or type-specific function name may be used. In the older versions of FORTRAN, and in subset versions, only the specific names are supported. For the sake of FORTRAN portability, the text will generally use specific names. A few commonly used functions are summarized in Table 2-1; additional functions are explained in Chapter 7. A list of all functions for reference purposes appears on the inside of the front cover. There are boxes to check off the functions available to you on your computer.

TABLE 2-1   Selected FORTRAN Intrinsic Functions

Generic name	Specific name	Type of argument	Type of function result	Function performed on expression
ABS	IABS	Integer	Integer	Take absolute value.
	ABS	Real	Real	
MAX	MAX0	Integer	Integer	Take largest value from list of integer values.
	AMAX1	Real	Real	Take largest value from list of real values.
MIN	MIN0	Integer	Integer	Take smallest value from list of integer values.
	AMIN1	Real	Real	Take smallest value from list of real values.
SQRT	SQRT	Real	Real	Take square root.
EXP	EXP	Real	Real	Exponentiate e to power represented by expression.
LOG	ALOG	Real	Real	Take natural log (to base e).
LOG10	ALOG10	Real	Real	Take log to base 10.

There is a set of trigonometric intrinsic functions (Table 2-2) to calculate the sine, cosine, etc., of angles. The argument for a simple trigonometric function is stated in radians of an angle, and can have a fractional part (which means it is real-type data); the result of the function is also a real quantity.

TABLE 2-2   Trigonometric Functions in FORTRAN*

Simple trigonometric functions		Arc functions		Hyperbolic functions	
Name	Function	Name	Function	Name	Function
SIN	Sine	ASIN	Arcsine	SINH	Hyperbolic sine
COS	Cosine	ACOS	Arccosine	COSH	Hyperbolic cosine
TAN	Tangent	ATAN	Arctangent	TANH	Hyperbolic tangent

* General and real argument names are the same; integer arguments are not allowed.

Self-Testing Exercise 2-1

1. Write the FORTRAN statements for the following formulas:

(a) $X = \sqrt{a + b}$

(b) $X = \sqrt[3]{\dfrac{a}{b}} + 2$

(c) $Y = e^x$

(d) $X = \sqrt{|y + 5|}$

(e) $Y = \log_e x$

(f) $r^2 = x^2 + y^2$ (find r)

(g) $A = \max(x^2, y^2)$

2. Write the formulas for the following FORTRAN statements:

(a) `X = ALOG (Y + Z)`

(b) `Y = SIN (ABS(A))`

(c) `DISCR = ABS(B**2 - 4.0 * A * C)`

(d) `Y = EXP( - (X**2))`

(e) `RHO = A * COS(THETA)`

(f) `X = SQRT (A + (B/C**D) * E * F + 1.0)`

Use of Integer-Type Data and Mixed-Type Arithmetic

In Chapter 1a, two types of variables and constants were identified—real constants and variables, which can have a fractional part, and integer constants and variables, which cannot have a fractional part. Real constants, for example, always have a decimal point (4.0, 3.1, 39.) even if the fractional part is zero. Integer constants have no decimal point (4, 7, 39). The distinction between the two types is useful in programming but can cause errors if the programmer does not understand internal representation and operational differences related to the types.

Internal Representation Differences for Real and Integer Data

An integer data item represents quantities that can be counted. It is always an exact computer representation of an integer value. It may represent only an integral value, such as 1, -1, 45, 18, 0, or -18. A real data item can represent fractional values such as those produced by measurement. A real data item in FORTRAN references a computer approximation of the fractional value of a real quantity. The difference between exact and approximate representation for integers and real quantities stems from the use of a binary number system internally in the computer. In other words, for integer data, the computer has a method of representing the value exactly (using the binary number system). For real data, the internal computer binary representation is sometimes exact and in all cases is very close, but there are some real fractions that cannot be represented exactly. The problem is similar to that of representing certain common fractions as decimal numbers. The fraction $\frac{4}{3}$ cannot be represented exactly as a decimal number but only reasonably close as 1.333. . . . To illustrate this point, two real data items were entered into a FORTRAN program in a popular computer; the decimal equivalent of the internal binary representation is shown alongside. Note that the first representation is exact and the second is not.

Input	Internal approximation
36.0	3600000000
19.63	1962999916

Since an integer-type variable can only represent integer values, any fractional part of a data item is lost when it is processed or stored as an integer variable. For example, when division is performed with integer-type data and a fractional part remains in the answer, the fractional part is dropped. The result of 7 ÷ 4 when both 7 and 4 are integers is 1 (instead 1.75); the result of 1 ÷ 3 is 0 (instead of 0.3333).

The approximate rather than exact representation of some real fractions is not normally a problem, and a programmer could write many programs without noting the result of approximate representation. Difficulty is most likely to occur when the program converts real data to integer representation, divides two integer variables, or makes any equality comparisons.

Conversion of Data between Real and Integer Types

There are two major reasons why data items may need to be converted from real to integer or from integer to real:

1. In some computations, only the integer portion of a value is desired. Converting from real to integer retains the integral portion and drops the fractional part.
2. Expressions cannot be executed with data having mixed types, because integer data items are represented in the computer differently from the real data items. In an expression having variables with mixed types, type conversions must be made before the computations in the expression can be processed. Note that a real expression may have an integer exponent without requiring conversion, but an integer variable with a real exponent is a mixed-type expression and one of them must be converted.

If the preceding reasons apply, why are the variables not defined as the needed type rather than converted from one type to another? The reason is that a variable may need to be used in different expressions with variables of different types.

Any conversion from one type to another can be handled in one of three different ways: (1) across the equals sign; (2) with an explicit intrinsic conversion function; or (3) during execution of mixed expressions using default procedures. Type conversion will occur when different types are mixed in expressions. The only issue is whether or not to program the conversions explicitly rather than to rely on default conversion procedures that might lead to unexpected results. The preferred method is using explicit intrinsic conversion functions.

In conversion across the equals sign, the expression on the right is evaluated and an answer obtained in the type used in that expression (real or integer). The answer is then converted and stored according to the type of the result variable on the left of the equals sign. Thus, I = X * Y will compute the real type product of X and Y, convert the result to an integer, and store it in the location assigned to the integer variable named I. Any fractional part from X * Y is lost. The weakness in the method is the lack of an explicit coding of what is to be done.

The preferred intrinsic function method is an explicit programming of conversion using intrinsic functions. As shown in Table 2-3, there is a function REAL (or

TABLE 2-3 Intrinsic Functions to Convert Data Types

Generic name	Specific name	Type of argument	Type of function result	Function performed on expression
REAL	FLOAT	Integer	Real	Convert from integer to real type
INT	IFIX	Real	Integer	Convert from real to integer (truncating the fractional part)

FLOAT) to convert from integer to real and a function INT (or IFIX) to convert from real to integer, REAL and INT are generic names, and FLOAT and IFIX are specific names for the intrinsic conversion functions. Remember that subset FORTRAN supports only specific names.

Examples

Statement	Result
I = 3.1417	I contains 3
R = 75	R contains 75.0
JIX = X * PRICE	JIX contains 3
where X = 3.5 and PRICE = 1.1	because result of X * PRICE = 3.85

Statement	Result
I = IFIX(3.1417)	I = 3
or I = INT(3.1417)	
R = FLOAT(75)	R = 75.0
or R = REAL(75)	
JIX = IFIX(X * PRICE)	JIX = 3
or JIX = INT(X * PRICE)	

If an expression contains mixed types and there is no explicit conversion, FORTRAN performs conversions as part of the execution of the statement. Integer variables in the mixed expression are converted to real values. It is generally not a good idea to rely on the automatic default conversion, since the programmer may not perceive the consequences of a mixed-type expression. It is better to code the conversion explicitly using the conversion functions. Note the following examples of mixed types in expressions:

Desired expression	Coding
X = A + K	X = A + FLOAT(K)
	or X = A + REAL(K)
I = K + A	I = K + IFIX(A)
	or I = K + INT(A)
X = I**A	X = FLOAT(I)**A
	or X = REAL(I)**A

A word of caution about converting real quantities to integer quantities by dropping the fractional portion: In a few cases, even though the real value should be a whole number, the approximate representation may be slightly less or slightly more by a very small amount. The difficulty is with those that are slightly less because the integer conversion will result in an integer 1 less than expected. Because of this possibility, a program may be written to add a small constant (say, 0.0001) to a real value before conversion to integer. For example, JIX = IFIX(A + 0.0001).

Although the discussion has taken several paragraphs, the rules for integer and real types in expressions are fairly simple. These are summarized below.

Rules for Integer and Real Types in Expressions

1. If integer and real data types are mixed in an expression, integer variables or constants will be converted to real. Good programming practice is to code these conversions explicitly rather than rely upon default.
2. In the statement $a = b$, if a is of a different type than b, the results of b will be converted to the type of a. If the conversion is from real to integer, the fractional part of the expression results will be truncated

and discarded. Preferred practice is to code conversions using intrinsic functions rather than using conversion with the equals sign.

3. Fractional parts from division of integer variables are truncated.
4. The allowable combinations of types in exponentiation are (a) integer expression with integer exponent, (b) real expression with real exponent, and (c) real expression with integer exponent. The exponent may be any arithmetic expression meeting these type restrictions.
5. An integer expression to a real exponent is a mixed-type expression. If used, the integer expression will be automatically converted to a real expression. Some older compilers will reject this form.

Self-Testing Exercise 2-2

1. Complete the following table:

Expression or statement	Valid or not valid; note if mixed type	If not valid, why; if mixed type, how converted
(a) A**2 + 1		
(b) A**(2 + 1)		
(c) A**(B + C/D)		
(d) A/B + D/3		
(e) IX + JX + 4		
(f) KX = A + BI		
(g) FUN = SQRT(A + AXEL/BETA)		
(h) X = (A + B)/((C + D) * E * IX)		
(i) X + Y = Z * ALPHA		
(j) JX = IX**A		
(k) X = A**I		

2. If A = 3.0, B = 2.5, IX = 3, and JX = 2, what will be the result of the following statements?
   (a) X = A/B
   (b) K = IX/JX
   (c) KIX = JX/IX
   (d) NIX = IX + 2/JX

3. Write statements using both intrinsic functions: generic and type-specific.
   (a) Take the absolute value of integer value KDATA.
   (b) Find the minimum for values of I, J, and K.

4. Convert the following by using the generic intrinsic function, then the specific intrinsic functions, and finally by coding a new variable name across the equals sign.
   (a) JIX to a real variable
   (b) DATA1 to an integer variable

5. Remove mixed mode by using explicit coding of conversion.
   (a) X = I * B**I
   (b) X = B + (C/J) + K**D

Explicit Type Statements

In Chapter 1a, it was explained that any variable name beginning with the letters I through N is assumed to represent an integer variable; names having any other first letter represent real variables. Defining the type of variable by the first letter is termed *implicit typing*. There is also a need for explicit typing to:

1. Define variable types other than integer and real
2. Override the implicit first-letter typing
3. Specify type explicitly rather than to rely on implicit typing

There are several types of variables in FORTRAN other than integer and real, and each has a unique representation in the computer. Character and logical types will be explained in this chapter; the remaining types will be described in Chapter 7. The explicit type statement has two forms: (1) the form for integer, real, and all other types except character type and (2) the form for character type. These are summarized in the box and explained below.

TYPE DECLARATION

The explicit type statement is required for character-type variables and types other than real or integer.

Real and integer type data
type v, v, . . .
declares all variables in list to be of specified type.
type may be REAL or INTEGER
The explicit type statement for real and integer variables overrides the implicit typing based on the first letter of the variable name.

Character-type data

CHARACTER v∗len, v∗len, . . .
where v is the variable name declared as storing character data and len is the maximum length of the string of characters to be stored. If the string being stored is less than maximum length, the string will be left-justified in the storage spaces and extra spaces at right will contain blanks. If len is not given, a length of one character is assumed.

CHARACTER∗len v, v, . . .
All variable names in list are declared as storing character and have the same length, len. A comma is optional following len.

Other data types
type v, v, . . .
type is LOGICAL (and other types explained in Chapter 7).

Real and Integer Type Statements

The form of the explicit type statement for real and integer types is

type v, v, . . .

where type is the type name. The names for integer and real types are INTEGER and REAL. For example, if ALPHA and IRATE are to be declared as real (IRATE would otherwise be integer), and TIMES and RATE to be declared as integer, the following statements are written:

```
REAL ALPHA, IRATE
INTEGER TIMES, RATE
```

The fact that the type declaration is required for some types but is optional for integer and real variables (that can use implicit typing) leads to two alternatives for programming style.

1. Explicit declaration of the type of all variables, including integer and real variables. Ignore implicit typing.
2. Use implicit typing for real and integer variables. Use explicit declaration only for variables requiring it.

Explicit typing of all variables is used in many computer languages, such as Pascal. It eliminates ambiguities as to type. It also eliminates the restrictions on naming that occur with implicit typing based on the first letter of the variable name. Current software development practice tends to the use of explicit typing for all variables. The only difficulty with this practice is that many FORTRAN programs have been written using implicit first-letter typing for integer and real variables. Maintenance of old FORTRAN programs requires that the programmer be aware of the rules for implicit typing.

An approach that may aid a student to become familiar with both explicit- and implicit-typing practices is to select variable names for student programs that are consistent with implicit typing for integer and real variables. This suggestion provides practice in associating names having a first letter of I, J, K, L, M, or N with integer types and names starting with other letters with real variables. Should a name starting with the wrong type letter be desired, it is used but explicitly typed in a type statement. When the program is completed, the other implicitly typed variables can then be added to the type statement to produce explicit typing for all real and integer variables. This suggestion will be illustrated in some of the example programs. In the list of variables, the type will be included with the description for all nonreal variables. For the short exercises in the text, type is defined by the first-letter implicit typing except where noted.

In the coding style followed in the text, type declarations will be placed in a program block following the program identification and variable identification blocks. The block is titled TYPE DECLARATION AND STORAGE BLOCK. (Other statements related to storage allocation—to be explained in later chapters—will be included in the block.)

Character Type Statement

The need to have integer variables to refer to integer quantities and real variables to refer to computer representation of real quantities has been explained. A first impression may be that storing characters (such as a letter, a name, or text) and referencing them by a variable name is not necessary in a language such as FORTRAN that is oriented to numeric computation. Providing descriptive labels on output, as described in Chapter 1a, is quite simple. The string of characters is enclosed in apostrophes in the output statement. In addition to descriptive labels, however, there are parts of a FORTRAN program that require variables that reference character data; in other cases, character data variables simplify programming. Two simple examples illustrate the need: the first is a program step in which the user is asked to input either a Y to indicate "yes" or an N to indicate "no." The input character is named and stored as a character variable. It can be compared to character variables (or character constants) for Y or N to determine which has been input. The second example is a program in which users identify themselves by input of their names. The name is then printed on the user output. When the name is input, it is stored as character data with a character variable name. For output, the character variable name is specified in the output command, and the character contents of the variable's storage location are output.

A character variable is defined by assigning a variable name to reference a string of characters. But since characters will have a storage representation form different from numbers used in computation, the FORTRAN program must define all variable names associated with character data as being character type. This is done with a character type statement. There is no implicit typing for character variables. The basic character type statement is in the form:

CHARACTER v∗length, v∗length, . . .

As an example, if HEAD1 references 15 characters and LABEL2 has 8 characters, the two names would be declared as referencing character data by the following:

```
CHARACTER HEAD1*15, LABEL2*8
```

In other words, a variable to be declared as character type must have a length (in characters) associated with it. Each character in the string of characters is counted (including blanks).

   If all the character variables in the list have the same length, the length specification need be stated only once before the variable list. In fact, the length immediately after the word CHARACTER applies to any variable in the list that does not have an explicit length following it.

CHARACTER∗length v, v, v, . . . (comma after length is optional)

As an example, if character variables H1, H2, and H3 are all of length 12, they can be declared by:

```
CHARACTER*12 H1,H2,H3
```

   When a character variable name has been declared, character data can be read by a list-directed input statement using the variable name. The character string being input must be enclosed in apostrophes. For example, a 12-character heading (called HEAD4) in the form 'XXXXXXXXXXXX' is to be read and then printed. The following statements are required:

```
CHARACTER HEAD4*12
READ *, HEAD4
PRINT *, HEAD4
```

Logical Type Statement

A fourth data type is logical type. A logical-type variable can store only one of two values. The two values that are stored are probably 1 or 0, but from the standpoint of the FORTRAN programmer, they are TRUE or FALSE. There are several uses for logical variables; one application is in programming the setting of a program switch that will be used in a selection of a program path later in the program. This will be explained later in the chapter.

   A variable name is defined as referencing a logical variable by a logical type statement. For example:

```
LOGICAL PAST
```

defines the variable name PAST as referencing logical data.

To assign a true or false value to a logical variable, the words .TRUE. and .FALSE. (preceded and followed by periods with no spaces) are used. The assignment statement

```
PAST  =  .TRUE.
```

assigns a value for true to the logical variable PAST.

Self-Testing Exercise 2-3

1. For a program, each set of input data is in the form 'XXXXXXXXXXXX', nnn, where the X's represent a character string and each n a digit of an integer number. Write statements to declare a character name for the string, read the data, and print the character string and integer number. Use LABEL1 and NSHARE for variable names.

2. The programmer wrote an entire program using the variable INTRST to refer to a real number and PYMNTN to refer to an integer value. Write type declarations to achieve the desired type.

3. Declare variables A, B, C, and D to be two characters in length.

4. Explain the difference between the following declarations:

```
CHARACTER*1, G,H,I,J
CHARACTER G,H,I,J
```

5. Declare the variable name SW1 to reference a logical variable and set it to a false value.

Selection among Alternative Processing Paths
Using the Block IF Statement

As explained in Chapter 1a, program logic is simplified by using only three program-coding structures:

1. Simple sequence
2. Selection
3. Repetition

Simple sequence was explained and used in Chapter 1; selection and simple repetition will be explained in this chapter; and repetition will be described in greater detail in Chapter 4.

Selection among alternative processing is programmed with the IF statement. There are essentially three forms of IF statements:

1. Block IF
2. Logical IF
3. Arithmetic IF

Each statement will be explained, but style preferences exist regarding usage. The block IF is preferred except for simple selection; in this case, the logical IF is used. The block IF statement may not be available in older versions of FORTRAN. In such cases, the logical IF provides a good alternative. Although the arithmetic IF is presented for comprehensiveness, its use is discouraged because it is error-prone.

Selection Structure

The selection structure consists of a logical expression that tests for a condition or a relation followed by two alternative paths for the program to follow. The program selects one program control path, depending on the results of the test (that is, the truth or falsity of the expression). After executing the instructions in one of the two program paths, the program continues with the statement following the two blocks of alternative instructions. This coding pattern can be termed IF. . .THEN. . .ELSE because the logic can be stated in if-then-else terms. For example, assume a condition P and sets of statements called C and D, as shown in Figure 2-1. The selection is described as follows: IF P (is true), THEN perform statements C; ELSE (if P is not true) perform statements D. The flowchart for the selection process consists of a decision symbol followed by two branches or paths, each with one or more process symbols to specify the processing to be performed for that branch. A frequent variation is to have one of the branches contain no processing. In that case the logic is: IF P (is true), THEN perform statements C; ELSE continue with the processing that follows the selection statements.

Describing the selection coding structure in the pseudocode of a program design language will follow the basic idea of if-then-else. Using the conventions of this text, the pseudocode statements for a selection include the following:

```
A statement of the test to be performed
    IF (statement of condition to be tested) THEN (processing to
        be performed if condition is satisfied)
    ELSE (processing  to  be  performed  if  condition  is  not
        satisfied)
```

The use of the capitalized words follows the convention explained earlier of capitalizing words that correspond to FORTRAN coding words. The indentation visually shows the parts of the selection structure.

The selection structure in FORTRAN can be coded in two ways:

1. *Block IF statement* This most closely matches the logic of the IF . . . THEN . . . ELSE logic of the selection structure in which one block of

Figure 2-1 Flowchart of selection program structure.

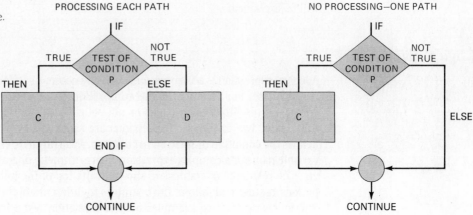

statements is executed if the condition is true and another block of statements is executed if the condition is false.

2. *Logical IF statement*   This statement is most useful if there is only one action if the condition is true and a continuation if the condition is not true.

In addition to the flow of program control with two alternative blocks, there are instances in which program control must be transferred unconditionally to another part of the program. Another less frequently used selection procedure is followed when a test in one part of the program results in a selection in another, later part. In the description of selection and transfer of control, the block IF will be explained first. This will be followed by a section on unconditional transfer, a section on use of the logical IF, and a section on delayed selection.

Block IF Statement

The FORTRAN statements to code a block IF selections structure consist of the following:

```
IF (logical expression) THEN
     statements to be processed for true block (IF block)
ELSE
     statements to be processed for false block (ELSE block)
ENDIF (or END IF)
```

The statements to be executed if the logical expression is true follow the THEN and are termed the *IF block;* the statements to be executed if the logical expression is false follow the ELSE and are termed the *ELSE block.* The ELSE and the ELSE block can be omitted if no processing is to occur if the expression is false. The ELSE, when used, should be the only statement on the line. Each IF. . .THEN. . .[ELSE]. . . must end with an ENDIF. Although the instruction may be written as two words, one word is preferred because it is less likely to be misunderstood. Indentation is recommended for statements in the IF block and the ELSE block to show the parts of the selection structure. Before illustrating the block IF, the programming of the logical expression will be explained.

Logical Expressions

A logical expression is an expression, such as a comparison for a relation, that is either true or false. For example, if the comparison is for equality of two variables, the comparison is either equal (true) or not equal (false). In the simplest type of logical expression, two arithmetic expressions are separated by a relational operator that defines the condition or relation to be tested. An arithmetic expression may be a single variable name or a complex expression with arithmetic operators, intrinsic functions, etc. The relational operators are shown at the top of the following page. Note that a period precedes and follows the operators to differentiate them from variable names. The following are two examples of how a relation test is used in coding a logical expression in a selection structure.

RELATIONAL OPERATORS

Operator	Representing
.LT.	Less than
.LE.	Less than or equal to
.EQ.	Equal to
.NE.	Not equal to
.GT.	Greater than
.GE.	Greater than or equal to

```
1. IF (A .GT. B) THEN
       PRINT *, 'BIG IS', A
   ELSE
       PRINT *, 'BIG IS', B
   ENDIF

2. IF (SQRT(Y) .LE. 5.0) THEN
       RESULT = 5.0
   ELSE
       RESULT = SQRT(Y)
   ENDIF
```

Character strings may also be compared by using relational operators. If the names are of unequal length, the shorter one is assumed to be made of equal length by adding blank space characters to the right end. For example, if two names are stored in NAME1 and NAME2 and the computer is testing to see if they are in alphabetical order, the instruction could be:

```
IF (NAME1 .LE. NAME2) THEN
    PRINT *, 'NAMES ARE IN ORDER'
ELSE
    PRINT *, 'NAMES OUT OF ORDER'
ENDIF
```

If NAME1 is equal to 'Davis' and NAME2 is equal to "Hoffmann," the equality comparison will be true and the printout will be 'NAMES ARE IN ORDER'.

A character constant (the value is used rather than a variable name) is written in single-quote (apostrophe) marks. A character constant may be used in making a comparison. For example, a test to see if an input is the word END would read:

```
IF (WORD .EQ. 'END') THEN
    PRINT *, 'END OF DATA'
ELSE
    PRINT *, 'NOT END OF DATA'
ENDIF
```

In many cases of decision making, more than one comparison is required to make a decision. If a decision requires comparing two or more relational expressions in FORTRAN, logical operators may be used to connect the comparisons for an overall answer. The basic logical operators are .AND., .OR., and .NOT.; additional logical operators are explained in Chapter 7. The logical operators .AND., .OR., and .NOT. have a meaning that is the same as English (when it is used precisely).

BASIC LOGICAL OPERATORS

Operator	Expression is true when
.AND.	Both relations are true.
.OR.	One or both of the relations are true.
.NOT.	Opposite is true.

A statement with the operator .AND. is true only if both relations connected by .AND. are true; a statement with the operator .OR. is true if either or both of the relations connected by .OR. are true. True means that the relationship is satisfied; for example, X. GT. Y is true if X is greater than Y. The operator .NOT. is used to indicate negation (opposite) of the relation.

The following example illustrates the difference between two operators. A society is evaluating two possible rules for deciding who should be admitted to an honors club. The first rule being considered is that a student has to have a club test score of greater than 76 *and* a grade-point average greater than 3.5. The second rule being evaluated is for admission if a student has a club test score greater than 76 *or* a grade-point average greater than 3.5. Using FORTRAN variable names of CTEST for club test scores and GPA for grade-point average, FORTRAN comparison statements for the two alternative decision rules are:

```
1.  IF ((CTEST .GT. 76.0) .AND. (GPA .GT. 3.5)) THEN
        PRINT *, 'ADMIT'
    ELSE
2.  IF ((CTEST .GT. 76.0) .OR. (GPA .GT. 3.5)) THEN
        PRINT *, 'ADMIT'
    ELSE
```

Statements can contain a number of relations connected by more than one logical operator. When more than one .AND. and .OR. are used in the same expression, the parenthesis rule (inside parentheses first) and a precedence rule can be applied. In the absence of parentheses, the following precedences are applied:

1. Arithmetic operations (using the precedence rule for them)
2. .NOT.
3. .AND.
4. .OR.

Operations having the same precedence are executed from left to right. For a clear program style, parentheses should be placed around the portions of the expressions connected by .AND. and .OR. even though they are not required.

The discussion about integer and real data as having exact versus approximate representation in a computer is relevant to a comparison for equality. The possible difficulty occurs with equality comparisons for data items that are almost equal but differ slightly because of approximate representation. This situation suggests care in use of equality comparisons for real variables and use of .GE. and .NE. rather than .EQ. (if appropriate). There is no problem with integer variable comparisons, so converting real variables that are whole numbers to integer equivalents (after adding a tiny rounding factor) will ensure a correct comparison for equality. Use of a tiny rounding factor will be explained in more detail later in this chapter.

As an example (assuming that A is a result of dividing 4 by 3), the following program segment will give a message that $4 \div 3$ is not equal to 1.333.

```
IF (A .EQ. 1.333) THEN
    PRINT *, 'A EQUALS 1.333'
ELSE
    PRINT *, 'A NOT EQUAL TO 1.333'
```

The following change in the first line of the IF statement will give an equality result for the comparison by changing it to an integer comparison:

```
IF (IFIX(A * 1000.0) .EQ. 1333) THEN
```

The use of logical operators as part of a logical expression is illustrated by the following examples:

```
IF ((PAY .GT. 45.0) .AND. (AGE .LT. 17.0)) THEN
    TALLY = TALLY + 1.0
ENDIF
```

This first example segment says to add 1 to TALLY only if PAY is greater than 45 and AGE is less than 17. Both must be true. If either or both are not true, the program continues with statements following the selection structure. There is no ELSE block.

```
IF ((HRS.LE.60.0).AND.(HRS.GT 0.0).OR.(KODE.EQ.1))THEN
    RATE = PTRATE
ELSE
    RATE = QSRATE
ENDIF
```

In the second example segment, the variable RATE will be set to either PTRATE or QSRATE, depending on the results of the test. If HRS is less than or equal to 60.0 and greater than zero, or if KODE is equal to 1, then set RATE to the value of PTRATE; otherwise (else), set RATE to the value of QSRATE.

The flowchart example on the next page illustrates the use of more than one processing statement in the IF and ELSE blocks. In the example, RPAY (regular pay) is computed at $4.10 per hour; for hours greater than 40, the OTPAY (overtime pay) is 1.5 times the $4.10 rate.

Nested Block IFs

In some programming situations, a succession of tests determines the action to be taken. There are two coding structures for a succession of tests. The first is an if-then-else selection within an IF block or an ELSE block. The second is an ELSEIF block that is used only in an IF block to code a sequence of tests that terminate when a condition is satisfied.

Placement of an if-then-else coding structure within an IF or ELSE block is illustrated by the example in the flowchart on the following facing page. In computing wages, if the shift code is greater than 1.0 (for other than day shift), the pay rate is

Flowchart	Program

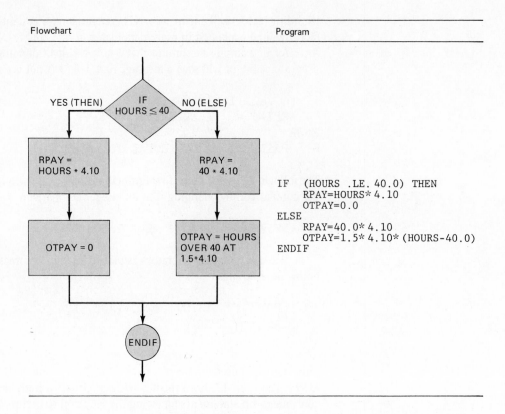

```
IF   (HOURS .LE. 40.0) THEN
        RPAY=HOURS* 4.10
        OTPAY=0.0
ELSE
        RPAY=40.0* 4.10
        OTPAY=1.5* 4.10* (HOURS-40.0)
ENDIF
```

$6.00 per hour. For the day shift (shift code = 1.0), the rate is $4.15 per hour; but if the day is Sunday (DAY = 7.0), there is a special premium of $3.00 per hour.

As a style comment, the first test of (SHIFT .GT. 1.0) is satisfactory except when SHIFT is in error (say SHIFT = 6.0 even though there is no shift greater than 4). It is wise to test for a value being within valid limits before making a test in which all other values are assumed to be valid. The test in this case might be IF (SHIFT .LE. 0.0 .OR. SHIFT .GT. 4.0) THEN error-handling statement.

The ELSEIF . . . THEN statement is used to code a sequence of one or more additional tests within the IF block before the ELSE result. It is not allowed in an ELSE block. ELSEIF is part of the IF block and does not use a separate ENDIF. The ELSEIF statement may be repeated for a series of tests, each with a separate action if the test result is true. The advantage of a series of ELSEIF statements is that the program tests each ELSEIF expression in turn. If the expression is not satisfied, the next test is performed; however, if the test is true, the action specified for that ELSEIF is taken and the program goes to the ENDIF at the end of the selection structure (skipping the ELSE block). If none of the IF or ELSEIF conditions or relations is true, the action specified in the ELSE block is processed. In other words:

```
IF (logical expression is true) THEN processing to be performed
    (and skip rest of selection structure); if false, continue
    with next test.
ELSEIF (logical expression is true) THEN processing to be per-
    formed (and skip rest of selection structure). If false,
```

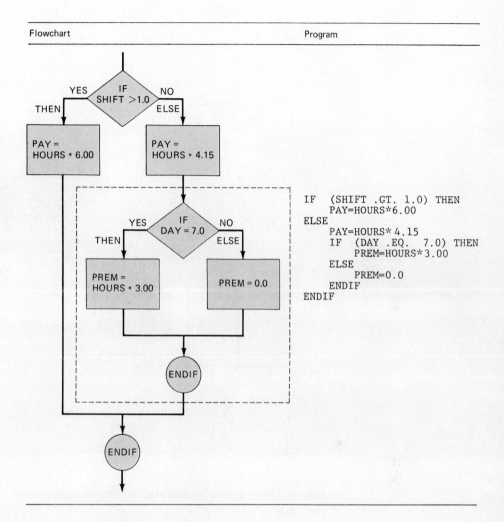

Flowchart	Program

```
IF  (SHIFT .GT. 1.0) THEN
    PAY=HOURS*6.00
ELSE
    PAY=HOURS* 4.15
    IF (DAY .EQ.  7.0) THEN
        PREM=HOURS*3.00
    ELSE
        PREM=0.0
    ENDIF
ENDIF
```

continue with the next ELSEIF. If all the IF and ELSEIF
tests turn out to be false, execute the statements in the
ELSE block.
ELSE
    Statements to be executed only if none of the IF or ELSEIF
    logical expressions was evaluated as being true.
ENDIF

The use of ELSEIF in programming a series of tests in which testing need not continue
if an expression is true is illustrated by the program segment on page 82 that prints
student grades based on exam scores:

90 to 100	A
80 to 89	B
70 to 79	C
Below 70	See instructor

Flowchart	Program

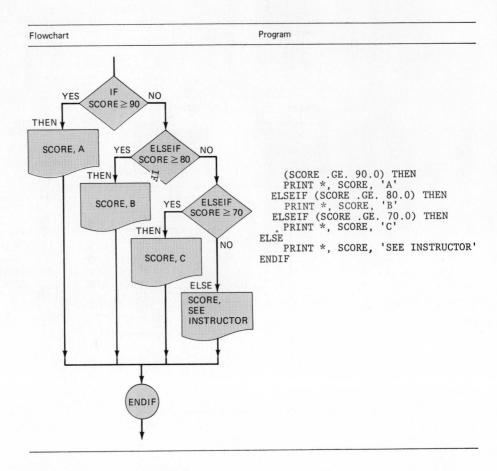

```
          (SCORE .GE. 90.0) THEN
             PRINT *, SCORE, 'A'
          ELSEIF (SCORE .GE. 80.0) THEN
             PRINT *, SCORE, 'B'
          ELSEIF (SCORE .GE. 70.0) THEN
             PRINT *, SCORE, 'C'
          ELSE
             PRINT *, SCORE, 'SEE INSTRUCTOR'
          ENDIF
```

Note that once a score is identified as being in a grade range, the remaining tests are not used.

By way of style comment, the tests of scores were written to test only greater than or equal to, since previous tests had logically eliminated the upper limit. But a good procedure would be to test explicitly for a score greater than 100.0 (an error). The other tests could also have been written to test for the entire range; for example, IF (SCORE .GE. 80 .AND. SCORE .LE. 89) THEN. . . . The test following the .AND. is redundant, but the program logic is made clearer. Unless efficiency is an important consideration, the full coding is preferred.

The various features of the block IF statement are summarized in the box on page 83.

Self-Testing Exercise 2-4

Write selection coding structures using the block IF for the following problems.

1. If the square root of $X^2 + Y^2$ is less than 100.0, the answer (ANSWR) is to be 12.0 * X. If it is greater than or equal to 100.0, the value of ANSWR is to be X^2. Print the answer.

2. Find the largest quantity represented by three variables: ALPHA, BETA, and GAMMA. Call the largest quantity BIG. If two are equal, either value may be used.
   (a) First write statements without using the AMAX1 (or MAX) function.
   (b) Then write statements using the AMAX1 function.

BLOCK IF STATEMENT	
| ```
IF  (logical  expression)  THEN
      statements for IF block
``` | Logical expression is a relation or condition that can be true or false (satisfied or not satisfied). |
| | All statements in the IF block are executed if the expression is true; statements in the ELSE block are executed if the expression is false. |
| ```
ELSE
      statements for ELSE block
``` | The ELSE should be the only word on the line. The ELSE and ELSE block statements are optional and may be omitted. |
| `ENDIF (or END IF)` | Each IF . . . THEN . . . [ELSE] must end with an ENDIF statement. |
| ```
ELSEIF (logical expression) THEN
      statements for ELSEIF block
``` | ELSEIF (or ELSE IF) statement is used to program a sequence of tests within the IF block. The IF logical expression is tested first; if true, the statements for the IF condition are executed and the remaining statements through the ENDIF are ignored. If false, the first ELSEIF expression is tested. If it is true, the statements for the ELSEIF are executed and the remaining statements through the ENDIF are ignored. If the IF and ELSEIF logical expressions are all false, the ELSE block statements are executed. The ELSEIF is part of the IF block and does not use a separate ENDIF. |

3. Two variables, NIX and KIX, should be unequal. Find the largest in absolute value (without regard to sign). Print out the largest. If they are equal, stop the program.

4. Find out if $-550 \le X \le 1000$. If X falls within these limits (between -550 and 1000), print out YES. If not, print out NO. Then halt the computer.

5. Test whether A is greater than B and greater than C, or whether A is less than D and equal to E. If so, print TRUE. If false, print FALSE.

6. If a code number (ICODE) is equal to 1 or 2, pay is computed as 3.75 times regular hours and overtime is set to zero. If the code is 3, pay is 4.15 times regular hours and overtime is 1.5 times 4.15 times overtime hours. If code is more than 3, ICODE ERROR and its value are printed.

Transferring Control within a Program

In some programs, the logic specifies a next instruction to be executed that is not next in sequence. It may be before or after the statement that transfers control. FORTRAN uses statement labels to identify the statements to which control can be transferred. The statement that transfers control unconditionally is the GOTO (or GO TO) statement. GOTO as one word is preferred for clearly documented program code.

Statement Labels in FORTRAN

FORTRAN statements may have a statement label, which is a number written in columns 1–5 of the coding sheet. The label is in a fixed position; it is never indented to the right of column 5 even if the statement it labels is indented. The statement label may be from one to five numeric digits. If there are less than five digits, it is customary
```

to right-justify them (leave the blanks at the left) within columns 1–5. The statement label numbers are coded by the programmer and used by the program; there is no connection with the line reference numbers often required for each statement in a program entered at a terminal or the line numbers added to the program listing by many compilers.

Any FORTRAN statement may be labeled, but only those statements that are referenced by another program statement *must* be labeled. For example, in Chapter 1b, none of the statements were labeled. A good practice is to use statement labels only when they are needed for reference or documentation, because excess statement labels make it more difficult to locate the statement label being referenced. The rules of the language allow the statement labels to be in any order, and they need not be sequential. In other words, the statement label numbers are identifying labels; they do not specify sequence. However, having statement label numbers in sequence or approximate sequence makes it easier to locate a referenced statement label number.

Figure 2-2 Outline of program form with block numbering.

```
*********            IDENTIFICATION BLOCK
*
*
*
*********
*                    VARIABLES IDENTIFICATION
*********
*
*
*********
*
*
*********
* BLOCK 0000         INITIALIZATION BLOCK
*********
*
      - - - - - - - - - -
      - - - - - - - - - -
      - - - - - - - - - -
*
*********
* BLOCK 0100         DATA INPUT AND INPUT VALIDATION BLOCK
*********
*
   101 READ *, Y,Z
      - - - - - - - - - -
      - - - - - - - - - -
*
*********
* BLOCK 0200         PROCESS BLOCK
*********
*
   201 X = Y + 2.0**2
      - - - - - - - - - -
      - - - - - - - - - -
*
*********
* BLOCK 0300         NORMAL OUTPUT BLOCK
*********
*
   301 PRINT *, X,Y,Z
      - - - - - - - - - -
*
*********
* BLOCK 0900         ERROR MESSAGE BLOCK
*********
*
      - - - - - - - - - -
      - - - - - - - - - -
      END
```

As explained, a disciplined style for a FORTRAN program will divide the program into logical blocks of code. A useful approach to labeling is to have each block of code start a new set of numbers. For example, the initialization block will be labeled with numbers in the 000s. It is often useful to label the first labeled statement in the block with the block number plus 1. The second block will use 100s, with the first labeled statement being 101, etc. This has the advantage that whenever a statement is referenced, its location in the program and the logical block to which it belongs are also identified. This is illustrated in Figure 2-2.

GOTO Statement

The GOTO statement is used to branch around one or more statements. The branching is unconditional; that is, it does not depend on any test or condition.

GOTO STATEMENT

GOTO s (or GO TO s)

where s is a statement label.

When a GOTO is encountered, the next statement to be executed will be the one labeled with the statement number s. After statement s is executed, control continues with the statements following s. Because GOTOs may make a program difficult to debug and maintain, they should be used with care. To aid in understanding the logic of a program, we have chosen to place a set of comments before most GOTOs explaining the nature of the branching as shown by the following example:

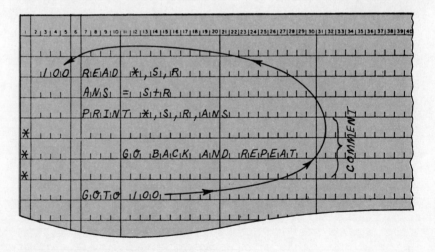

Selection of Alternative Processing Paths Using the IF Statement

In addition to the block IF, FORTRAN has two other IF statements that can be used for selection among alternative program paths: the logical IF statement and the arithmetic IF statement. The logical IF is the more important of the two; in fact, we do not recommend use of the arithmetic IF statement. It is only explained so that you can understand FORTRAN programs that use it.

Logical IF Statement

The logical IF consists of a test of a logical expression followed by an executable FORTRAN statement. The logical expression to be tested is, for example, a relation between two variables or two arithmetic expressions. The relation is coded by one of the relational operators or logical operators explained earlier in the chapter. The FORTRAN statement in the IF statement following the logical expression is executed only if the logical expression is true (is satisfied). Following execution of that statement, processing continues with the next statement after the IF statement. If the logical expression is false, the executable statement in the logical IF is not executed; the program goes to the following statement. As an example of a logical IF, assume that a program segment is to print a warning only if the value of a weekly paycheck is greater than $1000 but processing continues after the warning.

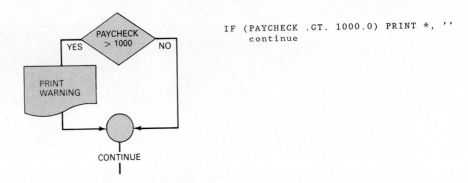

```
IF (PAYCHECK .GT. 1000.0) PRINT *, ''
     continue
```

In a second example, a logical IF combines with a GOTO to transfer control to another part of the program if there is a negative paycheck.

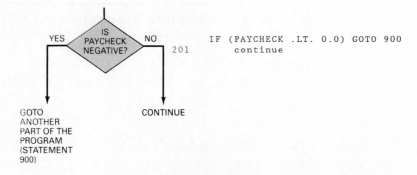

```
IF (PAYCHECK .LT. 0.0) GOTO 900
     continue
```

LOGICAL IF STATEMENT

IF (e) st

where e is a logical (relational) expression and st is almost any executable statement. If the relation is true, execute the statement; otherwise, do not execute the statement and continue with the statement following the IF statement.

The logical IF is a simpler construction than a block IF if only one action is required for one branch. The two examples above illustrate the one action for one branch situation. However, the simple logical IF statement can be used in more complex selection situations and can code the same logic as a block IF. This is

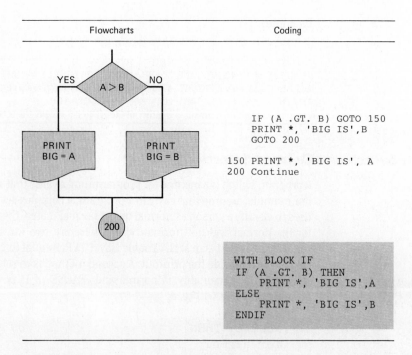

Flowcharts	Coding

```
IF (A .GT. B) GOTO 150
PRINT *, 'BIG IS',B
GOTO 200

150 PRINT *, 'BIG IS', A
200 Continue
```

```
WITH BLOCK IF
IF (A .GT. B) THEN
    PRINT *, 'BIG IS',A
ELSE
    PRINT *, 'BIG IS',B
ENDIF
```

illustrated by coding to find the largest of two real quantities A and B and to assign the largest value to BIG. This problem was illustrated earlier with the block IF. Since it may be helpful to compare the more efficient block IF coding, this is included.

In the example, there are two alternative processing statements for the two branches. The logical IF requires a GOTO; the block IF does not. The example illustrates one possibility of making an error in coding a logical IF that is not likely to occur with a block IF. Unless the action of the statement following the logical IF is to be executed in both cases, there must be a GOTO statement for one of the branches to go around it. For example, if the program was coded

```
IF (A .GT. B) PRINT *, 'BIG IS', A
PRINT *, 'BIG IS', B
```

the result would be that PRINT *, 'BIG IS', B is always executed since this statement is executed whether A or B is larger. To avoid such errors and to write clear coding when using the simple logical IF, it is sometimes desirable to have a set of two or more logical IF statements even though this causes some redundant processing. For example, the problem of finding the larger of A or B could be coded with a set of two logical IF statements. The clarity of the logic more than offsets the additional processing:

```
IF (A .GT. B) PRINT *, 'BIG IS', A
IF (B .GE. A) PRINT *, 'BIG IS', B
```

Note that the coding causes B to be printed if the two variables are equal in value.

The logical expression in a logical IF statement can include logical operators. Examples of statements that include both relational and logical operators are shown below.

Examples

```
IF ((PAY .GT. 45.0) .AND. (AGE .LE. 17.0)) TALLY = TALLY + 1.0
```
Add 1 to TALLY only if PAY .GT. 45 and also AGE .LE. 17 (both are true).
```
IF ((HRS .GE. 60.0) .OR. (OT .EQ. 10)) GOTO 10
```
Transfer control to statement 10 if either of the relational statements is true.

Program Switch and Delayed Selection

A program switch is a method for programming a value that will affect a later selection. For example, assume that early in a program, a complex set of selection statements is used to classify a person as normal or not normal. Later, the printouts will be different for the normal and not normal types. There are two ways to program this delayed selection. The first is to set a variable (say, PTYPE) equal to 1 or 2 and test the numeric value later to decide the printout. A second method is to set a logical variable equal to .TRUE. if the personality is normal and .FALSE. if it is not normal. Later in the program, the test will read:

```
IF (NORMAL) THEN
     for normal
ELSE
     for not normal
ENDIF
```

Arithmetic IF Statement

The arithmetic IF is not recommended because it tends to be error-prone. It is never necessary because the logical IF can be used. However, it was frequently used in older FORTRAN programs. Therefore, it will be explained so that FORTRAN programs written by those employing the feature can be understood.

> **ARITHMETIC IF STATEMENT**
>
> IF (expression) s_1, s_2, s_3
>
> where the expression may be a variable name or arithmetic expression. If the expression, when evaluated, is negative (that is, less than zero), control goes to the first statement label listed; if zero, to the second statement label; and if positive, to the third. Statement labels are separated by commas.

Two examples illustrate the arithmetic IF:

IF statement	Explanation
IF (X − 2.0) 100, 200, 400	IF X is less than 2.0, go to 100; if X equals 2.0, go to 200; if X is greater than 2.0, go to 400. By subtracting 2.0 from X, a negative condition is obtained in the first case, a zero for X equals 2.0, and a positive condition for anything greater than 2.0.
IF (X − 6.0) 113, 113, 210	If X ≤ 6.0, go to 113; if greater than 6.0, go to statement 210.

Validating Input Data

The selection structure programmed by the IF statements allows the coding of an important program block: validation of input data. Perhaps the most error-prone part of using a computer program is the preparation of the input data. Good program design suggests, therefore, that a program include features that are useful in detecting erroneous or incomplete input data. Two techniques should be employed where feasible.

1. Print out (echo) the input data for visual review. There may be a printout especially for validation purposes, or the input data may be printed as part of the final output. Printout of input data was used in the example programs in Chapter 1b. Echoing of data with labels is vital when input is from a file of data, but echoing of input data with labels is useful even with interactive input, especially if several data items are entered at once, because there is a possibility of not recognizing an error at the moment of input.
2. Test the input data to check for data items that do not meet the criteria for valid data.

The testing for valid data is based on the fact that it is possible, in many cases, to specify criteria for input data. For example, the data for hours worked might be specified as not negative or zero and not greater than 65.0. A test for validity could consist of three separate tests or a single, composite test, such as:

```
IF ((HOURS .LE. 0.0) .OR. (HOURS .GT. 65.0)) THEN
    PRINT *, HOURS, 'HOURS ERROR'
```

During processing, it is sometimes desirable to program a test to avoid possible division by zero. For example, a computation of pay as a percentage of bonus would, if bonus were zero, produce a machine execution error and abort the job. Coding to prevent this execution error might read:

```
IF (BONUS .EQ. 0.0) THEN
    PRINT *, 'ERROR. BONUS IS ZERO.'
ELSE
    PRATE = PAY/BONUS
ENDIF
```

Data validation is often overlooked in FORTRAN program design because users of the program are assumed to be able to enter correct data. This overlooks the many human possibilities for input errors or misunderstanding of input requirements. A validation module is therefore a vital part of a well-designed FORTRAN program.

Self-Testing Exercise 2-5

Use a simple logical IF statement (not a block IF) to code the following operations.

1. If the square root of $X^2 + Y^2$ is less than 100.0, the answer (called ANSWR) is to be 12.0 * X. If it is greater than or equal to 100.0, the value of ANSWR is to be X^2. Print the answer.

2. Find out if X is between -550 and 1000 inclusive ($-550 \leq X \leq 1000$). If so, print YES; otherwise, print NO. Then halt the computer.

3. Write a combined input and input validation block to test input data and reject (with a message) a negative or zero rate (RATE) or a rate greater than 15 percent. Stop the processing if there is an error.

4. Rewrite problem 3 with a block IF.

Processing More Than One Set of Input Data

A line of data items stored in a file or entered at a terminal (followed by pressing ENTER or RETURN) constitutes a set of data for FORTRAN input. The sequence program structure used in Chapter 1 works well for a single set of input data, but it is very cumbersome if more than one set is to be read and processed. Since each READ statement reads only one set of data (using the statements explained so far), processing 10 different sets of input data on 10 different lines would require 10 sets of processing statements, each with a READ statement, and each set of data has unique variable names. A more efficient program design is to write the program so that the READ statement and its related processing statement are used over again for each set of input data. This method is called *repetition* or *looping,* a fundamental technique in programming. A preferred method of repetition using the DO statement will be explained in more detail in Chapter 4; the repetition procedure described in this chapter is a simple IF loop that provides an introduction to repetition.

A Simple IF Loop

Assume a program segment that is to read values called X and Y from a file or terminal input, compute the sum (called Z), and print the values assigned to X, Y, and Z. This is to be repeated for several sets of X and Y inputs. The repetition could be programmed with a GOTO statement to transfer control back to the first statement in the set as shown in the following flowchart.

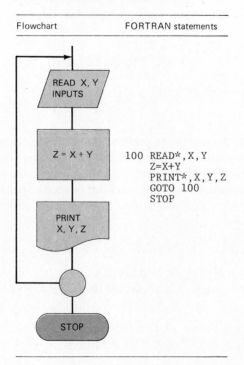

Flowchart   FORTRAN statements

```
100 READ*,X,Y
    Z=X+Y
    PRINT*,X,Y,Z
    GOTO 100
    STOP
```

The logic repeats the processing over and over using a new input card for each execution. The difficulty is that the repetition never terminates—it is an endless loop because there is no logic to cause it to stop looping. A program written in this way may eventually be abnormally terminated by the operating system, but this is not a satisfactory way to come to a stop.

A simple method for coding the end of a repetition is to use an IF statement to test whether or not the set of statements has been executed the appropriate number of times. Three methods of coding the test for termination when reading input data illustrate the concept.

1. Use a unique termination value for the input data item following the last set of data to be processed. Examples of such values are a negative value (if no regular value will be negative) or 999 (if no regular input would have this value). The coding and flowchart for a negative value are:

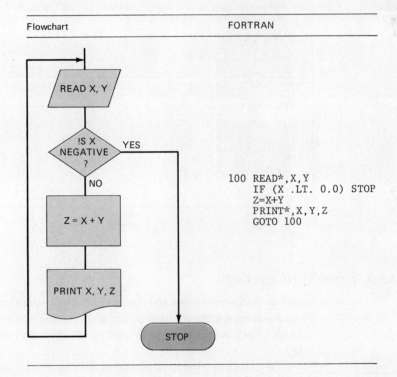

Flowchart   FORTRAN

```
100 READ*,X,Y
    IF (X .LT. 0.0) STOP
    Z=X+Y
    PRINT*,X,Y,Z
    GOTO 100
```

2. Establish a counter for input items. Keep track of the items read, and terminate when the required number have been processed. For example, if the input data set counter is called ICOUNT and 10 items are to be processed, the flowchart and coding could be as shown on page 92.

3. In interactive execution, have the program ask the user whether or not more data items are to be entered. The response (such as Yes or No or Y or N) can be tested to decide whether to repeat the loop. This will be illustrated in mathematical example 2 in Chapter 2b where the response Y or y causes the program to accept more data.

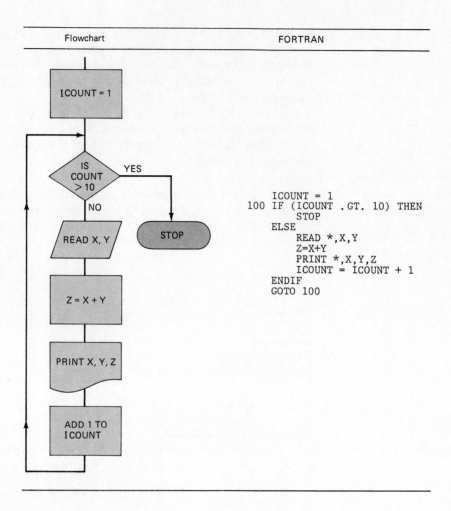

Flowchart	FORTRAN

```
          ICOUNT = 1
100  IF (ICOUNT .GT. 10) THEN
          STOP
     ELSE
          READ *,X,Y
          Z=X+Y
          PRINT *,X,Y,Z
          ICOUNT = ICOUNT + 1
     ENDIF
     GOTO 100
```

First- and Last-Time-Through Logic

In coding both simple loops and the more complex repetitions explained in Chapter 4, a major source of program logic errors occurs in the processing of the first data item through a block of code that will be used repeatedly and in the handling of the last data item.

The first-time-through errors generally result from failing to initialize properly. Logic that works perfectly once started will not give correct results if begun incorrectly. Two programming situations illustrate the need for first-time-through logic.

1. *Obtaining the largest value so far* If, as each data item is processed, the program tests it to determine if it is the largest value so far and stores the largest value, the instructions might read:

PLARGE = AMAX1 (DATA, PLARGE)

This instruction stores the larger of DATA and the previous PLARGE in PLARGE (which is then the largest so far). But what is PLARGE the first time the comparison is made? If it is zero and all the data items are negative, the result will be zero, which is not correct. To ensure that the test will work properly at the first comparison, PLARGE must be initialized so that the first data item will be larger. This can be done by initializing PLARGE with the first data value in the set of data values to be compared.

2. *Adding to previous sum*   In many programs, a sum is accumulated by a statement of the form:

```
SUM = SUM + DATA
```

In essence, this statement adds current value of DATA to the previous value of SUM. In order for the logic to work properly, SUM must be zero the first time through. If the first DATA amount is 5.0, then the SUM after the first execution will be 5.0 (but only if SUM is zero the first time through). Some (but not all) compilers set all storage to zero before the program execution, but do not depend on it.

These two examples illustrate the first-time-through situations. These situations are usually relatively simple to analyze and program if the programmer is alert to first-time-through problems.

The last-time-through problem may occur for several reasons. As with first-time-through logic, the problem is easily solved if recognized. Two major possibilities are given below.

1. *Last input in error*   When an input is found to be in error, there may be special processing of it before returning to read the next item. However, when the last input item is the one in error, another input should not be read.

2. *Last input item not read*   A fairly easy error to make and overlook is to program a count for records to be read and make the test so that the last set is not read. For example, refer to example 2 in the previous section with a termination test based on a record count of 10 and a count (ICOUNT) that started at 1. If the test was written as shown below, only nine sets of data would be read.

```
IF (ICOUNT .GE. 10) THEN
    STOP
ELSE
```

Using a File for Input Data

The alternative to input of data at a terminal in interactive execution is reading from a file of data prepared using a text editor or a file that represents the output data from another program. There are several types of files, and programming of files can be quite complex. Files are covered in detail in Chapter 6. For Chapters 2 through 5, we will use very simple sequential files, meaning the sets of data (records) are accessed from the file one after another in the order they were prepared (written).

The only programming requirement with sequential files is that the program must be able to identify the file to be used. As explained in the introduction, each file has a name and this name is used to specify the file the program is to use. This is done in FORTRAN with an OPEN statement. The simplest form of the OPEN statement for sequential files is OPEN (file device number, FILE = 'name of file'). The OPEN command specifies that file specifications will follow, enclosed in parentheses. The first specification is the unit number (an integer) assigned to the file device. The second specification consists of FILE = followed by the name assigned to the file enclosed in apostrophes. There are other optional specifications, but when they are not used, the default specifications are for a sequential file.

OPEN STATEMENT

OPEN (olist)

where the olist is a list of specifiers for the features of the file. If not specified, the file is a sequential access file. For simple files, the specifiers are:

unit number
FILE = 'character string name of file'

An example of an OPEN statement is:

```
OPEN (7, FILE = 'DATA2')
```

This specifies that the program is to use a file on device number 7 (an arbitrary number assigned to it) and the file name that was given to the file when it was created is DATA2.

The OPEN statement initiates operating system procedures to identify the file, check the file device, assign storage space for the file specifications and file input, and perhaps close the file device to other programs. The logical extension of the OPEN statement is a CLOSE statement to release the file device, release the file storage space, etc.

The CLOSE statement can be programmed explicitly, or closing may be handled by the operating system without the CLOSE statement (implicit programming). For simple sequential files, implicit closing of files is often satisfactory. Implicit closing will be used in the example programs for Chapters 2 and 3. Explicit closing will be illustrated in the payroll program in Chapter 4b. The CLOSE statement has several options to be explained in Chapter 6; only the simplest form for use with sequential files is explained here.

CLOSE STATEMENT

CLOSE (unit)

where the unit refers to the unit number specified for the file in the OPEN statement.

Other optional specifications will be explained in Chapter 6.

An example of a pair of OPEN and CLOSE statements (OPEN at the beginning of the program and CLOSE at the end of file use) are shown below. The statements assume a file is labeled 'DATAFL4' and is on device number 7.

```
OPEN (7,FILE = 'DATAFL4')
 .
 .
 .
CLOSE (7)
```

Planning and Designing a Program with Multiple Cases and Exceptions

In Chapter 1b, the explanations of the use of pseudocode and a program flowchart in program planning described a two-step planning and design process based on a single case (a single set of input data). In this chapter, statements have been introduced that allow the program to repeat the processing using more than one set of input data (multiple cases); the statements also allow more computer input validation and more complete handling of exceptions. The logic of program planning and design is therefore expanded as follows to include these more complex problem situations.

1. Plan the general logic of processing for the simple case (one set of output from one set of normally expected data) to the level of detail useful for the specific problem.
2. Add a control structure to the simple case to handle multiple cases (multiple sets of input). Include logic required for first- and last-time-through processing.
3. Modify control structure and add logic for input validation and handling of input errors.
4. Add logic for handling exceptions and unusual cases, including cases in which zero or negative data values are exceptions.

This expanded program planning and design procedure is illustrated in Chapter 2b in connection with the pseudocode for general example 2.

Introduction to Testing and Quality Assurance for a Program

Having written a program, the programmer (and user) needs assurance that the program is correct and performs as expected. Testing is required because program logic can become complex due to selection instructions and the variety of logical expressions used for deciding on selection. Testing and quality assurance of programs can use a variety of techniques. This section will describe the nature of the testing and quality-assurance process, explain the development and use of a set of test data—data designed specifically to test the program—and introduce debugging during compilation.

Testing and Quality-Assurance Process

With a very simple FORTRAN program, testing is quite simple. However, for larger and more complex FORTRAN programs, there is a need for a process of testing and quality assurance that proceeds concurrently with the program design, programming, and debugging.

Programming	Testing and quality-assurance process
1. Problem recognition and algorithm selection	1. Check literature for existence of tested algorithm. Use a tested algorithm, if available.
2. Program design (for example, flowcharting and/or pseudocode)	2. Develop testing strategy and design of initial set of test data.
3. Program coding	3. (a) Desk checking. The programmer manually traces a few data items through the program (at the desk before compilation). (b) Program reading (peer review). It is frequently helpful to have other programmers (or fellow students who are programming) read a program to check for errors in logic, adherence to good style, etc.
4. Compilation	4. Use compiler diagnostics to identify coding errors.
5. Debugging	5. Make corrections in design and code.
6. Testing	6. Use test data to identify logic errors and provide assurance of program correctness.

Development and Use of Test Data

Data for testing a program should be designed to test all paths through the program. If a program consists of a simple sequence (such as the programs in Chapter 1b), a single set of data will test the program. In a program with selection structures, a separate set of test data needs to be provided for each path through the program. For example, assume a program with the following structure (shown in Figure 2-3). With one selection structure, there are two paths through the program. If these two paths are two processing paths for a payroll program that has one computational procedure for less than or equal to 40 hours and another procedure for over 40 hours, one set of test data should test for 40 hours and a second set of test should test for over 40 hours. These two sets of test data are not sufficient because a frequent source of error in programs is at the boundary value specified in the decision block; in the example, the boundary value is 40. It might be quite easy for the programmer to code IF (HOURS .LT. 40.0) rather than IF (HOURS .LE. 40.0). If the boundary value itself is not tested, this easily made error would not be detected. For this reason, it is recommended that

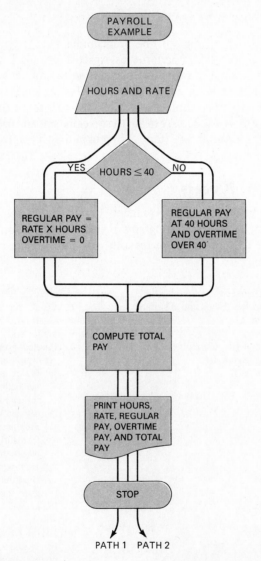

Figure 2-3 Paths through a simple payroll program for testing the program.

test data include data at the boundary value, the boundary value minus one, and the boundary value plus one. Plus or minus one means plus or minus the appropriate increment which may be a fraction or an integer. In the simple example, this will require three sets of test data with hours data of 39, 40, and 41 (if whole hours are used).

The testing of all processing logic includes the use of invalid data to test the data validation logic. In other words, a complete set of test data will include:

1. Normal case testing of all boundary values and boundary values plus one and minus one.
2. Abnormal or invalid cases. These should include tests for all error conditions being tested in data validation and a test for last-input-in error.

Debugging Programs during Compilation

The output from compilation is useful in removing coding-type errors (and program entry errors that may not have been noticed in checking the FORTRAN source program before submission). The errors that can be detected by the compiler are language-use errors. However, a student should be aware that the error message from the compiler correctly identifies the existence of an error, but in a significant number of cases the computer is unable to specify the true cause of the error and may instead specify an incorrect cause.

Self-Testing Exercise 2-6

1. Find the errors in the following program (all documentation lines are omitted). There are 10 inputs (with and without errors).

```
 1         INTEGER COUNT
 2         COUNT = 1
 3   100   READ COUNT, PAY
 4         IF (PAY .GT. 300.0) GOTO 900
 5         BONUS = SALARY * 100.0
 6         PRINT *, PAY, BONUS
 7         COUNT = COUNT + 1.0
 8         IF (COUNT .GE. 10) STOP
 9   900   PRINT *, 'ERROR. PAY TOO LARGE.', PAY
10         GOTO 100
11         END
```

2. After finding errors, recode the above program using a block IF and correct program design. Draw a flowchart for your solution.

Precision and Accuracy in Computing

Accuracy has to do with measurement. For example, suppose we wish to measure a large wooden table. Using three methods of measurement, we arrive at different accuracy.

Method of measurement	Accuracy
By eye	Within 1 foot
By using a hand span	Within 3 inches
By using a measuring tape	Within $\frac{1}{16}$ inch

Precision refers to how many digits are used to record (store) the result. For example, if the common fraction $\frac{4}{3}$ is to be recorded as a decimal, there is no theoretical limit to the trailing 3s; the limit imposed by the computer structure (or other recording of the data) is the precision for FORTRAN.

1.3	2-digit precision
1.333	4-digit precision
1.33333	6-digit precision

To understand the nature of precision, assume that only a fixed number of places is available for hand computation. Using only three or six places, solve $\frac{1}{6} + 30$. The decimal point (shown by $\wedge$) will be allowed to float, and there will be rounding before digits are dropped. The results are as follows:

Three-place precision	Six-place precision
$\frac{1}{6} =$ 1 6 7	1 6 6 6 6 7
$30 + \frac{1}{6} =$ 3 0 2	3 0 1 6 6 7

In hand computation, the person doing the computing will usually vary the precision from problem to problem, but a computer is generally designed to operate with a fixed precision. High-level-language compilers generally reflect the precision of the computer for which they are written. The precision can and does vary among computers. There are generally methods for changing the precision for FORTRAN computations. The standard FORTRAN method for greater precision is to specify double precision (explained in Chapter 7). With some FORTRANs, there is a nonstandard method for reducing precision (to save storage) or to increase it to double precision. As an example, in one popular microcomputer FORTRAN, an integer variable will take either 2 bytes or 4 bytes depending on a storage specification provided at compilation or a type statement for the variable of INTEGER*2 or INTEGER*4. Two bytes can store in the range +32,767, and 4 bytes store about nine digits. A nonstandard type specification of REAL * 8 is equivalent to specifying double precision for a real variable.

An example will illustrate how FORTRAN programs have different results when compiled and executed with different precision. Peter Minuit paid Indians $24 for Manhattan Island in 1626. If the Indians had invested the $24 at 6 percent compounded quarterly (0.06/4.0 per quarter), what sum would the Indians have had after 350 years in the USA bicentennial year of 1976? The FORTRAN statement is:

```
    AMT = 24.0 * ((1.0 + .06/4.0))**(350.0 * 4.0))
or  AMT = 24.0 * (1.015**1400.0)
```

Exponentiation to the 1400th power is done by logarithms, but the result is so large that it is very much affected by the precision used by the computer. The results obtained from two different computers illustrates the concept.

Computer	Result
Medium precision	27,058,163,712
High precision	27,081,355,025

The problem was rerun on the medium-precision computer but specifying a larger double precision (explained in Chapter 7); the result was 27,081,351,168, which is closer to the precision obtained on the large, high-precision computer.

This example should not be a cause for alarm. There are only a few problems where precision will be a significant factor. But the FORTRAN programmer should be aware of precision for those cases in which it is important. In microcomputer FORTRAN, the programmer is expected to be aware of precision requirements and specify larger or smaller precision, if necessary, by increasing the storage size used.

The maximum precision obtainable inside the computer is not necessarily the precision obtained at output. In the case of list-directed output, the output precision is defined by the compiler writer; the programmer has no control over it. For output using FORMAT (explained in Chapter 3), the computer will provide only the output precision specified by the FORMAT statement (but is limited to the precision of the internal representation).

Self-Testing Exercise 2-7

1. Write and evaluate a short program to generate a real number (called ANUM). Divide the number by 100 and call the result RESLT. Multiply RESLT by 100.0 and name the product RESLTM. Use the IFIX intrinsic function to obtain the integer portion of RESLTM (and call it IRESLT). Next, round RESLTM before converting to integer by adding 0.0001. Call the converted result IROUND. Print ANUM, RESLTM, RESLT, IRESLT, and IROUND using list-directed output. Repeat for the 11 real numbers from 100 to 110. Identify differences due to precision and binary stored values that only approximate some decimal numbers. Note the effect of integer conversion with and without a small correction quantity before conversion. Note also that differences can be greater or less than the expected value.

Suggestions for the **FORTRAN** Programmer

Because so much emphasis is placed in the text on good programming style, it may be useful to review the concept of a good program. Writing a good program is not merely writing language statements in correct form. The statements need to code a suitable solution procedure (a computing algorithm) that has been carefully designed. The coding should be done in a clear manner following a disciplined style. The statements need to be coded correctly, i.e., use the language correctly. These three important requirements can be understood by two analogies:

Analogy 1
A term paper on "Privacy and the Computer" has (assuming appropriate knowledge of the subject has been acquired by the student-writer) three elements that affect the result:

1. The planning of an organization for the paper. This should have logical parts, each part with an objective, and able to fit the overall structure of the paper. This design is reflected in a clear outline of the topics to be included. This phase is similar to the development of a computer solution procedure which meets the needs posed by the problem.
2. The organization of the paper into paragraphs with headings, subheadings, indentation, underlining, etc. This is similar in concept to computer programming style.

3. The writing of sentences in correct grammatical form. This is the same as coding of correct statements in the program.

Analogy 2

A student is to develop a computer solution procedure for finding the square root of a number. The three steps in the process are:

1. Find or develop a solution procedure. The student finds that the Newton-Raphson algorithm is already known and well-defined. This method can be described for this problem in a flowchart or in pseudocode. Organize the solution procedure for program clarity.
2. The program for the Newton-Raphson method can be divided into logically separate functions. For example, the separate activities in the solution procedure might be identified as:
    (a) Read input value and validate; that is, test for invalid values such as negative or zero.
    (b) Initialize all values for the computational procedure.
    (c) Perform the iterative procedure to find the square root.
    (d) Print out the input value and the square root.
3. The algorithm is coded in correct FORTRAN statements.

The programming style suggestions from Chapters 1 and 2 are listed below. The first seven suggestions summarize the guidelines described in Chapter 1, which should be reviewed; the remainder summarize good practice as explained in this chapter.

1. Analyze the problem and design the program before beginning to code instructions. If you do not understand the problem and the solution procedure, you cannot tell the computer what to do. Useful alternative design and planning methods are program design language (pseudocode) and program flowcharts. A suggested four-step process in planning and designing a program is:
    (a) Plan the general logic of processing for one simple normal case to the level of detail useful for the problem.
    (b) Add a control structure to the simple case to handle multiple cases. Include logic required for first-time-through and last-time-through processing.
    (c) Modify the control structure and add logic for input validation and handling of input errors.
    (d) Add logic for handling exceptions and unusual cases, including negative or zero values (if not allowed).
2. Use FORTRAN coding paper to aid in writing instructions in proper form.
3. Use a block structure to divide the program into logical segments. Include a PROGRAM IDENTIFICATION block and a VARIABLES IDENTIFICATION block for clear documentation. The style selected for this text is to have a block name line preceded and followed by a line consisting of 10 asterisks. For the block name line, there is an asterisk in column 1, a block number (BLOCK *nnnn*) starting in column 3 for all numbered blocks, and the block name starting in column 23. To be manageable, blocks should be less than 50 statements long.
4. Use explanatory comments at the beginning of each logical block. Use comments freely inside the blocks. Following the text style, set off each group of one or more inside-block comment lines by a blank comment line before and after. The inside-block comment lines are indented to column 11.
5. Use parentheses to avoid ambiguity. Do not rely upon unfamiliar precedence rules.

6. Consider a printout (echo) of input data as a visual check against incorrect input.
7. Print labels to clearly identify all output values.
8. Validate input data to make sure it falls within the limits assumed for the program. Provide suitable error messages and correct or reject bad data.
9. Use the block IF whenever appropriate. Also, use the logical IF. Do not use the arithmetic IF.
10. Check for incorrect logic following a basic logical IF. Remember that unless the action of the IF is to transfer control, the statement following the IF will be executed for both selection paths.
11. When coding tests of conditions, do not assume a value for any remaining condition. Make an explicit test.
12. Use care in equality tests of real variables. Consider .GE. or .LE. or conversion (with rounding factor) to integer value prior to comparison.
13. Provide explicit error stops or error messages for instances when conditions that should never occur actually do occur.
14. Code for clarity, not for a minimum number of coding lines.
15. Explicitly initialize variables where needed for first-time-through processing.
16. A program should be checked out by running it with comprehensive test data for which the results are known. Test carefully the first- and last-time-through logic, logic at and around boundary values, input validation, and handling of exceptions including errors in the last set of data.

Summary

The basic intrinsic functions were explained. These reduce coding requirements for common operations. The intrinsic functions have a generic name as well as specific names that identify the type of data being produced (such as integer or real). Integer data is important in FORTRAN because there are situations where integer data is needed and because the characteristics of integer arithmetic are often useful. Modern FORTRAN compilers allow mixed types in an expression but convert them to a compatible type before execution. Good programming style is to code the conversions with intrinsic conversion functions rather than to rely upon automatic conversion. There are type statements to override the implicit first-letter typing of integer and real variables and to declare the type for variable names for character data and logical data.

The selection structure is coded by the IF statement. The block IF follows the general selection pattern of IF . . . THEN . . . ELSE. For selection with only one action if the test is true, a logical IF may be more appropriate. An unconditional transfer of control is programmed with a GOTO. A delayed transfer is programmed with a logical program switch.

Data validation should normally be included in well-written programs. A simple IF loop can be used to perform repetitive processing. When loops are used, it is important to carefully code the logic so that the program will work correctly the first time through and the last time through. The program should be tested using desk checking and test data. The concepts of precision and accuracy in computing were explained and contrasted. Style guidelines for Chapters 1 and 2 were summarized.

Answers to Self-Testing Exercises

Exercise 2-1

1. (a) X = SQRT (A + B)
   (b) X = (A/B + 2.0)**(1.0/3.0)
   Exponentiating to the $\frac{1}{3}$ power is the same as taking the cube root. As will be

explained more fully in the chapter, the exponent must be real or it would turn out to be zero. The parentheses around the exponent are necessary. Why?

(c) Y = EXP (X)

(d) X = SQRT (ABS (Y + 5.0))

(e) Y = ALOG (X)

(f) R = SQRT (X**2 + Y**2)

Note that the square root of the right side was taken, since no expression is allowed on the left side.

(g) A = AMAX1 (X**2, Y**2)

2. (a) $x = \log_e(y + z)$

(b) $y = \sin|a|$

(c) $d = |b^2 - 4ac|$

(d) $y = e^{-x^2}$

(e) $\rho = a \cos \theta$

(f) $x = \sqrt{a + \dfrac{b}{c^d}\, ef + 1.0}$

Exercise 2-2

1.

Valid or not valid; note if mixed type	If not valid, why; if mixed type, how converted
(a) Valid, mixed	Will be converted to A**2 + 1.0.
(b) Valid (integer arithmetic for integer exponent is valid)	
(c) Valid, real type	
(d) Valid, mixed	Converts to A/B + D/3.0.
(e) Valid integer type	
(f) Valid, mixed	Result is converted to integer type.
(g) Valid real type	
(h) Valid, mixed	Better to code as X = (A + B)/((C + D) * E * FLOAT (IX))
(i) Not valid	Expression (X + Y) to left of equals sign not allowed.
(j) Mixed	Integer may not have real exponent, so compiler will convert to JX = FLOAT(IX)**A or some older compilers will reject it.
(k) Valid (integer exponent allowed)	

2. (a) 1.2   (b) 1   (c) 0   (d) 4

3. (a) J = ABS (KDATA)
       J = IABS (KDATA)
   (b) M = MIN(I, J, K)
       M = MINO(I, J, K)

4. (a) REAL(JIX)
       FLOAT(JIX)
       AJIX = JIX
   (b) INT(DATA1)
       IFIX(DATA1)
       IDATA1 = DATA1

5. (a) X = FLOAT(I) * B**I or X = REAL(I) * B**I
(I in exponent need not be made real because an integer exponent does not cause a mixed-type expression.)
(b) X = B + (C/FLOAT(J)) + FLOAT(K)**D or
X = B + (C/REAL(J)) + REAL(K)**D

Exercise 2-3

1. CHARACTER LABEL1*12
READ*LABEL1,NSHARE
PRINT*LABEL1,NSHARE

2. REAL INTRST
INTEGER PYMNTN

3. CHARACTER*2 A, B, C, D

4. They both declare variables G, H, I, J to be variable names for character data of one character each.

5. LOGICAL SW1
SW1 = .FALSE.

Exercise 2-4

1. IF (SQRT(X**2 + Y**2) .LT. 100.0) THEN
        ANSWR = 12.0 * X
ELSE
        ANSWR = X**2
ENDIF
PRINT *, ANSWR

2. (a) IF (ALPHA .GE. BETA .AND. ALPHA .GE. GAMMA) THEN
        BIG = ALPHA
    ELSEIF (BETA .GE. ALPHA .AND. BETA .GE. GAMMA) THEN
        BIG = BETA
    ELSE
        BIG = GAMMA
    ENDIF
(b) BIG = AMAX1(ALPHA,BETA,GAMMA)

3. IF (NIX .EQ. KIX) THEN
        STOP
ELSEIF (ABS(NIX) .GT. ABS(KIX)) THEN
        PRINT *, NIX
ELSE
        PRINT *, KIX
ENDIF

4. IF ((X .GE. −550.0) .AND. (X .LE. 1000.0)) THEN
        PRINT *, 'YES'
ELSE
        PRINT *, 'NO'
ENDIF
STOP

5.
```
   IF ((A .GT. B .AND. A .GT. C) .OR. (A .LT. D .AND. A .EQ. E)) THEN
        PRINT *, 'TRUE'
   ELSE
        PRINT *, 'FALSE'
   ENDIF
```

6.
```
   IF (ICODE .EQ. 1 .OR. ICODE .EQ. 2) THEN
        RPAY = RHRS * 3.75
        OTPAY = 0.0
      ELSEIF (ICODE .EQ. 3) THEN
        RPAY = RHRS * 4.15
        OTPAY = 1.5 * 4.15 * OTHRS
   ELSE
        PRINT *, 'ICODE ERROR', ICODE
   ENDIF
   STOP
```

IF block · ELSEIF block · ELSE block · IF...ELSE with ENDIF

Exercise 2-5

1.
```
   IF (SQRT(X**2 + Y**2) .LT. 100.0) ANSWR = 12.0 * X
   IF (SQRT(X**2 + Y**2) .GE. 100.0) ANSWR = X**2
   PRINT *, ANSWR
```

   The above answer is clear and complete but does repeat processing of the test. An alternative answer which is more efficient but more complex is:

```
       IF (SQRT(X**2 + Y**2) .LT. 100.0) GOTO 110
       ANSWR = X**2
       GOTO 120
   110 ANSWR = 12.0 * X
   120 PRINT *, ANSWR
```

2.
```
   IF ((X .GE. - 550.0) .AND. (X .LE. 1000.0)) PRINT *, 'YES'
   IF ((X .LT. - 550.0) .OR. (X .GT. 1000.0)) PRINT *, 'NO'
   STOP
```

3. Without block IF

```
       READ *, RATE
       IF ((RATE .LE. 0.0) .OR. (RATE .GT. 0.15)) GOTO 150
   120 normal input processing
       GOTO 200 (to skip around next statements)
   150 PRINT *, RATE, 'RATE NEG, ZERO, OR TOO LARGE'
       STOP
   200 continue with normal processing
```

4. With block IF

```
   READ *, RATE
   IF ((RATE .LE. 0.0) .OR. (RATE .GT. 0.15)) THEN
        PRINT *, RATE, 'RATE NEG, ZERO, OR LARGE'
        STOP
   ENDIF
   (continue with normal processing)
```

Exercise 2-6

1. Errors are:

Line 2 This is a count initialization error (in connection with test in line 8). Trace it through. It will terminate after reading nine good records.

Line 3 READ statement has no asterisk or unit to read from. COUNT is read, but it has been defined in line 2.

Line 7 Putting the increment in this place in the program means error inputs are not counted. Since COUNT is integer (line 1), the statement should not increment with a real constant.

Line 8 When COUNT is less than 10, the error message in line 9 is printed even though there is no error.

Line 10 This, in connection with line 4, represents a last-record-in error situation. If the last input is in error, there is a transfer back to read another record (after error message), but there is no more data.

2. A solution is shown by the flowchart below and the program on the next page.

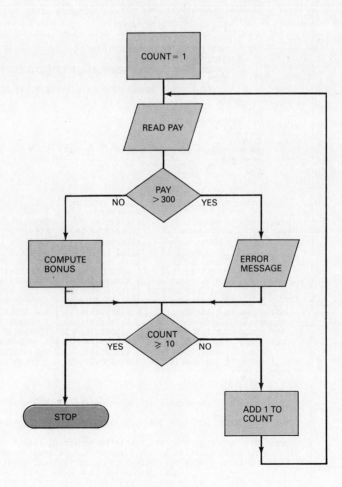

```
        INTEGER COUNT
        COUNT = 1
100     READ *, PAY
        IF (PAY .GT. 300.0) THEN
            PRINT *, 'ERROR. PAY TOO LARGE', PAY
        ELSE
            BONUS = PAY * 100.0
            PRINT *, PAY, BONUS
        ENDIF
        IF (COUNT .GE. 10) THEN
            STOP
        ELSE
            COUNT = COUNT + 1
            GOTO 100
        ENDIF
```

Self-Testing Exercise 2-7

I.

```
************
*                    PROGRAM QUIZ 2-7
************
      ANUM = 100.0
100  IF(ANUM .LE. 110.0) THEN
         RESLT = ANUM/100.0
         RESLTM = RESLT * 100.0
         IRESLT = IFIX(RESLTM)
         IROUND = IFIX(RESLTM + 0.0001)
         IF(RESLTM .EQ. ANUM) THEN
            PRINT *, '   EQUAL',ANUM,RESLTM,RESLT,IRESLT,IROUND
            ELSE
            PRINT *, 'NOT EQUAL',ANUM,RESLTM,RESLT,IRESLT,IROUND
         ENDIF
      ELSE
         PRINT *, 'END'
         STOP
      ENDIF
      ANUM = ANUM + 1.0
      GOTO 100
      END
```

Result of test for equality of (a) and (b)	(a) Real whole numbers from 100.0 to 110.0	(b) Quantity (a) first divided by 100.0 then multiplied by 100.0	(c) Quantity (a) divided by 100.0	See below (d)	(e)
EQUAL	1.000000000E+02	1.000000000E+02	1.00000000	100	100
EQUAL	1.010000000E+02	1.010000000E+02	1.00999999	101	101
EQUAL	1.020000000E+02	1.020000000E+02	1.01999998	102	102
EQUAL	1.030000000E+02	1.030000000E+02	1.02999997	103	103
EQUAL	1.040000000E+02	1.040000000E+02	1.03999996	104	104
NOT EQUAL	1.050000000E+02	1.049999924E+02	1.04999995	104	105
NOT EQUAL	1.060000000E+02	1.059999924E+02	1.05999994	105	106
NOT EQUAL	1.070000000E+02	1.070000076E+02	1.07000005	107	107
NOT EQUAL	1.080000000E+02	1.080000076E+02	1.08000004	108	108
EQUAL	1.090000000E+02	1.090000000E+02	1.09000003	109	109
EQUAL	1.100000000E+02	1.100000000E+02	1.10000002	110	110
END					

(d) Result of conversion of real quantity (b) to integer quantity.

(e) Result of adding 0.0001 to real quantity before integer conversion.

NOTE: Four of the 10 real quantities resulting from division by 100.0 followed by multiplication by 100.0 are no longer equal to the original real whole numbers. When the integer value of the real quantities in (b) are taken, two of the integer quantities are one less than the original whole numbers. By adding a very small quantity (0.0001) to the real quantity before conversion, the integer conversion yields correct integers.

Questions and Problems

1. Define the following terms:
   (a) compilation
   (b) desk checking
   (c) input validation
   (d) intrinsic function
   (e) program reading

2. Describe two methods of input validation.

3. Describe the testing and quality-assurance procedures that accompany the development of a FORTRAN program.

4. A program is coded with one simple selection. How many sets of data are necessary to test the program fully? How many are necessary if the program has two simple selections?

5. Write the FORTRAN expressions for the following:
   (a) X^a
   (b) X^i
   (c) X^{i-1}
   (d) e^r
   (e) $X^{\frac{1}{3}}$
   (f) X^{-4}
   (g) $X^{i/j}$
   (h) $\dfrac{1}{X^2}$

6. What is the result of each of the following statements, given the stated values for the variable?
   (a) $X = Y + Z/A$ $\left.\right\}$ $Y = 3.0, Z = 4.5, A = 2.0$
   (b) $IX = Y + Z/A$
   (c) $I = J/K$ $\left.\right\}$
   (d) $I = L/J + K$ $\left.\right\}$ $J = 3, K = 9, L = 10$
   (e) $I = J + L/K - L$

7. Write the formulas, given the following FORTRAN statements:
   (a) `Y = SQRT (X**2 + 2.0)/(1.0 - X**N)`
   (b) `X = THETA + SIN(THETA)`
   (c) `Y = 1.0/X`
   (d) `E = ((A**2 + B**2)**(1.0/2.0))/A`
   (e) `X = A**B * C + D * E/F * G**2`

8. Write the FORTRAN statement to solve the formula for each of the following:
   (a) $j = \sqrt{v}$
   (b) $a = |x + y|$ where $|\ |$ means the absolute value
   (c) $x = \dfrac{a(-b)}{c(-d)}$
   (d) $s = \dfrac{p}{q} + \dfrac{3r}{s}$

9. Eliminate mixed-mode arithmetic in the following by the use of intrinsic functions:
   (a) `IX = A + JX`
   (b) `N = XK + JX`
   (c) `X = IX**K`

(*d*) `X = X**I`
(*e*) `X = R**X + NIX`

10. Write a program segment to find the value of COST when COST is a step function of volume (*a*) first without a block IF and then (*b*) with a block IF.

If VOL is between 0 and 100	COST = 200 + 0.3 × VOL
If VOL is over 100 but not 1000	COST = 300 + 0.3 × VOL
If VOL is over 1000 but not over 5000	COST = 350 + 0.25 × VOL

11. Identify and correct the logical errors in the following:

(*a*)   `IF (A .GT. B) SMALL = A`
            `SMALL = B`
(*b*)   `IF (HOURS .LT. 0.0 .OR. HOURS .GT. 65.0)GOTO 150`
            `PAY = HOURS * 2.5`
     `150   PRINT *, HOURS, 'ZERO OR NEG INPUT'`
            `STOP`
            `PRINT *, 'HOURS', HOURS, 'PAY', PAY`

12. Write data validation statements for the quadratic formula—read the necessary variables from a file and validate the data as suitable for processing; that is, validate that $b^2 - 4ac$ is not negative (which would result in an error in attempting to take the square root). Print the input variables (with labels). Print error messages if data is invalid. The formula is

$$\frac{-b \pm \sqrt{b^2 - 4ac}}{2a}$$

13. Write a program segment to validate an input data item PRICE. If it is zero, negative, or greater than 3.0, it is to be rejected. Print an error message that gives the value and specifies the reasons for rejection.

Example Programs and Programming Exercises Using Intrinsic Functions, IF Selection, and Data Validation

General Notes on Chapter 2 Examples
Numbered Processing Blocks
Pointer Comments for Backward GOTOs
Terminating the Program
A GOTO Pseudocode Convention
Type Declaration and Storage Block
Methods of Input for Data

General Program Example 2—Payroll Computation
Problem Description for General Example 2
Program Documentation for General Example 2
Planning and Designing the Program for General Example 2 with Pseudocode
Notes on General Example 2

Mathematical Program Example 2—Table of Areas and Moments of Inertia of Hexagonal Sections
Problem Description for Mathematical Example 2
Program Documentation for Mathematical Example 2
Notes on Mathematical Example 2

Programming Exercises
Description of Assignment
Mathematics and Statistics
Business and Economics
Science and Engineering
Humanities and Social Sciences
General
Interactive Scientific and Engineering

The first example program is for the same payroll application as the general example in Chapter 1b, but additional requirements have been added that utilize the features presented in this chapter. The second program is a mathematical example of calculating the properties of hexagonal sections. The two programs not only illustrate different types of problems but also differences in program design. One program reads data from a file in batch execution (general example 2), and the other has interactive input during execution (mathematical example 2). Alternatives in use of type statements and termination of program execution are also illustrated. The documentation for the two examples contains both a pseudocode description and flowcharting to provide experience in these techniques. Following the examples are programming exercises.

General Notes on Chapter 2 Examples

The two examples utilize intrinsic functions, IF selection, and data validation. Statement numbers are also used as labels on some statements. Additional style considerations are the use of more than one logical (numbered) block of processing statements, the use of pointer comments with backward GOTOs, a convention for GOTOs in pseudocode, and a type declaration and storage block. The examples use simple IF loops to read and process several sets of input data.

Numbered Processing Blocks

As the number of processing statements becomes larger and the number of processing functions increases, it is good programming style to divide a program into more than one group of statements. These groupings (program blocks) are identified with a heading describing the block. An example is "COMPUTATION AND OUTPUT BLOCK." It is also useful to assign a number series to each of the blocks to specify the number series allowed for labeling statements in the block. We have chosen to number the initialization block as 0000. The first block after that is numbered 0100, and any statements in the block are labeled between 101 and 199; the next block is 0200, and the statements, if labeled, use labels ranging between 201 and 299. The block number can be placed anywhere in the block heading; we have placed it in columns 3–12 at the left side of the block heading line as BLOCK *nnnn*.

It is frequently useful to have a separate block for error messages. A convention we have chosen is to assign 900 (or 9000 for larger programs) as the error block number. This means that any reference to a 900 or 9000 number is to an error message.

The advantage of the block number and block number series is in clearly identifying the statement to which a GOTO (or other transfer statement) transfers control. A statement GOTO 310 anywhere in the program is immediately understood as transferring control into block 300.

Pointer Comments for Backward GOTOs

The most understandable design for a computer program is usually a program that has no backward transfers of control, that is, no GOTOs transferring to earlier program statements. It is virtually impossible to achieve such a program design for all FORTRAN programs. Many FORTRAN programs will need to transfer backward (essentially a "go back" statement). It is necessary, for example, when the program is to be repeated with new input data. This case is illustrated in both example programs.

In order to make a backward GOTO very clear, we include a comment line just before the GOTO describing what the GOTO is to accomplish (with a blank comment line on either side of the GOTO comment). The words GO BACK may be used in the comment to clearly mark a backward GOTO.

In the flowcharts, some of the backward GOTOs use a connector to avoid too many lines on the chart. The small circle has an identifying letter in it. The GOTO point has an arrow as well as a circle ⟶ Ⓐ and the point A to which control is going has the same letter as well as an arrow to the entry point Ⓐ ⟶

Terminating the Program

The two example programs read more than one set of data. They read and process input data until termination is indicated (usually by reaching the end of the data to be processed). There are several ways to program tests for end-of-data termination. Two simple ways are illustrated in the two example programs:

1. Test for a data value that terminates the input (general example 2).
2. Ask program user if more data is to be input. Mathematical example 2 illustrates the use of such a question during interactive data input and execution.

In the first example (general example 2), a special end-of-data record contains a negative value (such as $-1, -1, -1, -1$) for the values of the four input items. It is placed in the file as the last record following the last data record to be processed. After each record is read and before normal processing, the ID data item is tested for a negative value to detect the end-of-data record. All four items are entered as negative values because list-directed input requires all values to be entered, but only ID is tested for negative value. In flowchart form, the logic of using such an approach is given on page 112.

The second example program (mathematical example 2) tests for an input data item that is entered in response to a question, "More data (Y/N)?" (line 85). An input of 'Y' or 'y' will cause the program to request new data; any other value will result in termination of program execution. List-directed input of character data must use an apostrophe before and after the character string. Therefore, the yes response is 'Y' or 'y' (enclosed in apostrophes as shown).

In general, a program will be abnormally terminated by the operating system when the program attempts to read data and no more data items are available. However, this default option is not good programming practice, and in a problem such as the general example, with default termination, the program would be aborted before the summary data could be printed. It is always better to provide explicit

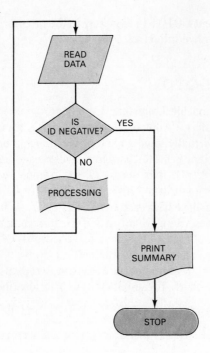

termination with end-of-program messages as in the example programs. Another method for termination using a different form of the READ statement will be explained in Chapter 3.

A GOTO Pseudocode Convention

The pseudocode description needs to provide for transfer of control (same principle as GOTO). The convention used in this text is to use a descriptive name in front of a block of pseudocode description. Any transfer of control in the program is planned with the pseudocode by writing transfer-type pseudocode with the name being the transfer point. The name is underlined. For example, a block of code might be named Summary; a pseudocode GOTO Summary is sufficient description for planning and documenting a program.

The pseudocode convention in the text for an IF test uses the IF block concept. IF and ELSE are used to identify the possible branches. If a branch has no processing, it is written as Else continue.

Type Declaration and Storage Block

As a matter of style, type declarations are coded in a separate program block placed in the program after the variables identification block. In the two example programs, this block illustrates type declaration for declaring variables as being integer even though the first letter specifies real (or, alternatively, real even though the first letter indicates integer). The variables could have been altered by using a different first letter, but we choose to declare them as real or integer to show the use of type declarations.

The two examples also illustrate the two different approaches to type statements—selective and complete. In the general program example, the type statement is used selectively only for those variables that are not correctly typed by the implicit first-letter convention. In the mathematical example, all variables are explicitly typed as real, integer, or character. In both programs, the variables identification block includes with the description the type of the variable if the first-letter implicit type is not correct.

Methods of Input for Data

The two programs are written with two different approaches to data input and handling of invalid inputs. The payroll general program example is written for input data from a file of data items (in list-directed form; i.e., items are separated by commas). There are no messages to prompt for input. When input data items are found to be invalid, a message is printed and the set of input items is not processed. If the payroll program (written for batch execution with a data file) were to be executed with interactive input, it would not be a good program design. The program would pause or an input prompt character would appear, but there is no message about what to input. In other words, a good program input design for batch input from a file is probably not a good program input design for interactive execution.

The mathematical example is written for interactive execution. There are messages to prompt input. If an input data item is tested and found to be invalid, it is rejected and a correct replacement is requested.

General Program Example 2—Payroll Computation

Problem Description for General Example 2

Paycheck amounts are computed for a specified number of employees. For data validation, input data is printed (echoed). Input data items are also validated as being within suitable limits. After calculations, net pay and gross pay are printed, net pay for each employee is checked for a positive pay amount, and negative net pay is noted by an error message. After all employees are processed, the total gross pay and total taxes for all the employees are printed along with the largest single gross pay amount. Values for the following variables are input for each employee:

Identification number (ID)
Hours worked (HRSWRK)
Wage rate (WGRATE)
Miscellaneous deductions (DEDUC)

The pension rate is 5 percent of gross pay, and taxes are 15 percent of gross pay. The number of employees is not specified; a negative value for ID ends input.

Program Documentation for General Example 2

The documentation consists of a pseudocode description (Figure 2-4), a program listing with simple output (Figure 2-5), and a program flowchart (Figure 2-6). Each symbol on the flowchart has at the upper right of the symbol the corresponding line numbers of the listing. This is primarily to aid you in reading the flowchart and comparing it to the program, but in some cases it may be a useful addition to the flowchart documentation.

Figure 2-4 Pseudocode description of program for general example 2—payroll processing.

	Program line numbers
`Declare types`	37
`Initialize pension rate at 5%, tax rate at 15%, totaling variables for gross pay and taxes at zero and largest value so far at zero`	43–48
`READ data record` for an employee	54
`Test for end-of-records, i.e., negative values for inputs IF ID negative, go to` PRINT summary `ELSE continue processing`	58
`PRINT input data with labels for visual validation`	59–61
`Validate input data for out-of-range conditions:`	
`Hours worked negative or greater than 60`	62
`Wage rate negative or greater than 10.00`	63
`Miscellaneous deductions negative or greater than 65.00`	64
`IF input data invalid, print error message and go to` READ data record	101–105
`ELSE continue with processing of input data`	
`Compute gross pay, taxes, and net pay`	65–67
`Select and store largest gross pay so far`	71
`PRINT net pay and gross pay values for this employee`	75
`Check for negative net pay`	76
`IF negative net pay, print warning message and continue with processing`	95–99
`ELSE continue with processing`	
`Add gross pay and taxes to accumulating totals`	77–78
`Go back to` READ data record `for an employee`	79
PRINT summary `totals for gross pay and taxes plus largest gross pay`	85–88
`STOP`	89

Planning and Designing the Program for General Example 2 with Pseudocode

The logic for planning a program described in Chapter 2a will be applied to general example 2 using pseudocode as the planning method. The same process can also be used with the program flowchart method.

1. Plan the general logic of processing to produce one set of output from normally expected input. Plan to the level of detail needed for the specific problem. For example 2, the appropriate level of detail might be as follows:

```
READ data for an employee
Compute gross pay, taxes, and net pay
Select largest gross pay so far
PRINT net pay and gross pay values for this employee
Add gross pay and taxes to accumulating totals
PRINT  summary  totals  for  gross  pay  and  taxes  plus
    largest gross pay
STOP
```

2. Add a control structure to handle multiple cases. Include logic required for first- and last-time-through processing. The statements from step 1 are at the margin and the statements added for multiple-case control are indented.

Statements from step 1
    Statements added to handle
↓   ↓ multiple cases   Explanation

Code	Explanation
Initialize pension rate at 5% and tax rate at 15%	As a matter of style, these constants are named instead of the constant values being used in the formula statement. Therefore, they must be set to the desired values.
Initialize totaling variables for gross pay and taxes	Totaling variables must be at zero for first-time-through logic.
Initialize largest value so far at zero	Largest value so far must be less than or equal to gross pay for first-time-through logic. Gross pay will be greater than or equal to zero, so largest value so far initialized at zero.
<u>READ data record</u> for an employee	As a pseudocode convention for this text, underlining one or more words at the beginning of a line means the line of code will be referenced by a transfer of control in another pseudocode statement.
Test for end—of—records IF ID negative, go to <u>PRINT</u> summary ELSE continue processing	There is a record with negative value for input item that marks the end of the input data. At end, transfer to statements to print the summary data.
Compute gross pay, taxes, and net pay	
Select largest gross pay so far	Current gross pay is compared with the largest gross pay so far and the largest of the two is made the new largest gross pay so far. Note the need to initialize for first time through with this logic.
PRINT net pay and gross pay values for this employee	
Add gross pay and taxes to accumulating totals	Since current value for gross pay and taxes are being added to accumulated amounts, the totaling variables were set to zero for first-time-through logic.
Go back to <u>READ data record</u> for an employee	When a record has been completely processed, control is transferred back to the pseudocode statement to '<u>READ data record</u> for an employee' to read the next record.
<u>PRINT summary</u> totals for gross pay and taxes plus largest gross pay	
STOP	

3. Modify control structure and add logic for input validation and handling of input errors. The logic for this is placed after the two statements to read data and increment record counter. The input validation consists of two major steps:

```
PRINT input data for visual validation
Validate input data for out—of—range conditions
   IF input data invalid, print error message and go to
      READ data record for an employee
   ELSE continue with processing of input data
```

If a programmer desires to specify more detail for the second validation step, the second pseudocode statement can be expanded to:

```
Validate input data for out-of-range conditions:
  Hours worked negative or greater than 60
  Wage rate negative or greater than 10.00
  Miscellaneous deductions negative or greater than 65.00
```

4. Add logic for handling exceptions and unusual cases, including cases in which data may be zero or negative. In this example, a net pay of negative is an unusual case and needs to be provided for. After printing net and gross pay, a test for negative net pay is inserted.

```
Check for negative net pay
  IF negative net pay, print warning message and continue
      with processing
  ELSE continue with processing
```

Note that the program logic allows the negative net pay to be printed, but a warning message is also printed.

The complete pseudocode for the planning of general example 2 is shown in Figure 2-4. Review the complete pseudocode for the program, and then read carefully through the FORTRAN program in Figure 2-5 noting the relationship of the pseudocode statements to the FORTRAN program. To aid in this comparison, the pseudocode statements are followed by the corresponding program line reference numbers from the program listing.

Notes on General Example 2

This payroll program is more complex than the one in Chapter 1b and requires additional features. The usual identification blocks are given. A type declaration and storage block is added for two type declarations that override the implicit first-letter type. For example, it allows us to call the largest gross pay LARGEP and have the name reference real data. Since the program is more complex, the computation has been divided into several blocks. The first block contains all the initialization instructions; given a block number of 0000, it is executed only at the beginning of the program. The grouping of initialization in a separate block assists the review of this important step. Note in line 48 that there is an OPEN statement to identify the name of the file 'DATA2' that contains the input data. Some FORTRAN systems allow this statement to be omitted and the file to be specified in a job control instruction. In other words, the job control instruction makes the connection between the program and the data file, and the OPEN statement is implied rather than being included.

There are additional blocks for read, compute, and print (block 0100), print summary and terminate (block 0200), and error messages (block 0900). Note we have written the block numbers at the left of the block name comment line containing the block name.

Referring to the program listing in Figure 2-5, the output requirements of the program are met as follows:

1. The output for each employee consists of four or five lines:
   (a) A blank line to separate each employee output (line 59).

(b) A labeled echo of input data (lines 60–61).

(c) Net pay and gross pay (line 21) or an error message if input is invalid (lines 75 and 101).

(d) If net pay is negative, a message not to issue a paycheck (line 95).

2. After all records have been read and processed, a summary is printed (lines 85–88). Each summary line consists of a label of two or three words over each value.

The input procedures assume a file of input records rather than interactive input. Therefore, there are no messages to prompt for input, and an input item that is in error does not cause the program to terminate. When an erroneous input item is detected in a set of payroll input items, an input error message is printed, the record is not processed, and the next record is read. The number of inputs to be read is not specified in advance. A record with negative values for the inputs is used to terminate the program.

The AMAX1 intrinsic function is used to select the maximum employee gross pay. The generic MAX name could have been used (if available). Note the program style in the use of the IF statements in lines 62–64 and 76. Simple logical IFs are used because there is only one action. The IFs are constructed so that the block of code that is normally expected to execute is placed after the IF and the error condition is a GOTO out of the normal flow.

As alternatives for coding this program, block IFs could have been used and the error messages included in the statements in the IF blocks. For example, the coding for lines 62–64, 103, and 105 could have been replaced by:

```
IF ((HRSWRK .LT. 0.0) .OR. (HRSWRK .GT. 60.0)) THEN
    PRINT *, 'ERROR IN INPUT DATA'
    GOTO 101
  ELSEIF ((WGRATE .LT. 0.0) .OR. (WGRATE .GT. 10.0)) THEN
    PRINT *, 'ERROR IN INPUT DATA'
    GOTO 101
  ELSEIF ((DEDUC .LT. 0.0) .OR. (DEDUC .GT. 65.0)) THEN
    PRINT *, 'ERROR IN INPUT DATA'
    GOTO 101
ENDIF
```

The code for lines 76, 95, and 99 could have been replaced by:

```
IF (PAYCHK .LE. 0.0) THEN
    PRINT *, 'NET PAY IS NOT POSITIVE. DO NOT ISSUE CHECK.'
ENDIF
```

The use of the error message block may make the code easier to read since normal processing flow is not interrupted by error messages; however, placement of messages in the block IF where the error test is made may sometimes be preferred (as will be illustrated in the mathematical example).

There are four IF statements that compare real data items. In Chapter 2a, there was a caution against equality comparisons of real data when the real data items being compared are the result of computations in the program, especially if they have a fractional part. These conditions do not occur with the comparisons in this program because the comparisons are greater than or less than, rather than equality.

Figure 2-5 Listing of FORTRAN program, sample input, and output for general example 2—payroll processing.

PROGRAM

```
 1 **********
 2 *                        PROGRAM IDENTIFICATION
 3 **********
 4 *
 5 *        This program computes paycheck amounts for employees
 6 *        and company totals.  It also finds the largest gross
 7 *        pay amount using an intrinsic FORTRAN function.
 8 *        Developed for file input (DATA2) and batch execution.
 9 *        Written 04/12/77 by T. Hoffmann  Rev. 12/16/81    3/09/87
10 *
11 **********
12 *                        VARIABLES IDENTIFICATION
13 **********
14 *
15 *        ID      = Employee identification number
16 *        HRSWRK  = Hours worked by each employee
17 *        GRSPAY  = Gross pay: $
18 *        WGRATE  = Wage rate: $/hour
19 *        PAYCHK  = Net paycheck amount:  $
20 *        TAXES   = Taxes due: $
21 *        DEDUC   = Miscellaneous deductions
22 *        TOTPAY  = Total gross pay for company:   $
23 *        TOTTAX  = Total taxes from all employees: $
24 *        LARGEP  = Largest gross pay for any employee (real)
25 *
26 **********
27 *                        CONSTANTS IDENTIFICATION
28 **********
29 *
30 *        PNRATE  = Pension contribution rate = 0.05
31 *        TAXRT   = Tax rate = 0.15
32 *
33 **********
34 *                        TYPE DECLARATION AND STORAGE BLOCK
35 **********
36 *
37        REAL LARGEP
38 *
39 **********
40 * BLOCK 0000             INITIALIZATION BLOCK
41 **********
42 *
43        PNRATE = 0.05
44        TAXRT = 0.15
45        LARGEP = 0.0
46        TOTPAY = 0.0
47        TOTTAX = 0.0
48        OPEN(7,FILE='DATA2')
49 *
50 **********
51 * BLOCK 0100             READ-COMPUTE-PRINT DETAIL
52 **********
53 *
54    101 READ (7,*) ID,HRSWRK,WGRATE,DEDUC
55 *
56 *                        TEST FOR FINAL DATA RECORD (-1,-1,-1,-1)
57 *
58        IF(ID .LE. 0) GOTO 201
59        PRINT *,' '
60        PRINT *, 'Employee ',ID,' worked ',HRSWRK,' hours'
61        PRINT *, 'at rate of',WGRATE,' and deductions of',DEDUC
62        IF((HRSWRK .LT. 0.0) .OR. (HRSWRK .GT. 60.0)) GOTO 905
63        IF((WGRATE .LT. 0.0) .OR. (WGRATE .GT. 10.0) ) GOTO 905
64        IF((DEDUC .LT. 0.0) .OR. (DEDUC .GT. 65.0) ) GOTO 905
65        GRSPAY = HRSWRK*WGRATE
66        TAXES = GRSPAY*TAXRT
67        PAYCHK = GRSPAY - TAXES - DEDUC - PNRATE*GRSPAY
68 *
69 *                        SELECT LARGEST GROSS PAY SO FAR
70 *
71        LARGEP = AMAX1(LARGEP,GRSPAY)
72 *
73 *                        CHECK FOR VALID PAYCHECK AMOUNT
74 *
75        PRINT *,' Net Pay = ',PAYCHK,' Gross Pay = ',GRSPAY
76        IF(PAYCHK .LE. 0.0) GOTO 901
```

```
 77   103 TOTPAY = TOTPAY + GRSPAY
 78       TOTTAX = TOTTAX + TAXES
 79       GOTO 101
 80 *
 81 **********
 82 * BLOCK 0200           PRINT SUMMARY AND TERMINATE
 83 **********
 84 *
 85   201 PRINT *, ' '
 86       PRINT *, '     TOTAL          TOTAL          LARGEST'
 87       PRINT *, '     PAY            TAX          GROSS PAY'
 88       PRINT *, TOTPAY,TOTTAX,LARGEP
 89       STOP
 90 *
 91 **********
 92 * BLOCK 0900           ERROR MESSAGE BLOCK
 93 **********
 94 *
 95   901 PRINT *, ' Net Pay Is Not Positive.  Do Not Issue Check.'
 96 *
 97 *                 GO BACK TO NORMAL PROCESSING
 98 *
 99       GOTO 103
100 *
101   905 PRINT *, 'Input Data outside validation limits.'
102 *
103 *          DO NOT COMPUTE PAY.  GO BACK FOR NEXT RECORD
104 *
105       GOTO 101
106       END
```

```
┌ID   ┌HRSWRK
│     │    ┌WGRATE
│     │    │   ┌DEDUC              SAMPLE INPUT
▼     ▼    ▼   ▼
35746,55.5,7.24,30.68
69587,10,4.67,27.50
35649,22,4.75,35.98
15768,3,6.28,24.68
27543,40,5.57,27.95
62475,37.5,8.24,65.34
-1,-1,-1,-1
```

SAMPLE OUTPUT

```
    Employee      35746 worked      55.50000000 hours
    at rate of      7.23999977 and deductions of      30.68000031
    Net Pay =     290.77597046 Gross Pay =     401.81997681

    Employee      69587 worked      10.00000000 hours
    at rate of      4.67000008 and deductions of      27.50000000
    Net Pay =       9.86000061 Gross Pay =      46.70000076

    Employee      35649 worked      22.00000000 hours
    at rate of      4.75000000 and deductions of      35.97999954
    Net Pay =      47.61999893 Gross Pay =     104.50000000

    Employee      15768 worked       3.00000000 hours
    at rate of      6.28000021 and deductions of      24.68000031
    Net Pay =      -9.60800076 Gross Pay =      18.84000015
    Net Pay Is Not Positive.  Do Not Issue Check.

    Employee      27543 worked      40.00000000 hours
    at rate of      5.57000017 and deductions of      27.95000076
    Net Pay =     150.28999329 Gross Pay =     222.80000305

    Employee      62475 worked      37.50000000 hours
    at rate of      8.23999977 and deductions of      65.33999634
    Input Data outside validation limits.

           TOTAL          TOTAL          LARGEST
           PAY            TAX          GROSS PAY
        794.66003418   119.19900513   401.81997681
```

Figure 2-6 Program flowchart for general example 2—payroll processing. (Numbers beside symbols refer to line numbers on program listing.)

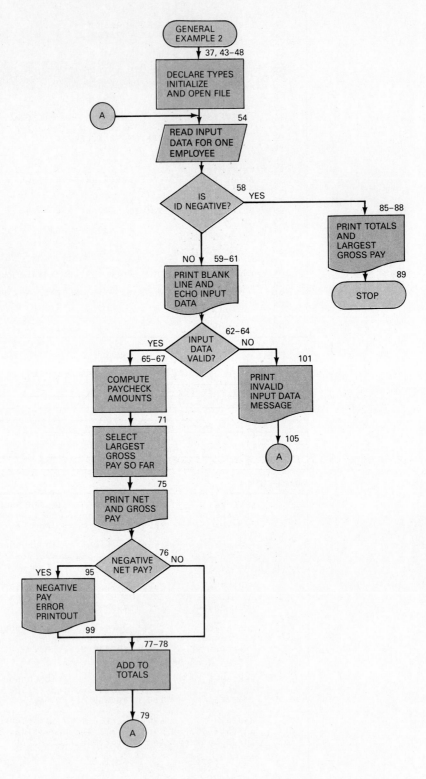

In summary, general program example 2 illustrates the following program features and conventions.

Selective use of explicit type declaration
Use of OPEN statement to specify file containing input data
Initializing of variables for first-time-through logic
Input expected in batch execution from file of records, so no messages to prompt input
Testing of input data value to decide on termination of program
Labeled echo of input data for visual validation
Data validation for range of values
Checking for an abnormal result
Error message with errors in either input data or results of processing and continuation of processing
Use of both IF . . . ELSE blocks and logical IF statements
Use of intrinsic function for finding the maximum
Use of GO BACK comments for GOTOs that go back to a previous block
Comparisons of real data
Error messages in a separate error message block

Mathematical Program Example 2—Table of Areas and Moments of Inertia of Hexagonal Sections

Problem Description for Mathematical Example 2

Compute a table of areas and moments for different hexagonal sections based on a hexagon with an initial width, a hexagon with a final width, and intermediate widths. The hexagons are assumed to have equal sides, i.e., to be "regular" hexagons. The input for the program consists of the initial hexagon width, the final hexagon width, and the number of widths to be computed after the initial width but including the final width. Input data values to be tested for errors include a final width that is less than the initial width and a number of widths to be computed that are not positive. Input of data and execution of the program are interactive. After a table of widths, areas, and moments is computed and printed, a message asks if another table is to be computed with new data. A reply of 'Y' or 'y' will cause the program to request new data; any other response will terminate the program.

The formulas to compute the area and moment of inertia for a hexagonal section are

$$A = \tfrac{3}{2} w^2 \tan a$$

where A = the area
w = the width of the hexagon
a = half the angle (in radians) between sides of the hexagon [Note that a is equal to $30\pi/180$, and π can be computed as 4 arctan (1)].

$$M = \frac{A}{12} \left[\frac{w^2(1 + 2 \cos^2 a)}{4 \cos^2 a} \right]$$

where M is the moment of inertia of a hexagonal section.

Program Documentation for Mathematical Example 2

The documentation consists of a pseudocode description of the program (Figure 2-7), a program flowchart (Figure 2-8), and a program listing (Figure 2-9). As in the general example, the line numbers alongside the program statements are placed at the upper right of flowchart symbols as a cross-referencing aid.

In drawing the flowchart, a general input/output symbol is used to indicate the combination of "display input prompt message" and "read data entered at keyboard."

Figure 2-7 Pseudocode description for mathematical example 2—table of areas and moments of inertia of hexagonal sections.

	Program line numbers
Explicitly declare all variable types	28–30
Initialize constant PI as 4 × arctangent of 1 and constant ANGLE as 30PI/180	36–37
PRINT heading for session outputs	43
PRINT initial width prompt requesting width of initial hexagon and READ initial width	45–46
PRINT input prompt requesting width of final hexagon and READ final width	47–48
Test for final width less than initial width	49
IF (final width is less than initial width) print error message and	50
go back to PRINT initial width prompt	51
ELSE continue	52
PRINT widths prompt requesting widths to compute after initial width and READ number of widths to be computed after the initial width	53–54
Test for positive number of widths to be computed	55
IF (widths to be computed not positive) print error message and	56
go back to PRINT widths prompt	57
ELSE continue	58
Compute step for calculating widths of hexagons between initial and final widths	59
PRINT heading for table outputs	60–61
Set current value of width to initial width	68
Compute area of hexagon using current value of width	69
Compute moment of hexagon using current value of width	70–71
PRINT width, area, and moment	72
Compute new current value of width by adding step increment	73
Test if final width has been printed so table is complete	78
IF (current value of width is greater than final width) GOTO PRINT new data prompt	78
ELSE go back to Compute area	
PRINT new data prompt to ask if a new table is to be printed with new data and READ reply	85–86
Test new data reply	91
IF yes, go back to PRINT initial width prompt	91
ELSE stop	92

This is to simplify the flowchart. Two separate symbols could have been used as shown below:

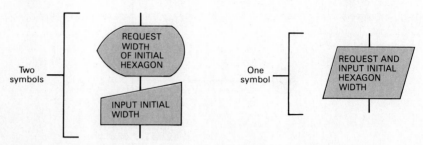

Notes on Mathematical Example 2

The program illustrates the use of FORTRAN trigonometric functions. Since trigonometric functions operate on data expressed in radians, it is necessary to calculate half the angle between sides of the hexagon in radians. That computation uses the value of pi, and the programmer can write the approximate value of pi as a constant (3.1416) or write a statement to compute it, as was done in the program, by using the arctangent function. The statement in line 36 computes pi as 4.0 * ATAN (1.0). Since the computation of pi and half the angle between sides of the hexagon are the same for any input data, they are computed in the initialization block.

The program illustrates complete, explicit typing of variables (lines 28–30). There is a type statement for the character variable, defining it as a one-character variable (since the user keys a one-character response). The variable NUMBER is explicitly declared as an integer variable, even though implicit typing would define it as integer. The remaining variables are explicitly declared as real variables, including INITIAL and MOMENT, which would otherwise be implicitly defined as integer variables.

The program is written for interactive execution so that input data is entered in response to prompts received by the user of the program at the terminal or visual display. Before each input of data, there is a message describing what is to be input (lines 45, 47, 53, and 85). Input data items are validated, and if an error is detected, a message is displayed indicating the nature of the error and requesting a correct input. The incorrect input is not processed.

The interactive program provides for an explicit termination of the program when all tables of areas and moments have been processed. The program asks (in line 85) "More data (Y/N)?" then tests the response to determine the action to take. Note in line 91 that the test includes either an uppercase letter 'Y' or a lowercase letter 'y' (enclosed in apostrophes). The apostrophes are required before and after list-directed character input data (although some FORTRAN implementations do not enforce it). The reason that both 'Y' and 'y' need to be tested for is that a person may key the response in either uppercase or lowercase and the computer codes for these are different. The testing of the response also illustrates another issue in programming. Even though the question asks for Y or N, what should be done if some other response is given? One possibility is to give an error message saying that the response is not a valid one. The other approach is to consider any input other than 'Y' or 'y' as indicating the program is to terminate. In this particular program, a default interpretation of "terminate" for any response other than 'Y' or 'y' seems appropriate. For FORTRAN implementations that enforce apostrophes around character data, lack of these will result in a system error aborting the program.

Figure 2-8 Program flowchart for mathematical example 2—table of areas and moments of inertia for hexagonal sections. (Numbers beside symbols refer to line numbers on program listing.)

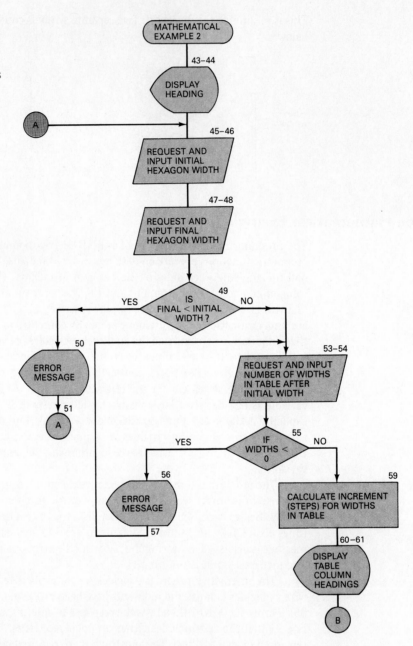

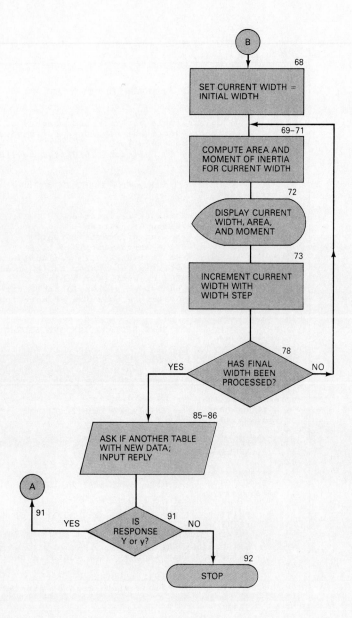

Figure 2-9 Listing of FORTRAN program and sample interactive input/output for mathematical example 2—table of areas and moments of inertia of hexagonal sections.

PROGRAM

```
 1 **********
 2 *                        PROGRAM IDENTIFICATION
 3 **********
 4 *
 5 *     Calculate table of areas and moments of inertia of
 6 *     hexagonal sections. Developed for keyboard input and
 7 *     interactive execution.
 8 *     Written by T. Hoffmann  10/03/86  rev. 3/09/87
 9 *
10 **********
11 *                        VARIABLES IDENTIFICATION
12 **********
13 *
14 *     AREA    = Area of the section
15 *     WIDTH   = Width of hexagon
16 *     MOMENT  = Moment of inertia (real)
17 *     PI      = pi = approximately 3.1416
18 *     ANGLE   = Half of angle (in radians) between sides of hexagon
19 *     INITIAL = Starting width for table (real)
20 *     FINAL   = Ending width for table
21 *     NUMBER  = Number of widths in table after initial width
22 *     REPLY   = Answer to question of more input data (character)
23 *
24 **********
25 *                    TYPE DECLARATION AND STORAGE BLOCK
26 **********
27 *
28       CHARACTER REPLY*1
29       INTEGER NUMBER
30       REAL INITIAL,MOMENT,AREA,WIDTH,PI,ANGLE,FINAL
31 *
32 **********
33 * BLOCK 0000       INITIALIZATION BLOCK
34 **********
35 *
36       PI = 4.0*ATAN(1.0)
37       ANGLE = 30.0*PI/180.0
38 *
39 **********
40 * BLOCK 0100       DATA INPUT AND VALIDATION BLOCK
41 **********
42 *
43       PRINT *, 'Table of Areas and Moments of Hexagonal Sections'
44 101 PRINT *
45       PRINT *, 'What is the initial width in the table? '
46       READ *, INITIAL
47       PRINT *, 'What is the final width in the table? '
48       READ *, FINAL
49       IF(FINAL .LT. INITIAL) THEN
50          PRINT *, 'Final width must be greater than initial width.'
51          GOTO 101
52       ELSE
53 103     PRINT *, 'How many widths after initial width? '
54          READ *, NUMBER
55       IF(NUMBER .LE. 0) THEN
56          PRINT *, 'Number of widths must be greater than zero.'
57          GOTO 103
58       ENDIF
59       STEP = (FINAL - INITIAL)/FLOAT(NUMBER)
60       PRINT *
61       PRINT *, '        Width          Area          Moment'
62 ENDIF
63 *
64 **********
65 * BLOCK 0200       COMPUTATION AND OUTPUT BLOCK
66 **********
67 *
68       WIDTH = INITIAL
69 205 AREA = (3.0/2.0)*WIDTH**2*TAN(ANGLE)
70       MOMENT = (AREA/12.0)*(WIDTH**2*(1.0 + 2.0*((COS(ANGLE))**2))
71 1        /4.0*(COS(ANGLE))**2)
72       PRINT *, WIDTH,AREA,MOMENT
73       WIDTH = WIDTH + STEP
74 *
```

```
75  *                        TABLE IS NOT COMPLETE UNTIL WIDTH EXCEEDS FINAL
76  *                        CHECK FOR COMPLETENESS, IF NOT DONE, THEN REPEAT
77  *
78          IF(WIDTH .LE. FINAL) GOTO 205
79  *
80  *********
81  * BLOCK 0300      CONTINUE OR TERMINATE BLOCK
82  *********
83  *
84          PRINT *
85          PRINT *, 'More data(Y/N)? '
86          READ *, REPLY
87  *
88  *                        IF MORE DATA, GO BACK TO BEGINNING.
89  *                        ANY REPLY NOT Y OR y WILL TERMINATE PROGRAM
90  *
91          IF ((REPLY .EQ. 'Y') .OR. (REPLY .EQ. 'y')) GOTO 101
92          STOP
93          END
```

SAMPLE INTERACTIVE INPUT/OUTPUT

```
Table of Areas and Moments of Hexagonal Sections

What is the initial width in the table? 4

What is the final width in the table? 9

How many widths after initial width? 6

        Width            Area            Moment
     4.00000000       13.85640717        8.66025352
     4.83333349       20.23131752       18.46195602
     5.66666698       27.80904198       34.88200760
     6.50000048       36.58958054       60.38710785
     7.33333397       46.57292938       97.83551025
     8.16666698       57.75908661      150.47697449

More data(Y/N)? 'y'


What is the initial width in the table? 8

What is the final width in the table? 3

Final width must be greater than initial width.

What is the initial width in the table? 3

What is the final width in the table? 8

How many widths after initial width? 0

Number of widths must be greater than zero.
How many widths after initial width? 5

        Width            Area            Moment
     3.00000000        7.79422903        2.74015856
     4.00000000       13.85640717        8.66025352
     5.00000000       21.65063667       21.14319801
     6.00000000       31.17691612       43.84253693
     7.00000000       42.43524551       81.22371674
     8.00000000       55.42562866      138.56405640

More data(Y/N)? 'n'
```

The number of entries in the table is specified by an initial width plus the number of widths to calculate after the initial width. In many cases, the result will be a table that contains one more or less entries than the specified "number of widths after the initial width." In the sample output, the first table contains only six entries, even though there should be seven. The reason for this is a precision error because the computer cannot represent $\frac{5}{16}$ exactly. We could have changed the program or changed the data used to avoid this result, but we left it to illustrate the kind of problems a programmer can experience. In line 78, there is a test to decide whether to continue computing table entries. Computation continues if the cumulative sum of the widths computed to that point is less than or equal to the final width for the table; otherwise, the table is finished. In this problem, the initial width was 4, the final width was 9, and the number of widths after the initial width was stated as 6. In order to have six entries between 4 and 9, the increment must be $\frac{5}{16}$, or .8333. . . . The computer cannot represent $\frac{5}{16}$ exactly and the resulting rounding errors resulted in a sixth entry equal to 8.16666698. When incremented by .83333349, it exceeded the final width of 9, and the table was ended without calculating the final entry with a width value of 9. In subsequent chapters, methods for handling such errors will be illustrated.

Backward GOTOs outside of the block are used in the program but are clearly marked before the GOTO statements (lines 88 and 89). Backward GOTOs within the same block (see block 0100) are not likely to be confusing, and therefore no comment lines are required. Block IFs are used in the program. Since there is only one action following the IF . . . THEN, a simple logical IF could have been used, but the logic is very clear with the IF . . . ELSE blocks.

In summary, mathematical program example 2 illustrates the following program features and conventions:

Complete, explicit typing of all variables
Interactive input requests and input
Input validation and interactive request for correct input
Error message following IF statement rather than in separate error message block
Simple IF loop for controlling the preparation of a table of values
Initialization of value incremented in IF loop for first-time-through logic
Use of trigonometric intrinsic functions
Use of explicit interactive termination requests and testing of reply

Programming Exercises

Description of Assignment

Select one or more problems (or take the problems assigned to you by the instructor). Use the statements from Chapter 1 as well as the statements explained in Chapter 2a. The program should be written in good style using the following features (except where inappropriate):

1. Use a style for input that is appropriate either to file input during batch execution or to keyboard input during interactive execution.
2. Use the block IF where appropriate or the logical IF statement.
3. Use at least one intrinsic function.
4. Use sensible variable names and type declarations as appropriate.
5. Echo input data for visual validation if it is not printed out as part of the normal output.
6. Use programmed validation of input data when specified in the problem.

7. Use an IF loop to read and process more than one set of input data. Select a method of termination that is appropriate to the mode of execution.
8. Check carefully first- and last-time-through logic.
9. Check carefully any equality comparisons of real data where one or both of the data items being compared result from computation.

The documentation should consist of the following:

1. Pseudocode description of program and/or program flowchart
2. Program listing
3. Results of program testing using both valid and invalid input

Chapter 3 will use these same problems but with additional requirements for formatting of output and handling of end and error conditions.

Mathematics and Statistics

1. For the angles given below, compare the value given by the intrinsic sine function with the value obtained using the five terms of the following series expansion for the sine. (*Hint:* Note that x must be in radians—1 degree equals $\pi/180$ radians.) Limit computations to positive angles less than $\pi/2$ radians.

$$\sin(x) = x - \frac{x^3}{3!} + \frac{x^5}{5!} - \frac{x^7}{7!} + \frac{x^9}{9!} - \cdots$$

Angle (degrees)
15
95
60
45

2. For each of the following sets of sample data, compute the standard deviation and mean absolute deviation (average of the absolute deviations from the mean). The means are 2, 8.8, 40.0, and 10.7 for set A, B, C, and D. *Hint:* Read the mean and number of data points in a set, and then read each data point in the set from a separate record.

A	B	C	D
−6	1.6	37.25	12.3
−12	6.3	39.4	8.0
8	12.4	45.61	17.4
14	9.3	38.0	6.5
13	8.0	35.78	9.3
7	7.7	42.65	
9	11.6	41.03	
−8	13.5	39.12	
10		43.66	
−15		37.5	

The formula for standard deviation is

$$\sqrt{\frac{\sum_{i=1}^{n} (X_i - \bar{X})^2}{n-1}}$$

where X_i are the data items and $\bar{X}$ is the mean.

3. The number of combinations c of n things taken m at a time is

$$c = \frac{n!}{m!(n - m)!}$$

For large values of m or n (say k), the factorial can be approximated by Stirling's formula:

$$k! = e^{-k}k^k \sqrt{2\pi k}$$

where $e = 2.7183$ and $\pi = 3.1416$. *Note:* This is valid only for positive, nonzero values of k. Compute c for the following using Stirling's approximation formula. Use the FORTRAN function for e.

n	m
6	4
0	5
40	30
50	70

Business and Economics

4. The formula for computing compound interest is

$$p = a \left(1 + \frac{i}{q}\right)^{nq}$$

where a = initial amount
$\quad\quad i$ = annual interest rate
$\quad\quad n$ = number of years
$\quad\quad q$ = number of times compounded each year
$\quad\quad p$ = value at end of n years

When q approaches infinity (continuous compounding), the equation becomes

$$p = ae^{in}$$

where $e = 2.7183$.

For each of the following initial amounts and an interest rate of 7 percent, compare the values after 1 and 10 years for compounding quarterly and continuously. Use the FORTRAN exponential function for e.

$a = 1000, 565, 2045$

5. The economic order quantity (EOQ) is given by the following:

$$EOQ = \sqrt{\frac{2\,as}{ic}}$$

where a = annual usage
$\quad\quad s$ = cost of placing an order
$\quad\quad c$ = unit cost
$\quad\quad i$ = annual carrying rate

For each of the following sets of data, compute the EOQ. Note that negative quantities or division by zero inside the square root are errors.

Set	a	s	c	i
1	10,000	11.75	.75	.20
2	1,000	3.50	1.25	.25
3	8,750	15.00	2.00	0
4	7,400	37.40	−1.30	.25
5	6,000	20.00	1.00	.20

6. Sales commissions c are computed as a multiple f of sales s in excess of quotas q. If goals are not met, no bonus is paid.

$$c = f(s - q)$$

For each of the following persons, compute the bonus and determine which one is the largest. Print a special message if quotas are not met.

Sales-person	Name	Goal	Actual	Bonus factor
1764	C. JONES	$400	$380	.2
2031	A. WHITE	300	340	.1
1	X. SMITH	375	395	.17
0773	J. ADAMS	380	420	.15
2114	K. JAMES	325	367	.19

Science and Engineering

7. The area of a triangle can be computed by the sine law when two sides of the triangle (a, b) and the angle θ between them are known.

$$\text{Area} = \tfrac{1}{2} ab \sin \theta$$

Given the following four triangular pieces of property, find their areas and determine which is largest. Omit computation if the angle is outside the range of 0 to 180 degrees.

Plot number	a	b	θ (radians)
1	137.4	80.9	.78
2	145.3	91.6	1.35
3	130.4	100.0	4.00
4	128.3	125.4	1.95

8. A projectile fired at an angle θ has a horizontal range R given by the following:

$$R = \frac{2v^2 \sin \theta \cos \theta}{g}$$

where v = initial velocity and g = 32.2 ft/s^2. Compute R for each of the following (limit angles to 0 to $\pi/2$ radians and v to positive values):

v	θ
200	20
200	70
200	45
175	160
1750	60

9. The period p of a pendulum is given by the following formula:

$$p = 2\pi \sqrt{\frac{L}{g}} \left(1 + \frac{1}{4} \sin^2 \frac{\alpha}{2} \right)$$

where $g = 980$ cm/sec^2
L = pendulum length
α = angle of displacement

Compute the periods of the following pendulums:

Pendulum number	L (cm)	α (degrees)
1	120	15
2	90	20
3	60	5
4	74.6	10
5	83.6	12

Humanities and Social Sciences

10. From the empirical study of learning, the following relationship was observed:

$$t_x = px^{-1}$$

where x = number of repetitions
t_x = cumulative average task time for the xth repetition
p = time to perform task the first time
l = learning factor

From this:

$$l = \frac{\log p - \log t_x}{\log x}$$

Compute l for each of the following situations (print warning if l is negative):

t_x	p	x
2.7	3.4	100
0.34	1.8	50
0.15	1.4	20
0.74	1.0	500
1.06	0.8	400

11. Population growth is often either geometric (for example, doubles every 10 years) or exponential (increases at an increasing rate). For geometric growth, the equation for population size p in year n is

$$p = a(1 + r)^n$$

where a is the initial population and r is the annual growth rate. For exponential growth a possible equation is

$$p = ae^{rn}$$

Given $a = 10,000$, for the following situations compute the population in year 10 and the relative increase for both formulas.

Situation number	r
1	.1
2	.2
3	.5
4	.67
5	.7

12. Air pressure is a function of altitude h. For each of the following locations, compute the air pressure p given that the relationship is

$$p = 14.7e^{-0.000038h}$$

Location	Elevation h (feet)
1 Denver	5280
2 Dead Sea	−1292
3 New York	55
4 New Delhi	760
5 Katmandu	4223

General

13. Given the currency exchange rates, compare the equivalent U.S. dollar value of a set of input amounts in non-U.S. currency (or vice versa). Use a coding scheme with positive and negative code numbers to indicate direction of convention.

Code	Currency	Offered for U.S. $1
1	German mark	1.837
2	English pound	1.523
3	Japanese yen	154.90

Negative codes mean opposite conversion (alternate non-U.S. currency to U.S. dollars). Identify which amount is the largest in U.S. dollars. Use the current rates (from *The Wall Street Journal*). Identify erroneous data (illegal codes).

Code	Currency value
1	6.50
3	8.95
2	6.42
−3	12.44
6	8.95
−2	6.43
−1	8.88
4	2.95
1	7.50

14. A customer goes to a food market to buy groceries. Compute item costs and the total grocery bill, and find the most costly purchase for the following purchase list:

Items	Unit cost	Number of units
1 Beef	$1.95	1.40
2 Potatoes	.85	6.75
3 Coffee	3.95	1.00
4 Candy	.15	12.00
5 Fruit	.98	7.95

15. Calculate the average temperature for each of the following weeks, and determine which is warmest. Omit temperatures greater than 100 or less than 60 degrees Fahrenheit, and print a warning message.

Week	Daily temperatures (°F)				
1 July 4–8	85	70	83	77	75
2 July 11–15	90	78	77	80	77
3 July 18–22	999	77	85	84	73
4 July 25–29	77	85	78	0	88

Interactive Scientific and Engineering

16. A tank having the shape of an inverted right circular cone of radius R and height h is initially filled with water. At the bottom of the tank is a hole of radius r through which water drains under the influence of gravity. The equation for the time t it takes to empty is

$$t = \frac{R^2}{5r^2} \sqrt{\frac{2h}{g}}$$

where g is the gravitational constant 32.17 ft/sec^2. Compute the time to empty tanks of the following dimensions:

Tank height	Tank radius	Hole radius
6.5	4.0	0.2
16.085	10.0	1.0
8.0	4.0	5.0
4.52	7.6	0.5

Check the input data for any logical inconsistency, such as a hole larger than the tank.

17. The length L of a belt needed to wrap around two pulleys of diameters D and d and whose centers are separated by a distance C is given by

$$L = \sqrt{4C^2 - (D - d)^2} + \pi \left(\frac{D + d}{2}\right) + (D - d) \sin^{-1}\left(\frac{D - d}{2C}\right)$$

Compute belt lengths for each of the following sets of data:

D	d	C
22	8	60
22	16	18
8	12	20

Validate the input data to make sure the distance between the pulleys is positive and not zero.

18. As in an automobile engine, a piston is connected to a crankshaft of radius r by a rod of length l. The velocity V of the piston as a function of the crankshaft angle A and revolutions per minute N of the shaft is approximately

$$V = 2\pi Nr \left[\sin A + \frac{r}{l} \sin A \cos A + \frac{1}{2}\left(\frac{r}{l^3}\right)\sin^3 A \cos A \right]$$

Compute the velocity in feet per minute for each of the following (remember that trigonometric functions use arguments in radians and π radians = 180 degrees):

N	A	l (inches)	r (inches)
3000	68	8	3
1800	95	12	4
1800	180	12	4
900	90	8	5
900	270	15	5

Validate data to ensure that the connecting rod is longer than the diameter of the crankshaft. Print out the angle in radians.

3 a

Format-Directed Input and Output

Records in FORTRAN Input and Output

Format-Directed Instructions
Input-Output Statements for Format-Directed Input and Output
Self-Testing Exercise 3-1
The FORMAT Statement
FORMAT Editing for Output
FORMAT Editing for Input
Self-Testing Exercise 3-2
Repetition of FORMAT Specifications
Horizontal Positioning Specifications
Missing Data Items
Self-Testing Exercise 3-3

Providing Descriptive Labels and Headings on Output
Apostrophe Edit Descriptor
H Edit Descriptor
Vertical Spacing with Control Characters
Self-Testing Exercise 3-4
Input, Storage, and Output of Characters
Self-Testing Exercise 3-5

Checking for End of Data and Data Error
Self-Testing Exercise 3-6

Handling Physical Records with Slash Editing
Reuse of FORMAT Specifications
Self-Testing Exercise 3-7

Rounding with FORMAT Specifications

Expressions in Output List

Additional Testing, Debugging, and Quality-Control Suggestions

Programming Style Suggestions

Summary

Answers to Self-Testing Exercises

Questions and Problems

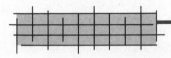

The list-directed input and output instructions explained in Chapter 1 are very simple to use but very limiting. FORTRAN provides for more flexible input and output using format-directed input and output. The commonly used features of format-directed input and output are explained in this chapter; additional features for external files of data on magnetic tape and optical or magnetic disks are explained in Chapter 6.

Records in FORTRAN Input and Output

To this point, input has consisted of sets of data items, each set entered on a separate line at a keyboard. In interactive execution, each line of data has been used immediately by the program. Alternatively, data lines have been entered prior to program execution and stored in a computer file. Output has used lines on a video display or a printer. In programming terminology, each line with input or each output line is a physical record. A *physical record* is a separable element of a storage or recording medium from which data can be read or on which data can be written.

A physical record may be fixed in size (length of input/output line or number of characters that can be stored) or variable in size. The physical records used so far were all fixed in length. The following are some characteristics of the fixed-length records that have been used in the first two chapters:

A line on the visual display (usually 80 characters)
A line on the terminal or PC printer (usually 80 characters)
A line on the high-speed printer (usually 120 to 130 characters)

Variable-length records do not have a fixed physical length; their length depends on the input and the program. Variable-length records will be explained in Chapter 6 in connection with tape and disk file specifications.

In contrast to a physical record is a logical record. A *logical record* consists of items of data that logically belong together. They may occupy less than one physical record, exactly one physical record, or more than one physical record. For example, a logical record may require two output lines (i.e., it requires two physical records). In the simplest cases, a FORTRAN READ or WRITE (or PRINT) statement will read or write one physical record (one line on the printer, one line of input from the keyboard, etc.). The use of more than one physical record by a READ or WRITE can be the result of implicit FORTRAN rules or can be explicitly specified. For example, list-directed input or output will implicitly use as many physical input records (lines) as necessary to provide the specified input or output records (display or printer lines) to contain the output. One of the functions of the FORMAT statement to be explained in this chapter is to explicitly specify the use of one or more physical input and output records.

Format-Directed Instructions

In format-directed FORTRAN, obtaining data from an input device or writing data on an output device requires a pair of statements: the input/output statement and the FORMAT statement. The input/output statement specifies what is to be done, what device (unit) is to be used, and what variables are involved. The FORMAT statement specifies the form of the data being read in or written out. The input/output statement and the FORMAT statement are identified as belonging together by assigning a unique statement label to the FORMAT statement and referencing it in the input or output statement. Following the style recommended in this text, the FORMAT statement label will be part of the number series for the block in which it appears. For example, a pair of statements might appear as follows (where 5 is a device number and 700 is a statement label number):

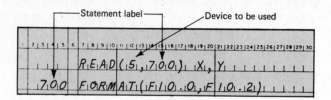

Input/Output Statements for Format-Directed Input and Output

The basic input/output statement with format-directed input/output describes (or implies) four specifications necessary for input or output:

1. The operation (read or write).
2. The device to be used (keyboard, display, printer, disk storage, etc.). FORTRAN assumes these devices have been assigned unit numbers (1, 2, 3, . . . , n).
3. The statement label of the FORMAT statement, which describes the format of the data to be input or output.
4. The variables to be input or output in the order to be read or written.

The basic specifications of device and FORMAT statement can be extended by other specifications, two of which will be explained later in this chapter and the rest in Chapters 4, 6, and 7.

There are two basic input/output statements—one for reading (input) and one for writing (output):

READ (u, fs) list
WRITE (u, fs) list

where u refers to the unit number assigned to the input or output device and fs refers to the label of the FORMAT statement to be used. The four specifications are provided as follows:

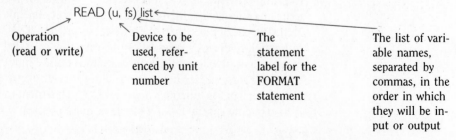

Examples

READ (5, 710) A, B, X	Read values for A, B, and X (in that order) using unit 5 and FORMAT statement 710.
WRITE (6, 720) X, A, B	Write values for X, A, B (in that order) using unit 6 and FORMAT statement 720.

Note that the space following each right parenthesis is optional. The text examples of FORMAT statements are numbered in the 700s. This is an arbitrary designation and has no special significance.

The unit specification in the input/output statement can be either an integer constant, an integer variable, or an asterisk. The asterisk refers to the standard input or output device defined for the computer system being used. All of the following are correct forms:

```
READ (5, 705) A, B, C
READ (NREAD, 705) A, B, C
READ (*, 705) A, B, C
```

If an integer variable such as NREAD is used, then it must be defined in the program as having a value equal to the desired unit. For example, if the unit number to be used in the above example is 5, then NREAD may be defined by a statement such as:

```
NREAD = 5
```

The input or output statement requires a unit number (or asterisk) to specify a terminal, printer, file storage device, etc. But what unit number should be used? There are no universally agreed-upon unit numbers, nor are any unit numbers specified in the FORTRAN standard. This means that a user of each implementation of FORTRAN must obtain the unit numbers assigned by that implementation. (There is a place to record these unit numbers for your computer on the inside of the back cover.) Although there are no universally agreed-upon standard numbers, the most generally used unit numbers are 5 for standard input device (such as terminal keyboard for interactive execution and standard file device for file input during batch execution) and 6 for standard output device (such as display, terminal printer, or high-speed printer). The asterisk may be used in place of a unit number to designate the standard input or output device.

One of the desirable features of FORTRAN is its portability such that a program written and run on one computer can be run without significant change on another computer. The use of different unit numbers at different installations can inhibit portability, but there are fairly easy ways to handle the differences. One way is to write all READ and WRITE statements with variable names for the unit designation (such as NREAD) and merely to change the statement that assigns a value to NREAD. The other way is to assign the desired value to an input or output device by the use of a job control instruction or the OPEN statement described in Chapter 2. In other words, each installation will have assigned default values, such as 5 or 6 for the terminal keyboard, printer, etc. These instructions to assign unit numbers are specific to each FORTRAN implementation, and thus must be obtained for the FORTRAN compiler being used. In the absence of other unit numbers, assume 5 for standard input and 6 for standard output (or use *).

There is an alternate form of the input and output statement that does not use the unit designation. It is included in the full 1977 FORTRAN standard and is provided in most implementations. In the name-designation form, READ means read from the standard device (generally terminal keyboard for interactive execution and standard file device for batch execution), and PRINT means to output using the standard device (generally display or printer). It is equivalent to using an asterisk or a unit number. Note that a comma must follow the FORMAT number in the name-designation form.

Unit-designation form	Name-designation form
READ (5, 705) A, B	READ 705, A, B
READ (*, 705) A, B	
WRITE (6, 710) A, B	PRINT 710, A, B
WRITE (*, 710) A, B	

The advantage of the name-designation form is that terminal and printer or other standard devices can be specified when the programmer does not know the unit number. In the first two chapters, the command (READ or PRINT) specified the standard device and the asterisk specified list-directed input/output (instead of FOR-MAT-directed input/output). However, the name-designation form is not always available in restricted versions such as subset FORTRAN. Since the unit-designation form is the more general form and always available, it is the preferred form.

In the unit-designation form, the asterisk can be used in place of the FORMAT statement number to specify list-directed input or output. The following are equivalent:

READ (5, *) A, B, C	All read one record containing values to assign to A, B, and C from
READ *, A, B, C	a standard input device using list-directed input.
READ (*, *) A, B, C	

In summary, the basic input/output instructions for format-directed input and output require only four elements: the command word (READ, WRITE), the input/output unit designation, the FORMAT statement label number, and the list of variable names in the order they are to be read, printed, displayed, etc.

BASIC INPUT/OUTPUT INSTRUCTIONS

Symbols used in description

u = unit designation (integer variable, integer constant, or asterisk) for input/output unit. Unit designations for various devices differ among implementations. Common usage is 5 for keyboard entry or standard file device and 6 for printer or display. Asterisk specifies standard device.

fs = statement label of FORMAT statement to be used with the input or output instruction. If an asterisk (*) is used in place of a statement number, the instruction is list-directed.

list = list of variables, which are to be read, printed, displayed, etc., in the order in which they are to be used. The variable names are separated by commas. There need be no spaces between items in the list, but spaces may be used for readability.

Form of instructions

READ (u, fs) list

Reads from an input unit the quantities associated with the listed variable names and puts them into storage for use by the program.

WRITE (u, fs) list

Writes variables using an output unit. Form of output varies with output unit and FORMAT statement having label fs.

Alternate forms without unit designation (not part of subset)

READ fs, list

Reads from standard input device the quantities associated with the listed variable names and puts them into memory. If fs = *, it specifies list-directed input from standard input device.

PRINT fs, list

Prints a line of output using the quantities represented by list of variable names in the form specified by FORMAT statement fs. If fs = *, it specifies list-directed output to the standard output device.

Examples

READ (5, 705) A, B, C READ 705, A, B, C READ (*, 705) A, B, C	Read data from input record on standard input device (assume it is unit 5 or *) containing values to assign to variable names A, B, and C. Read according to the format specified by statement 705.
WRITE (6, 710) I, BETA PRINT 710, I, BETA WRITE (*, 710) I, BETA	Write one record on standard output device (assume it is unit 6 or *) with the quantities from variable names I and BETA. Use format specified by statement 710.

Self-Testing Exercise 3-1

1. Explain the meaning of the following input-output statements, assuming unit number 5 is keyboard and unit number 6 is printer.
   (a) READ (5, 700) A, B, C
   (b) PRINT 710, X, Y, Z
   (c) WRITE (NRITE, 720) L, N, P
   (d) READ 730, Q, Z, T
   (e) WRITE (6, *) X, Y, IX

2. A FORTRAN program has been written using unit numbers 1 for standard file storage and 3 for printer. The program is now to be run on a computer with default unit numbers 5 for standard file storage device and 6 for printer. How is this change made?

The FORMAT Statement

The purpose of the FORMAT statement is to describe the specific form of the data being read or written. The FORMAT statement describes data in the same way for all input/ output media. The same FORMAT statement can define data to be read from a keyboard, written to a file storage device, or to be printed on the printer as long as the form of the data is the same in all cases. One FORMAT statement can be used by more than one input or output statement. The FORMAT statement does not have to appear next to the input/output statement using it. The statement label is sufficient identification, so that the FORMAT statement can be written before or after the input/output command using it. Some programmers put a FORMAT statement next to the first input/output statement referencing it; others group all FORMAT statements together at the beginning or end of the program. A convention used in this text is to place each FORMAT statement closely following the first input/output statement that references it and to use a statement label from the numbers in that block.

In order to describe the form of the data for input/output, three elements must be specified or implied:

1. *Type of editing*   This can specify real, integer, real with exponent editing, logical, or character data. (Other less common types will be explained in Chapter 7.)
2. *Field size*   This is the number of print positions on printer paper, display position on a video display, or character positions on other storage media that is available for reading, storing, or printing the quantity.
3. *Location of decimal point*   This is expressed as number of places from the right of the field. This element is eliminated from the FORMAT specification for integer quantities and character data (because it has no meaning).

The FORMAT statement consists of the statement label (columns 1–5), the word FORMAT (normally beginning in column 7), and then the sets of specifications separated by commas. The group of specifications is enclosed in parentheses. Spaces may be used freely to improve readability. Examples (to be explained later) are:

1	2	3	4	5	6	7 8 9 10 11 12 13 14 15 16 17 18 19 20 21 22 23 24 25 26 27 28 29 30 31 32 33 34 35 36 37 38 39 40
	1	0	9			FORMAT (F10.2,F5.1)
	2	0	9			FORMAT (F7.0,I1/2)
	3	0	9			FORMAT (E15.8,E15.8,F10.2)

As illustrated by the examples, each specification set consists of three elements: a single-letter edit descriptor, field size, and decimal location. The three elements in the specification F10.2 are useful in seeing how the three elements are contained in the specification.

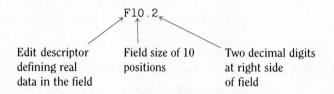

Edit descriptor	Field size of 10	Two decimal digits
defining real	positions	at right side
data in the field		of field

The first part of the specification is the single-letter edit descriptor. The four most commonly used edit descriptors are F, E, and I for numeric data and A for character data. Additionally, L is used for logical data. The three numeric data edit descriptors will be explained in this section. The character-data and logical-data descriptors are described in a later section. Additional descriptors for other data types are explained in Chapter 7.

FOUR COMMON EDIT DESCRIPTORS

Letter	Type of quantity	Form	Where
F	Real	Fw.d	w = field size
E	Exponent form of real	Ew.d	d = positions to right
I	Integer	Iw	of decimal
A	Character	Aw or A	

The next part of the FORMAT specification is the field size in numbers of spaces or columns. This is the maximum number of character spaces or columns the quantity can occupy. The data quantity need not use all of the field; the unused positions are filled with blanks. The field size for numeric output should allow space for characters such as the sign and, for real output, a decimal point. For example, the field size for the following real and integer outputs are computed as follows (the E edit descriptor will be explained later):

Type of variable	Form of data		Sign	Integer digits	Decimal point	Digits in fraction	Total	Edit specification
					Minimum field size			
Real	± ddd.dd	=	1	3	1	2	7	F7.2
Real	± ddd.	=	1	3	1	0	5	F5.0
Integer	± dddd	=	1	4	0	0	5	I5

The third part of the FORMAT statement (not used with the I edit descriptor) is the location of the decimal point in the field. The field specification and decimal point specification are used in input in a slightly different way than in output. The use in output will be discussed first, and then the differences will be noted.

FORMAT Editing for Output

The handling of numeric data on output is quite simple in the normal case. However, there are special rules for a field size that is too large or too small for the data. Also, the first position on the printed line may not be available if it is used for vertical spacing control. This feature will be explored later in the chapter. It will be convenient to separately describe integer data, real data with F edit descriptor, and real data with E edit descriptor.

For integer data, no decimal point is printed, the quantity is right-justified (number starts at right side of field), and unused positions to the left are blank. A minus sign will print for a negative quantity, but a plus sign will not print for a positive quantity. If the field size is too small for the quantity (for example, a field defined as I4 and a quantity to be output of 39,764), there is an error condition called *overflow*. In cases of overflow, the output for the field consists of asterisks to indicate the overflow error.

Examples

Specification	Data	Output (b indicates blank)
I6	−479	bb−479
I10	3	bbbbbbbbb3
I4	36754	****

Note that a field specification that is larger than needed is one method of leaving space between output items. Another method will be explained later. As an example of the uses of I specifications, the following statements will produce data and blanks in columns as illustrated.

```
    WRITE (6, 700) IX, JIX, KIX
700 FORMAT (I10, I5, I6)
```

where the value for IX is −37454; for JIX, 495; and for KIX, 1159.

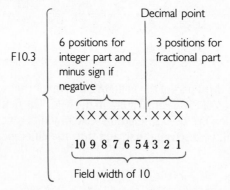

For real output using the F edit descriptor, the computer right-justifies in the field. The integer digits are positioned to the left of the decimal point, and the fractional digits are positioned to the right. As shown in the following example, a printing specification of F10.3 will place the decimal point in the fourth position from the right.

When using the F specification for output, the following conditions can occur for the integer portion and fractional portions of the F specification field:

1. Digits in result to be output do not fill the field:
   (*a*) Integer portion
   (*b*) Fractional portion
2. Digits in result to be output exceed positions in field:
   (*a*) Integer portion
   (*b*) Fractional portion

These conditions will be explained and illustrated.

1. Digits do not fill field.
   (*a*) If digits in integer portion do not fill all positions, the unused positions to the left are filled with blanks. For example, 98.5 and F10.1 = bbbbbb98.5. The integer portion must be large enough to include a minus sign when the output quantity is negative. It is good programming practice in writing specifications to allow for a negative sign even when only positive values are expected.
   (*b*) If fractional digits do not fill the fractional portion of the field, the remaining positions to the right are filled with zeros. For example, 347.56 and F10.5 = b347.56000.

2. Digits exceed positions available.
 (a) When the number of integer digits exceeds the available field width to the left of the decimal, there will be overflow resulting in output of a field of asterisks. For example, 67943.2 to be printed with a FORMAT statement F8.4 will cause overflow, and the output will be a field of asterisks.

			Field positions
d = 4	Fractional digit position (d)	=	4
67 943.2000	Decimal point	=	1
Field size of 8	Remaining for integer position =		3
Overflow digits	Total =		8

 (b) If the number of fractional digits exceeds fractional field size (specified by d portion of specification), the excess digits will be truncated after rounding. No error indication occurs. For example, 7.6543 printed with F8.2 will print 7.65, and 3.9462 with F8.2 will print 3.95. This is a useful method for rounding output.

The E, or exponent, form of output editing is preferred in all cases where the result is very large, is very small, or has an unknown range of magnitude. In output with the E format, the result is expressed as a decimal fraction plus an exponent that indicates the number of places the decimal point of the fraction should be moved to the right (for a positive exponent) or to the left (for a negative exponent). The E specification indicates the number of positions in the E result field and the number of positions (digits) in the fraction.

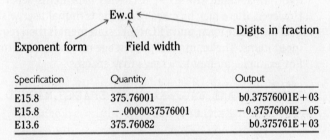

Specification	Quantity	Output
E15.8	375.76001	b0.37576001E + 03
E15.8	− .0000037576001	− 0.3757600IE − 05
E13.6	375.76082	b0.375761E + 03

The zero to the left of the decimal point in the E form of output is optional, so some implementations of FORTRAN produce it; others do not. In the text explanations, we will use it, but keep in mind that it is not always implemented.

The form of the exponent can vary with different implementations of FORTRAN and different sizes of exponents. The following are all standard: E ± nn or ± 0nn for exponents of 99 or less, and ± nnn for exponents between 99 and 999, where the n's stand for the digits in the exponent. Note that all forms use four output positions. For illustration purposes, we will use E ± nn.

If we assume a leading zero, an E specification requires at least seven digit positions more than the size of the fraction to allow for the sign of the fraction, the zero, the decimal point, and the four positions for the exponent. If there is no leading zero, only six positions are required beyond the fraction size. (Assume seven for all problems.) If the field size for output is more than required, the result will be right-justified and blank spaces will be inserted at the left. If the number of digits in the specified fraction size is less than the number of digits stored in the computer, the quantity will be truncated after rounding, as in the third variable in the last example. A specification for an E field that is adequate in most cases is E15.8.

The following examples illustrate how data characters and blank spaces are positioned when integer data items are output with I edit specifications and real data items are output using F and E edit specifications.

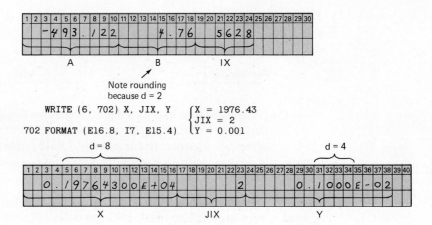

FORMAT Editing for Input

FORMAT editing may be used for both input from files and input from terminals. If input data items are being entered from a terminal, it is generally simpler to specify a free format input (READ *, list) with data items separated by commas or spaces. However, there may be cases when the terminal user wishes to enter data in a fixed-field formatted form, and a FORMAT statement is then required to specify the different input items. The input prompt message may be used to mark the field sizes for input. For example, an input message may specify:

```
ENTER ID AND WAGE-RATE IN SPACES MARKED BY *:
******** ***.**
```

The FORMAT statement is treated differently with a READ statement than with a WRITE or PRINT statement in three cases. First, with data in an input line from a terminal or input lines from a file, no provision need be made for an input sign or decimal point unless it occupies columns by being recorded. If an input value is negative, the sign must be entered as a leading minus sign, but if the values to be input are positive, no sign is needed. Within a field, blanks may precede the negative sign, but zeros must not be entered to the left of the sign.

The second difference is related to blank spaces in the input field. If every space in each input field contains a numeric digit, decimal point, or a plus or minus sign, the interpretation is clear. (No other characters are allowed; no commas can be used to mark thousands, etc.) If there are blanks in some or all of the character positions in an input field, they are interpreted as follows:

1. *All blanks*   No data entered in a field is interpreted as a zero value for the input

items. For an input field specified by F3.0, input of bbb (all blanks on input) is interpreted as 000.

2. *Leading blanks* Ignored. A field specified as I6 with input of bbb198 is the same as 000198.

3. *Blanks embedded in a numeric item* Ignored. A field specified as I6 with input of b1b9b8 is interpreted as 198.

4. *Trailing blanks* Ignored. If the field specification is F6.2, input of b1456b is interpreted as 14.56.

It is generally less error-prone to enter the decimal point with a data item or input than to rely on format specifications to insert the decimal point.

The third difference for input is in the form of input data for E format reading. The E is optional; if E is used, a plus sign is optional. However, clear input forms should be used to avoid mistakes. The following two sets of data are all valid, the items in the set showing different ways to represent the same quantity:

Examples

Set 1	Set 2
13795.2E12	.2684E01
13795.2 + 12	2684. − 3
.137952 + 17	26.84E − 1

Note that the exponent changed when the decimal point was moved. A number entered in an E format may also be read by an F specification.

The following examples illustrate the rules for input FORMAT specifications.

1. Several data items are entered on input without spaces between. Variable names are assigned as shown. No decimal points are entered, but the locations of the implied decimal points are shown by the carets; for example, X = 9.8, Y1 = 789.4, YJ = 1.094, YK = 86765.4, and KIX = 88.

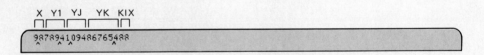

The statement to read these variables is the following. (Note that no allowance is made for a sign or a decimal point in the input field size because none appears in the data.)

       READ (5, 201) X, Y1, YJ, YK, KIX
    201 FORMAT (F2.1, F4.1, F4.3, F6.1, I2)

Note that spaces between specifications are optional and are used for readability only.

2. Applying the rules for reading input, a quantity in a line of data (input record) will be read as indicated using the given format:

Quantity in punched card	Format specifications to read data	Read as	Comments
[grid: 325 in columns 8–10]	I3	000	Because I3 reads only columns 1–3 and data is in columns 8 to 10.
[grid: 325 in columns 8–10]	I10	0000000325	Leading spaces = zeros.
[grid: 325 in columns 1–3, 457 in columns 5–7]	I3, I4	325 and 0457	
[grid: 325 in columns 1–3]	I10	325	Trailing spaces are ignored.
[grid: 375.56 in columns 5–10]	F5.2, F5.2	000.03 and 75.56	Only first 5 columns read with first format specification.
[grid: 375.56 in columns 5–10]	F10.2	00000375.56	Leading spaces = zeros.
[grid: 375.56 in columns 3–8]	F10.0	0375.56	Decimal point in input item overrides format. Trailing spaces are ignored.

The basic approach to input and output has now been explained. The rules for the FORMAT statement for numeric data are summarized in the box.

FORMAT STATEMENT FOR NUMERIC DATA

General form
fs FORMAT (list of specifications separated by commas), where fs is a format statement label. Spaces before and after parentheses and between specifications are optional.

Form of specifications

Fw.d	Real variable	w stands for field size
Ew.d	Exponent form	d stands for number of decimal positions to right of
Iw	Integer variable	decimal

Fitting data to field size
1. Data is justified to the right in the field on output. On input, trailing blanks are ignored, but a field of all blanks is interpreted as zero. In the case of real data input, a decimal position in the input data overrides a FORMAT-specified decimal position.
2. If integer positions of an output are greater than the integer portion field size, an overflow error condition results and a field of asterisks is output.
3. If significant digits in the fractional portion exceed the number of positions in the fraction field to the right of the decimal point, the remaining quantity is rounded and the excess digits are truncated.
4. Using the E form can ensure maximum accuracy without overflow. The d portion should be the same as the number of significant digits, and the field width should be at least 7 higher.

Self-Testing Exercise 3-2

1. Read the following data from an input record. The data items are referenced by the variable names ALPHA, BETA, IOTA, and JIX.

Note that the sizes of the fields, including blank spaces at the left, are:

Variable	Field size	Input Positions	Characters of data including sign position
ALPHA	10	1–10	10
BETA	9	11–19	9
IOTA	7	20–26	7
JIX	7	27–33	6

2. Print the above variables in reverse order. Use minimum space but allow for sign. Leave two spaces between ALPHA and BETA, not counting the sign position. Leave the first position on the line blank (not counting a space for a sign).

3. Print the variables IOTA and BETA. Do not print the fractional portion of BETA. Do not use a field size larger than absolutely necessary, but provide 10 spaces (not counting the space allowed for a sign) before the first quantity and between the actual quantities as printed.

4. What will be the result of the following set of WRITE and FORMAT statements if X = 1.0375 and IYEAR = 95?

```
      WRITE (6, 701) IYEAR, X
701 FORMAT (I10, F10.2)
```

5. What is the minimum specification for printing the following variables? (Remember to allow for decimal point and one space for sign.) Nonzero integers are represented by X's.

Form of variable	To be printed as	FORTRAN FORMAT specification
(a) XXXXXXXX	XXXX.XX	
(b) XXXX0000	XXXX.0	
(c) − XXX.XXXXX	− XX.XXXXXX	
(d) XXXXXXXX	.XXX	
(e) XXXX	XXXX	
(f) − XXXXXXX0000000.	− 0.XXXXXXX0E + 14	

Repetition of FORMAT Specifications

When several variables for input or output have the same specifications, a single specification can be repeated by placing an integer number in front of it. For example 7F10.3 means that the F10.3 specification is to be used seven times in succession.

If we enclose a set of specifications in parentheses and place an integer number in front of the set, the set will be repeated the number of times indicated: 3(F10.0, I3) is the same as (F10.0, I3, F10.0, I3, F10.0, I3).

The following examples illustrate the repeat feature. The repetitive use of the specifications stops when the list of variables to be input or output has been processed. In other words, the program uses only as many of the FORMAT specifications as are needed for the list of variables.

Examples of FORMAT repeat are:

FORMAT	Effect
FORMAT (I3, 7F10.0)	I3 and repeat F10.0 up to seven times.
FORMAT (5(I3, F10.0), F10.0)	Repeat (I3, F10.0) five times; then use F10.0
FORMAT (I3, 5(F10.0, I2))	I3 and repeat (F10.0, I2) up to five times.
FORMAT (7I2, 3(F10.0, I3))	Repeat I2 up to seven times, and then repeat (F10.1, I3) up to three times.

Horizontal Positioning Specifications

Specifying excess positions in a field width causes blanks to be inserted in a line, but this is sometimes cumbersome. An alternative is the wX specification, which causes w positions to be skipped (and filled with blanks). For example, on output a FORMAT (1X, I3, 10X, I3) puts a blank in the first position, prints data in the next three positions, skips the next 10 (makes them blank), and prints in the following three positions.

A Tc specification is a tabulating specification that positions the input or output device at the *cth* character position. For example, writing a FORMAT (T50, F10.2) will output starting at position 50 on the line. Note that T50 means to start input or output at position 50, not to skip 50 and start 51.

The wX and Tc edit specifiers apply to input as well as to output. For example, the following READ instructions read the data for Y in columns 51 to 60 and the data for IY in columns 71 to 75.

```
     READ (5, 100) Y, IY
100 FORMAT (T51, F10.0, 10X, I5)
```

> **HORIZONTAL POSITIONING**
>
> wX   Skip w positions to the right.
>
> Tc   Tabulate to position c; that is, move to position c where next input or output will begin. Available only with full FORTRAN.

Missing Data Items

Data items in an input line or record are provided to the computer in either list-directed form separated by spaces or commas or in formatted form. If an error is made in input and a data item is not entered, the result depends on whether the input is list-directed or formatted.

In list-directed input, a missing data item in a list will result in the next value being used instead. All subsequent values will be input to the wrong variable. The search for more input items will continue to the next line (input record); in other words, the search for list-directed input items to satisfy the input variable list does not stop at the end of a physical record. For example, assume that by input we want to set A = 10, B = 20, C = 30, and D = 40 but the items in the input record are 10, 30, 40 (value of 20 for B is missing) and there is the following input statement:

```
READ *, A, B, C, D
```

The first value of 10.0 will be assigned to A, the second value of 30.0 to B, and the third value of 40.0 to C. The program calls for one more input value (for D); the first item on the next line of input will be used.

In formatted input, data items are read from specified columns (fields) in the input record. If a data item is placed in the wrong field, it will be interpreted as input for the variable associated with the field. If the entire field is left blank, it will be interpreted as having a value of zero (for a numeric variable). There is no searching for a missing variable if there is no numeric value in the field assigned to it. For example, assume the same values of 10.0, 20.0, 30.0, and 40.0 for A, B, C, and D, formatted input with specification of 4F10.0, and input as follows:

```
bbbbb10.0|bbbbbbbbbb|bbbbbb30.0|bbbbbb40.0
```

The second field is blank, so the input operation results in variable B being assigned a value of zero.

If the field is all blank, the variable value is zero; if there are trailing blanks or blanks inside the data item, these are ignored. As an example of the handling of blanks within a data value, assume the following input statements:

```
    READ (5, 700) I, J, K, A
700 FORMAT (3I2, F5.2)
```

If the input values should be

```
I J K   A
23174596028
```

but through an input error, the input for J is 7 instead of 17 and there is a blank in the value for A

```
I J K   A
2374596b28b
```

then the input value will be interpreted as follows:

I = 23	
J = 74	Instead of 17 because 1 missing
K = 59	Instead of 45 because 4 used for J
A = 6.28	Because the two blanks embedded in the field are ignored, whereas an entire field of blanks is interpreted as zero

Because of the consequences of missing data items or data in the wrong columns, list-directed input is less error-prone for interactive keyboard entry. For formatted input, the consequences of missing data or data in the wrong column reinforce the need for echoing of input and validation of input items for valid range of values, invalid zero value, etc. It also suggests that entering decimal points in the input data items is desirable in order to reduce the risk of misinterpreting input data.

Self-Testing Exercise 3-3

What is the effect of each of the following FORMAT specifications?

1. FORMAT (5(F6.0), 3I4)

2. FORMAT (3I2, 4F10.0, 2E15.8)

3. FORMAT (4(I3, F10.0), I3)

4. FORMAT (I5, 10X, F10.2)

5. FORMAT (19X, F10.2, 20X, I3)

6. FORMAT (T20, F10.2, T50, I3)

Providing Descriptive Labels and Headings on Output

It is frequently desirable to provide descriptive labels and headings on output (primarily printed output). A program to compute the variance and standard deviation of an array of numbers might have an output such as the following:

```
THE VARIANCE IS                  XXXXXX.XX
THE STANDARD DEVIATION IS          XXX.XX
THE NUMBER OF OBSERVATIONS IS         XXX
```

The descriptive character output illustrated above is sometimes termed *Hollerith output* (named after Herman Hollerith, an early pioneer in automated data processing). FORMAT specifications permit any combination of letters, numbers, and special characters on a line of output. There are essentially four methods for providing headings and other character output.

1. A set of characters in list-directed output enclosed in apostrophes
2. Apostrophe edit descriptors in the FORMAT statement
3. The H edit descriptor in the FORMAT statement
4. Character data stored internally and referenced by variable names

The first method for descriptive labels and headings in list-directed output was explained in Chapter 2. The second and third methods, the apostrophe and H edit descriptors, are essentially identical in purpose and space. The H edit descriptor is the older method and tends to be error-prone. The apostrophe method is therefore recommended. The apostrophe and H edit descriptors are also used to control vertical spacing. The fourth method, explained in this section, involves input, storage, and output of character data.

Apostrophe Edit Descriptor

The apostrophe edit descriptor method is used within the parentheses that enclose the FORMAT specification. The characters to be output are enclosed in apostrophes. What is inside the apostrophes is printed or displayed. If the field to be output contains an apostrophe, two consecutive apostrophes are used to specify an apostrophe in the printed or displayed output. The first position in the output is not printed if it is used for vertical spacing. As a general rule for consistency (even for terminal output), make position 1 of the output line contain a blank character. Its use in vertical spacing control is explained later.

Examples

```
       WRITE(6,700)
  700  FORMAT(' NOW IS THE TIME.')

       WRITE(6,710)
  710  FORMAT(' I CAN''T DO IT.')
```

The apostrophe specification may be placed among a list of format edit specifications, or it may be the sole specification provided in the FORMAT for the WRITE (or PRINT) statement. For example, if the answer is the variable X, which has a specification of F10.2, two alternatives for the set of WRITE and FORMAT statements to print or display the following are given below:

THE ANSWER IS $\boxed{\pm\text{XXXXXX.XX}}$

```
       WRITE(6,700) X
  700  FORMAT(' THE ANSWER IS   ',F10.2)

       WRITE(6,700) X
  700  FORMAT(' THE ANSWER IS',F12.2)
```

The difference in the two FORMAT statements illustrates a programming choice. The first apostrophe specification provides for two spaces after the word IS. The second format shows how the blanks after the word IS can be provided by making the field size for the output of the variable X two spaces wider. Since the number on output is right-justified, the additional two spaces appear at the left. The Hollerith line starts at the left side with the first position kept blank. A heading such as ANALYSIS PROGRAM, to be centered on a page with 132 printing spaces, is written with a WRITE or PRINT statement having no variables list, as follows:

```
      WRITE (6, 700)
  700 FORMAT (58X, 'ANALYSIS PROGRAM')
```

Note that it was simpler to skip the 58 spaces to the center than to include these in the apostrophe specification. The T specification could also have been used to start the heading in column 59 (same as skipping over 58 spaces).

```
  700 FORMAT (T59, 'ANALYSIS PROGRAM')
```

H Edit Descriptor

The use of the H edit descriptor for character output is quite simple but is not recommended because it tends to be error-prone. It involves writing out the output exactly as it is to appear (including blanks) and then counting the number of character positions occupied. The number of character positions plus an H are written in front of the characters to indicate that the specified number of positions following is not to be translated, but is to be moved exactly as written to the output line. For example, to print THE ANSWER IS, which takes up 14 positions (if the first position is left blank), the H specification is:

```
  700 FORMAT (14H THE ANSWER IS)
```

Programming errors often occur because the count of the positions is wrong.

The separating comma in the FORMAT statement, necessary after an E, F, or I specification, is optional (but desirable) following the H and apostrophe edit specifications.

CHARACTER OUTPUT FROM FORMAT

Apostrophe edit   Enclose characters to be output in apostrophes. Two consecutive apostrophes are used to specify apostrophe in output.

H edit   Precede the characters to be output by wH, where w is the number of characters following H that are to be output.

Comma following apostrophe edit or H edit characters is optional.

Vertical Spacing with Control Characters

On line printers running under FORTRAN (but not on many terminals, small printers, or video displays), the first column on the line is not printed; that position is used for vertical spacing or carriage control of the printer. In cases when it is used by the printer, the output is formatted so that column 1 is blank unless vertical spacing control other than single spacing is desired. To implement vertical spacing control, a special character is assigned to the first position by an appropriate FORMAT statement. The usual method for including this in the FORMAT is to specify a one-character Hollerith field for output to column 1. The vertical spacing control characters are shown in the box:

VERTICAL SPACING WITH CONTROL CHARACTER

First position on line printer output line is used for vertical spacing control. The character is usually placed in the first position by a character output using either apostrophe or H edit methods.

Character	Vertical spacing before output
Blank	One line (single space)
0 (zero)	Two lines (double space)
1	To first line of next page
+	No advance

Note: Many terminals, displays, and small printers do not use a carriage control character. In such a case, the character in the first position is displayed (except in list-directed output).

The following examples illustrate the use of the vertical spacing control characters.

```
700 FORMAT ('1')
```
Advances paper to the first line of next page.

```
710 FORMAT ('0')
```
Double-space.

```
720 FORMAT ('1', 'THE ANSWERS')
```
Advance to first line of next page, and print THE ANSWERS on the first line.

Since a blank in the first position of any line of output on a line printer is used for normal single spacing, single-spaced lines should have a format in which the first character is a space. The X edit descriptor can be used to skip the position (leaving it blank), or a blank can be established by apostrophe or H edit methods. Excess leading spaces in F or I edit descriptors may also leave a blank but are dangerous because large values may fill the first space. The following three examples have the same effect of single spacing.

```
701  FORMAT(' THIS  IS PAGE ',I2)
201  FORMAT(/X, 'THIS  IS PAGE ',I2)
701  FORMAT(' ', 'THIS IS PAGE ',I2)
```

Self-Testing Exercise 3-4

Write a set of WRITE and FORMAT statements to provide the following lines of output. Write using the recommended apostrophe edit descriptors. A line is assumed to have 132 spaces.

1. ←——25——→ THE TOLERANCE IS bbXXX.XX

2. ←——10——→ AMOUNT OF SAVINGS IS $ XXX.XX

3. NUMBER IS XXXX

4. THE END. (With vertical spacing of 2 lines before printing)

5. ←—5—→ ITEM ←——10——→ AMOUNT

6. PAYROLL REPORT (centered at top of page)

Input, Storage, and Output of Characters

There will be situations where characters cannot be placed in a FORMAT statement because the characters to be used are variable. In such cases, it may be desirable to input the characters and store them for later use.

Character data can be stored in the computer and therefore can be referenced by name. The character string GBD can be referred to by NAME just as the data 147.6 can be referred to as VALUE. Each character in the character string occupies one character storage unit. The length of a character data item is the number of character positions (including embedded blanks) in the string. For example, "I WILL' occupies six positions.

As explained in Chapter 2, variable names that reference character data do not have a special first letter; they are declared explicitly as being of type CHARACTER. The declaration not only specifies a name as being a character variable name but also specifies the maximum number of characters that can be stored and referenced by the variable name. The maximum number of characters stored and referenced by a name can range from one to a very large number (limit set by the implementation of FORTRAN). As an example, the following type declaration defines the variable name HEAD as referencing locations that can store 15 characters, SUBHED as a variable that can reference 8 characters, and MSGE01 as a variable that can reference 20 characters.

```
CHARACTER HEAD*15, SUBHED*8, MSGE01*20
```

Declaring variable names for character data does not put any characters in the storage locations to which the names are assigned. This must be done by other instructions. A common method is to read the character data from input (entered at a keyboard or from records in a file). The reading of character data can use list-directed input or format-directed input.

When character data is read using a list-directed READ statement (with no FORMAT statement), the variable list contains a variable name that has been declared as character. The character data input is enclosed in apostrophes. For example, to read HI THERE! and store it in GREETN using list-directed input requires the following:

```
CHARACTER GREETN*9
READ *, GREETN
```

The data entered at the keyboard or in the file record would be enclosed in apostrophes in the form:

```
'HI THERE!'
```

If the greeting is to be printed, the list-directed method would include the character variable in a PRINT statement:

```
PRINT *, GREETN
```

The output will be the characters stored under the variable name GREETN but not the apostrophes. The output will be arranged according to the rules for list-directed output. In this case, the characters will be printed in columns 2–10 (list-directed output always leaves column 1 blank).

If formatted input or output statements are used, the variable names referencing character data must be declared as CHARACTER type. The FORMAT statement includes an A edit descriptor for fields for input or output of character data. The form is the A descriptor followed by the length of the character data field. If the length is not specified, the declared length in the CHARACTER-type declaration applies. For example, if NAME is defined by a declaration of CHARACTER NAME*10, the following two FORMAT statements will both define a format field of 10 characters:

```
      WRITE (6, 750) NAME
750   FORMAT (1X, A10)        Explicit field length of 10 characters for output of contents of vari-
                              able NAME
750   FORMAT (1X, A)          Implicit field length of 10 characters based on type declaration
                              length of 10 characters for variable NAME
```

If the FORMAT specification and the declared length of the variable name in the CHARACTER type statement do not match, the following rules govern what will be stored for input or printed for output.

1. Input
   (a) When the length specified by the A edit descriptor is greater than the declared length for the variable, the rightmost characters will be taken from the input field until the storage declared for the variable is full.
   (b) When the length specified by the A descriptor for input is less than the length of the declared size of variable storage, the data characters that are read are stored at the left side of the set of storage positions and the unused positions at the right are filled with blanks.

2. Output
   (a) An output field size larger than the number of characters stored for the output variable will result in leading blanks to fill the output field.
   (b) An output field size smaller than the number of characters declared for the character variable will result in the characters from the leftmost positions of storage being used.

As an example, assuming the following:

```
Declaration:        CHARACTER LABEL1*10
Input statement:    READ (5,700) LABEL1
Input data:         NOW IS THE TIME        (Note that this is 15
                                              characters.)
```

The characters that will be input and stored in the 10 storage positions of LABEL1 under three different FORMAT specifications are shown below:

FORMAT		Data stored in LABEL1 (10 positions)	
FORMAT (A10)	or (A)	NOW IS THE	(Takes exactly 10 characters starting at left)
FORMAT (A15)	(larger)	S THE TIME	(Takes rightmost characters from input field)
FORMAT (A6)	(smaller)	NOW ISbbbb	(Takes 6 leftmost characters and fills field with blanks)

The *output* for different FORMAT specifications, when NOW IS THE is stored in LABEL1 and the statement is WRITE (6,700) LABEL1 are the following:

FORMAT		OUTPUT	
FORMAT (A10)	or (A)	NOW IS THE	
FORMAT (A15)	(larger)	bbbbbNOW IS THE	(Leading blanks to fill field)
FORMAT (A3)	(smaller)	NOW	(Use specified number of stored characters starting at left)

THE A EDIT DESCRIPTOR

A w defines a character variable field on input or output containing w characters (including space characters). When no w is specified, the field size is made equal to the declared length for the variable name in the READ or WRITE statement.

When w is not equal to the length of the storage assigned to the variable name by the CHARACTER type declaration:

Input

w > length	Store rightmost characters of input to fill length.
w < length	Store w characters of input at left of variable storage and fill the remainder of storage with blanks.

Output

w > length	Use leading blanks to fill output field.
w < length	Use leftmost w characters.

Self-Testing Exercise 3-5

1. Read an input 'WE ARE ALL ENLISTED' using list-directed read. Declare the variable as CHARACTER type, and print the character string using formatted output. Leave the first character on the line blank. Show the form of the input.

2. Repeat question 1 but use formatted input. Show the input.

3. Use the specifications in question 2, but use the following A edit descriptors. Indicate the content of storage on input and the content of the output line when printed.
   (*a*) Input using:
      (1) A19 but length declared as 10
      (2) A20
   (*b*) Output assuming A19 on input and using:
      (1) A20
      (2) A10
      (3) A

4. Using the specifications in question 2, print a line that says: bbbbb WE ARE ALL ENLISTED, I THINK.

5. The program produced the following output even though the data stored in variable YAK (declared as CHARACTER YAK*5) was YETTI.

bYE

The blank is in position 1. What is your diagnosis? *Hint:* What are the FORMAT specifications that would have produced that result?

6. Write all necessary FORTRAN statements (including CHARACTER type declarations) to perform the following:

Read a phrase 'WHAT IS TRUE?', store it, and print it in reverse order "TRUE IS WHAT?' *Hint:* Use four variables to store the four parts of the phrase that must be manipulated.

Checking for End of Data and Data Error

If the number of data records (such as records in a file) to be input is variable, the program should test for the end of the data. An attempt to read a data record when there are no more input records causes the operating system that manages the computer to abort the job and provide a message indicating an abnormal termination. Rather than an abnormal termination, an explicit, programmed termination procedure is preferred. The two methods for explicit termination when the number of records is not known are:

1. Use the value of an item in a special end-of-data record (explained in Chapter 2)
2. Use an END specification in the READ statement

The form of the END specification in the READ statement is END = s, where s is the label of the statement to which control should go when the READ statement is executed but all data records have already been read. The specification is placed after the unit number and FORMAT statement label inside the parentheses in the READ statement. To identify the end of a set of data records in a file, the computer software that writes the file of records when they are created and stored normally writes a special end-of-file record with an end-of-file code (meaning the end of the records in the file). When the computer reads this end-of-file record while attempting to read data records, the END = s statement is executed. As an example, the READ statement below is executed until there are no more data records (i.e., the READ statement reads the end-of-file record), at which time control goes to the statement labeled 400. Spaces are optional and are used only for readability.

```
READ (5, 700, END = 400) A, B, C
```

END-OF-DATA SPECIFICATION IN INPUT STATEMENT

END = s

where s is the label of the statement to which control passes when all data has been read but a READ command is attempted and no data record is available.

The specification is placed after the unit number and FORMAT statement label in the input statement.

If a data input is not readable with the specified format, such as alphabetic characters in an integer field, the operating system aborts the job with some data error message. To avoid this type of termination and to keep the control in the program, full 1977 FORTRAN provides a data-type error specification in the READ statement. The form is ERR = s where s is the label of the statement to which control is to transfer if a data error is encountered. The specification is placed after the unit number and FORMAT statement label inside the parentheses of the READ statement. It can be before or after the END specification. The statement to which control is sent if there is a data-type READ error should output an error message and take appropriate action, such as returning to read the next record. For example, if the input record shown below is read by the following statement, there will be a data-type error.

```
READ (5, 701, END = 801, ERR = 901) NIX, X
701 FORMAT (I5, F5.0)
```

The decimal point in an I edit field is a data error.
Reading this input record will cause transfer to statement 901.

```
1.65 3764.
```

DATA-TYPE ERROR SPECIFICATION IN INPUT STATEMENT

ERR = s

where s is the label of the statement to which control passes when a data-type error is encountered.

The specification is placed after the unit number and FORMAT statement label (and before or after the END specification if used) in the input statement. Available only in full FORTRAN.

Self-Testing Exercise 3-6

1. Write READ and IF statements to read all data records, each record having variables ID, HOURS, and RATE in columns 1 to 5, 6 to 7, and 8 to 11. There is a trailer record after the last data record with 99999 in the ID field. At end, go to 500.

2. Write a READ statement to perform the same result as question 1, but use the END feature and omit the trailer record with 99999 for ID.

3. Write a READ statement to perform the same results as in question 2 but also with a data error specification transferring to 910 if a data error is encountered.

Handling Physical Records with Slash Editing

One FORMAT statement has thus far been assumed for each line of output, each input record read, etc. FORTRAN allows considerably more versatility in input and output. Lines, records, etc., may be skipped, and a single FORMAT statement may be used for more than one line of output.

The slash (/) is used in a FORMAT statement to terminate the current physical record. The closing right parenthesis of the FORMAT statement also terminates the current physical record. Using more than one slash causes multiple records to be skipped. The slash can be written anywhere in the FORMAT statement. Examples are:

```
FORMAT (/ /, 3F10.0)
FORMAT (I2, /, F10.0)
FORMAT (I2, F10.0, /)
```

Since the closing parenthesis also terminates a physical record (and therefore can be thought of as a slash), rules can be formulated for the effect of slashes.

USE OF SLASHES IN FORMAT

1. The use of *n* slashes at the beginning or end of a FORMAT causes *n* physical records to be skipped.
2. A slash in the middle of a FORMAT causes the current record to be terminated and a new physical record to be brought into use (starting at the beginning of the new record).
3. More than one slash in the middle of a FORMAT terminates the current record and causes *n* − 1 of the following records to be skipped.
4. Commas before and after the slashes in the FORMAT specifications are optional.

Examples of the Use of Slashes

FORMAT (with READ)	Effect
`FORMAT (F10.0 / I3)`	Reads two values from a set of two records; the first record has a data item with specifications of F10.0, and the second uses I3.
`FORMAT (3F10.0 /)`	Reads a record with three F10.0 values, then skips a record.
`FORMAT (/ / / F6.3)`	Skips three records and uses F6.3 for variable on fourth.

FORMAT (with WRITE or PRINT)	Effect
`FORMAT (1X, F10.0 /)`	Prints one value on a line with specification of F10.0, and then skips one line.
`FORMAT (1X, 3F10.0, /, 1X, I3)`	Prints three values on a line using F10.0, skips to the next line, and prints a value using an I3 specification.
Commas optional	
`FORMAT (1X, F10.0, / / /)`	Prints using F10.0, then skips three lines.

Note the placement of a blank space as first character of line for vertical spacing control by use of a 1X specification.

Reuse of FORMAT Specifications

At this point, it is appropriate to consider what happens if the number of variables in the input/output list is not equal to the number of specifications in the FORMAT statement. There can be:

1. Fewer variables in the input or output list than edit specifications (too many specifications)
2. More variables in the input or output list than edit specifications (not enough specifications)

In the case of too many specifications, the specifications required for the input or output list are used and all remaining edit specifications are ignored and not used. For example, the following WRITE statement lists three variables, but the FORMAT statement has five specifications. This will result in the output as shown (if I = 40, J = 12, and K = 19 and there is an asterisk at the beginning and end defined by '*'):

```
    WRITE (6,700) I, J, K
700 FORMAT (1X, '*', 5I4, '*')
```

Output:

```
* 40  12  19
```

There is no second asterisk on the line of output. There were only three variables, so only three of the five I4 specifications were used; the remaining two I4 edit specifications were not used, so the program never reached the last '*' specification, which was therefore ignored.

If there are not enough edit specifications to edit all variables in the input or output list, the edit specifications will be reused. However, reuse of specifications can affect use of physical records for input or output, because the rightmost parenthesis in the FORMAT statement is a specification to terminate the current physical record. When the end of the format specifications are reached without exhausting the list of variables, the current record is terminated, a new record is brought into use, and the format specifications are repeated. However, the program goes back only to the most recent unmodified left parenthesis in the format specifications (a specification in parentheses without a repeat number in front of it) and begins at that point for the repeating of the specifications. For example:

```
READ (5,700)   J, A, B, C,
```

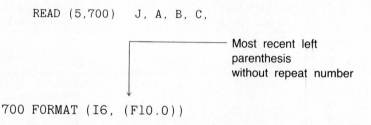

Most recent left
parenthesis
without repeat number

```
700 FORMAT (I6, (F10.0))
```

This will read J and A from the first record, but the list is not exhausted, so the specifications must be repeated with a new record. Because of the repeat at unmodified parenthesis rule, only F10.0 is repeated in the above example, not the entire specification. The list is still not exhausted, and F10.0 is again repeated with a new record. In other words, the example reads from three records: J and A on record 1, B on record 2, and C on record 3. The following examples for FORMAT (and a WRITE statement) illustrate the repeat at unmodified parenthesis rule.

`(I3 / (F10.0) )`	Prints I3 value on one line, goes to the next line, and prints an F10.0 value. If more variables, it continues printing one F10.0 to a line until the output list is exhausted.

`(I2 / (3F10.0) )`	Prints I2 value on one line, then prints three values with F10.0s per line until the output list is exhausted.
	
	`I2`
	`F10.0  F10.0  F10.0`
	`F10.0  F10.0  F10.0`
	`F10.0  F10.0  F10.0`

The effects of too few or too many specifications can be summarized as:

Condition	Effect	Example
More specifications than variables in the list	Extra specifications are ignored.	READ (5, 700) A, B, C 700 FORMAT (5F10.0) Uses only the first three specifications.
More variables than specifications	When specifications are exhausted (that is, the right parenthesis of the FORMAT is reached, which terminates the current record), a new record is brought into use, and the FORMAT specifications are repeated at the most recent unmodified left parenthesis.	WRITE (6, 700) A, B, C 700 FORMAT (1X, 2F10.0) Write output on two lines with A and B on first line and C on second line.

What happens if the FORMAT specifications call for a total of field widths (a logical record) greater than one physical record? The result is implementation-dependent. For some, the first physical record is used in its entirety, and another physical record is brought into use for the remainder. For others, the result may be a fatal error that aborts the job. It is poor practice to have logical records larger than physical records.

Self-Testing Exercise 3-7

Explain the effect of each of the following FORMAT specifications.

1. (I5 / F10.0)

2. (F10.0 / / / F10.0 /)

3. (/ / / F10.0)

4. (F10.0, / / / / /)

Rounding with FORMAT Specifications

Before we conclude the discussion of FORMAT editing, the impact of FORMAT rounding needs to be mentioned. It is especially important to be aware of rounding errors in business or accounting reports where totals often need to be the exact sum of individual items. For example, the gross pay amount for each individual listed in a payroll report should be rounded to the nearest penny, and the total gross pay for the report should be equal to the sum of the individual pay amounts, yet this may not happen in some situations.

The FORMAT specifications result in rounding in cases where the underlying data contains more digits than are printed out. For example, if pay rate is 5.764 per hour and hours worked are 37, the gross pay is 213.268. If this amount is printed out as dollars and cents for a report, a format of F8.2 will result in an output of 213.27 because the result is rounded and the excess digit is then truncated and not printed. But if the original unrounded data items are used to prepare the sum, there could be small differences. This can be seen from the example on the next page.

Gross pay	Printed as F8.2
213.268	213.27
312.177	312.18
249.266	249.27

Total 774.711   (774.72)

⌠ Unrounded   ⌠ Sum of
   sum   rounded
                 outputs

(774.71)

⌠ Rounded sum

In the majority of programming situations, the rounding of output under format control does not create any special problem. However, when situations arise such as the above example, it is important to understand the reason for it. It is, of course, possible to round and truncate the stored data so that it matches the output. In the example below, GRSPAY has an initial value of 213.268. Three statements are used to round the stored value to the nearest penny. The stored amount for summing is then identical to the amount printed. Even though these three statements could be combined, it is rather cumbersome and a different approach to handling the problem is shown in Chapter 5b in connection with the payroll program.

	GRSPAY	
	213.268	
`GRSPAY = GRSPAY + .005`	213.273	Add rounding factor.
`GRSPAY = REAL (INT (GRSPAY * 100.0) )`	21327.	Multiply by 100 to make the integer portion include cents, change to integer to truncate remainder, and then change back to real number.
`GRSPAY = GRSPAY / 100.0`	213.27	Divide by 100 to restore to dollars and cents.

Expressions in Output List

A feature of the 1977 full FORTRAN is the use of expressions in the output list. The expression, a constant or an arithmetic expression, is evaluated and the resulting value is output as specified by the format. For example, to print the value of a variable called A, its square, and its square root, only an output statement need be used:

```
WRITE (6, 700) A, A**2, SQRT(A).
```

Additional Testing, Debugging, and Quality-Control Suggestions

Testing and debugging a program to remove all errors is a significant part of the total programming time, taking perhaps one-fourth to one-third of the time required to produce a complete, tested, documented program. In addition to the test data explained in Chapter 2, the test should include data which violates the input format specifications (if ERR is used).

Placing FORTRAN statements to print output headings in the initialization block means that they are executed before computation. This aids debugging because output of the heading indicates progress to that point.

In general, a program to be executed in batch processing should be written to reject erroneous inputs but to continue processing the rest of the input data. If rejected in validation, the contents of an input should usually be printed; when rejected because of data-type error, the erroneous record contents cannot be printed but are identified by an input record number. Error messages may be printed in place of a regular line of output or may be printed in an error message area (say, to the right).

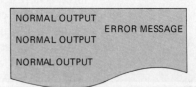

In the case of interactive input and execution, the program should reject erroneous input and request a corrected input of the record in error. If a large number of input items were entered in one line at the keyboard and only one or two are in error, the interactive program may be written to request corrected input only for the invalid item(s). The item to be corrected should be plainly labeled.

Where the number of input items can be reasonably large (say, over 10), it is good programming practice to count the records that are read and to print a message at the end of the output identifying the number of records that were processed, perhaps dividing the count into accepted and rejected records.

In debugging, it is often useful to insert temporary debugging statements in the program. These are generally PRINT statements that print out intermediate results before and after important program processing or before IF statements. It is convenient to use list-directed PRINT statements for this purpose. If there are a number of these PRINT statements, each statement should include a Hollerith output of the number assigned to the debugging statement. For example, debugging statement number 8 outputting results of J and X might be: PRINT *, '8', J, X. When the program is debugged, these PRINT statements are removed. To make removal easy, it is helpful to put an identifying statement label on each temporary statement that clearly marks it as one of the statements to be removed. For example, the statement PRINT *, '8', J, X might be labeled with a 9998:

```
9998 PRINT *, '8', J, X
```

Programming Style Suggestions

Style suggestions related to format-directed input and output are summarized below:

1. Place the FORMAT statement as nearly adjacent to the input/output statement as possible.
2. Use the apostrophe edit descriptor instead of the H descriptor.
3. Print headings as early as possible in the program. This output at the beginning provides evidence during debugging that the program has executed to this point.

4. Remember to leave column 1 blank on output. Either begin a line with an explicit one-blank-character specification, or skip the first position by an X edit specification. Do not rely upon an extra width I, F, or E edit descriptor.
5. Use END specification and ERR specification (if available) in READ statements.
6. Use formatted output for more readable results.
7. Use list-directed output for temporary PRINT statements inserted to print out results during debugging.
8. For input, selection of format-directed or list-directed mode is dependent on the data. For example, list-directed data is much simpler to input from a terminal or personal computer keyboard. If format-directed input is used for interactive input, consider a prompt message which defines the exact field lengths and formats for the input items.
9. Keep a record count. Print the record count at the end of the program. The record count can also specify accepted and rejected records.
10. For batch processing, print error messages that identify the record in error, the reason for the error, and whether or not the record is rejected. Consider a printout of the contents of the rejected input record.
11. For interactive input, the program should reject erroneous input and request a corrected input of the record in error. Invalid input records should not be processed.

Summary

The chapter has described the FORTRAN instructions to control input and output using the FORMAT statement. When a FORMAT statement is employed in a program, the READ or WRITE statement specifies the FORMAT statement by a FORTRAN statement reference. The FORTRAN statement specifies the form of the data by a set of edit descriptors, which include the type of data (integer, real, or exponent form of real data), the number of record positions allowed for the data items, and the decimal point position for real data. Horizontal movement (skipping over record positions) is specified by an X edit descriptor or by a T-tabulating edit descriptor.

Providing descriptive labels and headings on output is done mainly with an apostrophe descriptor that defines the characters to be output. Vertical spacing while printing on a line printer is specified by a character in column 1 of a line. Input and output of characters that are assigned to a character variable name are specified by an A edit descriptor.

It is convenient to be able to operate on data where the number of input records is unspecified. The chapter has described the use of the END specification in the READ statement. Another specifier, ERR, is used for transfer of control when input data does not match format-type specifications. As part of the FORMAT statement specifications, a slash (stroke) is used to terminate the use of the current physical record and to skip physical records. In addition to variables, the output statement list may contain expressions.

Answers to Self-Testing Exercises

Exercise 3-1

1. (a) Read from the keyboard (assume unit number = 5) values for the variable names A, B, and C. The format of the data is defined by FORMAT statement 700.
   (b) Print output on the printer consisting of values stored in variable name locations X, Y, and Z. Use format described by FORMAT statement 710.

(c) Write values for variables L, N, and P according to FORMAT statement 720 using unit number NRITE. If the printer has a unit number of 6, a value of 6 for NRITE will result in the instruction using the printer.

(d) Read, using the keyboard (no unit designation), values to be assigned to variable names Q, Z, and T. The format of the data on the input line is given by FORMAT statement 730.

(e) Write in list-directed form on unit 6 (the printer) the values for variables X, Y, and IX.

2. The input/output statements may be rewritten, but this is not necessary. A better approach is to use a job control instruction to assign unit 1 as the standard file device and unit 3 as the printer.

Exercise 3-2

1.
```
      READ (5, 710) ALPHA, BETA, IOTA, JIX
710 FORMAT (F10.2, F9.2, I7, I7)
```

2.
```
      WRITE (6, 720) JIX, IOTA, BETA, ALPHA
720 FORMAT (I7, I7, F9.2, F12.2)
```

3.
```
      WRITE (6, 730) IOTA, BETA
730 FORMAT (I17, F17.0)
```

The result will be (IOTA = 6 for data, 1 for sign, and 10 leading blanks for field size of 17; BETA = 5 for data, 1 for decimal, 1 for sign, and 10 leading blanks for field size of 17):

bbbbbbbbbb824341bbbbbbbbbbb53429.

4. The result will be:

bbbbbbbb95bbbbbbb1.04   (X is rounded and truncated to two digits in fractional part.)

5. (a) F8.2   (c) F10.6   (e) I5
   (b) F7.1   (d) F5.3   (f) E15.8

Exercise 3-3

1. Repeat F6.0 five times (parentheses are redundant), and then repeat I4 three times.

2. Uses three of I2, four of F10.0, and two of E15.8.

3. The set of I3, F10.0 is used four times followed by I3.

4. Use first five positions for integer output, skip next ten positions, and then use next ten positions as F10.2.

5. Skip 19 positions from the normal starting position of 1. Start at position 20 with F10.2 (20–29 and move to 30 for next field), skip 20 positions (30–49 and move to position 50 for next field), and then use three positions with I3.

6. Same effect as 5. Start at position 20 with 10.2 then do I3 starting at position 50.

Exercise 3-4

1.
```
      WRITE (6, 721) TOLER
721 FORMAT (25X, 'THE TOLERANCE IS', F8.2)
```

2.   WRITE (6, 722) SAVIN
  722 FORMAT (10X, 'AMOUNT OF SAVINGS IS $', F7.2)

3.   WRITE (6, 723) NMBER
  723 FORMAT (' NUMBER IS', I5)

4.   WRITE (6, 724)
  724 FORMAT ('0', 'THE END.') or ('OTHE END.')

5.   WRITE (6, 725)
  725 FORMAT (5X, 'ITEM', 10X, 'AMOUNT')

6.   WRITE (6, 726)
  726 FORMAT ('1', 58X, 'PAYROLL REPORT')

Exercise 3-5

1.   CHARACTER MESAGE*19
     READ *, MESAGE
     WRITE (6, 710) MESAGE
  710 FORMAT (A20) [Could also have been FORMAT (1X, A19)]

Input in form 'WE ARE ALL ENLISTED'

2.   CHARACTER MESAGE*19
     READ (5, 700) MESAGE
  700 FORMAT (A19)
     WRITE (6, 710) MESAGE
  710 FORMAT (A20)

Input in form WE ARE ALL ENLISTED starting in column 1 of input file record or keyboard interactive input.

3. (*a*) Content of storage (b = blank):
    (1) L ENLISTED
    (2) WE ARE ALL ENLISTEDb
  (*b*) Content of output line:
    (1) bWE ARE ALL ENLISTED
    (2) WE ARE ALL
    (3) WE ARE ALL ENLISTED   (Note that the first character is not blank and may not actually print since the position is used for carriage control.)

4.   WRITE (5, 710) MESAGE
  710 FORMAT (5X, A19, ', I THINK.')

5. If YAK is declared as a five-character variable and it contains YETTI, then an output specification of A2 will use only the leftmost two characters (YE). The heading blank was probably the result of a separate first-column specification prior to the A2 specification, e.g., FORMAT('',A2. . . . .).

6. Define four variables of CHARACTER type with lengths as shown:

	Length
B1 = WHAT	4
B2 = bISb	4
B3 = TRUE	4
B4 = ?	1

```
    READ (5, 101) B1, B2, B3, B4
101 FORMAT (3A4, A1)
    WRITE (6, 102) B3, B2, B1, B4
102 FORMAT (1X, 3A4, A1)
    STOP
    END
```

Note: The repeat character (CHARACTER*4) was used to specify the first three character variables as being of the same length of 4. If this program is to be executed in batch, it would be good practice to print out the input record as well as the result line.

Exercise 3-6

1.
```
    READ (5, 700) ID, HOURS, RATE
700 FORMAT (I5, F2.0, F4.3)
    IF (ID.EQ.99999) GO TO 500
```

2.
```
    READ (5, 700, END = 500) ID, HOURS, RATE
700 FORMAT (I5, F2.0, F4.3)
```

3.
```
    READ (5, 700, END = 500, ERR = 910) ID, HOURS, RATE
700 FORMAT (I5, F2.0, F4.3)
```

Exercise 3-7

1. The I5 is used for value on first file record or line, F10.0 for value on second. If list of variables is not exhausted, the next file record or line will use I5, etc.

2. First file record or line has one value F10.0; it is terminated and the next two records or lines are skipped. Then F10.0 is used for the next record. If list is not exhausted, the next record or line is skipped and the FORMAT is repeated.

3. Skips three file records or lines and then uses F10.0. If repeated, it will skip three records or lines again.

4. Uses F10.0 and then skips five lines or file records.

Questions and Problems

1. Explain three methods of identifying which input or output unit is to be used with a READ or WRITE statement.

2. Differentiate between physical and logical records.

3. Explain two methods for testing end of data.

4. Complete the following table using minimum FORMAT specification:

Data as found on record	Format to read	Desired printing	Format for printing
(a) XXX.XXX		XXX.XXX	
(b) XXX		XXX.0	
(c) .XXXXE + 17		0.XXXXE + 17	
(d) − .XXXXE + 5		− XXXX0.	
(e)	F5.2		F5.1

5. What is the effect of the following FORMAT specification sets?
   (a) `('0')`
   (b) `(3F10.0, 3/)`
   (c) `(1F10.0)`
   (d) `(I6, 2(I7))`
   (e) `(3F10.0, 4(I3))`
   (f) `(3F10.0, 5E15.8)`
   (g) `(I6, F10.0)`
   (h) `(I6 / F10.0)`
   (i) `(5(F10.0, I7))`
   (j) `(F10.4, F10.3, / / / I6)`
   (k) `(I10, 10X, F13.2)`
   (l) `(50X, I3)`
   (m) `(T50, I3)`

6. Print a heading AXYZ COMPANY centered within 80 spaces at the top of a page. Double-space and center 12/31/88 below the heading.

7. Write sets of WRITE and FORMAT statements to make the following outputs. Leave first position on line blank in all cases.
   (a) 52 spaces ANALYSIS PROGRAM
       $\longleftrightarrow$

   (b) CHI SQUARE TEST IS XX.XX
   (c) PART NO. 20 spaces QUANTITY 10 spaces AMOUNT
              $\longleftrightarrow$ $\longleftrightarrow$

   (d) PROGRAM DATA IS INCORRECT.

8. Write statements to read a 10-character heading from columns 36 to 45 on a file record and to print it using the printer at columns 76 to 85.

9. Explain what happens if there are too many format specifications. Also explain what happens if there are more variables in the list than edit specifications in the FORMAT statement.

10. Write all necessary FORTRAN statements (including character type declarations) to read the phrase 'HOW NOW, BROWN COW' and print on two lines as:

```
HOW NOW?
    BROWN COW!!
```

3b

Example Programs and Programming Exercises Using Format-Directed Input and Output

General Notes on Chapter 3 Examples
Use of Input and Output Layouts
Error-Control Features

**General Program Example 3—
Payroll Reports**
Problem Description for General Example 3
Program Documentation for General Example 3
Notes on General Example 3

**Mathematical Program Example 3
—Tables of Ordinates of the
Normal Curve**
Background Explanation for Mathematical Example 3
Problem Description for Mathematical Example 3

Program Documentation for Mathematical Example 3
Notes on Mathematical Example 3

Programming Exercises
Description of Assignment
Mathematics and Statistics
Business and Economics
Science and Engineering
Humanities and Social Sciences
General
Interactive Scientific and Engineering

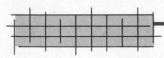

The example programs and exercises in this chapter use the features presented in Chapters 1 and 2 as well as the format-directed input and output explained in Chapter 3a. The two examples—payroll reports and tables of ordinates of the normal curve—show the use of formatting in two different environments. Both examples are instructive; the payroll report is particularly useful in showing the use of formatting features for a report prepared from file input. The mathematical example illustrates formatting with an interactive application.

General Notes on Chapter 3 Examples

Examine the sample outputs for the two programs (Figures 3-7 and 3-11). The outputs were formatted to use only 72 spaces instead of the full width of the printer paper. The limit on output size made the output suitable for exhibits in the text without significant reduction in size. Also, the outputs fit easily on the lines of a visual display or terminal printer.

Use of Input and Output Layouts

The use of input and output layouts is illustrated for the payroll report program but not for the table of ordinates program. In many FORTRAN programs, the input and output is simple enough that layout forms are not needed. As output becomes more complex, layouts are useful, especially output layouts.

The layouts (such as Figures 3-1 and 3-2) allow the placement of data on input and output media to be identified. On output, it helps line up headings and data amounts. A useful convention followed by many programmers is to mark the maximum field to be occupied by each data item by 9s or X's. The 9s are used to indicate numeric digits. Decimal points are written at the position occupied on output. The X's indicate alphanumeric character output such as labels and headings.

Four very important points to remember in regard to input data as illustrated in the example programs are:

Figure 3-1 Input line layout for general program example 3—payroll reports.

INPUT LINE – GENERAL EXAMPLE 3 – PAYROLL

ID	EMPNME	HRSWRK	WGRATE	DEDUC	NOT USED
99999	XXXXXXXXXXXXX	9999	9999	99999	

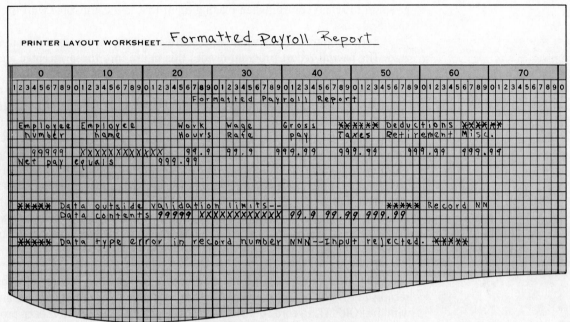

Figure 3-2 Layout for detail report for general program example 3—payroll reports.

1. Data items in FORMAT-directed input are not delineated by commas or blanks (as they were for the list-directed inputs of Chapters 1 and 2).

2. The input format for data items should be designed for ease of data entry. For example, if a text editor is being used for entering input records for a file, the input fields can be marked with tabs. Data entry starts at the beginning of the field. When the data item has been entered, the operator presses the TAB key to position entry at the beginning of the next field in the input format. Pressing the TAB twice will skip over a field (leaving it blank). Leaving spaces at the end of a field means that data entry of the next item does not begin until the operator presses the TAB key. This procedure is less error-prone than entering a continuous string of data items without any separation and reduces the probability of an error in one field affecting subsequent fields. In Figure 3-1, there are two spaces at the end of each field to provide for explicit TAB use to move to the next field after entering a data item.

3. Data items are assigned by the FORMAT statement to a specific set of positions on each line used for input. The data items must be placed in the assigned set of positions.

4. For real data, if the decimal point is entered with the input, it overrides the input format decimal point specification. A data item with a decimal point may be placed anywhere in the field assigned to it. Unused positions may be left blank.

Error-Control Features

Both programs use the END and ERR specifications in the input statement. With the END feature, an attempt to read input after the last data record transfers control to the statement number given by the END specification. This is an effective method to use when the number of inputs may vary. The ERR feature is used because it allows the program to retain control when reading input that is incompatible with the format specifications.

Both programs print a summary statement stating the number of input records read. The payroll report program divides this figure into those accepted and those rejected.

Note the use of error messages that print the contents of the record or identify the record number of an input data record that is in error. The error message for an input data item that does not meet the validation limit tests is instructive (see lines 82 to 84 in the payroll report program). Although the input data items are tested individually, only a single error output is used. The exact nature of the error is not specified. This approach is satisfactory for most fairly simple input validation. However, in more complex validation, it may be useful to have a separate error message for each error detected. The error message shows the output without any special formatting. The printing of the record contents (perhaps with spaces between data items) usually allows the error to be noted; an alternative is to label the parts of the input data being printed out.

The two programs illustrate the use of programmed error-control procedures. The END specification reduces the likelihood of an error in reading all input data records in a file. The ERR specification handles the case of input that is incompatible with the FORMAT. Record counts aid in verifying that all records have been processed. A missing data item in a set of input data can frequently be detected by testing for a zero value. The payroll program tests for missing numeric item values in input by testing for zero values for those formatted inputs that should not be zero. Testing for zero values is also important if the variable is used in a division operation. Error messages aid in correction of input errors.

General Program Example 3—Payroll Reports

Problem Description for General Example 3

Compute employee pay information for an unspecified number of employees (but less than 15), and print formatted output for each individual and a summary. Input consists of an employee's ID number, the employee's name (up to 12 characters long), hours worked, wage rate, and miscellaneous deductions. Hours worked in excess of 40 are paid at 1.5 times the regular rate. In addition to miscellaneous deductions, there are deductions for pension (5 percent of gross pay) and taxes (15 percent of gross pay). The total for all employees—hours worked, gross pay, taxes, retirement contributions, deductions, and net pay—are printed on a separate page following the last employee printout. Input data items are validated, including a test for missing (zero) numeric input items. Error messages are printed when errors are detected and invalid records are not processed.

Program Documentation for General Example 3

The documentation consists of an input layout (Figure 3-1), an output layout (Figure 3-2), a pseudocode description of the program (Figure 3-3), a program flowchart (Figure 3-4), a listing of the program (Figure 3-5), a list of input data used in testing the program (Figure 3-6), and a sample output (Figure 3-7) that includes program handling of error inputs.

Figure 3-3 Pseudocode description of general program example 3—payroll reports.

```
WRITE heading for employee data
Initialize counters and constants
READ an employee record
   IF (END) go to Summary
   IF (ERR) WRITE message, increment total record counter,
      increment not accepted record counter, and go back to READ
Increment total record counter
Validate input data
   Hours worked > 0.0 and ≤ 60.0
   Wage rate > 0.0 and ≤ 10.0
   Misc deductions ≥ 0.0 and ≤ 65.0
   IF invalid, print data validation message, increment not
      accepted record counter, and go back to READ employee record
   Else continue
Increment counter for valid records
Compute overtime hours
IF overtime hours
   Calculate gross pay with overtime at 1.5 times regular rate
ELSE
   Calculate gross pay at regular rate
Compute taxes and retirement contribution
Compute total deductions
Compute net pay
Update cumulative totals
WRITE detail for an employee
Test for negative net pay
   IF negative, print warning message
   Else continue
Go back to READ employee record
Summary
WRITE heading for summary
WRITE cumulative totals
WRITE number of valid, invalid, and total records
STOP
```

The input layout (Figure 3-1) is designed for planning and documenting the placement of the input data on an input line (and planning entry of input). Its use is optional because most FORTRAN programs have simple input. Note the use of the 9s and X's (as with output layout) to define the contents of the fields and the caret (^) to indicate the decimal location (if not entered).

The output layout (Figure 3-2) has already been mentioned. It is especially helpful in this case in laying out the headings and lining up the data under the headings. The two types of error messages are also shown on the layout. Layout forms usually have 132 to 140 positions horizontally; the layout form in Figure 3-2 has been trimmed to 80 positions because, as explained, the outputs in the text are all designed to fit on 72 positions.

The list of input data used to test the program is important documentation of the testing performed. At each change or correction in the program, the test data list provides a useful review of the prior testing, which can be expanded, if desired, and repeated with the changed program.

Figure 3-4 Program flowchart for general program example 3—payroll reports. (Numbers beside symbols refer to line numbers on program listing.)

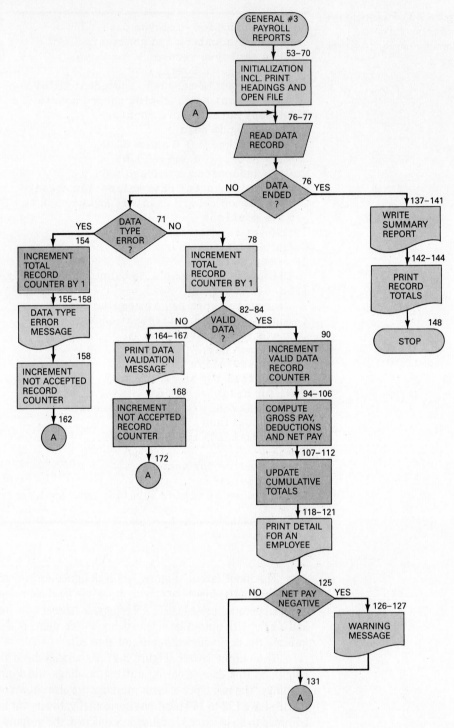

Test data items are designed to test each branch in a program. This requires three test data items for each branching instruction: the boundary value, the boundary value plus one, and the boundary value minus one. Negative and zero values should also be included in a test. Therefore, a complete set of test data items for program 3A will include the items described on page 179.

Figure 3-5 Listing of FORTRAN program for general program example 3—payroll reports.

```
 1 **********
 2 *                              PROGRAM IDENTIFICATION
 3 **********
 4 *
 5 *    Compute paychecks for employees and print formatted
 6 *    reports about individual pay amounts and company totals.
 7 *    Developed for file input (DATA3) and batch execution.
 8 *    Written by T. Hoffmann  4/22/77   rev. 1/06/82  3/14/87
 9 *
10 **********
11 *                              VARIABLES IDENTIFICATION
12 **********
13 *
14 *    ID      - Employee identification number
15 *    HRSWRK  - Total hours worked
16 *    GRSPAY  - Gross pay: $
17 *    WGRATE  - Wage rate: $/hour
18 *    PAYCHK  - Net paycheck amount: $
19 *    TAXES   - Taxes due: $
20 *    DEDUC   - Miscellaneous deductions
21 *    EMPNME  - Employee name (character)
22 *    OTIME   - Hours of overtime worked (excess over 40.0)
23 *    TDEDUC  - Total of all deductions by employee
24 *    RETIRE  - Retirement contribution by employee
25 *    TOTHRS  - Total hours worked by all employees
26 *    TOTRET  - Total retirement contribution by all employees
27 *    TOTPAY  - Total gross pay for company : $
28 *    TOTTAX  - Total taxes from all employees :$
29 *    TOTCKS  - Total of all paychecks
30 *    TOTDUC  - Total of all deductions
31 *    RECS    - Number of records read (integer)
32 *    NACEPT  - Number of error free records
33 *    NOTACP  - Number of not acceptable records
34 *
35 *****                         IDENTIFICATION OF CONSTANTS
36 *
37 *    PNRATE  = Pension contribution rate = 0.05
38 *    TAXRT   = Tax rate = 0.15
39 *
40 **********
41 *
42 **********                     TYPE DECLARATION AND STORAGE BLOCK
43 *
44       CHARACTER EMPNME*12
45       INTEGER RECS
46 *
47 **********
48 * BLOCK 0000                   INITIALIZATION BLOCK
49 **********
50 *
51 *                             PRINT HEADER/TITLE LINE
52 *
53       WRITE(6,2)
54    2 FORMAT(26X, 'Formatted Payroll Report' )
55       WRITE(6,3)
56    3 FORMAT('0',2('Employee '),5X,'Work  Wage',4X,'Gross',3X,6('*'),
57    1    ' Deductions ',6('*')/2X,'Number',4X,'Name',8X,'Hours',
58    2    '  Rate',5X,'Pay',4X,'Taxes  Retirement  Misc.')
59       PNRATE = 0.05
60       TAXRT = 0.15
61       NACEPT = 0
62       TOTPAY = 0.0
63       TOTTAX = 0.0
64       RECS = 0
65       TOTHRS = 0.0
66       TOTRET = 0.0
67       TOTCKS = 0.0
68       TOTDUC = 0.0
69       NOTACP = 0
70       OPEN(7,FILE='DATA3')
71 *
```

Figure 3-5 continued

```
 72 **********
 73 * BLOCK 0100          READ AND VALIDATE EMPLOYEE DATA
 74 **********
 75 *
 76 101 READ(7,102,END=401,ERR=901) ID,EMPNME,HRSWRK,WGRATE,DEDUC
 77 102 FORMAT(I5,2X,A12,2X,F4.1,2X,F4.2,2X,F5.2)
 78     RECS = RECS + 1
 79 *
 80 *                     VALIDATE INPUT DATA
 81 *
 82     IF(HRSWRK .LE. 0.0 .OR. HRSWRK .GT. 60.0) GOTO 910
 83     IF(WGRATE .LE. 0.0 .OR. WGRATE .GT. 10.0) GOTO 910
 84     IF(DEDUC .LT. 0.0 .OR. DEDUC .GT. 65.0) GOTO 910
 85 *
 86 **********
 87 * BLOCK 0200          COMPUTE GROSS AND NET PAY
 88 **********
 89 *
 90     NACEPT = NACEPT + 1
 91 *
 92 *                     COMPUTE OVERTIME, IF ANY
 93 *
 94     OTIME = HRSWRK - 40.0
 95     IF(OTIME .GT. 0.0) THEN
 96             GRSPAY = WGRATE*(40.0 + 1.5*OTIME)
 97        ELSE
 98             GRSPAY = HRSWRK*WGRATE
 99     ENDIF
100 *
101 *          COMPUTE EACH TYPE OF DEDUCTION AND NET PAY TOTALS
102 *
103     TAXES = TAXRT*GRSPAY
104     RETIRE = PNRATE*GRSPAY
105     TDEDUC = DEDUC + TAXES + RETIRE
106     PAYCHK = GRSPAY - TDEDUC
107     TOTPAY = TOTPAY + GRSPAY
108     TOTTAX = TOTTAX + TAXES
109     TOTHRS = TOTHRS + HRSWRK
110     TOTRET = TOTRET + RETIRE
111     TOTDUC = TOTDUC + TDEDUC
112     TOTCKS = TOTCKS + PAYCHK
113 *
114 **********
115 * BLOCK 0300          PRINT DETAIL
116 **********
117 *
118     WRITE(6,301) ID,EMPNME,HRSWRK,WGRATE,GRSPAY,TAXES,RETIRE,DEDUC
119 301 FORMAT('0',2X,I5,2X,A12,F7.1,F6.2,1X,2F8.2,1X,2(3X,F6.2))
120     WRITE(6,304) PAYCHK
121 304 FORMAT(' Net pay equals',6X,F6.2)
122 *
123 *                     CHECK FOR VALID PAYCHECK AMOUNT
124 *
125     IF(PAYCHK .LE. 0.0) WRITE(6,303)
126 303 FORMAT('+',28X,'Net pay is not positive.',
127 1               ' Do not issue check')
128 *
129 *                     GO BACK AND READ ANOTHER EMPLOYEE RECORD
130 *
131     GOTO 101
132 *
133 **********
134 * BLOCK 0400          PRINT SUMMARY AND TERMINATE
135 **********
136 *
137 401 WRITE(6,402) TOTHRS,TOTPAY,TOTTAX,TOTRET,TOTDUC,TOTCKS
138 402 FORMAT('1','*****',18X,'Summary Totals',17X,5('*')/
139 1     ' Hours',4X,'Gross    Taxes    Retirement    Deductions',
140 2     2X,'Paychecks'/' Worked',4X,'Pay',11X,'Contribution'/
141 3     '0',F6.2,2F8.2,5X,F5.2,2X,2(6X,F6.2))
142     WRITE(6,403) NACEPT,NOTACP,RECS
143 403 FORMAT(//10X,'Records accepted',I3,5X,'Records rejected',I3/
144 1    10X,'Total records',I4)
145 *
146 *                     NORMAL TERMINATION
147 *
148     STOP
```

Figure 3-5 concluded

```
149  *
150  **********
151  * BLOCK 0900          ERROR MESSAGE BLOCK
152  **********
153  *
154  901 RECS = RECS + 1
155      WRITE(6,902) RECS
156  902 FORMAT(//' ***** Data type error in record number',I3,
157     1    '--Input rejected. *****')
158      NOTACP = NOTACP + 1
159  *
160  *               GO BACK AND READ ANOTHER EMPLOYEE RECORD
161  *
162      GOTO 101
163  *
164  910 WRITE(6,911) RECS,ID,EMPNME,HRSWRK,WGRATE,DEDUC
165  911 FORMAT('0','***** Data outside validation limits--input ',
166     1    'rejected ***** record',I3/7X,'Data contents ',
167     2    I5,2X,A12,2X,F5.1,2X,F5.2,2X,F6.2/)
168      NOTACP = NOTACP + 1
169  *
170  *               GO BACK AND READ ANOTHER EMPLOYEE RECORD
171  *
172      GOTO 101
173  *
174      END
```

1. Test for proper handling of end of data. This will be done without additional coding by checking the execution of a set of records.
2. Test for proper handling of data-type error. This will be performed by entering a test record with alphabetic characters as the employee number (ID).
3. Test for valid data:
   (a) Hours worked (HRSWRK) of:
       (1)   0.0 (invalid) ⎫ Zero and negative
       (2) −1.0 (invalid) ⎭
       (3) 60.0 (valid) ⎫
       (4) 59.9 (valid) ⎬ Boundary value ± 0.1
       (5) 60.1 (invalid) ⎭
   (b) Wage rate (WGRATE) of:
       (1)   0.0 (invalid) ⎫ Zero and negative
       (2) −10. (invalid) ⎭
       (3) 10.0 (valid) ⎫
       (4)   9.99 (valid) ⎬ Boundary value ± 0.01
       (5) 10.01 (invalid) ⎭
   (c) Miscellaneous deductions (DEDUCT) of:
       (1)   0.0 (valid) ⎫ Zero and negative
       (2) −0.1 (invalid) ⎭
       (3) 65.00 (valid) ⎫
       (4) 64.99 (valid) ⎬ Boundary value ± 0.01
       (5) 65.01 (invalid) ⎭
4. Test for overtime computation:
   (a) Hours worked (HRSWRK) = 39.9 (no overtime) ⎫
   (b) Hours worked = 40.0 (no overtime) ⎬ Boundary value ± 0.1
   (c) Hours worked = 40.1 (overtime) ⎭
5. Test for zero and negative paycheck. Use hours worked, pay rate, and miscellaneous deductions that will provide a net paycheck amount (PAYCHK) of:
   (a) 0.0
   (b) Negative

```
ID       NAME           HRS    RATE   DEDUC  PURPOSE OR EXPECTED OUTPUT
-----    --------------  ----   ----   -----  ------------------------------------
23456    T. HOFFMANN    40.0   3.57   27.95  Valid.  Net pay should be $6.29
15786    RALPH JONES    39.9   6.28   24.68  Valid.  Gross pay should be $250.57
15968    W. RONG        14.4   2)KM   45.68  Error.  Nonnumeric data in numeric field
36985    J. JOHNSON     22.0   0275   03598  Valid.  Format sets decimal point for
                                                     deductions.
JKLUI    ONA                                  Error.  Nonnumeric data in numeric field.
69852    T. NAMAN       10.0   2.67   27.50  Valid.  Net pay negative.
35748    L. SMITH       40.1   9.94   30.68  Valid.  Gross pay equals $399.09.
62475    F. MORLOCK     37.7   8.24   65.34  Error.  Deductions greater than 65.00


                                             Five records accepted.
                                             Three records rejected.
```

Figure 3-6 Input test data with purposes noted for general program example 3.

Figure 3-7 Sample output for general program example 3—detail and summary payroll report.

DETAIL OUTPUT

```
                          Formatted Payroll Report

Employee Employee       Work   Wage   Gross   ****** Deductions ******
 Number   Name          Hours  Rate    Pay    Taxes  Retirement  Misc.

  23456   T. HOFFMANN   40.0   3.57   142.80  21.42     7.14     27.95
Net pay equals        86.29

  15786   RALPH JONES   39.9   6.28   250.57  37.59    12.53     24.68
Net pay equals       175.78


***** Data type error in record number  3--Input rejected. *****

  36985   J. JOHNSON    22.0   2.75    60.50   9.08     3.03     35.98
Net pay equals        12.42


***** Data type error in record number  5--Input rejected. *****

  69852   T. NAMAN      10.0   2.67    26.70   4.01     1.34     27.50
Net pay equals        -6.14  Net pay is not positive. Do not issue check

  35748   L. SMITH      40.1   9.94   399.09  59.86    19.95     30.68
Net pay equals       288.59

***** Data outside validation limits--input rejected ***** record  8
       Data contents 62475  F. MORLOCK      37.7   8.24   65.34
```

SUMMARY OUTPUT

```
*****               Summary Totals           *****
Hours    Gross    Taxes  Retirement   Deductions  Paychecks
Worked    Pay             Contribution

152.00  879.66  131.95     43.98       322.72      556.94


        Records accepted  5    Records rejected  3
        Total records     8
```

In other words, a complete test of this very small program requires at least 21 different sets of input data. It is understandable why it is difficult to completely test very large programs. Even for small programs, a smaller set of test data may be used, focusing on the most significant error possibilities. The test data items in Figure 3-6 are not a complete set; they only illustrate how to set up a test data list with expected output defined for each.

Notes on General Example 3

The usual identification blocks are present. The computational section has been divided into six logical blocks with block numbers. In the initialization section, printing the detail report heading is done first. This also has advantages for debugging, since it is useful to have some output from a program as early as possible to provide an indication that the program has compiled and begun execution.

The variable RECS has been created to keep count of the total records read. This assists in locating erroneous input records and in ensuring that all records which were intended to be processed have been processed by comparing the final count to the intended value. The initial value and the locations of the increment instructions for the counter must be carefully considered. Note that this is done right after reading the record (line 78), but if there is a data error, the ERR specification causes a transfer and this line is never reached. Therefore, the counter is alternatively incremented with statement 901 at line 154 just before the data error printout. Separate counters are also kept for not accepted and accepted records.

Updating the totals could be done before or after the printing of the pay information. However, grouping the computations in a block makes the program more readable and easier to debug.

Output formatting can be a very lengthy and tedious job. It is often useful to print lines of asterisks or other symbols as part of output, but writing out long lines of them in FORMAT statements can be time-consuming and error-prone. An alternative is the use of repetition counts. The following are equivalent methods for programming a set of five asterisks to be printed on an output line:

```
FORMAT (' ', '*****')
FORMAT (' ', 5('*'))
```

There is an illustration of the use of a repeat for asterisks in the example payroll program. In FORMAT statement 3 at line 57, the specification 6 ('*') is used to output ******. The heading "Employee" which is repeated is written with a repetition specification. See line 56 for the 2('Employee ') specification.

There are several examples of vertical and horizontal spacing in the payroll program. Note that the program is written for a printer that responds to vertical spacing characters in format position 1. Some personal computer printers do not. The examples include top of page, double-line spacing, starting a new line, single spacing, and no spacing (overprinting).

Top of page　The second report of the two payroll reports should begin on a new page of paper, that is, at the top of a page. In FORMAT statement 402 at line 138, the top of page is specified by a '1' in format position 1.

Spacing between print lines　Two alternative methods are illustrated for spacing, inserting blank lines between printed lines:

1. In FORMAT statements 403 at line 143 and 902 at line 156, two slashes are used before output to create two blank lines. In statement 911 at line 167, a blank line is specified after printing by a slash at the end of the format.
2. In FORMAT statements 3 at line 56, 301 at line 119, 402 at line 141, and 911 at line 165, a '0' is placed in format position 1 to obtain double spacing.

Starting a new line   More than one line of output is specified in the format list by a slash. This is illustrated in FORMAT statement 402 at lines 138–141 in which three lines of headings, double spacing, and a line of output are all specified by a single FORMAT statement. To separate the lines, a slash specification is placed in the format list each time there is to be a new physical record (new line).

Single spacing   The normal spacing is for the printer to move one vertical space at the beginning of a format specification. This occurs if column 1 of the format contains a space (blank). When using a single FORMAT statement to produce multiple lines, it is important to make sure the first position of each new line is blank. This is illustrated in FORMAT statement 402 at lines 138–141. Note the beginning of each new line (statement lines 139 and 140) contains a blank. When the position of the output guarantees that position 1 is blank, there is no need to have an explicit blank. This is illustrated in FORMAT statement 2 at line 54 in which the first 26 columns are skipped which guarantees position one is blank.

Printing on the same line   In FORMAT statement 303 at line 126, the message is to be printed on the same line (overprinted). A plus sign is used in format position 1 to specify no advance of the paper, which results in printing on the same line used by the prior print statement.

Positioning a heading   The report heading is to start in column 27. In FORMAT statement 2 at line 54, this is specified by a skip specification to skip over 26 columns. This could also have been programmed as T27 (to tab to and start in column 27).

The problem of rounding with the format on output is illustrated in this program. The payroll detail is printed out as dollars and cents using a format with two places to the right of the decimal point. The printed totals are the same as the sum of the individual outputs rounded at printing except for total taxes. The rounding difference is not corrected in this simple program. An approach to correcting this type of rounding error situation is described in Chapter 5. The sum of the individual taxes as printed is 131.96, whereas the total is shown as 131.95. The difference arises from rounding individual amounts but summing unrounded amounts for the total as follows:

Unrounded taxes (gross pay × 0.15)	Rounded output
21.42|00	21.42
37.58|55	37.59
9.07|50	9.08
4.00|50	4.01
59.86|35	59.86
Total 131.94|90	131.96
Outputs 131.95	

Mathematical Program Example 3—Tables of Ordinates of the Normal Curve

Background Explanation for Mathematical Example 3

The normal curve is a bell-shaped symmetrical curve which describes the frequency distribution for large numbers of phenomena in nature and in scientific experiments. It is important in statistical analysis because many statistical techniques rely upon an assumption of a normal distribution of the characteristics being sampled, tested, etc. The x-axis, or abscissa, for a normal curve is a standardized value representing the number of standard deviations around the average for the characteristic being studied (ages, heights, weights, etc.). The standard deviations have a midpoint value at 0.0 with 99.9 percent values occurring in the range from 3.0 to -3.0. The ordinates, or y values, of the normal curve represent the height of the normal curve for any given x value. Because the normal curve is symmetrical, the y value is identical for the same positive or negative value of x.

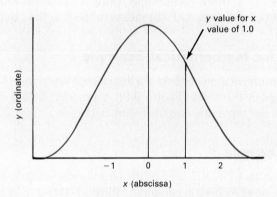

The value of the ordinate y is not useful by itself. It will be useful in calculating areas under the normal curve (in Chapter 4b). Therefore, the main value of this program to calculate a table of ordinates of the normal curve is to introduce the concept of the normal curve and how the ordinates can be calculated for any x value. Since the calculation of the ordinates will be required in order to calculate the area under the normal curve, it may be useful to look ahead and consider why it is important to be able to calculate the areas. In many problems in statistical analysis, it is necessary to calculate the percentage of occurrences that are less than or greater than an x value. For example, in a study of human height, it may be useful to calculate what percentage of humans have a height greater than 6 ft. It is also required in some analyses to calculate the percentage of the normal curve that occurs between two values of the characteristic. For example, in a study of weights of individuals, it may be necessary to calculate the percentage of individuals whose weight is between 110 and 130 lb.

A table of ordinates of the normal curve represents the y values for a given set of x values. The x values represent standard deviations around the mean. Therefore, the x values should be in the range from 4.0 to -4.0 and in most cases will be between 3.0 and -3.0.

Problem Description for Mathematical Example 3

Produce formatted tables of the ordinates of the normal curve based upon interactive input of an initial x value, an incremental value for x, and number of entries desired. Validate input data for number of entries not zero, negative, or greater than 20. Use END and ERR specifications. Terminate the program execution based on a response to a query.

The formula for calculating the ordinates, or y values, for the normal curve is

$$y = \frac{1}{\sqrt{2\pi}} \, e^{-x^2/2}$$

where y = the ordinate for a given value of x

       x = the value on the abscissa expressed in terms of standard deviations around the mean value of zero

    2π = 6.2832; the approximate value of π (3.1416) will be used in this program

      e = the base of the natural logarithms

In FORTRAN, this is programmed using the function EXP for the exponential function. In other words, EXP (B) means to use B as the exponent for the value of e.

Program Documentation for Mathematical Example 3

The documentation consists of a pseudocode description of the program (Figure 3-8), a program flowchart (Figure 3-9), a program listing (Figure 3-10), and sample interactive input and output (Figure 3-11).

Notes on Mathematical Example 3

The constant PIROOT used in the formula was computed using the SQRT function. The value of 2π used in computing PIROOT (that is, 6.2832) is not used elsewhere in the program, so no variable name was assigned to it (see line 37).

The program illustrates issues in the design of interactive programs. There is a clear, unambiguous message asking for each of the inputs required for the program (lines 44–49). The END = specification is included in the READ statement at line 45 and the ERR = in the one at line 49. Since the program is terminated by an explicit response to a question as to whether more tables are to be computed, the END = specification is not likely to be activated. However, from a terminal or a personal computer, it is usually possible to press one or more keys to indicate an end to a session. An end-of-session keystroke instead of a regular input at line 45 will probably activate the END = specification. The ERR = is activated by input of data that does not match the type of the variable in the READ statement. When there is an error in input data, the program can reject the entire set of data and start over or only reject the item in error and ask for a new input of that item. Rejecting only the input in error is illustrated for a data-type error for number of lines in the table (see lines 88–89 and 93). After the error message, the program returns to request the number of table lines again be entered. The rejection of the entire set of data is illustrated by how the program responds when the input value for the table length exceeds the limits of the program (line 53). There is an error message, and the program then institutes the end-of-program question (see lines 95–97 and 101). If another table is to be computed, the program starts at the beginning (lines 78–82).

Figure 3-8 Pseudocode description of mathematical program example 3—tables of ordinates of normal curve.

```
Initialize constants
PRINT request for beginning X value and READ it
IF no input data, STOP
ELSE continue
PRINT request for increment size and READ it
PRINT request for number of lines in table and READ it
Check for noninteger number of lines
IF noninteger data, PRINT error message
    PRINT error message
    Go to PRINT request for number
ELSE continue
Test for valid input data for number of values—not zero, negative,
    or ≥ 20
IF input data for number of values to compute not valid
    Print error message and GO to check for more problems
ELSE
    Continue
WRITE problem title
Initialize step counter to one
IF step counter greater than NVALUS
    Go to check for more problems
ELSE
    Compute ordinate Y
    WRITE X, Y
    Increment X by X increment and step counter by one
    GO back to IF step counter
Check for more problems
IF none
    STOP
ELSE
    Go back to PRINT request for beginning X
```

An issue in program design is how much to specify in the request. The program only accepts a table size from 1 to 20, but the input request does not give this information. A complete input request might include the specifications (including the fact that it had to be an integer value). On the other hand, the program "teaches" the user through the error message if the limit on lines is exceeded. The input of x value is an illustration of expectations about user expertise. There is nothing in the request that gives reasonable limits to a beginning x value. If the program is being used by knowledgeable people, the x value limits would add unnecessary verbiage to the request; if the users are neophytes, the limits might be very useful.

Even though the interactive session provides a question and a recording of the data entered in response, an additional error control is to provide a heading to the output that echoes the input data. This is done in the table heading. The initial x value is echoed as well as the increment. The number of table lines is used to calculate an ending value for the table, thus providing another check for the user of the program.

The inputs to the program are list-directed. As noted previously, this mode is favored for interactive input. The outputs, on the other hand, are programmed using FORMAT statements to give a more readable output. Note the use of // at the beginning of FORMAT statements 110 and 113 (lines 56–57 and 59) to double-space before the

Figure 3-9 Program flowchart for mathematical program example 3—tables of ordinates of normal curve. (Numbers beside symbols refer to line numbers on program listing.)

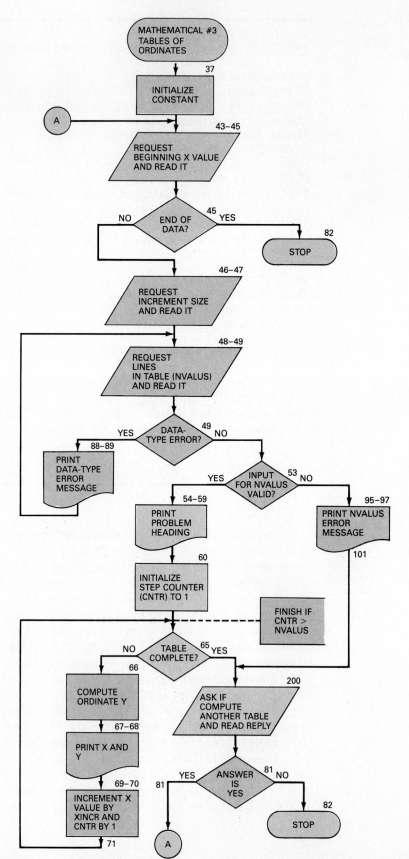

Figure 3-10 Listing of FORTRAN program for mathematical program example 3—tables of ordinates of normal curve.

```
 1 **********
 2 *                       PROGRAM IDENTIFICATION
 3 **********
 4 *
 5 *      Calculate tables of ordinates of the normal curve.
 6 *      Developed for keyboard input and interactive execution.
 7 *      Written by T. Hoffmann 05/03/77 rev. 01/06/82    03/09/87
 8 *
 9 **********
10 *                       VARIABLES IDENTIFICATION
11 **********
12 *
13 *      NVALUS  - Number of values to compute
14 *      CNTR    - Counter to record number of values computed
15 *      XVALU   - Value of X to use in computation of YVALU
16 *      YVALU   - Value of the ordinate corresponding to XVALU
17 *      XINCR   - Increment of X
18 *      EVALU   - Last value of X in table of ordinates
19 *      REPLY   - Y or N answer to input query
20 *
21 *****                   IDENTIFICATION OF CONSTANTS
22 *
23 *      PIROOT  - Reciprocal of the square root of two pi (6.2832)
24 *
25 **********
26 *                       TYPE DECLARATION AND STORAGE BLOCK
27 **********
28 *
29        CHARACTER REPLY*1
30        INTEGER CNTR,NVALUS
31        REAL XVALU,YVALU,XINCR,PIROOT,EVALU
32 *
33 **********
34 * BLOCK 0000        INITIALIZATION BLOCK
35 **********
36 *
37        PIROOT = 1.0/SQRT (6.2832)
38 *
39 **********
40 * BLOCK 0100        READ - COMPUTE - PRINT BLOCK
41 **********
42 *
43 101 PRINT *
44        PRINT *, 'What is the beginning X value? '
45        READ (5,*,END=205) XVALU
46        PRINT *, 'What should be the increment size? '
47        READ *, XINCR
48 107 PRINT *, 'How many lines in the table? '
49        READ (5,*,ERR=901) NVALUS
50 *
51 *                       TEST FOR VALID TABLE LENGTH
52 *
53        IF(NVALUS .LE. 0 .OR. NVALUS .GT. 20) GOTO 910
54        EVALU = XVALU + XINCR*FLOAT(NVALUS-1)
55        WRITE(6,110) XVALU,EVALU,XINCR
56 110 FORMAT(//,7X,'Tables of Ordinates of the Normal Curve'/
57      1    3X,'From ',F6.2,' to ',F6.2,' in increments of ',F5.1)
58        WRITE(6,113)
59 113 FORMAT(//15X,'X Value',4X,'Y Value')
60        CNTR = 1
61 *
62 *                       IF NVALUS NOT COMPUTED, CALCULATE NEXT ORDINATE.
63 *                       IF THEY HAVE BEEN, THEN CHECK FOR NEW TABLE
64 *
65 124 IF(CNTR .GT. NVALUS) GOTO 200
66        YVALU = PIROOT*EXP(-XVALU*XVALU/2.0)
67        WRITE(6,125) XVALU,YVALU
68 125 FORMAT(16X,F6.2,5X,F6.4)
69        XVALU = XVALU + XINCR
70        CNTR = CNTR + 1
71        GOTO 124
72 *
```

Figure 3-10 continued

```
73 **********
74 * BLOCK 0200        TERMINATION BLOCK
75 **********
76 *
77 200 PRINT *
78     PRINT *, 'Compute another table(Y/N)? '
79     READ (5,201) REPLY
80 201 FORMAT(A)
81     IF ( REPLY .EQ. 'Y' .OR. REPLY .EQ. 'y' ) GOTO 101
82 205 STOP
83 *
84 **********
85 * BLOCK 0900        ERROR MESSAGE BLOCK
86 **********
87 *
88 901 WRITE(6,902)
89 902 FORMAT(/,' Data Error. Number of lines must be integer. ')
90 *
91 *                   GO BACK TO RE-READ NUMBER OF LINES IN THE TABLE
92 *
93       GOTO 107
94 *
95 910 WRITE(6,911)
96 911 FORMAT(//'***** Data limit error for number of values *****'/7X,
97    1   'Number of Table Lines Must be Between 1 and 20 inclusive.')
98 *
99 *                   GO BACK AND ASK WHETHER TO COMPUTE ANOTHER TABLE
100 *
101       GOTO 200
102 *
103       END
```

output line. After the table headings are output, each computation of y is printed along with the corresponding x value (lines 67–68).

The calculation of the values for the table is repeated until the table is complete. To find out if the table is complete, a counter is established (CNTR in line 60) which is incremented after a y value is calculated and a line printed (line 70); it is tested against the number of values to be calculated (an input) before calculating a new y value (line 65).

This program again illustrates the fact that disciplined, well-documented programs require many lines of program code beyond the basic computations. For example, in this program of 103 lines:

63 lines are comment lines to clearly document the program.
24 lines perform the basic input/computation/output.
 8 lines are associated with error control.
 8 lines are used to provide labeled, spaced output.

Programming Exercises

Description of Assignment

Select one or more problems (or take the problems assigned to you by the instructor). Write the program including the following features.

1. A heading for the output.
2. Labels and/or headings on lines of output.
3. Use END, if available, to control program transfer at end of data input from a file, or use a termination query reply for interactive input.
4. Data validation with error message. Include some form of printout of input data.

Figure 3-11 Example of interactive input and output for mathematical program example 3—tables of ordinates of the normal curve.

```
What is the beginning X value? -1.4

What should be the increment size? 0.7

How many lines in the table? 8

          Tables of Ordinates of the Normal Curve
   From  -1.40 to   3.50 in increments of   0.7


            X Value      Y Value
            -1.40        0.1497
            -0.70        0.3123
             0.00        0.3989
             0.70        0.3123
             1.40        0.1497
             2.10        0.0440
             2.80        0.0079
             3.50        0.0009

Compute another table(Y/N)? Y


What is the beginning X value? -2.7

What should be the increment size? 0.7

How many lines in the table? 212


**** Data limit error for number of values *****
      Number of Table Lines Must be Between 1 and 20 inclusive.

Compute another table(Y/N)? Y


What is the beginning X value? -2.7

What should be the increment size? 0.7

How many lines in the table? 12



          Tables of Ordinates of the Normal Curve
   From  -2.70 to   5.00 in increments of    0.7


            X Value      Y Value
            -2.70        0.0104
            -2.00        0.0540
            -1.30        0.1714
            -0.60        0.3332
             0.10        0.3970
             0.80        0.2897
             1.50        0.1295
             2.20        0.0355
             2.90        0.0060
             3.60        0.0006
             4.30        0.0000
             5.00        0.0000
Compute another table(Y/N)? N
```

(Alternative: Rather than rejecting some data, you may wish to accept the data and give a warning message.)

5. Error message for data-type error. Include record number. If ERR is not available on your compiler, omit this step as well as the test data item with a data-type error.

6. If file input is used, keep a record count. Print it at the end of the program. If appropriate, print a separate count for accepted and rejected items.

7. Identify data values for a complete set of test data. Test the program using all test data items (or if large, using a subset that performs critical tests).

Mathematics and Statistics

1. The natural logarithm (base e) of X can be approximated by the following series:

$$\log_e(X) = \frac{X-1}{X} + \frac{1}{2}\left(\frac{X-1}{X}\right)^2 + \frac{1}{3}\left(\frac{X-1}{X}\right)^3 + \cdots$$

Prepare a table for $X = 0.5, 2.0, 6.0$, and π that compares the computed series value for the first 20 items with the values from the ALOG intrinsic function. The table format should be as follows:

```
          SERIES VS. INTRINSIC FUNCTION
             FOR NATURAL LOGARITHM

X              SERIES      FUNCTION      DIFFERENCE
               VALUE       VALUE

  .50000

 2.00000

 6.00000

 3.14159
```

2. The following formulas describe properties of portions of circles, with radius r and central angle θ in degrees.

$$\text{Area} = \pi r^2$$

$$\text{Length of arc} = \frac{\pi r \theta}{180}$$

$$\text{Length of chord} = 2r \sin \tfrac{1}{2}\theta$$

$$\text{Area of segment} = \frac{\pi r^2 \theta}{360} - \frac{r^2 \sin \theta}{2}$$

Prepare a table giving each of these properties for input data values for r and θ as follows:

r	θ
10.0	65
5.0	97
12.4	134
15.2	12

The table should have the following headings for the outputs:

```
                      PROPERTIES OF CIRCLES
                        LENGTH      LENGTH     AREA OF
   R       THETA    AREA   OF ARC    OF CHORD   SEGMENT
```

3. The sum of the first N numbers is $N(N + 1)/2$. The sum of the squares of the first N numbers is

$$\frac{N(N + 1)(2N + 1)}{6}$$

The sum of the cubes of the first N numbers is

$$\frac{N^2(N + 1)^2}{4}$$

For values of N of 3, 7, 10, 12, and 13, prepare a table of these three sums in the following format:

```
N                 SUM               SUM OF           SUM OF
                                    SQUARES          CUBES
```

Business and Economics

4. The annual payment p to repay a loan of b dollars for t years at an interest rate of i percent is given by

$$p = b\,\frac{i(1 + i)^t}{(1 + i)^t - 1}$$

Prepare a repayment table of the following form showing the payment, interest, and loan balance for each of three loans:

```
        REPAYMENT SCHEDULE FOR LOAN OF $ XXXX
          AT A RATE OF XX PERCENT FOR XX YEARS
               ANNUAL PAYMENT IS $ XXXX.XX

   PAYMENT      INTEREST     PRINCIPLE     BALANCE
   NUMBER                                  DUE
```

The data items to be used are:

Loan amount	Interest rate (%)	Length of repayment period
$ 10,000	12	7
100,000	14	12
50,000	16.5	4

Note: The annual interest due is computed on the outstanding balance before the payment.

5. As transactions are received by a bank, they are entered as to transaction type (D for deposit and W for withdrawal), amount, and account number. The following four accounts exist:

Account number	Beginning balance
3201	$ 652.87
4331	127.95
1604	6043.80
1134	1097.81

The entry records have the following format:

Record columns	
1	Transaction type
2–10	Amount
11–15	Account number

Read in the following input data:

W	250.17	3201
D	458.24	4331
W	1265.86	1604
W	27.18	3201
S	784.33	1134
D	685.32	3201
W	537.00	4331
D	16.84	1134
W	484.39	1604
W	127.45	1134

Prepare a report showing invalid transactions and summarizing for each account the ending balance and the number of each type of transaction. *Hint:* A character data item can be compared with a character constant, for example, IF(CODE .EQ. 'W') THEN. . . .

```
                         TRANSACTION SUMMARY

INVALID TRANSACTIONS    [If none, print a line saying so.]

ACCOUNT SUMMARY

ACCOUNT          BEGINNING          NUMBER OF          ENDING
NUMBER           BALANCE            TRANSACTIONS       BALANCE
```

Referring to problem 6 in Chapter 2, assume the input data is in the following format:

Input columns	Item
1–4	Salesperson number
5–14	Salesperson name
15–18	Sales goal
19–22	Actual sales
23–24	Blank
25–30	Bonus factor

Prepare a report in the following form:

```
                        SALES COMMISSION REPORT

NAME OF                 PERCENT OF
SALESPERSON             GOAL ATTAINED           COMMISSION
```

Note: Remember to print message "FAILED TO MEET GOAL" if a person fell short of the stated goal. Also check for invalid input.

Science and Engineering

7. Air pressure p declines as altitude h increases. The approximate relationship is

$$p = 14.6 \times 10^{-0.0164h}$$

where p is expressed in pounds per square inch and h in thousands of feet. Prepare a table of this function for h values of 4, 10, 35, 70, and 100.

```
   HEIGHT            PRESSURE
(1000 OF FT.)    (LBS./SQ. FT.)
      4.0
     10.0
     35.0
     70.0
    100.0
```

8. A projectile fired at an angle θ given an initial velocity of v_0 will travel a distance r according to the following formula:

$$r = \frac{v_0^2 \sin 2\theta}{g}$$

where g is the acceleration constant of 32 ft/s². It will be in motion for a time t given by

$$t = \frac{2v_0 \sin \theta}{g}$$

and reach a maximum height h of

$$h = \frac{v_0^2 \sin \theta}{g}$$

For all angles from 20 to 70 degrees in 10-degree increments and initial velocities of 200, 400, and 1000 ft/sec, produce tables of the following form:

```
       PROJECTILE CHARACTERISTICS

   (INITIAL VELOCITY EQUALS 200. FT/SEC)

ANGLE        RANGE        TIME        HEIGHT
```

9. Produce a table showing the weight of cylindrical drums produced out of materials of various types and thicknesses. The area is obtained from the formula

Area $= 2\pi r(r + h)$ $r =$ radius; $h =$ height

The drums are from 2.5 to 3.5 ft in diameter in half-foot increments, and the height is 4.5 ft. The specifications for material are:

Material	Thickness	Weight, lb/ft²
Steel	0.0908 in	3.70
Brass	0.0908 in	3.884
Copper	0.0908 in	4.110
Steel	0.0201 in	0.820
Brass	0.0201 in	0.860
Copper	0.0201 in	0.910

Assume input in the following format:

Column	Contents
1–15	Material
16–20	Blank
21–25	Weight

Produce output as shown below:

```
            WEIGHT OF CYLINDRICAL DRUMS
               4.5 FEET HIGH

                     DIAMETER (FEET)
MATERIAL             2.5      3.0      3.5

STEEL .0908"

BRASS .0908"

COPPER .0908"

STEEL .0201"

BRASS .0201"

COPPER .0201"
```

Humanities and Social Sciences

10. Each degree of latitude represents approximately 68.84 miles. For each of the towns, given the input data, compute how far north of the equator it is and produce a tabular output:

```
     DISTANCE FROM EQUATOR
       FOR SELECTED CITIES

CITY                MILES
```

Use the following data:

City	North latitude
London	51°30′
Minneapolis	44°58′
Honolulu	21°18′
Cairo	30°31′
Fairbanks	64°50′
New York City	40°40′

Assume input in the following format:

Column	Contents
1–22	City name
23–25	Blank
26–27	Latitude (degrees)
28	Blank
29–30	Latitude (minutes)

11. A transition matrix shows the percentage of people of each class who will switch to the other classes or remain in their own each year. An example is switching political parties.

Party	Republican	Democrat	Independent
Republican	0.5	0.1	0.4
Democrat	0.1	0.6	0.3
Independent	0.2	0.2	0.6

Given that the system starts with 1000 Republicans, 1500 Democrats, and 2000 Independents, prepare a table for the next 10 years showing the number of each type. Assume an input format (one input per line of matrix):

Column	Contents
1–15	Party
16–20	Blank
21–23	Percentages (no decimal points)

Produce an output report:

```
              PARTY MEMBERSHIP BY YEARS

YEAR   REPUBLICANS   DEMOCRATS   INDEPENDENTS

 0        1000         1500         2000
 1        1050         1400         2050
 2
 3
 4
 5
 6
 7
 8
 9
10
```

12. Personalized letters are desired to increase participation in a political survey. The input consists of names and addresses, and the output is a personalized letter. Assume the following output:

```
Mr. & Mrs. _____name_____

_____street address_____

_____city, state_____

Dear Mr. & Mrs. _____name_____

      You have been selected as representative of the people in

___city___ to assist us in determining public sentiment toward

the federal budget. The ___name___ family, we feel, as citizens

of ___state___ will want to have a part in this important project.
```

Prepare a program to write such letters using the following input data:

Jones	1838 W. Vliet Street	Madison, Wisconsin
Smith	125 E. 75 Avenue	Kansas City, Kansas
Johnson	4501 S. Custar Road	St. Paul, Minnesota
Alvarez	3286 N. 125 Street	Seattle, Washington
Vilas	5101 E. Ontario Blvd.	Miami, Florida

Assume an input format:

Column	Contents
1–10	Name
11–15	Blank
16–40	Street address
41–45	Blank
46–57	City
58–68	State

General

13. A professor must prepare a grade report in the following format:

```
PROFESSOR:
    your name

                              DATE: today's date
             STUDENT GRADE REPORT

                  FINAL      FINAL      COURSE
STUDENT NAME      EXAM       SCORE      GRADE
```

Student grades are entered to a file or interactively in the following format:

Column	Entry
1–20	Name
21–25	Quiz 1 grade
26–30	Quiz 2 grade
31–35	Homework grade
36–40	Final exam grade

The final score = 0.2(quiz 1) + 0.2(quiz 2) + 0.3(homework) + 0.3(final exam). Letter grades are assigned as follows:

Final score	Letter grade
0–49	F
50–59	D
60–79	C
80–89	B
90–100	A

For the following set of students and grades, prepare a common grade report.

Name	Quiz 1	Quiz 2	Homework	Final exam
J. C. Johnson	90	85	95	93
L. W. Juergens	82	65	88	84
C. B. Smile	75	70	83	71
L. W. Thatcher	80	69	74	74

14. A company has a fleet of many different automobiles. It gathers data on the operating costs of each one to produce a report.

```
          GASOLINE OPERATING EXPENSE REPORT

                  TOTAL      MILES PER     COST PER
AUTO      ID      MILES       GALLON        MILE
```

Based on the following input data format and input data, prepare a report:

Column	Contents
1–10	Car type
11–15	Car ID number
16–20	Blank
21–25	Starting mileage
26–30	Ending mileage
31–32	Blank
33–35	Gallons put into tank
36–40	Cost of fill-up

Car	ID	Starting mileage	Ending mileage	Gallons	Cost
Ford Wagon	0123	6,718	7,204	21.2	28.62
Ford Sedan	1854	8,179	8,415	8.7	11.31
Chevy 2-door	7835	10,012	10,341	10.6	13.67
Chevy 2-door	6114	7,315	7,784	15.6	19.97
Ford Wagon	1005	5,663	5,902	9.6	12.76

15. If inventory on hand falls below the reorder point, a replenishment order is placed. The amount to be ordered Q is given by the following formula:

$$Q = \sqrt{\frac{2AS}{ci}}$$

where A = annual usage
S = setup cost
c = unit cost
i = interest rate for carrying inventory

The reorder of point R equals $L \times U$, where L is the lead time in weeks and U is the weekly usage. Print an output report that shows the reorder point and order quantity for each of the following items. (*Note:* The quantity to order at reorder point should be in whole units.) Use the headings shown:

INVENTORY REPORT

ITEM NUMBER	DESCRIPTION	REORDER POINT	REORDER QUANTITY			
Item number	Description	Lead time	Set-up cost	Unit cost	Interest rate	Annual usage
1124	Washer	1.6	1.25	0.001	0.10	200
2106	Cone subassembly	2.4	35.00	125.00	0.15	5,000
4603	Socket	3.0	6.25	7.25	0.10	12,000
5119	Plug	1.8	4.37	1.39	0.15	650
7732	Engine	4.2	45.50	650.78	0.20	3,050

The format for the input is

Column	Contents
1–5	Item number
6–10	Blank
11–30	Description
31–35	Lead time
36–40	Blank
41–45	Setup cost
46–55	Unit cost
56–57	Blank
56–60	Interest rate
61–65	Usage

Interactive Scientific and Engineering

16. The heat flow Q from an insulated pipe is given by the following formula:

$$Q = \frac{2\pi kL(T_i - T_o)}{\log_e (D_2/D_1)}$$

where L = pipe length
T_i = temperature inside

T_o = temperature outside (ambient temperature)
D_2 = outer diameter of the pipe (with insulation)
D_1 = diameter of pipe (without insulation)
k = thermal conductivity factor of the insulation

Construct a series of tables of heat flow versus thickness of insulation in half-inch increments from 1 to 3 inches for the following situations:

T_o	T_i
150	850
75	850
750	650
100	1000

The program should accept any pipe length and diameter, but for this example, assume a pipe 50 ft long which has a diameter of 8 in. Similarly, assume a thermal factor of 0.035. Check input data to ensure the inside temperature exceeds the outside temperature.

17. For a cylindrical tube of outside diameter D_o and an inside diameter of D_i, the moment of inertia is

$$\frac{\pi(D_o^4 - D_i^4)}{64}$$

and the radius of gyration is

$$\frac{\sqrt{D_o^2 - D_i^2}}{4}$$

For any external tube diameter and initial thickness, prepare a table of each of these properties, incrementing the thickness by a step given by the program's user. Terminate the table when the tube becomes a solid. Validate that the initial values are reasonable.

18. In addition to the velocity of the piston (described in problem 18 in Chapter 2), the displacement D of the piston is given by

$$D = r[1 - \cos(A) + \left(\frac{r}{2l}\right)\sin^2(A) + \left(\frac{r}{2l}\right)^3 \sin^4(A)]$$

Prepare a table of displacement and velocity versus crankshaft angle from 0 to 360 degrees in uniform increments of size specified by the user. The program should be able to accept any crankshaft radius, connecting rod length, and rotation speed. As an example, use the same values as in problem 18 in Chapter 2.

4a

Repetition Program Structure, Subscripted Variables, and DO Loops

Subscripted Variables
Arrays and Matrices
Form of FORTRAN Subscripts
Use of Subscripts
Self-Testing Exercise 4-1

DO Statement
Concept of Repetition or Looping
Form of the DO Statement
Use of the DO Statement
Rules for Using the DO Statement
Self-Testing Exercise 4-2

Implied DO Loops in Input/Output
Self-Testing Exercise 4-3

Initializing Data Values with the DATA Statement
Self-Testing Exercise 4-4

Style Guidelines for Arrays and DO Loops

Summary

Answers to Self-Testing Exercises

Questions and Problems

A very important program design and coding element is the repetition structure used to program the repeated execution of a block of instructions. The repetition structure is implemented in FORTRAN by the DO loop. Many repetition problems are simplified by the use of subscripted variables, and thus the FORTRAN notation for subscripted variables will be explained before describing the DO loop.

Subscripted Variables

Subscripts are frequently used in mathematical formulations, and therefore it is important to understand this method of identifying data items. The mathematical concept of subscripts can be directly applied to FORTRAN.

Arrays and Matrices

A list of quantities that can be grouped together can be thought of as a one-dimensional array. A quantity in the list is identified by a name given to the entire list, as well as by a number that refers to the position in the list occupied by the quantity. Mathematical notation uses a lowered number, hence the term *subscript*. For example, sales by customers would form a single-dimension array as shown in Figure 4-1. If S is used to denote sales, the sales to customer 3 can be identified as an array element S_3, sales to customer 4 as S_4, etc.

A two-dimensional array, or rectangular array (often called a *matrix*), provides a twofold classification. For example, a classification of persons by height and weight would result in a rectangular array. A single name can be used to refer to the matrix, and when any particular element or classification in the array is referred to, the name

Figure 4-1 Single-dimension array.

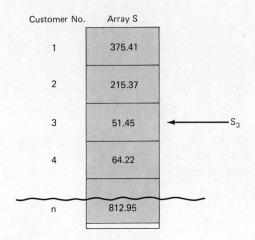

201

Figure 4-2 Two-dimensional array.

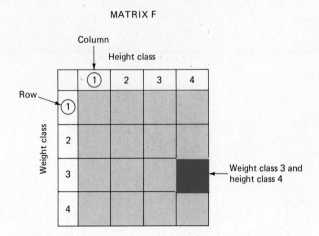

MATRIX F

is used with subscripts designating row and column. By convention, the row is always written first and the column second. For example, if F is used to refer to the twofold classification of females, $F_{3,4}$ refers to the number of those who are in weight class 3 and height class 4, as illustrated in Figure 4-2.

A threefold classification uses three subscripts. The first subscript refers to the row, the second to the column, and the third to the level. For example, a classification by weight, height, and age will result in the three-dimensional array shown in Figure 4-3. If the entire classification by weight, height, and age is termed C, persons falling into weight class 2, height class 4, and age class 1 are identified as $C_{2,4,1}$. The classifications are listed as subscripts in order by row, column, and level.

In short, subscripts are used to identify one out of a related set of items. All items in an array have the same name because they are all in the same category. The subscript identifies a specific element within the array.

Although it is often useful to visualize subscripts as referring to simple lists, rectangular arrays, or three-dimensional arrays, full FORTRAN allows seven subscripts (subset FORTRAN allows only three). Since spatial visualization does not work well for arrays with more than three dimensions, another way to think about sub-

Figure 4-3 Three-dimensional array.

MATRIX C

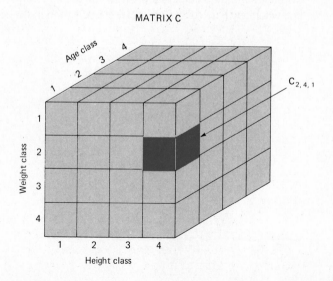

scripted variables is as an index to a list. For example, a two-dimensional array with three rows and two columns can be thought of as a list with an index to each entry as shown below.

Subscript	Row	Column	Data indexed by row and column
(1,1)	1	1	—
(1,2)	1	2	—
(2,1)	2	1	—
(2,2)	2	2	—
(3,1)	3	1	—
(3,2)	3	2	—

The concept of a list indexed by the subscripts can be extended to many subscripts. For example, four subscripts with each one having a range from 1 to 2 result in a list with 16 entries indexed by the subscripts (10 items of the list are shown below):

First subscript	Second subscript	Third subscript	Fourth subscript
1	1	1	1
1	1	1	2
1	1	2	1
1	1	2	2
1	2	1	1
1	2	1	2
1	2	2	1
1	2	2	2
2	1	1	1
2	1	1	2

Note that in the list, the fourth subscript changes through its entire range before the value for the third subscript is changed, and so on.

Form of FORTRAN Subscripts

Standard mathematical notation for subscripts uses numbers or letters written below the level of the symbol to which they apply, hence the name *subscript*. But since neither the keyboard nor the printer in a computer system may be equipped to handle lowered characters, subscripts are represented in FORTRAN as a set of numbers enclosed in parentheses that follow immediately after the name. The subscripts are separated by commas. The previous array examples would appear in FORTRAN as S(3), F(3, 4), and C(2, 4, 1). As explained above, the number of subscripts is limited to three in subset FORTRAN and to seven in full FORTRAN.

The name of an array consists of from one to six characters (same rules as for a simple variable name). The first letter of the array name identifies the data items in the array as being integer or real. Or array names may be declared in a TYPE statement as referencing storage locations holding integer-, real-, or character-type data items without regard to the first letter of the name.

When array names are used in FORTRAN statements, they are followed by subscripts to identify the specific data item or element in the array (except in special cases). The subscripts referring to elements in the array must have an integer value, since positions in an array can only be whole numbers. The integer values for subscripts can be specified by integer variables, integer constants, or integer expressions. The subscript expression follows the general rules for arithmetic expressions.

GENERAL FORM OF SUBSCRIPTS

A (iek$_1$)
A (iek$_1$, iek$_2$)
A (iek$_1$, iek$_2$, iek$_3$)

A = any array name. First letter of array name identifies array variables as integer or real in same way as variable names, unless name is declared as different type. A character array must be declared as CHARACTER.

iek = integer variables, integer expressions, or integer constants as subscripts. Full FORTRAN also allows array element references as subscripts.

Subscripts are separated by commas. The number of subscripts is limited to three in subset FORTRAN and to seven in full FORTRAN. Spaces are optional for readability.

Examples of Allowable Array References

Array reference	Comments
ALPHA (9)	References the 9th element in array ALPHA.
BETA (1, 7)	References the element in row 1 and column 7 of array BETA.
IOTA (I, J, K)	References the element in Ith row, Jth column, and Kth level of array IOTA. In order to locate the element, the program must have values for I, J, K.
GAMMA (M, 3)	References the Mth row and third column of array GAMMA. A value for M must be known before execution of statement.
Y (7 * KIX, 8)	Value of KIX is multiplied by 7 to arrive at row number; column is 8th.
Z (NIX+3, JIX)	Add 3 to value of NIX to compute row number; number of column is the value of JIX.
DELTA (K, 3, 2, 2)	References the Kth, 3rd, 2nd, 2nd, item in the array defined by the name DELTA.

Examples of Array References Not Allowed

Variable	Why not allowed
ALPHA (X)	Cannot be a real subscript; code as ALPHA (INT(X))
X(NIX, YIX)	Cannot be a real subscript; code as X(NIX, INT(YIX))

Use of Subscripts

Each time the compiler program translating the FORTRAN source statement to machine language encounters a variable name, it assigns a memory location to it. An array name presents a problem because the number of memory locations to be assigned to it is not always apparent from the program. In fact, the number may vary, depending on the problem being run. To allow the compiler to assign the correct number of memory locations for an array, the programmer must specify the maximum size of the array. The statement for doing this is the DIMENSION statement, which may appear any place in the program before the first use of the array name. However, it is usually good practice to put all DIMENSION statements at the beginning of the program in a type declaration and storage allocation block.

The basic form of the DIMENSION statement is the word DIMENSION followed by the dimension declarations for each array being described. The dimension declaration consists of the array name followed by parentheses that enclose the maximum values for each dimension of the array. For example, if there are three arrays A, B, and C, the first of which is a simple column of 15, the second is 4 × 5, and the third is 3 × 4 × 6, the DIMENSION statement would appear as follows:

```
DIMENSION A(15), B(4, 5), C(3, 4, 6)
```

To illustrate the meaning of the above statement, the three dimensions for C are the maximum number of rows, columns, and levels that will be needed by the program to store data elements under the array C name.

In 1977 subset FORTRAN (and previous versions of the language), the array declarations in the DIMENSION statement can use only integer constants, and all array dimensions are assumed to start with 1 and end with the number specified as being the maximum dimension. In other words, A(15) declares an array with elements numbered from 1 to 15; B(4, 5) declares an array with elements numbered from 1 to 4 for the rows and from 1 to 5 for the columns.

The full 1977 FORTRAN allows the dimensions to be expressed as an upper and lower bound in the form L:U, where the value of either bound may be positive, negative, or zero. The value of the upper bound must be greater than the value of the lower bound. The lower-bound/upper-bound dimension is not necessary, since the program can always include instructions to convert to standard dimensions starting at 1, but the bounds are very convenient in some problem situations. For example, data (called D) for the years 1945 to 1959 can be referenced by subscripts as D(1) to D(15), but it is probably more meaningful to use D(1945) to D(1959). This is done by a DIMENSION D(1945:1959). Other situations arise in which subscripts would be more meaningful if started at zero or with a negative number. An interest problem over 10 periods might have computations for time zero. An experiment might generate data to be identified as starting at -10 and going to $+20$. DIMENSION statements for these two cases would be:

```
DIMENSION PERIOD (0:10)
DIMENSION EXPRNT (-10:20)
```

The number of storage locations allocated by the DIMENSION statement is only enough to meet the range specified. The computer translates from the subscripts used to the storage location. In the above examples, 11 locations would be provided for PERIOD and 31 for EXPRNT.

Another feature of full 1977 FORTRAN is the use of constant expressions (expressions using constants and plus or minus operators) and exponentiation in dimensions. For example, in full FORTRAN, H(5 + 30, 10), and K(10**2) are allowed.

Type declarations and DIMENSION statements are placed in the same program block for convenience. There is no rule as to which should be first. Also, the dimension for a variable can be incorporated in the type statement. For example, REAL X(10, 10) specifies X as a real array with dimensions 10 × 10. For clarity, we prefer to use separate DIMENSION and type statements rather than combination statements, with the type statements first.

Care should be taken not to dimension larger than necessary for the maximum set of data. A DIMENSION X(100, 100, 100) calls for 100 × 100 × 100 memory locations. Although valid in form, this requirement for 1 million memory locations exceeds the internal capacity allowed for a FORTRAN program on most computers.

When an array name is used in an executable statement, it must always be used with a subscript to identify the desired location. The only exception to this rule is a specialized input/output situation in which an array name without a subscript refer-

> **BASIC FORM FOR DIMENSION FOR ARRAYS**
>
> DIMENSION A (k), A (k_1, k_2), A (k_1, k_2, k_3), A (k_1, k_2, . . . , k_n)
>
> If more than one array is dimensioned, the variables are separated by commas.
>
> A = any array name
> k = an integer constant
> k_1, k_2, k_3, . . . = the maximum number of rows, columns, levels, etc.
>
> 1977 standard FORTRAN allows up to seven dimensions; 1977 subset FORTRAN allows up to three dimensions; 1977 full FORTRAN allows a dimension to be declared as an upper and lower bound:
>
> k_L:k_U where k_L must be less than or equal to k_U
>
> 1977 full FORTRAN also allows an expression using integer constants as a dimension.

ences the entire array (to be explained later in the chapter). Two short sample problems illustrate two types of uses for arrays.

Array Example 1

Use Input Data to Compute Subscript

The first problem is a program to tally the number of students whose grade-point averages fall into each of five categories. The array called TALLY has five categories:

Category	Grade point
TALLY(1)	0.0–0.99
TALLY(2)	1.0–1.99
TALLY(3)	2.0–2.99
TALLY(4)	3.0–3.99
TALLY(5)	4.0

The program reads a record with the grade-point average for a student given on it. This variable, called GPA, is in the form X.XX. The END condition causes the tallies to be printed. After reading the input, the next step is to determine which category the student's grades are in and to add 1 to the tally for that category (Figure 4-4). Note that the data itself is used to provide the subscript category by which it is classified. The statement I = INT(GPA + 1.0) thus provides the proper integer for the tally statement. (The INT or IFIX function is redundant but clarifies the logic.)

Array Example 2

Select Variable in a Loop

The second problem is to sum 100 quantities stored in an array called X. The quantities have been read and placed in the array by instructions not shown. A simple IF loop is used to repeat the processing using a new value at each repetition, as shown in Figure 4-5. The test for termination of the loop is an IF statement, which is placed at the beginning of the loop. If subscripts were not available, the program to add 100 numbers would require statements listing all 100 variable names. In order to understand the logic of Figure 4-5, trace the value of JIX and SUM when data values for X(1), X(2), and X(3) are 9.0, 11.0, and 20.0.

Figure 4-4 Program segment for tally grade-point problem.

```
*********
*                          STORAGE ALLOCATION
*********
*
      DIMENSION TALLY(5)
*
*********
* BLOCK 0000            INITIALIZATION BLOCK
*********
*
      TALLY(1) = 0.0
      TALLY(2) = 0.0
      TALLY(3) = 0.0
      TALLY(4) = 0.0
      TALLY(5) = 0.0
*
*********
* BLOCK 0100            READ AND TALLY GPA CATEGORY
*********
*
*                       (VALIDATION OF INPUT DATA NOT SHOWN)
*
  100 READ(5,110,END=300) GPA
  110 FORMAT(F5.2)
      I = INT(GPA + 1.0)
      TALLY(I) = TALLY(I) + 1.0
*
*                       GO BACK TO READ ANOTHER DATA RECORD
*
      GOTO 100
*
*********
* BLOCK 0300            OUTPUT (NOT SHOWN)
*********
*
```

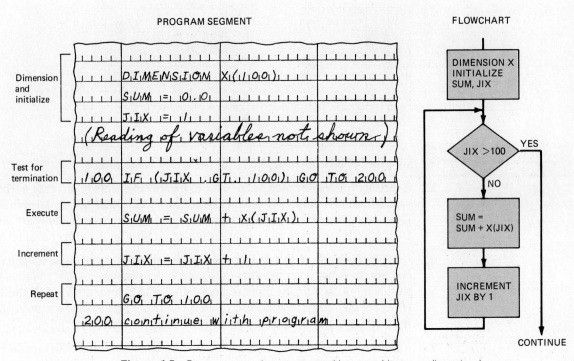

Figure 4-5 Program segment to sum quantities stored in a one-dimensional array.

Self-Testing Exercise 4-1

1. State whether the following statements or expressions are valid or invalid. If invalid for some FORTRANs, state why.

Statement or expression	Valid or invalid for full 1977 FORTRAN	Valid or invalid for subset FORTRAN
(a) DIMENSION C(100), NIX (100)		
(b) A (14, NIX, X)		
(c) A (JIX * KIX)		
(d) ALPHA (10, 10, 5)		
(e) DIMENSION ALPHA (100), BETA (100, 10)		
(f) GAMMA (A + 5.0)		
(g) DELTAS (I*5)		
(h) Y (5, 10, 4, 3)		
(i) DIMENSION BETA (0:15, −5:10)		
(j) DIMENSION TBL (10**3, 5*5)		

2. Write the DIMENSION statements for the following arrays:
   (a) An array of 100 sample observations
   (b) A two-dimensional array to classify persons by sex and by one of 10 occupations
   (c) An array to classify business firms by one of eight size groups, one of 15 types of business groups, and one of five location classes
   (d) Four arrays A, B, C, and D, each having 15 entries

3. Give the subscripted variable names by which the following matrix array elements are identified.

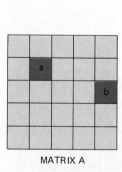 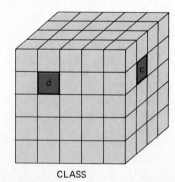

MATRIX A   CLASS

4. Give the DIMENSION statements for the arrays in question 3.

5. A variable NX is to be used as an index to identify elements in an array A which has values from 0 to 8. Array A is dimensioned by DIMENSION A(0:8). Assume that the lower-bound/upper-bound dimensions are not available and show an alternate DIMENSION statement and a reference to an element in the array based on NX.

6. Using logic similar to that in Figure 4-5, write program segments to initialize a loop counter, to dimension three lists (A, B, and C) for five values each, and then to read pairs of numbers from five input records (F10.2, F10.2) into lists A and B. Multiply the corresponding entries A and B to create a list C. The DO statement to be presented next is a simpler way to code these operations, but this exercise is useful.

7. A list is to be defined for keeping track of the number of automobiles on the road by using two fuel categories, three car size categories, two safety categories, and five

manufacturer categories. Considering this as a list indexed by subscripts, how many different data items are represented. Give the subscripts for the eighth, fourteenth, and thirty-first items in the list?

DO Statement

The DO statement or DO loop is one of the most powerful features of FORTRAN. It greatly simplifies the writing of program repetition (also called program loops).

Concept of Repetition or Looping

Looping is repetition based on program modification. A set of one or more instructions is executed a number of times, each time altering one or more variables in the set, so that each execution is different from the preceding one. The effect of looping is to reduce substantially the number of instructions required for a program.

The repetition structure (looping) is implemented in FORTRAN by the DO statement. Loops can be written in FORTRAN without the DO statement by coding separate statements to perform the functions of loop control (see Figure 4-5), but the DO loop form is generally preferred.

The DO loop repetition structure follows the DO WHILE logic explained in Chapter 1 (see Figure 4-6). The repetition is said to continue WHILE the condition governing the loop is true; when it is not true, the repetition ceases.

Figure 4-6 Flowchart of DO WHILE repetition structure.

1977 STANDARD FORTRAN DO WHILE

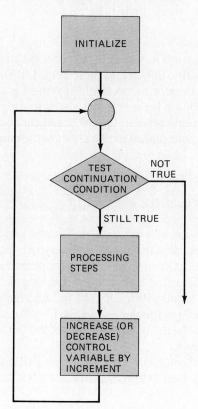

The logic of a DO WHILE or DO loop includes the following procedures:

1. Initialize the loop control variable to the first value.
2. Test to see if the loop control variable is within the limit for continuation. If it is within the limit, continue with the loop; if it exceeds the limit, branch out of the loop.
3. Execute the set of statements in the loop.
4. Modify the loop control variable.
5. Go back to the beginning of the loop (step 2).

Form of the DO Statement

The DO statement is a repetition command that simplifies the writing of loops. It automatically initializes the loop variable, tests to see if the variable is within the limit for continuation, passes control to the statements to be executed (or branches out of the loop), modifies the loop variable, and branches back to the start of the loop.

The DO loop structure begins with a DO statement, which identifies in order the following elements required for the loop execution:

1. The statement label of the last or terminal statement of the set of statements included in the loop. In other words, the DO statement is the statement at the beginning of the loop; the terminal statement, with its statement label, is the last statement in the loop (it defines the range of the loop).
2. The variable controlling the loop (the DO control variable).
3. The initial value of the DO control variable.
4. The limit-of-continuation value for the DO control variable.
5. The increment by which the DO control variable will be changed each time the loop is executed.

The terminal statement in a loop can be any executable statement except a transfer-of-control statement (GOTO, DO, and, in most cases, IF). To avoid ending a loop with a transfer-of-control statement, a CONTINUE statement is often written as the last loop statement in every DO loop because it adds clarity to the program structure. Also, for clear style, the statements between the DO statement and the CONTINUE statement may be indented (say, four spaces) to visually show the range of the loop. For example:

```
DO 150 I = 1, 10, 2
    C(I) = A(I) * B(I)
    WRITE (6,700) A(I), B(I), C(I)
150 CONTINUE
```

In the above example, the DO statement says that the statements from the DO statement through the statement labeled 150 should be executed repeatedly based on the DO control variable I. The loop is repeated as long as I is not greater than 10. The DO control variable I begins with a value of 1 and is incremented by 2 at the end of each execution of the loop. As in the above example, the DO control variable can be used in statements within the loop. The general form of the DO statement is summarized in the box on the next page.

In most cases, the number of executions for a DO loop is clear; DO 100 I = 1, 5 executes the loop five times. If the terminal value is less than the initial value, the loop is not executed. (Older FORTRAN compilers may execute the loop once.) The number of executions is computed from the integer value of

$$\frac{\text{Terminal value } - \text{ initial value } + \text{ increment}}{\text{Increment}}$$

Thus the loop specified in DO 100 M = 5, 18, 3 is executed five times:

$$\frac{18 - 5 + 3}{3} = 5$$

The basic, most simple form of the DO statement uses only positive integer variables and integer constants for the loop parameters and only an integer variable for the DO control variable. As extensions to the basic DO loop specifications, the subset of 1977 FORTRAN allows negative parameters. The full 1977 FORTRAN also allows the following:

A real variable as the control variable
Real variables as parameters
Real or integer expressions as parameters

DO STATEMENT

DO statement in 1977 full FORTRAN

DO s v = vek$_1$, vek$_2$, vek$_3$ If vek$_3$ is omitted, it is assumed to be 1

where s = statement label of the last statement in the loop (the terminal statement).
    v = DO control variable, which may be a real or integer variable.
   vek = parameters, which may be integer or real variables, constants, or real or integer expressions. Parameters may be negative.
   vek$_1$ = initial parameter, that is, the initial value of the loop variable.
   vek$_2$ = terminal parameter, that is, the maximum value the loop variable can be and have the loop processing continue.
   vek$_3$ = incrementation parameter, that is, the increment value by which the loop variable is to be modified. If vek$_3$ is not stated, it is assumed to be 1.

DO statement in subset FORTRAN

DO s i = ik$_1$, ik$_2$, ik$_3$ If ik$_3$ is omitted, it is assumed to be 1

where i = integer variable as the DO control variable.
   ik = integer variable or integer constant for initial, terminal, and increment parameters. Parameters may be negative.

Placement of a comma after the statement label in the DO statement is allowed but is not usually written because historically it was not permitted.

A repetition structure involving a DO loop can be described in the pseudocode of a program design language. A statement defining the nature of the loop is followed by the statements in the range of the loop, which are indented to aid visual definition of the range. The end of the loop is explicitly defined by an End of DO or End DO pseudocode statement. The pseudocode statements in the loop should explain clearly the processing to be performed. Words, mathematical expressions, or combinations may be used. These alternatives will be illustrated in the chapter.

Figure 4-7 Flowcharting a
DO loop.

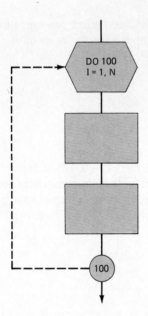

In flowcharting a DO loop, the programmer can write the flow diagram in terms of the DO loop statement itself. The terminal statement label, control variable, initial value, terminal value, and incrementation value are specified within a special processing symbol. A dotted line may be used to visually define the range of the DO loop as shown in Figure 4-7.

A DO loop can contain DO loops within its range. This is termed *nesting*. When nesting one DO loop inside another, the inner DO loop must be entirely contained within the range of the outer DO loop. However, the loops may have the same terminal statement, but, as a matter of clear style, we use a separate CONTINUE for each loop. There is no specified limit to the number of DO loops that can be nested. The inner loop is repeated the specified number of times each time the loop in which it is contained is incremented. For clear program design, the inner DO is indented to show the relationship and range of the inner DO loop to the outer DO loop. As an example, assume a program segment to sum the elements in an N × 5 matrix.

```
      SUM = 0.0
      DO 110 I = 1, N
          DO 100 J = 1, 5                        Range of    Range of
              SUM = SUM + A(I, J)                 inner DO    outer DO
100       CONTINUE
110   CONTINUE
```

Each time the outer loop is executed, the inner loop is executed 5 times. Therefore, the outer loop is executed N times and the inner loop 5 * N times.

Use of the DO Statement

The following examples illustrate and explain the way the DO statement is used in programming the repetition structure. The examples also illustrate the rules for DO loops and the style suggestions for clarity in programming.

Figure 4-8 DO example I.

PROGRAM SEGMENT	FLOWCHART	PSEUDOCODE

SUM = 0.0 — INITIALIZE SUM = 0.0 — Initialize SUM = 0.0

DO 100 K = 1, 210, 2 — DO 100 K = 1, 210, 2 — DO for k from 1 to 210 by 2

SUM = SUM + DELTA (K) — ADD DELTA (K) TO SUM — Add Delta_k to SUM

100 CONTINUE — 100 — End of DO

Note that SUM has to be set to zero before the loop is entered if it is to be used as the accumulator variable.

DO Example I
Write a DO loop to sum variables in an array DELTA with odd-numbered subscripts between 1 and 210 (Figure 4-8). Note the initial subscript is 1 and the increment is 2, so the subscripts used in the addition statement will be 1, 3, 5, 7, ...

DO Example 2
Multiply two arrays A and B, with N entries in each, to form a new array C (Figure 4-9). Note the computation is with two subscripted variables and the result is stored in a subscripted variable.

DO Example 3
Read K records with a variable X in each record in columns 1–10 in the form 99.99. Find the arithmetic mean (average) of the numbers (Figure 4-10). The READ statement is executed each time through the loop (100 times). A simpler form will be

Figure 4-9 DO example 2.

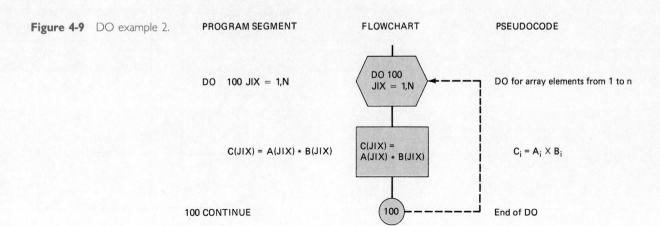

PROGRAM SEGMENT	FLOWCHART	PSEUDOCODE

DO 100 JIX = 1,N — DO 100 JIX = 1,N — DO for array elements from 1 to n

C(JIX) = A(JIX) * B(JIX) — C(JIX) = A(JIX) * B(JIX) — $C_i = A_i \times B_i$

100 CONTINUE — 100 — End of DO

Figure 4-10 DO example 3.

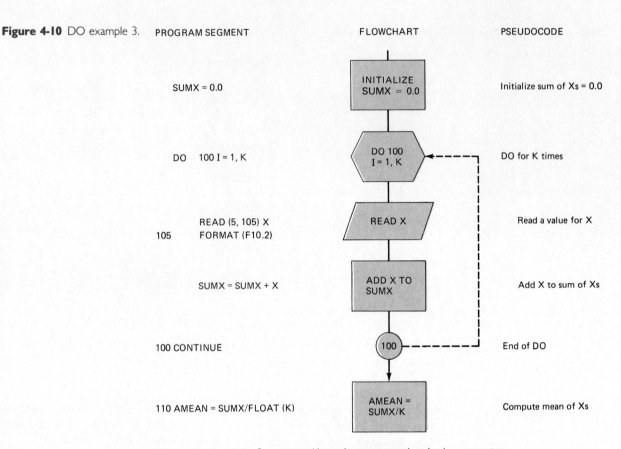

PROGRAM SEGMENT | FLOWCHART | PSEUDOCODE

SUMX = 0.0 — INITIALIZE SUMX = 0.0 — Initialize sum of Xs = 0.0

DO   100 I = 1, K — DO 100 I = 1, K — DO for K times

READ (5, 105) X
105   FORMAT (F10.2) — READ X — Read a value for X

SUMX = SUMX + X — ADD X TO SUMX — Add X to sum of Xs

100 CONTINUE — 100 — End of DO

110 AMEAN = SUMX/FLOAT (K) — AMEAN = SUMX/K — Compute mean of Xs

Note that the loop index I was not used in any loop statement but simply as a counter.

Figure 4-11 DO example 4.

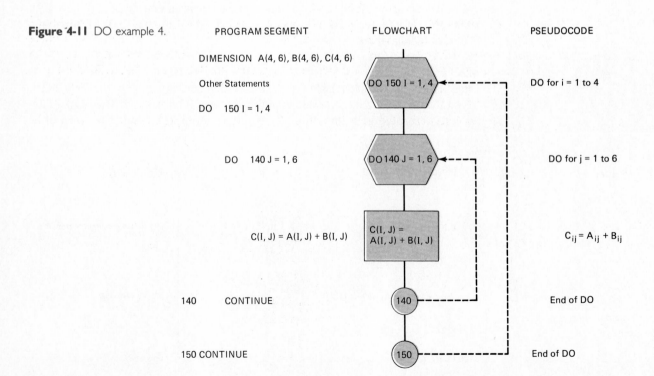

PROGRAM SEGMENT | FLOWCHART | PSEUDOCODE

DIMENSION A(4, 6), B(4, 6), C(4, 6)

Other Statements — DO 150 I = 1, 4 — DO for i = 1 to 4

DO   150 I = 1, 4

DO   140 J = 1, 6 — DO 140 J = 1, 6 — DO for j = 1 to 6

C(I, J) = A(I, J) + B(I, J) — C(I, J) = A(I, J) + B(I, J) — $C_{ij} = A_{ij} + B_{ij}$

140   CONTINUE — 140 — End of DO

150 CONTINUE — 150 — End of DO

described later in the chapter. The loop variable is used as a counter to keep track of the number of records.

DO Example 4

Add two 4 × 6 matrices A and B to form matrix C; that is, C(1, 1) = A(1, 1) + B(1, 1), etc. (Figure 4-11). The purpose of this example is to illustrate the fact that the order in which the program will perform the computation is defined by the DOs. The J values go through a cycle from 1 to 6 each time I changes by 1. Thus the order of computation in Example 4 will be:

```
C(1, 1) = A(1, 1) + B(1, 1)
C(1, 2) = A(1, 2) + B(1, 2)
C(1, 3) = A(1, 3) + B(1, 3)
C(1, 4) = A(1, 4) + B(1, 4)
C(1, 5) = A(1, 5) + B(1, 5)
C(1, 6) = A(1, 6) + B(1, 6)
```
I is set to 1, and J loops from 1 to 6.

```
C(2, 1) = A(2, 1) + B(2, 1)
C(2, 2) = A(2, 2) + B(2, 2)
etc.
```
I is set to 2, and J loops from 1 to 6 again.

```
C(3, 1) = A(3, 1) + B(3, 1)
C(3, 2) = A(3, 2) + B(3, 2)
etc.
```
I is set to 3, and J loops from 1 to 6 for the third time.

```
C(4, 5) = A(4, 5) + B(4, 5)
C(4, 6) = A(4, 6) + B(4, 6)
```
1 is set to 4, and J loops from 1 to 6 for the fourth time.

DO Example 5

Compute how much $1000 invested today will return in 10 years if the interest rate is 10, 11, 12, 13, 14, or 15 percent and interest is compounded annually. The formula is $1000(1.0 + r)^{10}$, where r is the interest rate. Print out each rate and amount. The program, flowchart, and pseudocode are shown in Figure 4-12. This illustrates the use of real data for DO parameters.

Figure 4-12 DO example 5.

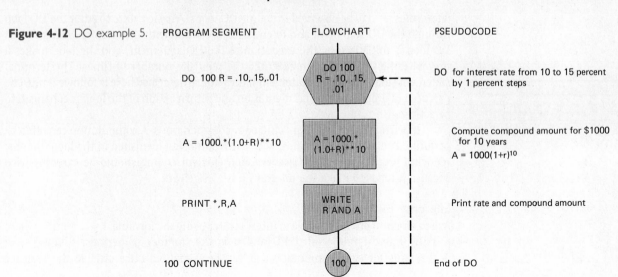

PROGRAM SEGMENT	FLOWCHART	PSEUDOCODE
DO 100 R = .10,.15,.01	DO 100 R = .10, .15, .01	DO for interest rate from 10 to 15 percent by 1 percent steps
A = 1000.*(1.0+R)**10	A = 1000.* (1.0+R)**10	Compute compound amount for $1000 for 10 years $A = 1000(1+r)^{10}$
PRINT *,R,A	WRITE R AND A	Print rate and compound amount
100 CONTINUE	100	End of DO

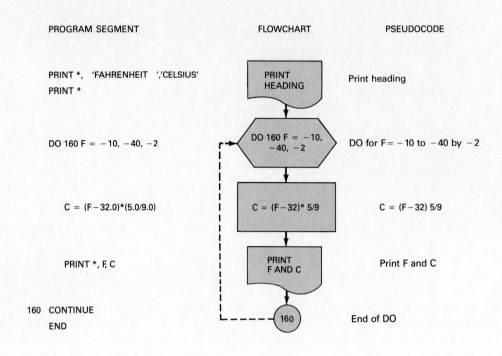

PROGRAM SEGMENT | FLOWCHART | PSEUDOCODE

PRINT *, 'FAHRENHEIT ','CELSIUS'
PRINT *

PRINT HEADING

Print heading

DO 160 F = −10, −40, −2

DO 160 F = −10, −40, −2

DO for F = −10 to −40 by −2

C = (F−32.0)*(5.0/9.0)

C = (F−32)* 5/9

C = (F−32) 5/9

PRINT *, F, C

PRINT F AND C

Print F and C

160   CONTINUE
END

160

End of DO

Figure 4-13 DO example 6.

DO Example 6

Print a table of Celsius equivalents for Fahrenheit temperatures from −10 to −40 by increments of −2. This illustrates the use of negative parameters (Figure 4-13).

Rules for Using the DO Statement

A few rules need to be observed in coding DO loops. A basic rule is to enter the DO loop through the DO statement and to end each execution with the terminal statement. A DO loop is initialized by the execution of the DO statement, and the loop makes a normal exit after it has been executed the requisite number of times. The terminal statement (the CONTINUE statement if the pattern described here is followed) must be executed in order for the incrementation and return action of the loop mechanism to be activated.

In writing loops, there are efficiency considerations. A computation can often be performed outside the loop once, with the result being furnished to the loop, thereby reducing processing time. However, such efficient coding should be carefully used because it tends to make the program logic less clear.

Efficiency Example

A program is to produce a table of interest rates using the formula $A = (1 + i)^n$, where i is the interest rate (called XI) and n is the number of periods. Since $1 + i$ is the same for each computation, it can be computed once outside the loop for

---

RULES FOR DO LOOPS

1. The parameters of a DO statement should not be altered by statements within the range of the DO. This includes the values for the control variable, the initial value, the terminal value, and the increment.

2. The control variable can be used in statements inside the range of the DO loops or it may be used only as a repetition counter. When exit is made from the loop, the current value of the control variable is available for use outside the loop.

3. DO loops must be entered only through the DO statement because that execution establishes the loop controls. Never transfer from a statement outside the range of a DO to the inside of the range of a DO. An inner-nested DO can transfer into the range of an outer DO because the inner DO is already within the range of the outer DO.

4. The iteration count for number of times the loop will execute is established as the integer value from [(terminal value − initial value + increment) / increment]. If negative, the count is set to zero. A count of zero means the loop will not be executed at all. (Older FORTRANs may execute the loop once.) Note that the iteration count formula allows an initial value larger than a terminal value if there is a negative increment value. (Older FORTRANs do not allow a negative increment.)

---

efficiency. But unless the tables are very large, the efficiency is not significant enough to justify loss of clarity.

Clear coding of loop	More efficient coding of loop
	FACTR = 1.0 + XI
DO 150 N = 1, L	DO 150 N = 1, L
A = (1.0 + XI)**N	A = FACTR**N
(other statements)	(other statements)
150 CONTINUE	150 CONTINUE

Self-Testing Exercise 4-2

1. Complete the table:

DO statement	Valid or invalid for 1977 full FORTRAN	If invalid for full or subset FORTRAN, explain why
(a) DO NIX I = 1, 7		
(b) DO 120, I = 1, NIX		
(c) DO 230 MIX = 1, J, K		
(d) DO 350 JANE = JOE, + 7		
(e) DO 450 K = 10, 8		
(f) DO 560 LUCK = 7, 7		
(g) DO 670 ILL = 7, 15, 3		
(h) DO 780 I = 1, N − 1		
(i) DO 890 X = 1, 10, 2		

2. At the completion of the following program loops, what will be the value of K, L, and M?

```
       M = 0
       DO  150 I = 1, 10
          K = I
          DO  140 J = 1,5
             L = J
             M = M + 1
140          CONTINUE
150    CONTINUE
```

3. How many times will the loops defined by the following DO statements be executed? Which statements are allowed by the 1977 standard FORTRAN but not allowed by 1977 subset FORTRAN standard? Show computation for iteration count using the formula.

(a) DO 3 I = 5, 5
(b) DO 3 I = 5, 1
(c) DO 3 I = 1, 5
(d) DO 3 I = 1, 5, 3
(e) DO 3 A = 0.1, 0.5, 0.2
(f) DO 3 A = 0.03, 0.30, 0.05
(g) DO 3 I = 5, 1, −2

4. In what order will the following program segment print out the subscripted variables from a three-dimensional array?

```
       DO  120  I = 1, 2
          DO  110  J = 1, 2
             DO  100  K = 1, 2
                WRITE (3,900) ARRAY (I, J, K)
100          CONTINUE
110       CONTINUE
120    CONTINUE
```

5. What will the following program segment do?

```
       DO  150  I = 1, 30
          SUM = 0.0
          SUM = SUM + A(I) * B(I)
150    CONTINUE
```

6. Which of the following DO loop nests in the figure below are valid?

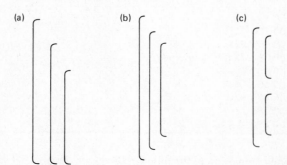

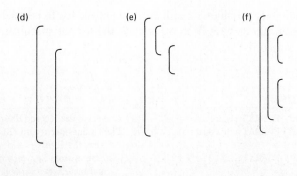

(d) (e) (f)

7. Write a program segment to sum the products from multiplying the elements in array LIX by the corresponding elements in array MIX. There are N entries in each.

8. Write a program segment to print out every other entry in the K-entry array DAD, starting with the second entry.

9. Write a program segment to shift the values in an array A so that $A(1) = A(2)$, $A(2) = A(3)$, etc. $A(N)$ should contain original value of $A(1)$. Be careful with $A(1)$.

10. Write a program segment to shift the values in the 25-entry array ALPHA so that $A(2) = A(1)$, $A(3) = A(2)$, etc., and $A(1) = A(25)$. It is easy to make a logic error, so be sure to check your logic carefully.

Implied DO Loops in Input/Output

In reading or writing subscripted variables, each subscripted variable may be listed, but this is very cumbersome. Another method is to include the READ or WRITE statement inside a DO loop, but this method is limited by the fact that each loop initiates a repeat of the input/output command. With formatted input/output, each repeat will use a new physical record. A very useful FORTRAN feature that may simplify input and output of subscripted variables is a form of the input/output statement called an *implied* DO *loop*.

The form of the implied DO loop input or output statement is similar to that of the DO loop. In fact, as many as three implied loops may be nested. The form is shown by the following examples:

```
READ (5, 700) (A(I), I = 1, N)
READ (5, 700) ((A(I, J), J = 1, M), I = 1, N)
```

Note that each of the loop parameter specifications is enclosed in parentheses. Note also the placement of the commas, particularly after the parentheses.

In addition to the fact that it is a shorter form, the implied DO loop has an advantage over the regular DO loop in that the resulting variables are treated as a single list so that input or output from physical records is entirely under FORMAT control. For example, READ (5, 700)(A(I), I = 1,100) will read the data items from 1 to 100 records, depending on the format specifications. Keep in mind that the closing parenthesis of the FORMAT statement terminates the current physical record. If additional variables are still available in the list to be read or written and the format specifications have been exhausted, the format specifications are used again with a new record.

FORMAT	READ instruction READ (5, 700)(A(N), N = 1, 100)
700 FORMAT (F10.0)	One value per record (100 records)
700 FORMAT (8F10.0)	Eight values per record (13 records with only four values from the 13*th*)
700 FORMAT (2F10.0 / F10.0)	Two values from first record, one variable value from second record, two variable values from third record, etc., because slash terminates use of a record (skips to next record)

The above example applies equally well to output. A program statement of the form WRITE (6, 700)(A(N), N = 1, 100) will write 100 values as specified by the FORMAT statement, for example, one value per line, eight values per line, etc.

The implied DO loop can therefore be considered as a DO loop that creates a list of input or output variables to be input or output under FORMAT control. Nested loops can be used in implied input or output DO loops. The outer loop is written last, and the innermost DO (the one that changes most rapidly) is placed next to the variable. The loops should be listed to match the arrangement of data. Example implied DO loop statements and order in which variables are read follow:

```
READ (5, 700) (A(I), I = 1, N)
A(1), A(2), A(3), . . . , A(N)

READ (5, 700) ((A(I, J), I = 1, M), J = 1, N)
A(1, 1), A(2, 1), A(3, 1), . . . , A(M, N)

READ (5, 700) ((A(I, J), J = 1, N), I = 1, M)
A(1, 1), A(1, 2), A(1, 3), . . . , A(M, N)

READ (5, 700) (((A(I, J, K), I=1, M), J=1, N), K=1, L)
A(1, 1, 1), A(2, 1, 1), A(3, 1, 1), . . . , A(M, N, L)
```

A special form of the implied DO can be used when an entire array is to be read or printed. The array name is written without subscripts or implied DO loops. The DIMENSION statement will already have specified both the fact that it is an array name and the size of the entire array to be read or written. This input or output form can be used only when the entire array is to be read or written in natural order, that is, in the column order (row varies most rapidly). For example, array Y dimensioned as (2, 2) will be processed by an implied DO in the order (1, 1), (2, 1), (1, 2), (2, 2). This form, in essence, creates a list of the entire array in natural order, and it is input or output under FORMAT control. Reliance upon default procedures such as the array name without subscripts are quite error-prone and should be used with caution. The explicit specifications in the implied DO loop are preferred style.

There is no special method for flowcharting implied DO loops. Since the effect is entirely contained within the READ or WRITE statement, it is probably satisfactory to merely indicate that data is to be read or written by the normal input or output symbol.

If additional detail is desired in the flowchart, the implied loop can be noted in the symbol, or an annotation symbol can be used.

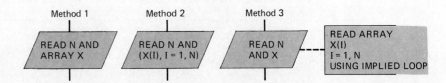

Self-Testing Exercise 4-3

Explain the effect of each of the following sets of statements. It may be helpful to review the section on "Reuse of FORMAT Specifications" in Chapter 3.

```
  1.        DIMENSION A (10, 10)
            READ (5, 700) A
      700   FORMAT (F10.0)

  2.        DIMENSION B (5, 5)
            READ (5, 710)  ((B(I, J) J = 1, 5), I = 1, 5)
      710   FORMAT (8F10.0)

  3.        DIMENSION C (6, 6)
            READ (5, 720) (C(1, J), J = 1, 6)
      720   FORMAT (6F10.0)

  4.        DO 130 K = 1, 3
               DO 120 J = 1, N
                  DO 110 I = 1, N
                     READ (5, 105) X (I, J, K)
      105            FORMAT (F10.0)
      110         CONTINUE
      120      CONTINUE
      130   CONTINUE

  5.        WRITE (6, 730) ((KIX (I, J), J = 1, 4), I = 1, 4)
      730   FORMAT (4I10, /)
```

Initializing Data Values with the DATA Statement

In many programs, there are variables that should be set to an initial value. This may be accomplished by input of data as the first step in the program, by assignment statements, or by a DATA statement. The DATA statement provides initial values for variables, entire arrays, and array elements.

Essentially, the DATA statement lists variables to which data values are to be assigned and then lists the data values to be assigned. The first data value is assigned to the first variable, etc. If an array name is used, it must have been dimensioned previously. If an array name is listed without a subscript or an implied DO loop, the entire array is used.

DATA STATEMENT

DATA nlist / clist / nlist / clist/   or   DATA nlist / clist /, nlist / clist /

nlist is a list of variable names, array names, or array element names; clist is a list of the values to be assigned. A value can be repeated by using an integer plus an asterisk in front of the value, the integer specifying the number of repetitions of the value. The nlist (in 1977 full FORTRAN, but not in 1977 subset FORTRAN) can be an implied DO statement.

The DATA statement is placed in the program after specification statements such as DIMENSION.

Examples

```
DATA A, B, I / 5.0, 3.5, 4 /
```
[Assigns 5.0 to A, 3.5 to B, and 4 to I.]
```
DATA A, B, C(3) / 3 * 10.0 /
```
[Assigns 10.0 to A, 10.0 to B, and 10.0 to C(3).]
```
DATA ALPHA / 50 * 0.0 /
```
[Places zeros in all 50 elements of array ALPHA.]
```
DATA (BETA(I), I = 11, 20) / 10 * 5.0 /
```
[Initializes (with value 5.0) elements 11–20 in array BETA. Note implied DO loop.]
```
DATA ((IGAMMA (I, J), I = 6, 10), J = 1, 15) / 75 * 0 /
```
[Initializes to zero the last five rows of elements in 10 × 15 array.]

The DATA statement must be placed after specification statements such as DIMENSION. In the style used in this text, the DATA statements will be placed after the type declarations and DIMENSION statements in a type declaration and storage allocation block. It is a useful statement, especially when an entire array or a number of variables used as accumulators are set to zero. For example, setting TALLY1, TALLY2, and a 100-element array GAMMA to 0 can be performed using assignment statements and a DO loop, but it is more efficient and very clear coding to use a DATA statement.

Without DATA statement

```
    TALLY1 = 0.0
    TALLY2 = 0.0
    DO  150 I = 1, 100
        GAMMA (I) = 0.0
150 CONTINUE
```

With DATA statement

```
DATA TALLY1, TALLY2 / 2 * 0.0 / GAMMA / 100 * 0.0 /
```

Note that the DATA statement could also have been written as (poor style):

```
DATA TALLY1, TALLY2, GAMMA / 102 * 0.0 /
```

Self-Testing Exercise 4-4

1. Use the DATA statement to initialize A to 40.1, B to 3.7, C and D to 1.0, and all elements in a 100-element array BETA to 0.

2. Use an implied loop in a DATA statement to initialize to 2.0 every other element between 15 and 49 in array ARRAY.

Style Guidelines for Arrays and DO Loops

As in previous chapters, the style guidelines reflect one example of good practice. There are alternative styles that may also result in clear, disciplined program coding.

1. Do not dimension an array to be excessively large.
2. Subscript values used in a program at execution generally are not checked to ensure that they do not exceed the maximum value dimensioned for the array. If such values are used, they may cause serious errors. In reviewing the logic of a program, check for this error.
3. In the variable identification block, use a separate array name section to clearly identify array names (see examples in Chapter 4b).
4. Clearly specify the DIMENSIONs for all arrays in a separate type declaration and storage allocation block.
5. End each DO loop with a CONTINUE statement. It is not required except when the last statement in the range of the DO loop would be a transfer of control. However, as a matter of style, the CONTINUE clearly marks the range of a DO loop.
6. As a matter of style, statements may be indented between the DO statement and the CONTINUE statement to define visually the range of the DO loop.
7. For nested DO loops, each inner loop may be indented. Each nested loop may end with a separate CONTINUE. Example:

```
      DO 130 I = 1, N
          DO 120 J = 1, M
              DO 110 K = 1, 5
                  SUM = SUM + A (I, J, K)
110               CONTINUE
120           CONTINUE
130 CONTINUE
```

Note: The statement labels are not indented for the indented CONTINUE statements, since statement labels must appear in columns 1–5.

8. Since the single letters I through N are often used as loop parameters, it is a practical matter of style to avoid using these single letters as simple variable or array names, and to reserve them for DO loop paramaters. In following this suggestion, it is not necessary to define these index variables in the variable identification block.
9. Use the DATA statement to initialize data items. Place DATA statements in a type declaration and storage allocation block.

Summary The repetition structure is very important in programming. In FORTRAN, it is implemented by the DO loop. Subscripted variables are frequently used in connection with loops to simplify the programming of processing of data items that can be grouped together and assigned a common name. Subscripts indicate data-item position in the array. The DIMENSION statement defines the maximum number of entries in an array.

The DO loop begins with the DO statement that specifies the range of the loop, the DO control variable, the initial value, the terminal value, and the increment. Good practice suggests that the terminal statement for a DO loop should be a CONTINUE statement and indentation should be used to define visually the statements inside the loop.

An implied DO loop may be contained within a READ or WRITE statement. This is very useful because it allows input and output to be completely under FORMAT control.

Data values, especially arrays, can be initialized to starting values by assignment statements, but a very useful alternative is the DATA statement.

Answers to Self-Testing Exercises

Exercise 4-1

1.

Valid or invalid for full FORTRAN	If invalid for some versions of FORTRAN, why
(a) Valid	
(b) Invalid	Real subscript (X) not allowed
(c) Valid	
(d) Valid	
(e) Valid	
(f) Invalid	Real subscript expression (A + 5.0) not allowed
(g) Valid	
(h) Valid	Subscripts limited to three in subset FORTRAN
(i) Valid	Not valid for 1977 subset FORTRAN
(j) Valid	Not valid for 1977 subset FORTRAN

2. (a) DIMENSION ARRAY (100)
   (b) DIMENSION PERSNS (2, 10)
   (c) DIMENSION BUSNES (8, 15, 5)
   (d) DIMENSION A(15), B(15), C(15), D(15)

3. (a) A (2, 2)
   (b) A (3, 5)
   (c) CLASS (2, 5, 2)
   (d) CLASS (2, 2, 1)

4. DIMENSION A(5, 5), CLASS (5, 5, 4)

5. DIMENSION A(9)
   A(NX + 1) Adding 1 to NX changes array references from 0–8 to 1–9.

6. Figure 4-14.

Figure 4-14 Program segment using loops to read and multiply array values.

```
*********
*                          STORAGE ALLOCATION
*********
*
      DIMENSION A(5),B(5),C(5)
*
*********
* BLOCK 0000              INITIALIZATION
*********
*
      I = 1
      J = 1
      K = 1
*
*********
* BLOCK 0100              READ DATA INTO ARRAYS
*********
*
  100 IF(I.GT.5) GOTO 200
      READ(5,150) A(I),B(I)
  150 FORMAT(F10.2,F10.2)
      I = I + 1
*
*                         GO BACK TO READ ANOTHER DATA RECORD
*
      GOTO 100
*
*********
* BLOCK 0200              MULTIPLY A TIMES B TO GIVE C
*********
*
  200 IF(J.GT.5) GOTO 300
      C(J) = A(J)*B(J)
      J = J + 1
*
*                         GO BACK TO START OF BLOCK
*
      GOTO 200
*
*********
```

7. Treating the subscript as an index to a list, there are $2 \times 3 \times 2 \times 5 = 60$ items.

		Fuel	Size	Safety	Manufacturer
(a) 8th item	(1, 1, 2, 3)	1	1	2	3
(b) 14th item	(1, 2, 1, 4)	1	2	1	4
(c) 31st item	(2, 1, 1, 1)	2	1	1	1

Exercise 4-2

1.

	Full 1977 FORTRAN	If invalid for full or subset FORTRAN, why
(a)	Invalid	Because a variable may not be used as a statement label.
(b)	Valid	Comma after statement label optional in 1977 standard.
(c)	Valid	
(d)	Valid	
(e)	Valid	Note that the terminal value is less than the initial value. The 1977 standard says execute zero times.
(f)	Valid	The loop will be executed once; count = $(7 - 7 + 1)/1 = 1$.
(g)	Valid	Note that the loop stops when the terminal value is exceeded. Therefore, this will be executed three times. Using the iteration count formula, the count = $(15 - 7 + 3)/3 = 11/3 = 3$.
(h)	Valid	Arithmetic expression allowed only in 1977 full FORTRAN, not subset.
(i)	Valid	DO control variable must be integer in 1977 subset FORTRAN.

2. K = 10, L = 5, M = 50

3. (a) 1 (5 − 5 + 1)/1 = 1
    (b) 0 (1 − 5 + 1)/1 = −3 = 0
    (c) 5 (5 − 1 + 1)/1 = 5
    (d) 2 (5 − 1 + 3)/3 = 2
    (e) 3 (.5 − .1 + .2)/.2 = 3 }
    (f) 6 (.30 − .03 + .05)/.05 = 6 }   Not allowed by subset FORTRAN
    (g) 3 [1 − 5 + (−2)]/−2 = 3

4. ARRAY (1, 1, 1), (1, 1, 2), (1, 2, 1), (1, 2, 2), (2, 1, 1), (2, 1, 2), (2, 2, 1), (2, 2, 2)

5. The program will end with SUM = A(30) * B(30). The initializing of the accumulating variable must be done outside the loop in which it is used.

6. Valid: *a, b, c,* and *f.*
    Invalid: *d* and *e.* Inner DO must be entirely within range of outer.

7.
```
     ISUM = 0.0
     DO 150 I = 1, N
        ISUM = ISUM + LIX (I) * MIX (I)
 150 CONTINUE
```

8.
```
     DO 160 I = 2, K, 2
        WRITE (5, 700) DAD(I)
 160 CONTINUE
```

9.
```
     TEMP = A(1)
     DO 100 I = 2, N
        A(I − 1) = A(I)
 100 CONTINUE
     A(N) = TEMP
```

10.
```
     TEMP = A(25)            (Possible alternative in 1977 full FORTRAN)
     DO 100 I = 1, 24            TEMP = A(25),
        K = 25 − I               DO 100 I = 24, 1, − 1
        A(K + 1) = A(K)             A(I + 1) = A(I)
 100 CONTINUE               100 CONTINUE
     A(1) = TEMP                 A(1) = TEMP
```

Exercise 4-3

1. One hundred values for A will be read from records. One value will be read from each record, arranged in natural order by columns; the row subscript will vary most rapidly.

    A(1, 1), A(2, 1), A(3, 1), . . .

2. Twenty-five values for B will be read, eight to a record, in row order:

    B(1, 1), B(1, 2), B(1, 3), . . .

3. Six values will be read from a record. These will form the first row of a 6 × 6 matrix.

4. This will read an N × N × 3 array, entered one to a record and arranged in natural order. The row varies most rapidly, column next, and level last.

5. The 16-value array KIX will be printed out with four columns values per line, double-spaced between lines (because the closing parenthesis does single spacing and the slash skips a line).

Exercise 4-4

1. DATA A, B, C, D / 40.1, 3.7, 2 * 1.0 / , BETA / 100 * 0.0 /

2. DATA (ARRAY (I), I = 15, 49, 2) / 18 * 2.0 /

Questions and Problems

1. Define or explain:
   (a) The purpose of the DIMENSION statement
   (b) Array
   (c) Matrix
   (d) Subscript

2. Write the DIMENSION statements for the following:
   (a) An array X with 59 entries
   (b) An array YES with 39 rows and 10 columns
   (c) An array to accept a threefold classification—by state, by 1 of 20 sizes of cities, and by one of two classes relating to growth in the past 10 years

3. A company wishes to classify SALES by salespeople (10 of them), by size of company (four size categories), and by product sold (eight of these). Set up the classification for SALES, and write a program segment to calculate totals by a salesperson.

4. Complete the table below.

DO statement	Valid or invalid for 1977 full FORTRAN	If invalid for subset FORTRAN, why
(a) DO 19 NIX = JIX, KIX, LIX		
(b) DO 100 FIX = 1, TRIX		
(c) DO 50 I = 1, N, L + 1		
(d) DO 30 I = 1, N, K		
(e) DO 17 I = 1, 4, 2		
(f) DO X J = 1, K		
(g) DO 150 Z = −10, 12		
(h) DO 200 Y = .15, .25, .05		

5. What is the purpose of the CONTINUE statement?

6. In what order will the first six subscripted variables be processed when N is 2 and M is 3?

```
    DO 102 I = 1, N
       DO 101 J = 1, N
          DO 100 K = 1, M
             A (K, J, I) = . . .
100       CONTINUE
101    CONTINUE
102 CONTINUE
```

Figure 4-15 Course-grade matrix for problem 7.

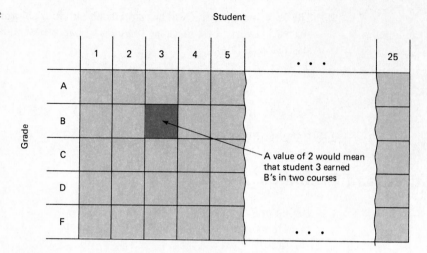

7. A matrix contains the number of A's, B's, etc., earned by each student in a class of 25. Each course is three credits. (See Figure 4-15.) Write a program segment to calculate the grade-point average for each student and for the class.

8. What is the effect of the following statements?

(a)
```
      READ (5, 700) (((A(I, J, K), K = 1, 3), J = 1, 5), I = 1, 3)
  700 FORMAT (F10.0)
```
(b)
```
      DIMENSION BETA (5, 5, 5)
      READ (5, 700) BETA
  700 FORMAT (F10.0 /)
```
(c)
```
      DIMENSION IOTA (8, 8)
      WRITE (6, 700) IOTA
  700 FORMAT (I10)
```
(d)
```
      DO 750 J = 1, N
          WRITE (6, 700) J, A(J)
  700     FORMAT (I10, F10.2)
  750 CONTINUE
```
(e)
```
      READ (5, 700) B(1, 1), B(3, 2), B(4, 1)
  700 FORMAT (F10.0)
```

4b

Example Programs and Programming Exercises Using Subscripted Variables and DO Loops

General Comments on the Example Programs

General Program Example 4— Payroll Reports
Problem Description for General Example 4
Program Documentation for General Example 4
Notes on General Example 4

Mathematical Program Example 4— Tables of Cumulative Normal Probability
Problem Description for Mathematical Example 4
Program Documentation for Mathematical Example 4
Notes on Mathematical Example 4

Programming Exercises
Description of Assignment
Mathematics and Statistics
Business and Economics
Science and Engineering
Humanities and Social Sciences
General
Interactive Scientific and Engineering

The example programs illustrate the use of data stored as arrays and referenced by subscripted variables, DO loops, and implied DO loops. The general example of payroll, designed for file input and batch execution, makes use of implied DO loops for input and output; the mathematical program, designed for interactive execution, uses DO loops in the computations. Both example programs should be reviewed because they illustrate different ways to use these features.

General Comments on the Example Programs

Both programs store data items in an array as they are computed. The stored array of data is then used for processing and output. Without the array, it is cumbersome to store lists, tables, or arrays of data.

The variables identification block has previously contained only variable names and constants identification. An array names section is added within the block to identify array names clearly. The DIMENSION statements are placed in the type declaration and storage allocation block.

In the flowcharts (which require more than one page), note the use of off-page connector references.

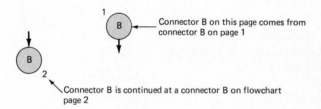

Some programmers use a special off-page connector symbol found on IBM flowchart

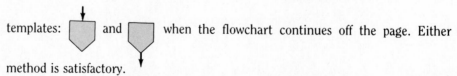

templates: and   when the flowchart continues off the page. Either

method is satisfactory.

There is no special flowchart symbol or notation to indicate implied DO loops with input or output. The flowchart need not show all details of the program coding, and in these programs, implied DO loops were not significant for the flow of program logic.

General Program Example 4—Payroll Reports

The program computes gross pay, deductions, and net pay, as with the previous programs. However, new techniques are used, such as reading from two input files and storing the valid input data in an array. This allows the program to delay printing the payroll reports until after all data records have been read. There are two separate reports. The Employee Paycheck Report lists the employees in an order different from the order of input.

Problem Description for General Example 4

The program reads employee pay data and produces two reports: (1) Paycheck Report: Table Values and Error Messages, an error and control report (see Figure 4-21), and (2) Employee Paycheck Report, a report of pay amounts (see Figure 4-16). There are two sets of input for the program on two separate input files (called DATA4D and DATA4E on input units 7 and 8). The first file contains five records with pairs of department numbers and names, one pair per record plus a record containing values indicating end of records. The second input file contains a record with the date of week the payroll ended plus employee data records, one record for each employee, giving ID number, name, department number where employed, hours worked, wage rate, and miscellaneous deductions. The program will process 14 or fewer valid employee input records.

The Employee Paycheck Report consists of a heading with a date for the payroll period, a line of output for each employee, and a total line (see Figure 4-16). The employees are not listed in order of input; rather, they are listed by department. Because the report does not have space for an error message if net pay is zero, negative, or over $300, there is a column for notes and a code in the column is used to reference an error message at the bottom of the report.

The error and control report (titled Paycheck Report: Table Values and Error Messages) produced during input validation consists of three parts (see Figure 4-21):

Figure 4-16 Example of Employee Paycheck Report from payroll reports program.

```
                Employee Paycheck Report
                  Week Ended 03/19/87

     Employee      ID   Dept    Gross    Total      Net    Notes
       Name              Name    Pay   Deductions

R. M. NELSON  42753   FIN    298.00   117.24    180.76

T. NAMAN      69852   ENGR    26.70    32.84     -6.14      A

L. SMITH      35748   ENGR   399.09   110.50    288.59

J. JOHNSON    36985   MKTG    60.50    48.08     12.42

P. HOFFMANN   23456   PROD   142.80    56.51     86.29

A. PETERSON   74365   PROD   294.02   113.43    180.59

RALPH JONES   15786   ACCT   250.57    74.79    175.78


              Totals  1471.68   553.40    918.29


   Notes
   A - Net pay is out of bounds. Do not issue check.
```

1. An echoing of the table of department numbers and names for visual validation.
2. Error messages identifying errors detected during input validation.
    (a) For invalid data (invalid department number), the error message identifies the cause of the rejection and the record number of the rejected record.
    (b) For data-type errors, the message identifies the record number.
    (c) For array overflow caused by excess employee data records, an excess data error message is printed and the program is terminated.
3. A record count of total records read and total records rejected.

Program Documentation for General Example 4

The documentation of program design is given by a pseudocode description (Figure 4-17) and a program flowchart (Figure 4-18). The program listing is given in Figure 4-19. Test data records used for the sample output are listed in Figure 4-20. The test data items merely illustrate the output and are not a complete test of the program. An example of a Paycheck Report: Table Values and Error Messages is shown in Figure 4-21, and an example of an Employee Paycheck Report is given in Figure 4-16.

Notes on General Example 4

The outputs from program example 4 are in much better form than previous reports. There are two separate reports, and there is a date on the reports. Error messages are removed from the detail report, headings are more meaningful, and the order of output is under program control.

The variables identification block has been enlarged to include a section identifying arrays (lines 16 to 27) and a section that names temporary variables (lines 49 to 52). Temporary variable names are used only in a short block of code and are not needed either before or after that block is executed. Such variables may function as temporary counters or, as in this case, to improve readability or efficiency. The reason for listing them in the variables identification is that if the program is later revised and modified, the same name should not be used as a variable name.

This program again illustrates selective use of the type statements. Three variable names are specified as type INTEGER: DEPT, DEPTS, and RECS (line 60). Note that DEPT refers to an array that stores integer values.

DIMENSION and DATA statements appear in the type declaration and storage allocation block. Some variables in the program are initialized by a DATA statement in line 64 and others by arithmetic assignment statements in lines 83–88. Although logically equivalent, these are handled differently by the FORTRAN compiler. The DATA statement method is generally preferred, but there are some restrictions in special cases that will be explained in Chapter 5.

It is always wise to clearly label a report with a heading that includes the date covered by the report (see lines 75–79). Another desirable technique (not used in this example) is to label the report with the date prepared or version number. In case there are errors and the report is rerun, the most recent output is clearly identified. The date for the report is the first input record with the file of employee data (line 75). This data record identifies the data file and is used for placing a date on the two reports.

Two input validation techniques are illustrated in the program: table printout for visual validation (lines 101–104) and checking input data against a table of valid values (lines 131–140). Tables of values used by the program are more sensitive (have

Figure 4-17 Pseudocode description of logic of general program example 4—payroll reports.

```
Dimension arrays for 6 departments and 15 employee records (5 de-
    partments, maximum of 14 accepted records and 1 potential
    error case for each)
OPEN data files
WRITE heading and date at top of page for Paycheck Report: Table
    Values and Error Messages
Initialize counters, summing variables and rates
READ set of allowable department numbers and names
WRITE table of department numbers and names for visual validation
WRITE error message heading
READ an employee record and test for end of data and data-type error
    If no more records, go to Print Detail Report, else continue
    If data-type error, increment record counter, print message, and
    go back to READ, else continue
Test number of accepted records
    If number exceeds limit of array storage, print excess records
    message and stop
    Else continue
Test for valid input data
    IF invalid, print error message and go back to READ
    Else continue
Test for invalid employee department number
    IF invalid employee department number, print message and go back
    to READ, else continue
Compute payroll data and store in arrays
    Compute overtime
    Compute gross pay, including overtime (if any)
    Compute taxes, pension contributions, all deductions
    Compute net pay
Add employee gross pay, total deductions, and net pay to totals
Increment accepted employee records counter by 1 and go back to READ
Print Detail Report
WRITE record counts at bottom of Paycheck Report: Table Values and
    Error Messages
WRITE heading and date for Employee Paycheck Report at top of new
    page
DO for all departments
    Select department numbers in order
    For each employee PRINT detail (Name, ID, Dept. Name, Gross Pay,
    Deductions, Net Pay)
    If net pay is outside limits (negative or > 300), PRINT error code
    on same line
End of DO
WRITE summary totals and error code explanation
CLOSE data files
STOP
```

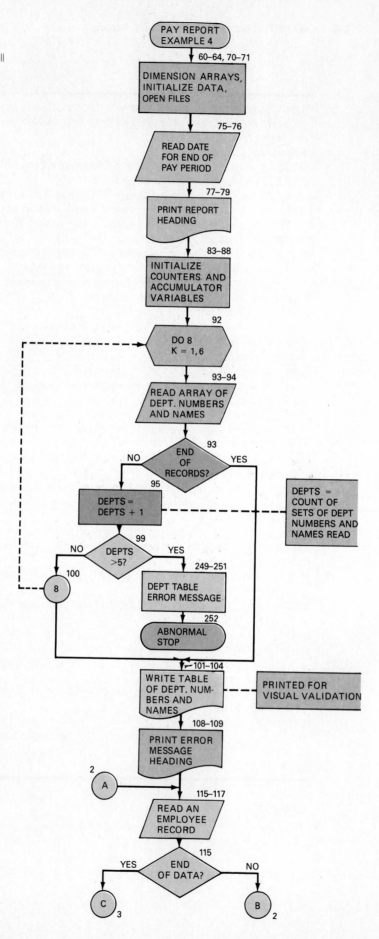

Figure 4-18 Program flowchart for general program example 4—payroll reports. (Numbers next to symbols are line numbers from program listing.)

PAY REPORT EXAMPLE 4

60–64, 70–71
DIMENSION ARRAYS, INITIALIZE DATA, OPEN FILES

75–76
READ DATE FOR END OF PAY PERIOD

77–79
PRINT REPORT HEADING

83–88
INITIALIZE COUNTERS AND ACCUMULATOR VARIABLES

92
DO 8 K = 1,6

93–94
READ ARRAY OF DEPT. NUMBERS AND NAMES

93
END OF RECORDS?

NO   YES

95
DEPTS = DEPTS + 1

DEPTS = COUNT OF SETS OF DEPT NUMBERS AND NAMES READ

99
DEPTS >5?

NO   YES

100
8

249–251
DEPT TABLE ERROR MESSAGE

252
ABNORMAL STOP

101–104
WRITE TABLE OF DEPT. NUMBERS AND NAMES

PRINTED FOR VISUAL VALIDATION

108–109
PRINT ERROR MESSAGE HEADING

2
A

115–117
READ AN EMPLOYEE RECORD

115
END OF DATA?

YES   NO

C 3

B 2

33

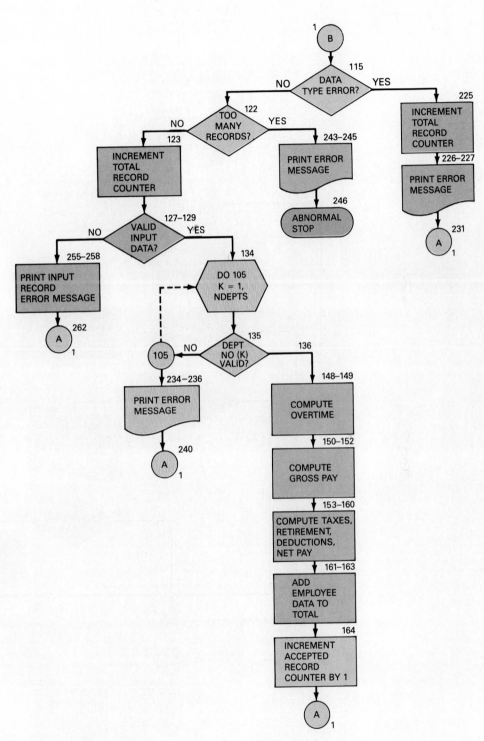

Figure 4-18 continued

Figure 4-18 concluded

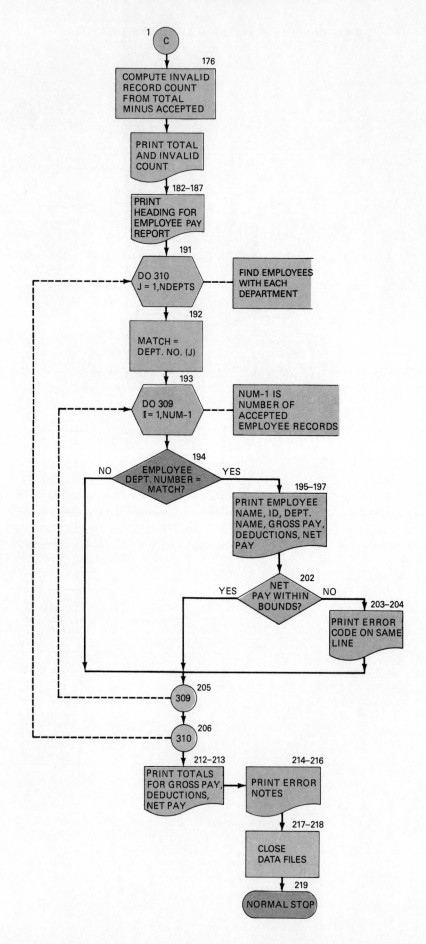

more error impact) than individual employee data records. If an employee data record has an error in hours worked, the error affects only one paycheck. If a table of values used in computation is in error, it can affect many paychecks. The table in this program is not used in computation, but many tables are used in that way. For example, a company may have different pay classses, and a table of pay rates may be input for use by the paycheck program. In addition to simple output and visual validation of tables, other techniques may be applied to tables used in computation. Control totals for rows, columns, and the entire table may be printed for manual comparison with the valid amounts. Any unauthorized changes in amounts or rates can be detected by this procedure.

Unlike the hours worked, pay rate, and deductions which can be checked against preestablished limits, many input items can only be checked to see if they are part of a set of valid values. This form of input validation is used in lines 131–140 to check the department numbers contained in the input data. If the department number in an input is not one of those in the department table, it is an invalid number. An error message is printed, the input record is rejected, and a new record is read (lines 234–240).

Validation of the paycheck amount for a negative amount is extended to test that the paycheck amount is within limits from zero to an upper limit (line 202). The testing for an upper limit illustrates how to combat those classic $1,000,005.37 "computer errors" described in newspaper articles. It is always good style to test, if possible, critical output data items to see if they are in a range of reasonable values.

As part of error control, two record counters are established for total records read and valid records and incremented (line 123 and line 164). Invalid records are computed. The first counter (RECS) keeps track of all records read, while the second (NUM) counts those accepted (error-free). These counters were initialized in lines 86 and 87. The initialization of NUM at 1 and RECS at zero illustrates the handling of a first-time-through problem. RECS is incremented after a new record has actually been read; NUM is set to the record number that the record will be if it is valid. Therefore, NUM is set at 1 for the first record to be read and thereafter the value of the record to be read. The reason for this is that value of NUM is the subscript for all processing associated with the record. If, however, the end of records is detected, a last-time-through condition occurs. At that point, NUM is set at the number of valid records plus 1; the computation of invalid records in line 176 reflects this by subtracting 1 (written as subtracting NUM and adding 1 which is equivalent).

Arrays are used to store data previously referenced by individual variable names. The arrays are both one- and two-dimensional. Conceptually, there are arrays for the department table, input data, and results. They are dimensioned in lines 62–63.

1. The department table arrays consist of 2 one-dimensional arrays with five entries containing the numbers and names for departments and a sixth for a record to detect array overflow for this table, that is, too many table entries.

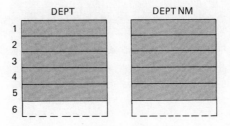

Figure 4-19 Listing of FORTRAN program for general program example 4—payroll reports.

```
 1 **********
 2 *                          PROGRAM IDENTIFICATION
 3 **********
 4 *
 5 *        This program computes employee paychecks based
 6 *        upon hours worked, wage rate and various deductions.
 7 *        It prints employee data (File DATA4E) grouped by
 8 *        departments (File DATA4D). Written for file input
 9 *        and batch execution.
10 *        Written 4/27/77 by T. Hoffmann   rev. 1/13/82  3/16/87
11 *
12 **********
13 *                          VARIABLES IDENTIFICATION
14 **********
15 *
16 *****                        ARRAY NAMES
17 *
18 *        ID      = Employee identification number (integer)
19 *        GRSPAY  = Gross pay: $
20 *        NAME    = Employee names (character)
21 *        NDEP    = Dept. Number where worked (integer)
22 *        DEPT    = List of department numbers (integer)
23 *        DEPTNM  = Corresponding list of department names (character)
24 *        PAYCHK  = Net paycheck amount: $
25 *        PAYDAT  = Payroll input data (hrswrk,wgrate,deduc)
26 *        TDEDUC  = Total of all deductions for an employee
27 *
28 *****                        SIMPLE VARIABLES
29 *
30 *        DEPTS   = Number of departments (integer)
31 *        RECS    = Number of records read (integer)
32 *        NUM     = Number of valid employee records accepted (integer)
33 *        NOTVLD  = Number of not valid employee records (integer)
34 *        OTIME   = Hours of overtime (excess over 40.0)
35 *        RETIRE  = Retirement contribution by employee
36 *        TAXES   = Taxes due: $
37 *        TOTNET  = Total of net pay amounts
38 *        TOTPAY  = Total gross pay for company: $
39 *        TOTDUC  = Total of all employee deductions
40 *        WKEND   = Date of week payroll ended (MM/DD/YY) (character)
41 *
42 *****                    IDENTIFICATION OF CONSTANTS
43 *
44 *        PLIMIT  = Maximum paycheck value to allow - $300.00
45 *        MAXEMP  = Maximum number of valid employee records - 14
46 *        PNRATE  = Pension contribution rate - 0.05
47 *        TAXRT   = Tax rate - 0.15
48 *
49 *****                    TEMPORARY VARIABLE NAMES
50 *
51 *        MATCH,PAYNET
52 *
53 **********
54 *                     TYPE DECLARATION AND STORAGE ALLOCATION
55 **********
56 *
57 *        Maximum number of valid employee records is 14 (MAXEMP)
58 *        Maximum number of departments is 5
59 *
60       INTEGER DEPT,RECS,DEPTS
61       CHARACTER NAME*12,DEPTNM*4,WKEND*8
62       DIMENSION DEPT(6),DEPTNM(6),ID(15),NAME(15),NDEP(15),
63      1    PAYDAT(15,3),GRSPAY(15),TDEDUC(15),PAYCHK(15)
64       DATA PLIMIT/300.0/MAXEMP/14/PNRATE/0.05/TAXRT/0.15/
65 *
66 **********
67 * BLOCK 0000               INITIALIZATION BLOCK
68 **********
69 *
70       OPEN(7,FILE='DATA4D')
71       OPEN(8,FILE='DATA4E')
72 *
73 *                     READ DATE AND PRINT HEADER
74 *
75       READ(8,1) WKEND
```

Figure 4-19 continued

```
76    1 FORMAT(A8)
77      WRITE(6,3) WKEND
78    3 FORMAT(' Paycheck Report: Table Values and Error Messages'/
79    1    20X,'Week Ended ',A8/)
80  *
81  *            ZERO ACCUMULATORS AND INITIALIZE COUNTERS
82  *
83      TOTPAY = 0.0
84      TOTNET = 0.0
85      TOTDUC = 0.0
86      RECS = 0
87      NUM = 1
88      DEPTS = 0
89  *
90  *            READ AND PRINT DEPARTMENT NUMBERS AND NAMES
91  *
92      DO 8 K = 1,6
93          READ(7,7,END=9) DEPT(K),DEPTNM(K)
94    7   FORMAT(I4,A4)
95          DEPTS = DEPTS + 1
96  *
97  *            TEST TO DETECT TOO MANY TABLE ENTRIES
98  *
99          IF(DEPTS .GT. 5) GOTO 908
100   8 CONTINUE
101   9 WRITE(6,10)
102  10 FORMAT(' Table of Departments'/3X,' Number    Name')
103     WRITE(6,11) (DEPT(K),DEPTNM(K),K=1,DEPTS)
104  11 FORMAT(5X,I4,4X,A4)
105  *
106  *                PRINT ERROR MESSAGE HEADER
107  *
108     WRITE(6,13)
109  13 FORMAT(///6X,'Error messages during data input'/)
110  *
111 **********
112 * BLOCK 0100        READ EMPLOYEE DATA
113 **********
114  *
115 101 READ(8,102,END=301,ERR=901) ID(NUM),NAME(NUM),
116   1     NDEP(NUM),(PAYDAT(NUM,K),K=1,3)
117 102 FORMAT(I5,2X,A12,2X,I4,2X,F4.1,2X,F4.2,2X,F5.2)
118  *
119  *            TEST TO PREVENT ARRAY OVERFLOW. IF ARRAY'S NOT FULL
120  *                GO ON TO CHECK DATA VALIDITY
121  *
122     IF(NUM.GT.MAXEMP) GOTO 906
123     RECS = RECS + 1
124  *
125  *                VALIDATE PAYROLL DATA
126  *
127     IF(PAYDAT(NUM,1) .LE. 0.0 .OR. PAYDAT(NUM,1) .GT. 60.0) GOTO 910
128     IF(PAYDAT(NUM,2) .LE. 0.0 .OR. PAYDAT(NUM,2) .GT. 10.0) GOTO 910
129     IF(PAYDAT(NUM,3) .LT. 0.0 .OR. PAYDAT(NUM,3) .GT. 65.0) GOTO 910
130  *
131  *            CHECK FOR VALID DEPARTMENT NUMBER IN EMPLOYEE RECORD
132  *                WHEN FOUND, PROCESS EMPLOYEE DATA
133  *
134     DO 105 K=1,DEPTS
135         IF(DEPT(K).EQ.NDEP(NUM)) GOTO 201
136 105 CONTINUE
137  *
138  *            ERROR -- NO MATCH FOUND FOR EMPLOYEE DEPT. NUMBER
139  *
140     GOTO 903
141  *
142 **********
143 * BLOCK 0200            COMPUTE GROSS PAY, DEDUCTIONS & NET PAY BLOCI
144 **********
145  *
146  *                COMPUTE PAY, INCLUDING OVERTIME, IF ANY.
147  *
148 201 OTIME = PAYDAT(NUM,1) - 40.0
149     IF(OTIME.GT.0.0) THEN
150             GRSPAY(NUM) = (40.0 + 1.5*OTIME)*PAYDAT(NUM,2)
151         ELSE
152             GRSPAY(NUM) = PAYDAT(NUM,1)*PAYDAT(NUM,2)
153     ENDIF
```

Figure 4-19 continued

```
154 *
155 *                       COMPUTE EACH TYPE OF DEDUCTION AND NET PAY
156 *
157       TAXES = GRSPAY(NUM)*TAXRT
158       RETIRE = GRSPAY(NUM)*PNRATE
159       TDEDUC(NUM) = PAYDAT(NUM,3) + TAXES + RETIRE
160       PAYCHK(NUM) = GRSPAY(NUM) - TDEDUC(NUM)
161       TOTPAY = TOTPAY + GRSPAY(NUM)
162       TOTDUC = TOTDUC + TDEDUC(NUM)
163       TOTNET = TOTNET + PAYCHK(NUM)
164       NUM = NUM + 1
165 *
166 *                       GO BACK TO READ ANOTHER RECORD
167 *
168       GOTO 101
169 *
170 **********
171 * BLOCK 0300              PRINT DETAIL BY DEPARTMENT GROUPING
172 **********
173 *
174 *                 PRINT SUMMARY OF DATA INPUT MESSAGES
175 *
176 301 NOTVLD = RECS - NUM + 1
177       WRITE(6,302) RECS,NOTVLD
178 302 FORMAT('0',I4,' Records read'/1X,I5,' Records in error')
179 *
180 *            PRINT HEADER/TITLE LINE FOR EMPLOYEE DETAIL REPORT
181 *
182       WRITE(6,303) WKEND
183 303 FORMAT('1',T17,'Employee Paycheck Report'/T19,'Week Ended ',A8/)
184       WRITE(6,304)
185 304 FORMAT(5X,'Employee',5X,'ID',3X,'Dept',3X,'Gross',4X,
186     1      'Total',6X,'Net',4X,'Notes'/7X,'Name',12X,'Name',4X,
187     2      'Pay',3X,'Deductions')
188 *
189 *          FOR EACH DEPARTMENT FIND EACH EMPLOYEE & PRINT DETAIL
190 *
191       DO 310 J=1,DEPTS
192         MATCH = DEPT(J)
193         DO 309 I=1,NUM-1
194           IF(NDEP(I).NE.MATCH) GOTO 309
195           WRITE(6,305) NAME(I),ID(I),DEPTNM(J),
196     1        GRSPAY(I),TDEDUC(I),PAYCHK(I)
197 305       FORMAT('0',2X,A12,I6,2X,A4,3X,F6.2,3X,F6.2,3X,F6.2)
198           PAYNET = PAYCHK(I)
199 *
200 *                  CHECK FOR VALID PAYCHECK AMOUNT
201 *
202           IF(PAYNET.GT.0.0 .AND. PAYNET.LE.PLIMIT) GOTO 309
203           WRITE(6,306)
204 306       FORMAT('+',57X,'A')
205 309   CONTINUE
206 310 CONTINUE
207 *
208 **********
209 * BLOCK 0400              PRINT SUMMARY AND TERMINATE
210 **********
211 *
212     WRITE(6,402) TOTPAY,TOTDUC,TOTNET
213 402 FORMAT(//20X,'Totals',3X,F7.2,2F9.2)
214     WRITE(6,403)
215 403 FORMAT(///5X,'Notes'/5X,'A - Net pay is out of bounds',
216     1      '. Do not issue check.')
217 410 CLOSE (7)
218     CLOSE (8)
219     STOP
220 *
221 **********
222 * BLOCK 0900              ERROR MESSAGE BLOCK
223 **********
224 *
225 901 RECS = RECS + 1
226     WRITE(6,902) RECS
227 902 FORMAT(//'*****',' ERROR IN EMPLOYEE RECORD NUMBER',I3,'*****')
228 *
229 *                  GO BACK TO READ NEXT EMPLOYEE RECORD
```

Figure 4-19 concluded

```
230 *
231     GOTO 101
232 *****
233 *
234 903 WRITE(6,904) RECS
235 904 FORMAT(//' ***** ERROR - DEPT. NO. NOT VALID IN ',
236   1     'EMPLOYEE RECORD NO. ',I4,2X,'*****')
237 *
238 *               GO BACK TO READ NEXT EMPLOYEE RECORD
239 *
240     GOTO 101
241 *****
242 *
243 906 WRITE(6,907) MAXEMP
244 907 FORMAT(///' ***** ERROR. ATTEMPTED TO READ ',
245   1     'MORE THAN',I3,' VALID RECORDS'/7X,'PROGRAM ABORTED. ')
246 *
247 *               CLOSE FILES AND ABORT RUN
248 *
249     GOTO 410
250 *****
251 *
252 908 WRITE(6,909)
253 909 FORMAT (///'***** ERROR. ATTEMPTED TO READ TOO MANY DEPARTMENT ',
254   1     'NAMES. *****')
255 *
256 *               CLOSE FILES AND ABORT RUN
257 *
258     GOTO 410
259 *****
260 *
261 910 WRITE(6,911) RECS,ID(NUM),NAME(NUM),(PAYDAT(NUM,I),I=1,3)
262 911 FORMAT('0','***** Data outside validation limits--input ',
263   1     'rejected ***** record',I3/7X,'Data contents ',
264   2     I5,2X,A12,2X,F5.1,2X,F5.2,2X,F6.2)
265 *
266 *               GO BACK AND READ ANOTHER EMPLOYEE RECORD
267 *
268     GOTO 101
269 *
270     END
```

Figure 4-20 Annotated input test data for general program 4.

```
1234FIN
4275ENGR
7269MKTG
7531PROD
8551ACCT
```

```
03/19/87
23456   P. HOFFMANN    7531   40.0   3.57   27.95
15786   RALPH JONES    8551   39.9   6.28   24.68
36985   J. JOHNSON     7269   22.0   0275   03598
23456   T. HOFFMANN    1596   40.0   3.57   27.95    Dept. no. not valid
69852   T. NAMAN       4275   10.0   2.67   27.50    Negative pay
35748   L. SMITH       4275   40.1   9.94   30.68
W. RONG              1596.   GEN                     Invalid data
42753   R. M. NELSON   1234   40.0   7.45   57.64
74365   A. PETERSON    7531   54.0   4.82   54.63
62475   F. MORLOCK     4275   37.5   8.24   65.34    Outside limits
```

Figure 4-21 Example of Paycheck Report: Table Values and Error Messages from payroll reports program.

```
Paycheck Report: Table Values and Error Messages
                Week Ended 03/19/87
Table of Departments
   Number    Name
   1234      FIN
   4275      ENGR
   7269      MKTG
   7531      PROD
   8551      ACCT


   Error messages during data input


***** ERROR - DEPT. NO. NOT VALID IN EMPLOYEE RECORD NO.     4  *****

***** ERROR IN EMPLOYEE RECORD NUMBER  7 *****

***** Data outside validation limits--input rejected ***** record 10
      Data contents 62475  F. MORLOCK     37.5   8.24   65.34

  10 Records read
   3 Records in error
```

2. Arrays for input data consist of 15 rows to accommodate 14 valid employee records as well as a potential error case. The use of these arrays allows all input data to be stored so that the error report can be prepared separately and the output can be in a different order than the input.

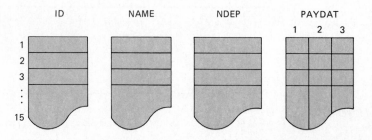

There is an array for identification numbers, an array for names, a number-of-department list, and a table for three different types of payroll data (previously called HRSWRK, WGRATE, and DEDUC). A reference to hours worked for the I*th* valid record is now PAYDAT(I, 1).

3. The arrays for results consist of 3 one-dimensional, 15-element arrays for gross pay, total deductions, and net pay.

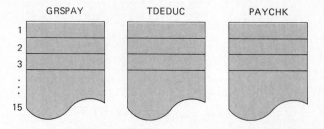

On input (lines 115–116), data items are assigned to rows in the different arrays by using the value of the valid input counter (NUM). Invalid data is not stored in the arrays. If the current value of NUM is 3, then a statement that reads ID(NUM), NDEP(NUM), etc., will place the ID in element 3 of the ID array, and NDEP in the third element of the array for number of department where employee works. If the data on input turns out to be invalid, the counter NUM does not change and the next input record is stored in the same locations, replacing the invalid input.

If a program attempts to store more data in arrays than has been allocated in the DIMENSION statement, there will be an error that may cause incorrect results or abnormal termination. Therefore, a program should be designed to prevent attempting to store too many data items in arrays. There are various methods for doing this. Note two cases in the sample program.

1. A specified number of sets of data items to be stored plus storage locations to detect overflow from input (too many input records). Since the program specifications define five departments, the department table arrays are dimensioned at six rows of storage locations for the five departments plus one row to use in detecting possible input overflow. The READ statement in the DO loop is executed up to six times, reading up to six records each with a set of data values. The READ statement at line 93 has an END = 9 specification, which will transfer control to the statement labeled 9 (line 101) if there are five or less inputs to the table. If a sixth entry is read (an error condition), line 99 transfers control to an error message and the program stops execution.

2. An unspecified number of data items to be stored but with a limit. Since the program description calls for an unspecified number of input pay records but not to exceed 14 accepted records, a count is established for accepted records stored in the various arrays. This count is tested against a limiting value at line 122. If a record is read after the limit has been reached, there are too many pay records in the input file. An error message is printed, and the program is aborted (lines 243–246).

The logic of using the final storage location for checking for too many input records will be traced in detail. Since the program is designed for a maximum of 14 or less valid records, there are no problems with less than or equal to the maximum number. After reading the last valid record, the program attempts to read another record (line 115) and finds none. This causes control to go to statement 301 for termination processes. But what happens if there is another record after the limiting number (an error)? The program stores each record in the array pending validation, so there must be a place for it. The program design question is whether or not the program should detect and report on the existence of more than the maximum number of valid input records. If the answer is "no," then the number of valid records that has been read can be used to stop the read operation prior to any extra record. If excess input records should be detected and reported, the program illustrates one method. Note that the procedure detects one extra input record; it does not detect the existence of more than one.

The program makes use of two implied DO loops for input and output. Review these:

		Lines
1.	PRINT table of department names	103
2.	READ employee data	116

In the print detail block, note the use of the local variable MATCH. The value of MATCH (line 192) is a function of the "outside" loop index J; it does not change with the "inner" loop I. To reduce execution time [to eliminate the necessity to reevaluate DEPT(J) for each change in I], a local temporary variable has been used. Similarly, PAYNET (line 198) has been set so that PAYCHK(I) need be referenced only once, not twice, in line 202. In this simple program, these temporary variables are not needed to reduce execution time, but are used to illustrate the technique of programming for efficiency.

Other payroll program features that are instructive include the following:

The use of a DO loop to locate the employees working in a department so the report can print the employees grouped by department (lines 189–195).

The explicit closing of the files in lines 217–218 that were opened at lines 70–71. Up to this point, implicit closing of files has been used.

The printing of a warning flag (a letter pointing to a note for the report) for net pay that is negative or exceeds the limit (lines 203–204). Note the use of the + in the FORMAT statement to put the "A" on the line with the net pay outside the limits.

Mathematical Program Example 4—Tables of Cumulative Normal Probability

This example is designed for interactive execution. It also illustrates the use of an array to hold the ordinates needed for Simpson's rule. In this case, the computation is numerical integration. As a review of this procedure, recall that integration means computing the area under a curve within an interval of the function. One approach to this is to divide the interval into small segments, to define each segment as a rectangle, and to compute the areas of each of these using the formula area = base × height. The areas for the segments are summed to give the area for the interval. For example:

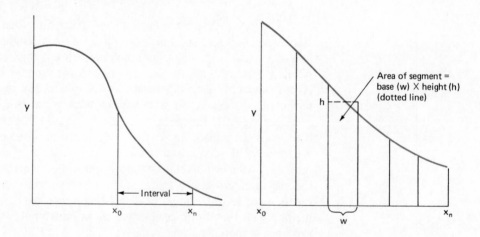

The difficulty with the approach is selecting an approximate height, since the heights of the two sides (given by the ordinates of the curve) are not the same. A simple method is to average the two heights. The area equation becomes

$$a_n = \frac{y_{n-1} + y_n}{2} w$$

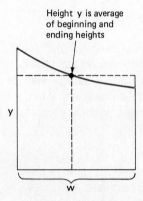

Height y is average of beginning and ending heights

While this averaging of the beginning and ending ordinates is a good approximation, it can be improved. If the curve is approximated by a second-degree polynomial, Simpson's rule provides a better measure of the area. The interval is divided into n segments (n must be an even number).

$$\text{Area} = \frac{w}{3} (y_0 + 4y_1 + 2y_2 + 4y_3 + \cdots + 4y_{n-1} + y_n)$$

The n ordinates are multiplied by 1, 2, or 4 (first and last ordinates by 1, even-numbered ordinates by 2, and odd-numbered ones by 4). The sum of these products is divided by 3 and multiplied by interval width w. It is not necessary to understand the formula to read the program; just accept it as the formula for computing the area.

Problem Description for Mathematical Example 4

The program is to calculate and print a normal probability table of positive Z values and corresponding probability of Z or less. The positive Z values represent multiples of the standard deviation greater than the mean. The probability of Z or less represents the cumulative probability of an item being included in the range containing all items up to Z standard deviations greater than the mean. These Z values are vital in statistical hypothesis testing, and tables of Z values are included in statistics texts.

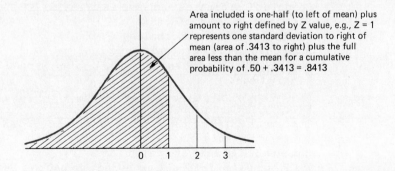

Area included is one-half (to left of mean) plus amount to right defined by Z value, e.g., Z = 1 represents one standard deviation to right of mean (area of .3413 to right) plus the full area less than the mean for a cumulative probability of .50 + .3413 = .8413

The program produces a new table with appropriate headings for each valid interactive input. The input defines the beginning of the table, the end of the table, and the interval between table entries for Z. The input is checked for invalid values— negative values or initial value greater than ending value. An invalid value results in an error message with rejection of the input and request for new input.

$$\text{Probability} = \int_{-\infty}^{Z*} f(Z) = 0.5 + \int_{0}^{Z*} \frac{1}{\sqrt{2\pi}} e^{-(X^2/2)}$$

The area under $y = f(Z)$ in the interval 0 to $Z*$ is to be computed using Simpson's rule. The distance on the x-axis between zero and the Z entry for which a probability is being computed is divided into 20 segments. The area is then computed using Simpson's rule with 20 values of y corresponding to the 20 values of x. Each ordinate (height) is computed as in the mathematical program in Chapter 3b.

$$\text{Ordinate} = \frac{1}{\sqrt{2\pi}} e^{-(X^2/2)}$$

Program Documentation for Mathematical Example 4

The documentation consists of a pseudocode program description (Figure 4-22), a program flowchart (Figure 4-23), a program listing (Figure 4-24), and an example of input and output from interactive execution of the program (Figure 4-25).

Notes on Mathematical Example 4

The program continues the practice followed in the previous interactive programs of using a response to a reply to decide on termination of execution. There is an explicit-type declaration for all variables. Input is list-directed; output is formatted.

In this case, the variable identification block has been augmented by a special section for listing array names (lines 16–19). An algorithm block has been added to

Figure 4-22 Pseudocode description of program for mathematical example 4—normal probability tables.

```
WRITE heading for session
READ set of inputs: start value, end value, and table increment
Validate data
    If invalid data, write error message, and go to Ask if
WRITE table heading
Set ZSTAR (Z value being computed) to start value for first entry
Set X to zero
Compute size of 20 X increments from zero to ZSTAR
Initialize sums to zero
Compute 20 ordinates and save in array
Sum first and last ordinate
Sum even-numbered ordinates
Sum odd-numbered ordinates
Compute TOTSUM of first sum plus 2 times second sum plus 4 times
    third sum
Probability equals 0.5 + (increment * TOTSUM)/3
WRITE ZSTAR and probability
Increment ZSTAR by table increment to set ZSTAR to next value of Z
    entry in table
Compare ZSTAR with end value for Z
    IF end value for Z not exceeded, go back to Set X
    ELSE continue
Ask if "compute another table?"
    IF "yes" go back to READ set of inputs
    ELSE STOP
```

Figure 4-23 Program flowchart for mathematical program example 4—normal probability. (Numbers next to symbols are line numbers from program listing.)

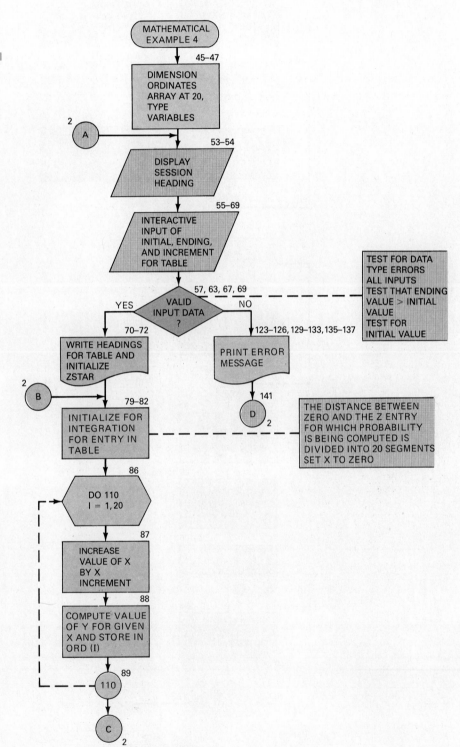

Figure 4-23 concluded

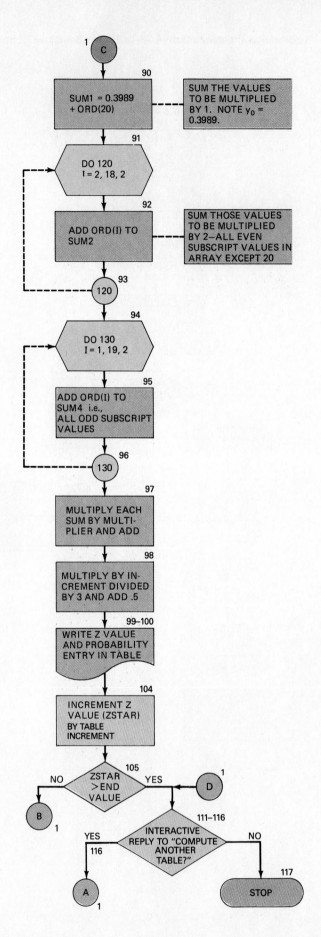

Figure 4-24 Listing of FORTRAN program for mathematical program example 4—normal probability tables.

```
 1 **********
 2 *                        PROGRAM IDENTIFICATION
 3 **********
 4 *
 5 *        Generate table of cumulative probabilities (area of the
 6 *        normal curve) less than Z for a set of positive values
 7 *        for Z. Interactive input of starting Z value, ending Z
 8 *        value, and Z value increment for table. Probability
 9 *        generated using Simpson's rule for numerical integration.
10 *        Written 04/30/77 by T. Hoffmann rev. 1/13/82   3/9/87
11 *
12 **********
13 *                        VARIABLES IDENTIFICATION
14 **********
15 *
16 *****                       ARRAY NAMES
17 *
18 *        ORD        - Ordinates of the normal curve
19 *
20 *****                     SIMPLE VARIABLES
21 *
22 *        VALU1      - Starting value for table of probabilities
23 *        VALU2      - Ending value for table
24 *        STPSIZ     - Step size (i.e. table increment)
25 *        ZSTAR      - Upper bound of integration interval
26 *        X          - Abscissa values in Simpson's rule
27 *        XINCR      - Integration interval
28 *        SUM1       - Sum of first and last ordinates
29 *        SUM2       - Sum of even ordinates
30 *        SUM4       - Sum of odd ordinates
31 *        TOTSUM     - Weighted total sum of all ordinates
32 *        PROB       - Normal probability value
33 *        REPLY      - Y or N response to "Compute another table?"
34 *
35 **********
36 *                        ALGORITHM - SIMPSON'S RULE
37 **********
38 *
39 *PROB=.5+(XINCR/3)*(ORD(0)+4*ORD(1)+2*ORD(2)+...+4*ORD(N-1)+ORD(N))
40 *
41 **********
42 *                        TYPE DECLARATION AND STORAGE BLOCK
43 **********
44 *
45      REAL VALU1,VALU2,STPSIZ,ZSTAR,X,XINCR,SUM1,SUM2,SUM4,TOTSUM,PROB
46      CHARACTER REPLY*1
47      DIMENSION ORD(20)
48 *
49 **********
50 * BLOCK 0000          INITIALIZATION AND INPUT BLOCK
51 **********
52 *
53      WRITE(6,1)
54    1 FORMAT(/7X,'Normal Probability Table Program')
55    6 PRINT *
56      PRINT *,'What is the initial Z value? '
57      READ (5,*,ERR=901,END=299) VALU1
58 *
59 *                        INITIAL VALUE MUST BE POSITIVE
60 *
61      IF (VALU1 .LT. 0.0) GOTO 920
62      PRINT *, 'What should be the ending value? '
63      READ (5,*,ERR=901) VALU2
64 *
65 *                        TERMINAL VALUE MUST EXCEED INITIAL VALUE
66 *
67      IF( VALU1 .GT. VALU2) GOTO 910
68      PRINT *,'What should be the table increment? '
69      READ (5,*,ERR=901) STPSIZ
70      WRITE(6,11)
71   11 FORMAT(/5X,'Normal probability table'//6X,
72      1    'Z Value   Probability of'/,18X,'Z or less'/)
73      ZSTAR = VALU1
74 *
75 **********
```

Figure 4-24 concluded

```
 76  * BLOCK 0100              COMPUTE PROBABILITY VALUES
 77  **********
 78  *
 79    101 X = 0.0
 80        XINCR = ZSTAR/20.0
 81        SUM2 = 0.0
 82        SUM4 = 0.0
 83  *
 84  *                         COMPUTE 20 ORDINATES IN TABLE INTERVAL
 85  *
 86        DO 110 I = 1,20
 87            X = X + XINCR
 88            ORD(I) = 0.3989*EXP(-X*X/2.0)
 89    110 CONTINUE
 90        SUM1 = 0.3989 + ORD(20)
 91        DO 120 I= 2,18,2
 92            SUM2 = SUM2 + ORD(I)
 93    120 CONTINUE
 94        DO 130 I = 1,19,2
 95            SUM4 = SUM4 + ORD(I)
 96    130 CONTINUE
 97        TOTSUM = SUM1 + 2.0*SUM2 + 4.0*SUM4
 98        PROB = 0.5 + XINCR*TOTSUM/3.0
 99        WRITE(6,138) ZSTAR,PROB
100    138 FORMAT(7X,F6.2,7X,F6.4)
101  *
102  *                         INCREMENT TABLE VALUE AND REAPPLY RULE
103  *
104        ZSTAR = ZSTAR + STPSIZ
105        IF(ZSTAR.LE.VALU2) GOTO 101
106  *
107  **********
108  * BLOCK 0200              TERMINATION BLOCK
109  **********
110  *
111    201 PRINT*
112        PRINT*
113        PRINT *, 'Do you want to compute another table (Y/N)? '
114        READ(5,202,END=299) REPLY
115    202 FORMAT(A)
116        IF( REPLY .EQ. 'Y' .OR. REPLY .EQ. 'y') GOTO 6
117    299 STOP
118  *
119  *********
120  * BLOCK 0900              ERROR MESSAGE BLOCK
121  *********
122  *
123    901 WRITE(6,902)
124    902 FORMAT(//'***** ERROR. VALUE MUST BE REAL NUMBER. *****')
125  *
126        GOTO 998
127  *
128    910 WRITE(6,917) VALU1,VALU2
129    917 FORMAT(//'***** ERROR IN DATA.'/,
130       1 ' Starting value of table,',F6.2,
131       2 ', must be less than ending value,',F6.2)
132  *
133        GOTO 998
134  *
135    920 WRITE(6,925) VALU1
136    925 FORMAT(//'***** ERROR IN DATA' /,
137       1    ' Starting value should be positive, not',F6.2)
138  *
139  *       GO BACK TO CHECK WHETHER USER WANTS TO CONTINUE
140  *
141    998 GOTO 201
142  *
143        END
```

Figure 4-25 Example interactive input and output for mathematical program example 4—normal probability tables.

```
       Normal Probability Table Program
What is the initial Z value? 0

What should be the ending value? 3.0

What should be the table increment? 0.25

   Normal probability table

   Z Value    Probability of
                 Z or less

     0.00        0.5000
     0.25        0.5987
     0.50        0.6914
     0.75        0.7733
     1.00        0.8413
     1.25        0.8943
     1.50        0.9331
     1.75        0.9599
     2.00        0.9772
     2.25        0.9877
     2.50        0.9937
     2.75        0.9970
     3.00        0.9986


Do you want to compute another table (Y/N)? Y

What is the initial Z value? -1


**** ERROR IN DATA
Starting value should be positive, not -1.00


Do you want to compute another table (Y/N)? Y


What is the initial Z value? KL

**** ERROR. VALUE MUST BE REAL NUMBER. *****

Do you want to compute another table (Y/N)? Y

What is the initial Z value? 2.5

What should be the ending value? 1.5

**** ERROR IN DATA.
Starting value of table, 2.50, must be less than ending value, 1.50

Do you want to compute another table (Y/N)? Y

What is the initial Z value? 0.25

What should be the ending value? 0.25

What should be the table increment? 1

   Normal probability table

   Z Value    Probability of
                 Z or less

     0.25        0.5987

Do you want to compute another table (Y/N)? N
```

explain the methodology (lines 36–40). Also a storage allocation block is used for the DIMENSION statement.

The initialization and input block reads a data record and checks it for several kinds of potential errors. The handling of the errors detected by the program should be noted. There are three error conditions with error messages:

1. Nonnumeric characters are input. The error message is that the VALUE MUST BE A REAL NUMBER, and the program terminates the current set of data and asks if another table is to be computed (lines 123–126).
2. Starting value for table is less than the ending value. There is an error message, the current set of data is rejected, and the program asks if another table is to be computed (lines 128–133).
3. Starting value is not positive. There is an error message, the negative starting value is rejected, and the program asks if another table is to be computed (lines 135–141).

Note that in all three cases, the approach to interactive execution is to give an error message, reject the incorrect data, and ask if another set of data is to be entered. There is no attempt to fix the data or do incomplete processing because the person entering the data can make an immediate correction.

The program also illustrates an iterative computation procedure using DO loop variables to select the values from the array (lines 86–96). Note the DO variable at line 91 selects the values in the even cells of the array, while the DO variable in line 94 selects the values from the odd cells. When one line of the table has been computed and printed, the next ZSTAR value is computed by incrementing it by the step size for the table (line 104), and if the table is not complete (line 105), the computation is repeated with the new value for ZSTAR. When the new computation is begun, the variables used to compute and accumulate the sums must be reset to zero (lines 79–82).

The computation block uses Simpson's rule by computing 20 equally spaced ordinates and saving them in an array at lines 86–96. (The zeroth ordinate is known to be 0.3989 from setting Z to 0 in the normal equation.) Three partial sums are created: one for those ordinates multiplied by 1 (zeroth and last), a second for the even-numbered ordinates (those to be multiplied by 2), and the third for the odd-numbered ones (those to be multiplied by 4). Note the use of the DO loops and the values of the DO parameters in lines 91 and 94 to select the values to sum. The total sum is computed (line 97) by multiplying the partial sums by their appropriate values and adding. A less efficient way of doing this would have been to put a 2 multiplier and a 4 multiplier in front of ORD in lines 92 and 95, respectively. This would have caused 18 multiplications. (Why?)

Programming Exercises

Description of Assignment

Select one or more problems (or take the problems assigned by your instructor). Use DO loops in the program to process data and to perform input and output of subscripted variables. Use a DATA statement for initialization where appropriate. Follow the style guidelines and prepare the following:

1. Pseudocode description
2. Program flowchart

3. Program listing
4. List of test data and expected results, testing for both valid and invalid data where appropriate
5. Sample output including results of testing of all error conditions

Mathematics and Statistics

1. For each of the following sets of n data points (X, Y), compute the correlation coefficients r.

$$r = \frac{n\Sigma XY - (\Sigma X)(\Sigma Y)}{\sqrt{[n\Sigma X^2 - (\Sigma X)^2][n\Sigma Y^2 - (\Sigma Y)^2]}}$$

Set 1		Set 2	
X	Y	X	Y
34.22	102.43	20	27.1
39.87	100.93	30	28.9
41.85	97.43	40	30.6
43.23	97.81	50	32.3
40.06	98.32	60	33.7
53.29	98.32	70	35.6
53.29	100.07	80	37.2
54.14	97.08		
49.12	91.59		
40.71	94.85		
55.15	94.65		

2. Pascal's triangle is a set of numbers having some very interesting properties. (Actually, Omar Khayyám wrote about them well before Pascal.) Arranged in the usual manner (as shown below), each number in the interior is the sum of the numbers on either side of it in the row above. Any row (labeling the top as row zero) contains the coefficients of the expansion $(a + b)^n$ or the ordered set of combinations of n things taken m (0, 1, 2, etc., from left to right) at a time. Write a program to compute and print the first 11 rows ($n = 0$ through 10) of Pascal's triangle. Printing need not be in the symmetric triangle form.

n						
0			1			
1		1		1		
2	1		2		1	
3	1	3		3		1
etc.			etc.			

3. Write a program using Simpson's rule to evaluate the gamma function (the generalization of the factorial) for the following set of values: $n = 0.05, 1.7, 2.0,$ and 1.5. *Hint:* Since $\log \frac{1}{x}$ where $x = 0$ is undefined, use a very small number in place of zero, such as $1.0E - 10$.

$$\text{Gamma} = \int_0^1 \left(\log \frac{1}{n}\right)^{n-1} \quad \text{for } n > 0$$

Business and Economics

4. Prepare tables of the form given below showing the size of a loan that is possible from different monthly payments ($100 to $500 in $50 increments) for a given number of months m at annual interest rates of 7, 8, 9, 10, 11, and 12 percent. Assume the monthly rate is one-twelfth the yearly rate. Read in m as 240 and 300.

```
Term in Months     NNN
                                   Annual interest rate
Monthly
payments       .07           .08          .09        . . .       .12

$100          XXXXX.        XXXXX.
 150          XXXXX.
 200
 250
 300
 .
 .
 .
 500
```

5. Prepare a table of the form shown below for given interest rates i and 1-year increments from 1 through 10 years showing the effect on an initial amount of $100 compounded annually, quarterly, monthly, weekly (assume exactly 52 weeks per year), daily (assume each year has 365 days), and continuously. Use i values of 7, 9, and 12 percent. (See problem 4 in Chapter 2 for formulas.)

```
NN Interest Rate
                          Frequency of compounding
Year      1           4         12     52     365     Continuous

 1      XXXX.XX    XXXX.XX
 2      XXXX.XX
 .
 .
 .
10
```

6. A business executive has the following portfolio of stocks at the start of a period and makes the given set of transactions during the period. Prepare a report showing her starting position, a summary of her transactions, and her final position. *Hint:* Reference the stocks by number rather than by name. You may wish to use current stock quotations.

Starting Portfolio

Stock number	Stock	Shares	Price/share
1	International Harvester	100	$33.50
2	White Consolidated	200	27.50
3	Texaco	100	29.25
4	Northern Natural Gas	300	44.00
5	National Distillers	500	24.25
6	Public Service of Colorado	200	29.75
7	Middle Southern Utilities	200	16.25

Transactions

Number	Stock	Action	Shares	Price
3	Texaco	Buy	100	$28.75
8	Anheuser-Busch	Buy	200	23.00
4	Northern Natural Gas	Sell	200	45.25
7	Middle Southern Utilities	Buy	100	17.00
9	IBM	Buy	100	61.50
1	International Harvester	Sell	100	32.00
3	Texaco	Buy	100	29.50
6	Public Service of Colorado	Sell	200	20.25
10	Control Data	Buy	100	21.25

Final Prices

Stock	Price	Stock	Price
International Harvester	$ 8.25	Public Service of Colorado	$13.75
White Consolidated	25.25	Middle Southern Utilities	12.75
Texaco	30.62	Control Data	31.38
Anheuser-Busch	22.25	IBM	61.50
Northern Natural Gas	47.50	National Distillers	22.37

Science and Engineering

7. A frequently encountered computer science problem is to sort an array of numbers into descending order of magnitude. One procedure for doing this is called the *bubble-sort technique.* The steps in it are as follows:

(*a*) Compare the first and second number. If the second is larger, switch the order of the numbers.

(*b*) Take the next number in the array, and compare it to its predecessor. If it is larger, switch positions and compare it to the next predecessor, making a switch if it is larger. Repeat until the selected number is not larger than a predecessor or it is in the first position.

(*c*) Take the next number after the previously selected one, and repeat step (*b*) until the last number has been selected and compared.

For example, the original set is 8, 9, 5, 11, 7. The arrows show exchanges; the dotted lines show comparisons without exchanges.

Column	0	1	2	3	4	5	6
Array	8	9	9	9	9	11	11
	9	8	8	8	11	9	9
	5	5	5	11	8	8	8
	11	11	11	5	5	5	7
	7	7	7	7	7	7	5

Each column shows the array contents after the comparison and/or switch. The underlined number is the one that had been selected for comparison with its predecessor.

Write a program to perform a bubble sort on any set of less than 100 numbers.

Use it to sort the following sets of data:

Set number		
1	2	3
66	−6	.156
85	−87	.951
86	−56	.537
45	−34	.015
77	2	.126
74	6	.672
57	43	
49	18	
62	85	

8. Prime numbers are those divisible without a remainder only by themselves and 1. To find all the primes less than 1000, one can start with 2 and divide all higher numbers by it, eliminating all that have no remainder and then moving to the next largest that has not been eliminated and dividing by it in the same manner. This is a straightforward method based upon the definition. However, it is very time-consuming because division is lengthy. A quicker way is to use the *sieve of Eratosthenes* procedure. Fill an array with values from 1 to 1000. Starting with the second entry, set to zero all multiples of it in the array (all multiples of 2). Proceed to the next nonzero number and repeat the process, etc. At the conclusion of this all the nonzero entries will be prime numbers. Write a program to implement this procedure and print out a table of primes.

9. Data is often more meaningful if graphed. Write a program to both tabulate and graph the curve of damped vibration.

    $$y = e^{-nx} \sin mx$$

    for the following values:

n	m	x range
0.2	1	0 to 3π
0.2	2	$-\pi$ to 2π
0.3	3	0 to 2π

    Hint: Create the graph sideways on the paper; that is, x is plotted vertically and y horizontally on the page. Use an array of one-character variables set to blanks, and insert an asterisk in the appropriate y position for each x.

Humanities and Social Sciences

10. Data described below from a questionnaire has been entered into a file in list-directed form.

Data description
Age: 0 = no response
Sex: 1 = female, 2 = male
Homeowner: 1 = yes, 2 = no, 0 = no response
Income (in thousands): 999 = none, 900 = no response
Political preference: 1 = Democrat, 2 = Republican, 3 = other, 0 = no response

Data

Age	Sex	Homeowner	Income	Politics
35	1	1	25	1
19	2	0	18	3
17	1	2	999	3
39	2	1	35	2
54	2	1	17	1
73	2	2	900	1
27	2	1	27	2
72	1	2	8	0
0	2	2	40	2
43	1	1	25	1
55	2	1	27	1
39	2	2	43	3
32	1	0	11	3
23	1	2	900	0
66	1	1	7	1

Tally responses and nonresponses and prepare the following tables:

Table 1

Age, years	Income (000)				
	Less than $5	$5–$9	$10–$15	$15–$19	Over $19
Less than 20					
20–29					
30–39					
40–49					
50–59					
60–69					
Over 69					

Table 2

Age	Sex		Homeowner		Politics		
	F	M	Yes	No	Democrat	Republican	Other
Less than 20							
20–29							
30–39							
40–49							
50–59							
60–69							
Over 69							

Table 3

Nonresponses
Age
Homeowner
Income
Political preference

11. One step in preparing a concordance is to search the text for a selected phrase or word. Write a program that reads a paragraph, calculates the frequency of a selected word, and prints a summary. Paragraphs are limited to 800 characters, including spaces and punctuation, appearing on 10 records. The paragraph is indented five spaces. *Caution:*

Only individual words that match the key word are to be counted, not longer words that contain the key letters. *Hint:* Establish an array of 80 single-character elements, and read, process, and print the lines of the paragraph one at a time (using input/output format of A80). Read in the key word as single characters into another array including a beginning and ending blank as part of the key word. Test for the series of letters, for example, blank, T, H, E, blank, from the key word array. Also check for key word followed by period.

Key word: THE

Paragraph:

Now is the time for all good men to come to the aid of their party. But let us not lose heart for there are 30 theocratic parties to console us.

Key word: LOVE

Paragraph:

Love is patient and kind; it is not jealous or conceited or proud; love is not ill-mannered or selfish or irritable; love does not keep a record of wrongs.

12. Given the following data on population and immigration for the United States, produce a table showing, for each decade, initial population, total increase, net immigration, and percent of increase attributable to immigration.

Period	Initial population (000)	Net immigration (000)	Period	Initial population (000)	Net immigration (000)
1870–1880	39,818	2,274	1920–1930	105,711	3,089
1880–1890	50,156	4,490	1930–1940	122,775	1,067
1890–1900	62,948	2,531	1940–1950	131,669	875
1900–1910	75,995	5,289	1950–1960	151,326	2,660
1910–1920	91,972	3,201	1960–1970	179,323	3,282

General

13. A matrix contains the number of A's, B's, etc., earned by each student. Each course is four credits. Write a program to calculate the grade-point (A = 4, B = 3, etc.) average for each student and for all students.

Student name	Number of courses for each guide				
	A	B	C	D	E
George Thiel	0	8	2	2	1
Craig Ebert	3	4	9	1	0
Dean Greco	1	5	3	0	0
Paul Hogan	5	8	9	0	1
David Sellman	7	1	0	2	0
Bonnie Link	5	3	3	1	0
Susan Frye	9	6	4	4	0
Larry Maxwell	3	8	2	0	0
Kathy Adams	7	1	4	2	1
Jill Swift	3	3	4	2	0
Rebecca Young	7	5	2	0	1
Dan Johnson	1	1	1	0	0
Mark Snyder	1	3	0	2	0
Steve Fisher	2	4	0	2	0
Sally Crown	6	6	7	1	0

14. Given any amount of a restaurant check up to $25 and any amount tendered up to $40, find the quantity and denomination of paper money and coins to return as change. Print the result in order from smallest to largest denomination. Print an error message if the amount tendered is less than the check.

Amounts

Check	Tendered
$ 2.13	$20.00
6.15	5.00
3.37	3.37
21.95	20.00
17.44	30.00

Hint: Results are obtained from largest to smallest, so save the results in an array for printing in small to large order.

15. Reprogram problem 13 of Chapter 3, and print the conversions in groups ordered by their codes as 3, 2, 1, -1, -2, -3.

Interactive Scientific and Engineering

16. There are several techniques for solving a set of simultaneous equations. The method of eliminating variables is known as the *Gauss-Jordan reduction* technique. Given a set of m equations in m unknowns (variables), the process involves dividing the first equation by the coefficient of the first variable and then using the resulting equation to eliminate the first variable (that is, reduce the coefficient to zero) from all the rest of the equations. Similarly, the process is repeated for the second variable from the second equation and so forth. (Rearrangement of the equations may be necessary if the ith variable in the ith equation has a zero coefficient.) At the conclusion of this process, the right-hand sides of the equations are the values of the variables in ascending order. For example,

$$
\begin{aligned}
X_1 + 2X_2 + 3X_3 &= 4 \\
4X_1 - 2X_2 + 7X_3 &= 6 \\
5X_1 + 4X_2 - 9X_3 &= -7
\end{aligned}
$$

$$
\begin{aligned}
X_1 + 2X_2 + 3X_3 &= 4 \\
- 10X_2 - 5X_3 &= -10 \\
- 6X_2 - 24X_3 &= -27
\end{aligned}
$$

$$
\begin{aligned}
X_1 \quad\quad + 2X_3 &= 2 \\
X_2 + .5X_3 &= 1 \\
- 21X_3 &= -21
\end{aligned}
$$

$$
\begin{aligned}
X_1 &= 0 \\
X_2 &= .5 \\
X_3 &= 1
\end{aligned}
$$

If at any stage no nonzero coefficient exists for a given variable, then there is no unique solution to the set. Write a program to solve the preceding problem, and test it with the following three sets of inputs:

$$
\begin{aligned}
3X_1 - 2X_2 &= 5 \\
2X_1 + 4X_2 &= -3
\end{aligned}
$$

$$-X_1 + 3X_2 + X_3 = 5$$
$$2X_1 - X_2 + 2X_3 = 3$$
$$X_1 + 4X_2 - X_3 = 6$$

$$-X_1 + 3X_2 + X_3 = 5$$
$$2X_1 - X_2 - 2X_3 = 3$$
$$X_1 + 4X_2 - X_3 = 6$$

17. There are numerous ways to code or encrypt a message. One of these is to swap or interchange pairs of letters. For example, if the original message is "This way out" and the letters "o" and "i" and "s" and "a" are interchanged the coded message becomes "Thoa wsy iut." More swaps result in an even more unintelligible phrase. Write a program to accomplish this task for a one-line message involving an arbitrary number of exchanges.

18. A polynomial of arbitrary order can be evaluated efficiently by rewriting it in an iterative form. For example, to evaluate the following fifth-order equation

$$f(x) = -0.7x^5 - 0.45x^4 + 1.8x^3 - 5.3x^2 + 8x + 3$$

we can evaluate instead the equivalent equation

$$f(x) = (\{[(-0.7x - 0.45)\,x + 1.8]\,x - 5.3\}\,x + 8)x + 3$$

using an array for the coefficients and a DO loop for the iterative evaluation of the expression in parentheses and not have to use powers of x explicitly. Write a program to implement this procedure for any equation up to the fiftieth order. Test the program by evaluating the above equation at the points 1, 4.5, and 13.

5a

FORTRAN Subprograms and Case Program Structure

Characteristics of Subprograms
Purpose and Use of Subprograms
Checking on Availability of Prewritten
   Subprograms
Two Types of External Subprograms

Function Subprogram
Self-Testing Exercise 5-1

Subroutine
Self-Testing Exercise 5-2

COMMON and EQUIVALENCE Declarations
Use of COMMON Storage
Blank COMMON
Named COMMON and Block Data Subprogram

EQUIVALENCE Declaration
Self-Testing Exercise 5-3

Case Program Structure
Self-Testing Exercise 5-4

Subprograms and a Structured Modular Design

Summary

Answers to Self-Testing Exercises

Questions and Problems

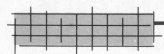

A *subprogram* is a separate program unit used (called) by a main program or by other subprograms. Subprogram capability is a very important feature of the FORTRAN language. It is implemented in two different ways: the function subprogram and the subroutine subprogram, both of which are explained in this chapter.

The three basic programming structures (sequence, selection, and repetition) have been presented in previous chapters. The sequence structure of one statement following another was described in Chapter 1. The selection structure for choosing between two program paths as implemented by the FORTRAN IF was explained in Chapter 2. The repetition programming structure using the DO loop was presented in Chapter 4. Although all programming may be performed using only the three basic structures, it is convenient to use a fourth programming pattern, the case structure, to select among multiple alternatives. The FORTRAN implementation of the case structure using the computed GOTO is described in this chapter.

Characteristics of Subprograms

As background for understanding the specific types of subprograms, the purpose and use of subprograms are explained and some general characteristics are described.

Purpose and Use of Subprograms

The purpose of subprograms is to simplify programming. Subprograms help to achieve this objective in two major ways:

1. *Reusable program elements* Processing functions that will be used more than once in the program (or used by more than one program) are written once and then used by programs needing the processing. Examples are subprograms to:
   (a) Generate random numbers
   (b) Calculate statistics (such as mean, variance, etc.)
   (c) Sort data into ascending or descending order
2. *Decomposition of programming tasks* Sections of the program are written as independent subprograms to reduce the complexity of the program design, to aid in testing the program, and to allow different programmers to work on different subprograms concurrently. For example, the instructions to print a report (which may be fairly complex) may be organized into a subprogram separate from the instructions to compute the data to be printed in the report.

The first objective of reusable program elements can be achieved through subprograms because each subprogram is treated as a separate program. This independence is reflected in the following features of a subprogram.

1. It can be compiled separately from the program using it.

2. The variable names in the subprogram refer to different storage locations (in other words, are different variables) than variables with the same names in programs that use the subprogram. If it is desired that these be the same, special instructions are available to make the names refer to the same storage locations.
3. Use of a subprogram is achieved by a simple program statement in the using (calling) program.
4. Transfer of data between a program using a subprogram (a calling program) and the subprogram is specified by special instructions in the calling program and the subprogram.

The second objective of decomposing programming into smaller, simpler tasks is also possible because the subprograms can be written and tested separately. In this approach, a large program is written as a main control program (the main program) that uses (calls) subprograms. In other words, the main control program ties together the major segments of the program that are written and tested as separate programs. A subprogram may also use (call) other subprograms.

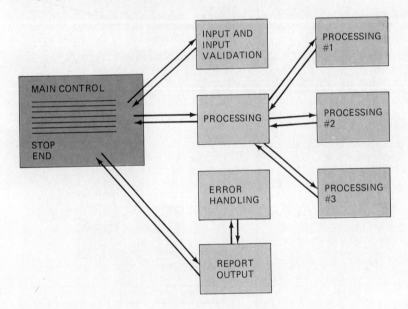

There are three sources for FORTRAN subprograms used by a main program or by subprograms.

1. *Intrinsic functions*   These are essentially internal subprograms that are part of the standard facilities of the language.
2. *User-written external subprograms*   These generally are unique to the program rather than being general subprograms.
3. *Library external subprograms*   These are part of a library of prewritten subroutines that may be made available.

If a program or subprogram invokes or calls a subprogram, the subprogram coding must be available to the calling program when it is executed. The following are the ways in which this may be accomplished for these three sources of subprograms.

1. *Intrinsic functions*   The compiler provides all necessary links to the internal intrinsic function subprograms. The programmer merely uses the intrinsic function name in a program statement in the calling program.

2. *User-written external subprograms*   These are included with the calling program, either by specifying their retrieval from storage or by including them with the job when it is submitted for compilation and execution. When subprograms are included in the compilation and execution job, each subprogram has an END statement, so that each will compile separately. The uniting of the subprograms and the calling program is done by job control instructions. For example, in a submission using program files, the structure is approximately as follows.

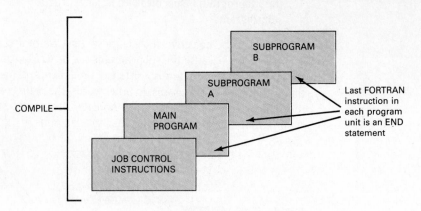

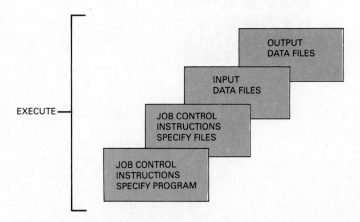

3. *Library external subprograms*   When a program calls for a subprogram that is part of a library of such programs, job control instructions are used to obtain the subprogram from the subprogram library and make it available to the program calling it.

When a large program uses a number of subprograms, it is good documentation practice to list in the comments at the beginning of each subprogram the program units that call upon the subprogram. This is especially helpful if the subprogram is altered, replaced, etc.

Checking on Availability of Prewritten Subprograms

It is very important for the programmer to be aware of the extensive libraries of prewritten subprograms that are easily available for use as part of a program being written. These are in addition to the standard intrinsic FORTRAN functions. A university computer center will usually have several hundred such subprograms developed by the center or obtained from an outside supplier. For example, a well-known library of subroutines is the IMSL (International Mathematical and Statistical Libraries, Inc.) library of mathematics and statistics subroutines. There are over 400 prewritten subprograms classified as follows:

Analysis of Experimental Design Data
Basic Statistics
Categorized Data Analysis
Differential Equations: Quadrature; Differentiation
Eigensystem Analysis
Forecasting: Econometrics; Time Series
Generation and Testing of Random Numbers; Goodness of Fit
Interpolation; Approximations; Smoothing
Linear Algebraic Equations
Mathematical and Statistical Special Functions
Nonparametric Statistics
Observation Structure
Regression Analysis
Sampling
Utility Functions
Vector, Matrix Arithmetic
Zeros and Extrema; Linear Programming

It is always wise to check on the availability of a prewritten routine before designing, coding, and testing a new subprogram. Most computer centers maintain a directory of available subprograms as well as documentation manuals describing each and the exact procedure for calling them.

Two Types of External Subprograms

There are two types of external subprograms with different characteristics:

1. *Function subprogram*   Although an external subprogram, a function subprogram is called by program coding that is similar to intrinsic functions. In the usual case, the statement calling the function subprogram specifies a list of variables and constants; the function subprogram returns a single result value to the calling program statement.
2. *Subroutine*   A subroutine is a more flexible subprogram. It does not *require* a parameter list, and there is no requirement that it return a single value as a result.

From this short description of the two alternatives, it can be seen that the subroutine is more flexible, while the function subprogram is likely to be limited to fairly simple mathematical computations similar in scope to those performed by intrinsic functions. Since a subroutine can be used for all situations, a function subprogram is a special case and is selected for those computations in which a function provides clearer, simpler coding and the constraints on its use are met.

Function Subprogram

The *function subprogram* is the method by which a programmer can write an external function to be invoked by other programs. Coded as a separate program unit, it is assigned a name by the programmer so that the function can be called using the name as a reference. A function subprogram is called into use by writing the name in a program statement followed by a list of values (variable names or constants) to be used by the function—the values separated by commas and enclosed in parentheses. The list of values are termed the arguments of the function.

As an example, a programmer may write a small program routine to find the largest value in a single-dimension array of n elements. The programmer decides to keep the routine as a separate program unit by defining it as a function subprogram and assigning it the name RAYMAX. Another program unit, such as a main program, may use the RAYMAX function with a program statement that uses the function name RAYMAX followed by the arguments enclosed in parentheses. Assuming the RAYMAX function is to operate on array ALPHA with N entries, the function call would read RAYMAX(ALPHA, N). The single value is returned by the function (largest value in the array) and used as specified in the complete statement. Two separate examples illustrate the way the example RAYMAX function subprogram is invoked by statements in the using (calling) program.

Example 1

```
                     ┌─┬──────────Arguments of the function
                     ↓ ↓
X = RAYMAX(ALPHA,N)+6.0
```

This example calculates the maximum value from the N values in array ALPHA, adds 6.0 to it, and stores the result in X.

Example 2

```
IF (BIG.LE.RAYMAX(Y,10)) GOTO 120
```

This statement compares the value of BIG with the largest value in the 10 values in array Y. If BIG is less than or equal to that value, control goes to statement 120.

The process of using a user-written function can now be summarized. The statements that invoke the function are in the calling program. The function program unit that does the processing is a separate subprogram. The calling program statement identifies the function subprogram to be used and defines the data to be used (normally with the argument list). The function subprogram operates on the data in the argument list and transfers a single value back to the calling program in place of the function call.

The function subprogram, written as a separate program unit, begins with an identifying statement. This first statement consists of the word FUNCTION followed by the programmer-assigned name of the function and a parameter list (or dummy arguments) of variables required by the function, with the variables separated by commas and the list enclosed in parentheses. The parentheses are required even if there are no arguments (an unusual case). The initial letter of the function name indicates the implicit type of the result to be returned from the function (integer or real). The type can be changed by an explicit type statement. Character or logical types can also be specified. If explicit typing is to be used for the function itself, the type specification is part of the first line defining the function name. For example, if a function FINDIT is to return an integer value, a function ALPHA to return a character value, and DECIDE is to return a logical value (TRUE or FALSE), they would be defined as follows as the first lines of the function definitions:

```
INTEGER FUNCTION FINDIT (parameter list)
CHARACTER FUNCTION ALPHA (parameter list)
LOGICAL FUNCTION DECIDE (parameter list)
```

When the function is used, the value of the variables or constants in the argument list in the calling statement of the using program are used in place of each corresponding variable in the parameter list of the subprogram. For this reason, these variables in the function definition are termed *dummy arguments* or *dummy variables;* they are replaced by the values of the actual variables in the argument list of the calling statement. The actual argument list must correspond in number of values and type with the parameter list of dummy arguments.

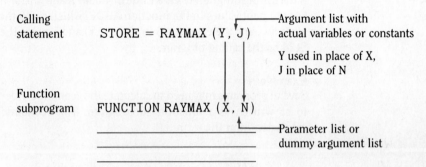

Calling statement   STORE = RAYMAX (Y, J)   Argument list with actual variables or constants

Y used in place of X, J in place of N

Function subprogram   FUNCTION RAYMAX (X, N)   Parameter list or dummy argument list

Program statements in a function subprogram follow the function-naming statement. One or more of the assignment statements in the subprogram must define the function name as the result variable, for example, function name = expression. An example of such a statement for the RAYMAX function is RAYMAX = BIG shown in the example below.

In the example RAYMAX function subprogram, there is an array named X and the number of entries in the array is N. Any array used in the subprogram must be dimensioned in the subprogram itself; thus array X is dimensioned in the example at a maximum of 100.

Outline	Example	
FUNCTION f(X_1, X_2, . . . , X_n)	FUNCTION RAYMAX(X, N)	
.	DIMENSION X(100)	
.	BIG = $-9.99E - 10$	
.	DO 100 I = 1,N	Function
.	BIG = AMAX1(X(I),BIG)	subprogram
.	100 CONTINUE	
function name = expression	RAYMAX = BIG	
RETURN	RETURN	
END	END	

A RETURN statement is put at the logical end of the function subprogram. If there is more than one logical end, there may be more than one RETURN statement. The RETURN signals that control is to return to the calling program from which the transfer to the subprogram was made. The END statement is required as the last statement or physical end of the subprogram. The END statement implies the RETURN statement, so the RETURN is optional if it would logically be the last statement before the END.

Example 3
As a simple case to illustrate both the form of the calling program and the form of the function, a simple program to read two values from an input record, sum them, and print the two inputs and the sum is written with a function subprogram to perform the summing operation.

Calling program	Function subprogram
READ *, A, B	FUNCTION ADDF (X, Y)
SUM = ADDF (A, B)	ADDF = X + Y
PRINT*, A, B, SUM	RETURN
STOP	END
END	

If the calling program reads a value of 4.0 for A and 3.5 for B, these values are provided as argument values to the function ADDF, which sums them (uses the value for A in place of X and the value for B in place of Y) and returns the sum of 7.5 to be stored in SUM by the calling program.

Example 4

Several programs may need to calculate the economic order quantity. This is therefore to be written as a function subprogram. The economic order quantity (EOQ) is calculated from the formula

$$EOQ = \sqrt{\frac{24VS}{AC}}$$

where V = average monthly usage in units
S = setup or order cost
A = carrying cost expressed as a decimal
C = variable cost per unit

SUMMARY OF SPECIFICATIONS FOR FUNCTION SUBPROGRAM

Notation

f = function name
e = expression

$x_1, x_2, \ldots, x_n$ = dummy arguments of the function
$a_1, a_2, \ldots, a_n$ = actual calling arguments of the function

Where defined	Externally defined in a separately compiled independent subprogram.
How defined	FUNCTION $f(x_1, x_2, \ldots, x_n)$ $f = e$ (at least one statement of this form in program) RETURN (at each logical exit from program) END
How named	Same as variable name—up to six characters, first letter determines type unless type declared as follows: Type FUNCTION $f(x_1, x_2, \ldots, x_n)$
How called into use	Appearance of name in an expression $v = f(a_1, a_2, \ldots, a_n)$
Number of outputs	One
Restrictions on form of calling argument	Type, number, and order of calling arguments must agree with the dummy arguments of the definition; argument may be a variable name, subscripted variable, array name, expression, or subprogram name.

269

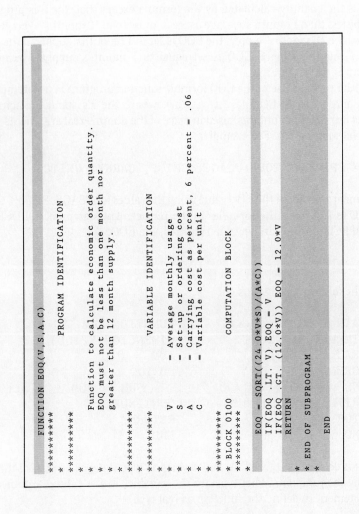

```
        FUNCTION EOQ(V,S,A,C)
***********
*              PROGRAM IDENTIFICATION
***********
*
*       Function to calculate economic order quantity.
*       EOQ must not be less than one month nor
*       greater than 12 month supply.
*
***********
***********
*              VARIABLE IDENTIFICATION
*
*       V     = Average monthly usage
*       S     = Set-up or ordering cost
*       A     = Carrying cost as percent, 6 percent = .06
*       C     = Variable cost per unit
*
***********
* BLOCK 0100    COMPUTATION BLOCK
***********
*
        EOQ = SQRT((24.0*V*S)/(A*C))
        IF(EOQ .LT. V) EOQ = V
        IF(EOQ .GT. (12.0*V)) EOQ = 12.0*V
        RETURN
*
** END OF SUBPROGRAM
*
**      END
```

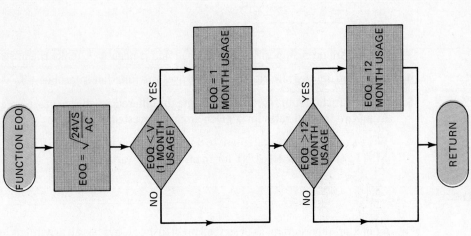

Figure 5-1 Function subprogram to calculate economic order quantity.

The EOQ is the quantity calculated by the formula except that, for this program, it must not be less than 1 month's average usage or more than 12 months' average usage. If it exceeds the 12 months' supply, the EOQ is set to 12 months' supply; if the EOQ is less than 1 month's supply, EOQ is set equal to 1 month's supply. The function subprogram is shown in Figure 5-1.

In order to make use of the EOQ formula function program in a statement, it is necessary only to write EOQ (a_1, a_2, a_3, a_4), where the a's stand for actual real arguments (variables or contants) used in place of the dummy real arguments V, S, A, and C of the subprogram. For example:

```
ORDER = SPECL + EOQ (USAGE, SETUP, CARRY, UNITC)
```

This statement will obtain the EOQ value using the values for USAGE, SETUP, CARRY, and UNITC as factors in the formula. In the replacement statement, ORDER is set equal to SPECL plus the single value returned, the EOQ.

Self-Testing Exercise 5-1

1. What do the following programs do?

```
***** MAIN PROGRAM *****        FUNCTION SUM (X)
      DIMENSION A(100)          DIMENSION X(100)
      READ (5, 700) A           SUM = 0.0
  700 FORMAT (10F8.0)           DO 100 I = 1, 100
      ANS = SQRT (SUM(A))           SUM = SUM + X (I)
      WRITE (6, 700) ANS    100 CONTINUE
      STOP                      RETURN
      END                       END
```

2. A function is defined as IBOY(X, A, J). What is the type (integer or real) of the result returned by the function? What type are the variables in the calling argument list? Write a statement to define the function as real type.

3. Write a function subprogram to find the positive, real root (if it exists) of a quadratic equation. The a term is always positive for this problem. The formula is

$$\text{Root} = \frac{-b + \sqrt{b^2 - 4ac}}{2a}$$

If there are no real, positive roots ($b^2 - 4ac$ is negative), make the answer equal 0.

4. Write a main program statement that uses the function in problem 3.

5. Write a function subprogram to calculate the difference between yearly interest earned using two interest rates for a given amount invested.

6. Write a main program statement to use the function in problem 5. Use variable names XINT1, XINT2, and AMOUNT for main program variables.

Subroutine

A function subprogram, as described previously, always has an argument list enclosed in parentheses and returns a single value to the program statement where it is used. In contrast, the *subroutine* subprogram removes these restrictions. The subroutine may have parameters, but it does not require them. It does not automatically return a value to the main program; it may simply alter the value of a variable or print out the contents of various locations.

The subroutine is a separate program that is defined by the word SUBROUTINE (starting in column 7) followed by a name and parameters (dummy arguments), which are not required. The name, up to six characters, has no type (integer, real, character, etc.) significance.

SUBROUTINE $f(x_1, x_2, \ldots, x_n)$ or SUBROUTINE f

_____
_____
_____
_____
_____

RETURN
END

The parameter list of the subroutine definition may include dummy array names as well as single variable names. If a dummy array name is used, the parameter array name must be dimensioned in the subroutine.

The subroutine is used by writing a CALL statement. If an argument list is needed, the actual arguments to be used must be of the same type and be listed in the same order as the parameter list of dummy arguments. A subroutine can call other subroutines or functions but cannot call itself.

    CALL $f(a_1, a_2, \ldots, a_n)$ for subroutine that was defined as having an argument list

or CALL f   for subroutine that was defined without an argument list

Example

To illustrate the form of both the calling program and the subroutine subprogram, the simple example will be used of a program that reads values for A and B, calls a subroutine to sum them, and prints the values for A, B, and the sum.

Calling program	Subroutine
| ```
READ *, A, B
CALL SUMIT(A, B, SUM)
PRINT *, A, B, SUM
STOP
``` | ```
SUBROUTINE SUMIT(X, Y, RESULT)
RESULT = X + Y
RETURN
END
``` |

When the calling program calls the subroutine, it provides the value of A and B to be used by the subroutine in place of X and Y. It also provides a variable name SUM that is equivalent to RESULT (both being third in the parameter list). When the subroutine calculates X + Y and stores it in RESULT, it actually stores the sum in SUM. Compare this form with the previous example on page 268 using a function.

Example

A program requires the ordering of several arrays in descending sequence by magnitude from the largest to the smallest value. The arrays are all one-dimensional, and the number of quantities in an array range from 10 to 100. The subroutine is written so that one of the arguments is the array name and the other is the number of entries. The subroutine program shown in Figure 5-2 is dimensioned to handle the largest array.

```
      SUBROUTINE ORDER(NTRIES,ARRAY)
**********
*                    PROGRAM IDENTIFICATION
**********
*
*      Subroutine to order an array from largest
*      to smallest value by interchange.
*
**********
*                    VARIABLE IDENTIFICATION
**********
*
*      ARRAY   = Array of 100 or less elements
*      NTRIES  = Number of entries in array
*      SAVE    = Temporary variable
*      LIMIT   = NTRIES minus one
*      INDEXL  = Array pointer
*
**********
*                    STORAGE ALLOCATION
**********
*
*      DIMENSION ARRAY(100)
*
**********
* BLOCK 0100        SORT BLOCK
**********
*
      IF(NTRIES .LT. 2) RETURN
      LIMIT = NTRIES - 1
      DO 110 I = 1,LIMIT
         INDEXL = I + 1
         DO 100 J = INDEXL,NTRIES
            IF(A(I) .GE. A(J)) GOTO 100
            SAVE = A(I)
            A(I) = A(J)
            A(J) = SAVE
 100     CONTINUE
 110  CONTINUE
      RETURN
*
* END OF SUBPROGRAM
*
      END
```

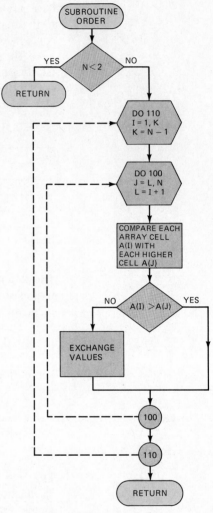

Figure 5-2 Subroutine program to order an array from largest to smallest value.

Note that the subroutine is general and will work for an array of 100 or less entries. The quantities are arranged by successive comparisons, shifting the larger values to the front until the array is ordered. A program needing to order an N-element array called GRADES merely writes the following statement:

```
CALL ORDER (N, GRADES)
```

After the array GRADES is ordered, control is returned to the statement following the CALL.

In flowcharting programs with subroutines, the subroutine program or module symbol is used to indicate a subroutine CALL.

A subroutine does not automatically return a single value to the calling program as does a function. However, the subroutine must be able to communicate with the calling program and transmit the results of the subroutine processing. This communication occurs in two ways—through the arguments in the subroutine call or by common storage (to be explained later in the chapter). Communication of computation results by arguments in the calling list and corresponding parameters in the subroutine declaration was illustrated by the first example. In that example, a single result was transferred through the argument list. This method is not limited to one result. For example, assume a subroutine that requires one value (Y) to be sent from the calling program and that provides two values (A1 and A2) returned as results. In the following program segment, the subprogram CALL causes the subroutine to use the storage locations for Y, A1, and A2 as the locations for B, C, and D. When the subroutine executes C = 50, it is actually executing A1 = 50.

Calling program	Subroutine
CALL COMP (Y, A1, A2)	SUBROUTINE COMP (B, C, D)
	C =
A1 and A2 now contain	.
quantities computed by	.
subroutine (identified in	D =
subroutine as C and D).	END

This means that the subroutine is not limited in the number of values that may be communicated back to the calling program by this method. These values may include arrays.

The communication between the subroutine and the main program need not include any computed result. In the sorting example, the subroutine sequenced data

SUMMARY OF SPECIFICATIONS FOR SUBROUTINE

Notation

f = subroutine name
e = expression

$x_1, x_2, \ldots, x_n$ = parameters in the function
$a_1, a_2, \ldots, a_n$ = actual calling arguments of the function

Where defined	Externally defined in a separately compiled independent program.
How defined	SUBROUTINE $f(x_1, x_2, \ldots, x_n)$
	or SUBROUTINE f
	Program steps
	RETURN (at each logical exit from program)
	END
How named	Same as variable name (up to six characters, etc.) except that the name of subroutine has no type significance.
How called into use	CALL statement
	CALL $f(a_1, a_2, \ldots, a_n)$
	or CALL f
Number of results	Any number
Restrictions on form of calling argument	Type, number, and order of actual calling arguments must agree with the dummy arguments of the definition. Argument may be a variable name, subscripted variable, array name, expression, or subprogram name; need not have an argument.

that was specified by an argument in the call to the subroutine, but there was no computed value returned to the calling program.

Self-Testing Exercise 5-2

1. Why should a subroutine be used instead of a function?

2. Write the function problem 5 from Exercise 5-1 as a subroutine. The problem was to write a subprogram to calculate the difference between yearly interest earned using two interest rates for a given amount invested.

3. Write a statement to use (call) the subroutine in question 2 if the main program variables are XINT1, XINT2, AMOUNT, and D (for the difference).

4. Write a subroutine that will interchange rows and columns of square matrices. The subroutine should handle matrices of size 20 × 20. Name the routine MOVE (remember that the name of the subroutine does not indicate type).

5. If, with reference to problem 4, the matrix to be rearranged is called ALPHA, what is the statement to perform the interchange of rows and columns? ALPHA must be 20 × 20 in size.

COMMON and EQUIVALENCE Declarations

Use of COMMON Storage

A variable name in a subprogram is not automatically related to a variable with the same name in the calling program. The two variables are assigned to different memory locations, and computations affecting one do not affect the other. The X's in the following example are completely independent (although they can be associated by the subroutine parameter list and subroutine call argument list).

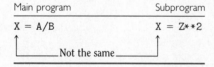

The use of a parameter list and arguments in the CALL statement is a clear, explicit method for associating the storage locations of the calling program with the processing performed by the subroutine. It is generally the preferred method. However, there are many instances in which it is convenient and desirable to have a variable name in both programs refer to the same memory location without having them appear in the argument lists. This is accomplished by the use of a special storage area designated as COMMON.

The use of common storage allows communication among independent program units. Instead of a list of variable names as arguments in the subroutine definition and subroutine CALL statement to specify data to be used and data names for results, the data required for processing and the results to be stored may be placed in common storage available to both calling program and subprogram.

Blank COMMON

The most frequently used common storage is also termed *blank* COMMON to distinguish it from a special form of common storage called *named* COMMON. A set or block of blank COMMON storage is defined by a blank COMMON declaration:

COMMON nlist

where nlist is a list of variable names or array names common to more than one program unit. An array name in a COMMON declaration defines the entire array as being in common storage. If any variable in a blank or named COMMON block is character type, all variables in that block must be character type. To declare both types of variables to be in COMMON, put the character variables in a named COMMON block (see next page).

The blank common storage sequence in all program units starts with the same storage location. The compiler assigns memory locations to the special blank common storage by sequentially assigning the variables listed in the COMMON declaration. The first variable in each list occupies the first position in common, the second (if an array of size 10) occupies the next 10 positions, etc. If there is more than one blank COMMON declaration, storage assignment for the next COMMON statement continues from the storage assignment of the previous statement. Because variables are associated by the order of appearance in the COMMON declaration, one or more COMMON declarations listing all variable or array names in the same order must be included in each subprogram having any (even one) of these common elements. One cannot list only those variables unique to a particular subprogram. Putting two variables in the same position in the COMMON declaration list of two different program units will result in their using the same memory location. If the variable and array names in all COMMON declarations are the same (the usual case), the COMMON declarations may be duplicated and a copy placed in each subroutine using any of the common variables.

Examples

Main program COMMON A, B, C Subprogram COMMON A, B, C	A, B, C in the main program reference same data as A, B, C in the subprogram.
Main program COMMON X, Y, Z Subprogram COMMON A, B, C	A, B, C in the subprogram reference the same data storage locations as X, Y, Z in the main program.
Main program COMMON D, G Subprogram 1 COMMON D, G, X Subprogram 2 COMMON D, G, X	If subprograms share X but it is not used by the main program, then the main program need not list X (since it is the last item, it is not required to keep other variables in same sequence), but recommended procedure is to have all COMMON declarations include the entire list.

An array included in a COMMON declaration must also be dimensioned in each program using the COMMON declaration. The dimensions must be the same for all using programs. Dimensioning may be done through DIMENSION statements or, alternatively, may be included in the COMMON declaration for the variable. This is recommended as being less error-prone. For example:

Single declaration (recommended)	Separate declarations
`COMMON X(100), Y(50)`	`DIMENSION X(100), Y(50)` `COMMON X, Y`

By following the style of including the dimension in the COMMON declaration, DIMENSION statements are used only to dimension variables not in common storage. This style aids in keeping common variables and local variables (applying only to a single program unit) clearly identified. Also, a variable name with dimension appearing in a COMMON declaration is clearly identified as being an array.

Named COMMON and Block Data Subprogram

Blank COMMON is useful in that it applies to all program units declaring COMMON. However, if data is shared only by some but not all of a number of subprograms, blank COMMON requires that the variables be accounted for in the COMMON declaration list of all subprograms with COMMON declarations. Also, variables in blank COMMON may not be initialized using the DATA statement.

An alternative common storage available in 1977 FORTRAN is the *named* COMMON. The form of the named COMMON declaration is to have a common block enclosed in slashes preceding the list of variable names to be declared as common.

COMMON / common block name / nlist

If no name appears between the slashes, the variables that follow are blank COMMON; in other words, // is the same as blank COMMON. A named COMMON block has a unique storage sequence that starts at the same location for all COMMON blocks using the same name. Named COMMON blocks in different subprograms using the same name must be the same size.

Examples

COMMON / A / X, Y, Z / B / M, N, F	Named common block A contains X, Y, Z and named common block B contains M, N, F.
COMMON / / R, S, T(100)	R, S, and array T are in blank COMMON.

If variables and array elements in common storage are to be initialized by the use of a DATA statement, these must be placed in named COMMON. The DATA statement is placed in a BLOCK DATA subprogram—a subprogram designed for this purpose. A BLOCK DATA subprogram is defined by the BLOCK DATA statement:

BLOCK DATA [symbolic name for block data subprogram (optional)]

The BLOCK DATA statement is followed by statements that define the data specified in named COMMON blocks. The BLOCK DATA subprogram contains storage specifications but does not contain any executable statements. The DATA statement is used to initialize variables, and DIMENSION, COMMON, and EQUIVALENCE (to be explained below) statements are used as appropriate. The last statement is END.

The reason for the BLOCK DATA subprogram is that named COMMON can be used by several program units, and thus no program unit can be relied upon to have the data initialization. The BLOCK DATA subprogram defines initialization at the global level of the entire set of programs and subprograms. An example of a BLOCK DATA subprogram is the following:

Example program unit using named COMMON	BLOCK DATA subprogram to initialize named COMMON
| ```
SUBROUTINE CALCUL
COMMON / BD / ALPHA (50), BETA, A
      .
      .
      .
      .
      .
RETURN
END
``` | ```
BLOCK DATA
COMMON / BD / ALPHA(50), BETA, A
DATA ALPHA / 50*0 / BETA / 1.0 /
END
``` |

Notice that the 50-element array ALPHA and the variables BETA and A are defined in two or more program units as being in named COMMON (named BD). The BLOCK DATA subprogram initializes ALPHA as zeros and BETA as 1.0. All the variable names in a named common block must be named in the named COMMON statement even if they are not initialized in the DATA statement. More than one named COMMON block may be initialized by DATA statements in the same BLOCK DATA subprogram.

COMMON DECLARATIONS AND BLOCK DATA SUBPROGRAM

Blank COMMON block

COMMON nlist   or   COMMON // nlist

where nlist is a list of variable names, array names, and array declarators. Variables in blank COMMON list may not be initialized with DATA statements.

Named COMMON block

COMMON / named common block name / nlist

BLOCK DATA subprogram

BLOCK DATA [name for BLOCK DATA subprogram (name optional)]

Statements such as DIMENSION, COMMON, EQUIVALENCE, type, or statements not yet explained (IMPLICIT, SAVE, PARAMETER). No executable statements.
DATA statement
END

BLOCK DATA is not included in subset FORTRAN

The BLOCK DATA subprogram is used to provide initial values for variables and arrays in named COMMON. If any variables in a named COMMON block are initialized, all variables in the block must be specified in the named COMMON declaration in the BLOCK DATA subprogram.

EQUIVALENCE Declaration

The EQUIVALENCE declaration is used within a program unit to indicate that two variables are to use the same memory location. The reason for this statement may be that, due to an error, two different names have been written for the same item. Or the reason may be to conserve memory space. Two or more variables used at different points in the program may be assigned to the same memory location if the earlier variables' values do not have to be preserved. Using the same name for the variables would cause them to share the memory location, but this may not be consistent with the naming scheme, etc., being used. Other reasons may also arise in individual programs. Entire arrays may be equivalenced. The form is:

EQUIVALENCE $(v_1, v_2, \ldots, v_n), (A_1, A_2, \ldots, A_n)$

where all the variable names or arrays listed inside each set of parentheses are to be assigned to the same memory location.

EQUIVALENCE should be used cautiously. It is possible to equivalence an element in an array to a nonsubscripted variable. Also, two arrays may be overlapped. These are error-prone uses and should be avoided.

Example

EQUIVALENCE (X, Y)	X and Y are to be assigned to the same memory location.
EQUIVALENCE (A(3), X)	X and A(3) are to reference the same location. Error prone!
EQUIVALENCE (I, J), (R, S)	I and J are the same, and R and S are the same.
Incorrect EQUIVALENCE (A(3), B(9))	This is incorrect because two array elements cannot be equivalenced.

The COMMON and EQUIVALENCE declarations should appear in the program ahead of any statements using the variables that they declare. A recommended order for these declarations (if any of the variables to be equivalenced are in COMMON) is

1. DIMENSION ⎫ Or, as recommended, include dimensioning in COMMON
2. COMMON ⎬ declaration
3. EQUIVALENCE ⎭

The DATA statement follows these specifications.

Self-Testing Exercise 5-3

1. Two subprograms and a main program all refer to the same set of three variables called X, IOTA, and CHI and to a 100-element array called SILLY by the two subprograms and DILLY by the main program. Write three statements for the three program units to declare these variables as COMMON (and dimension the arrays).

2. In a subroutine called SORT to sort an array, the array to be sorted is called X and dimensioned as 100. The main program also refers to the array as X and dimensions it as 100. Write statements to associate the two arrays X, (a) using the argument lists and (b) using COMMON declarations. Also, dimension the arrays.

3. Redo the answers to problem 2 assuming the name of the array is X in the subroutine and A in the main program.

4. Redo the answer to problem 1 putting the variables in named COMMON and initializing all variables to zero.

Case Program Structure

The case program coding structure is an extension of the IF and block IF selection structures. In the case structure, there are normally more than two program paths, one of which is selected (Figure 5-3). The case structure is useful because in many problems there are different processing actions to be performed on different classes or types of data. Each programming path may be termed a case. For example, the selection of a processing path for the different cases may be based on a code or other characteristic of the data. The multiple path selection can be programmed in FORTRAN by a set of IF statements or ELSEIF statements, but is usually more clearly programmed by the computed GOTO statement.

The computed GOTO transfers control to one of several program statements based on the value of an integer variable (or integer expression). The specifications are summarized in the box.

COMPUTED GOTO STATEMENT

GOTO $(s_1, s_2, s_3, \ldots s_n)[,]i$

i = integer variable (or integer expression in 1977 full FORTRAN)
s_i = statement label

GOTO can also be written as GO TO. If the value of the integer variable (or the integer expression) is 1, control transfers to the first statement listed; if the value is 2, control goes to the second statement, etc. If the integer value is less than 1, or greater than n (number of statements listed), control goes to the statement following the computed GOTO.

The maximum number of statement labels is not defined by the standard, but some compilers have limits. The comma following the right parenthesis, separating it from i, is optional in 1977 standard. Integer variable is required for i by 1977 subset FORTRAN; any integer expression is allowed by 1977 full standard.

A statement number can be repeated in the list so that, for example, both a value of 1 and a value of 3 will transfer control to the same statement. An integer value less than 1 or greater than the number of statements listed will cause the statement following to be executed; this is useful in error control. By always placing an error-control or error-message statement following a computed GOTO, the out-of-range condition is easily detected and reported. Some simple examples illustrate the form of the statement.

Figure 5-3 Case structure.

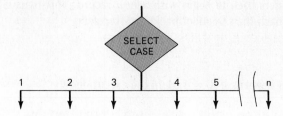

Computed GOTO Example 1

A program will perform one of four types of statistical analysis based on a code of 1 to 4 input by the user. The input value is assigned to ICODE. The statement labels for the four cases are 201, 301, 401, and 501. The case statement to select the processing path is:

```
GOTO (201, 301, 401, 501), ICODE
```

Computed GOTO Example 2

A program should transfer control to 410 if JVALUE is 1 or 2, to 450 if JVALUE is 3 or 4, and to 600 if JVALUE is 5. If JVALUE is zero, negative, or more than 5, print an error message.

```
GOTO (410, 410, 450, 450, 600), JVALUE
PRINT *, 'JVALUE OUT OF RANGE', JVALUE
```

Computed GOTO Example 3

A program to analyze the distribution of amount of sales by invoice may set up the following four categories (it is assumed that no sale exceeds $2999):

Less than $500
$500 to $999.99
$1000 to $1999.99
$2000 to $2999.99

If sales are negative, zero, or even $2999.99, then control should go to an error statement (number 910). Sales are input in the form XXXX.XX. A partial program and flowchart are shown in Figure 5-4.

The computed GOTO in the example could have been written as a single statement:

```
GO TO (. . . .), INT(1.0 + SALES / 500.0)
```

It was written in two steps for clarity in the example. In Figure 5-4, the INT (or IFIX) function that takes the integer portion of the result is redundant because there will be truncation across the equals sign to the integer variable K. However, use of an explicit function reduces the chance of error in understanding and maintaining the program. Note how the statement following the computed GOTO specifies transfer to an error-handling block.

To clarify the cases following a computed GOTO, it is useful to precede the beginning of each case (before each statement label specified in the computed GOTO) by a comment line that indicates the case to which the coding to follow applies. This is illustrated in Figure 5.4.

There must be GOTOs following each tally instruction. Note that all the GOTOs are forward to a single statement at the end of the group (statement 250), which transfers back to begin with a new record. This is usually a clearer programming approach than frequent backward transfers.

Self-Testing Exercise 5-4

1. What happens if X = 4.51 in the execution of

```
GOTO (100, 200, 310, 450, 710) INT(X)
```

```
*****
*                PROGRAM IDENTIFICATION
*****
*
*        Sales tally program.
*        Tally sales by category
*        (1) means less than $500
*        (2) means $500 to $999
*        (3) means $1000 to $1999
*        (4) means $2000 to 2999
*
*****
* BLOCK 0100      PROGRAM BEGINNING
*****
*
*        (DETAIL NOT SHOWN)
*
*
*****
* BLOCK 0200      READ AND TALLY
*****
*
   200 READ(5,201,END=300) SALES
   201 FORMAT(F7.2)
       K = INT(1.0 + SALES/500.0)
       GOTO (210,220,230,230,240,240),K
*
*               ERROR CASE
*
       GOTO 910
*
*               CASE 1
*
   210 T1 = T1 + SALES
       GOTO 250
*
*               CASE 2
*
   220 T2 = T2 + SALES
       GOTO 250
*
*               CASE 3
*
   230 T3 = T3 + SALES
       GOTO 250
*
*               CASE 4
*
   240 T4 = T4 + SALES
*
*        GO BACK TO READ ANOTHER RECORD
*
   250 GOTO 200
*****
* BLOCK 0300      OUTPUT BLOCK
*****
```

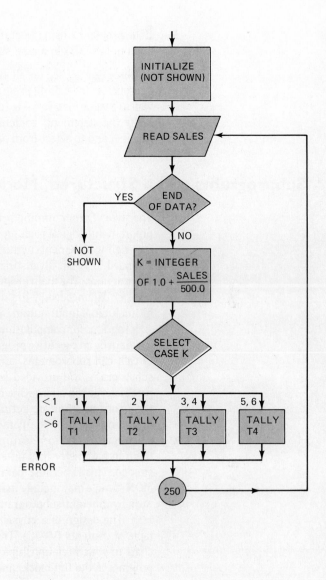

Figure 5-4 Partial program and flowchart for sales-tally program.

2. An input code (called ICODE) is either 2, 3, 4, or 5. Different processing is to be performed in each case (statement 200, 300, 400, and 500). If ICODE is one or less, or greater than 5, go to 900. Write a computed GOTO to perform this case selection.

3. Redo problem 2 with an ICODE of 0, 1, 2, and 3.

4. A programmer following the full 1977 FORTRAN standard writes a computed GOTO as follows:

```
GOTO (100, 200, 400, 600), IX + 2
```

The statement is rejected. Rewrite in FORTRAN acceptable to both subset and full versions.

5. Code problem 2 using IF statements. This illustrates the power and simplicity of the computed GOTO in a case situation.

6. A subroutine is used for all error messages. Before transferring to the error-message subroutine, the calling program defines a code from 1 to 6 for one of six messages as well as a value for a variable (call it XERR) that is to be printed with the error message. Write the statements to define the code, to call the subroutine, to define the subroutine, and to select from among the message cases.

Subprograms and a Structured, Modular Design

The style of programming presented to this point has emphasized the division of the program into logical parts and labeling each part as a block with a block number series for labeling statements within the block. The concept of logically defined blocks can be extended to physically distinct blocks in a program. The physically distinct blocks are subprograms. The main program is written to direct the use of the subprograms and to transfer data needed by the subprograms. This concept can be implemented partially by including input/output and error messages in the main program and using subprograms for computations. It can be implemented completely by having the main program be an executive program with only statements that decide which subprogram to call, call subprograms, and terminate the program. All data items needed by the subprograms are provided by variables in COMMON or by including them in the parameter list in subroutine calls or in function parameter lists. Responses needed by the main program are returned by storing them in variables in COMMON or by specifying them in the parameter lists for the subprogram. In providing data for subprograms and in returning results, there is generally a preference for including them in parameter lists unless there is a clear reason for putting them in common storage. This is because parameter lists are clear and unambiguous, whereas COMMON storage may include many unrelated data items that may be affected in unknown ways by different subprograms.

The design of a physically modular program is often documented by a visual table of contents (VTOC). This is similar to a hierarchy diagram or an organization chart in which relationships are shown by lines (and sometimes arrows). The main program is the top block, and modules called by it are at the second level. Modules called by the second level are shown at a third level. The only diagramming issue is how to show a program module that is used at the second level and is also used by a third level module, etc. The simplest approach is to repeat the program module in the

Figure 5-5 Visual table of contents for FORTRAN program with executive module and subprograms.

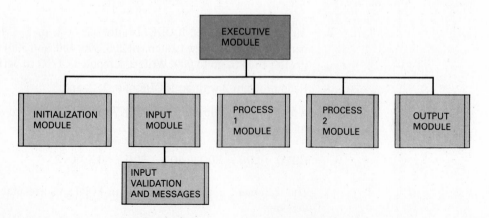

diagram in each place but to put a notation (such as a slash in the upper left corner or an asterisk) that indicates this is a repeat of a module represented earlier (Figure 5-5).

The question of how completely to subdivide a program into subprograms is answered on the basis of using the program structure that provides the clearest, most error-free, easiest-to-maintain design. As programs become larger and more complex, the value of subprograms increases.

Summary

Subprograms are an important programming technique useful for reducing the complexity of large programs, for separate writing and testing of parts of programs, for making use of prewritten routines, etc. The two types of subprograms are function subprograms and subroutines.

The function subprogram returns a single value to the main program. It is used for coding user-defined functions. It is invoked by using the function name, together with arguments, in an expression.

The subroutine subprogram is a separate program that is invoked by a CALL statement. The parameters of the CALL statement are variable names for data to be used by the subroutine and data names assigned to receive the results (if not in common storage). A subroutine may return no result, one result, or multiple results.

The COMMON declaration is an alternate method for two or more subprograms to communicate. Common storage assignments allow different subprograms to access the same storage locations, thereby using the same data.

The case structure is an extension of the selection structure in instances where multiple cases can be identified by integers between 1 and n. The case coding structure for selecting among multiple program paths for different cases is implemented in FORTRAN by the computed GOTO.

Answers to Self-Testing Exercises

Exercise 5-1

1. The function subprogram SUM sums the elements of a 100-entry array. The main program reads the array A, takes the square root of the sum of A returned by the function, and prints the result.

2. The function IBOY returns an integer result; the variables in the calling argument list are real (X), real (A), and integer (J). The statement to define the function as real type is

   ```
   REAL FUNCTION IBOY (X, A, J)
   ```

3. ```
   FUNCTION ROOT (A, B, C)
   DESCR = B**2 - 4.0 * A * C
   IF (DESCR .LE. 0.0) THEN
       ROOT = 0.0
   ELSE
       ROOT = -B + SQRT(DESCR) / (2.0 * A)
       IF (ROOT .LT. 0.0) ROOT = 0.0
   ENDIF
   RETURN
   ```
   ```

4. X = A**2 + ROOT (X, Y, Z)

5. FUNCTION DIFF (RATE1, RATE2, AMT)
DIFF = AMT * (RATE2 − RATE1)
RETURN (optional)
END

6. D = DIFF (XINT1, XINT2, AMOUNT)

Exercise 5-2

1. The subroutine need not have arguments; the functions must have at least one argument. The subroutine returns any number of results; the function subprogram returns one result. The function is used in an assignment statement; the subroutine is called by a single, separate statement.

2. SUBROUTINE DIFF (RATE1, RATE2, AMT, RESULT)
RESULT = AMT * (RATE2 − RATE1)
RETURN (optional)
END

3. CALL DIFF (XINT1, XINT2, AMOUNT, D)

The result of the call is to make D in the main program equal to the RESULT in the subroutine.

4.
```
      SUBROUTINE MOVE (B)
      DIMENSION B(20, 20)
      DO  110 I = 1, 20
         L = I + 1
         DO 100 J = L, 20
            TEMP = B(I, J)
            B(I, J) = B(J, I)
            B(J, I) = TEMP
100      CONTINUE
110 CONTINUE
      RETURN (optional)
      END
```

5. CALL MOVE (ALPHA)

Exercise 5-3

1.

Main program	COMMON X, IOTA, CHI, DILLY (100)
Subprogram 1	COMMON X, IOTA, CHI, SILLY (100)
Subprogram 2	COMMON X, IOTA, CHI, SILLY (100)

2. (*a*) Argument list

Subroutine	SUBROUTINE SORT (X)
Main program	CALL SORT (X)

(b) Common

Subroutine	SUBROUTINE SORT	
	DIMENSION X (100) ⎤	or COMMON X(100)
	COMMON X ⎦	
Main program	DIMENSION X (100) ⎤	or COMMON X(100)
	COMMON X ⎦	
	CALL SORT	

3. (a) Subroutine   SUBROUTINE SORT(X)
       Main program   CALL SORT (A)
   (b) Subroutine   SUBROUTINE SORT
                     DIMENSION X(100) ⎤ or COMMON X(100)
                     COMMON X   ⎦
       Main program   DIMENSION A(100) ⎤ or COMMON A(100)
                     COMMON A   ⎦
                     CALL SORT

Note that since A and X were both the first item in COMMON, they will occupy the same storage and therefore be equivalent.

4. Main program   COMMON / G1 / X, IOTA, CHI, DILLY (100)
   Subprogram 1   COMMON / G1 / X, IOTA, CHI, SILLY (100)
   Subprogram 2   COMMON / GI / X, IOTA, CHI, SILLY (100)
   BLOCK DATA
   COMMON / G1 / X, IOTA, CHI, DILLY (100)
   DATA IOTA / 0 / X, CHI / 2 * 0.0 / DILLY / 100 * 0.0 /
   END

Exercise 5-4

1. It will go to statement 450 because X will be truncated to 4. It could also have been coded in two steps.

   ```
   JX = INT (X)
   GOTO (100, 200, 310, 450, 710), JX
   ```

2. Subtract 1 from ICODE to make it within limits of 1, 2, 3, and 4.

   ```
       GOTO (200, 300, 400, 500) ICODE −1
   900 for out of limits
   or  ICODE = ICODE − 1
       GOTO (200, 300, 400, 500), ICODE
   900 for out of limits
   ```

3. Add 1 to ICODE to make it fit the form of 1, 2, 3, or 4.

   ```
       GOTO (200, 300, 400, 500), ICODE + 1
   900 for out of limits
   or  ICODE = ICODE + 1
       GOTO (200, 300, 400, 500), ICODE
   900 for out of limits
   ```

4. ```
   I = IX + 2
   GOTO (100, 200, 400, 600), I
   ```
   ```

5.
```
IF (ICODE.LT.2.OR.ICODE.GT.5) GOTO 900
IF (ICODE.EQ.2) GOTO 200
IF (ICODE.EQ.3) GOTO 300
IF (ICODE.EQ.4) GOTO 400
IF (ICODE.EQ.5) GOTO 500
```

6. Main program
```
JCODE =
XERR =
CALL (JCODE, XERR)
```

Subprogram
```
SUBROUTINE (KODE, XMSSG)
GOTO (100, 200, 300, 400, 500, 600), KODE
```

Questions and Problems

1. What is the difference between the function subprogram and subroutine?

2. What is the difference between the COMMON and the EQUIVALENCE statements?

3. What is the effect of each of the following statements or declarations?
   (*a*) CALL WILMA
   (*b*) CALL MOM (DAD, KIDS, SIS)
   (*c*) EQUIVALENCE (TEEN, SILLY, CRAZY)
   (*d*) FUNCTION NICE (I, J, K)
   (*e*) SUBROUTINE COME (X, Y, Z, B)
   (*f*) X = TALLY (GAMMA1, GAMMA2)

4. Make X in a main program equal to $\sqrt[3]{A^2 + B^2}$. Do this step using two different methods: a function subprogram and a subroutine (using two methods for transferring the answer). Write complete subprograms but show only the necessary segment of the main program.

5. Write a main program segment to read *n* (say, 10) data items in F10.2 fields and print the input. Write a subroutine to order the data items from smallest to largest. Code statements for the main program to call this subroutine and then print out the ordered array. For a small array, interchange sorting is satisfactory. In interchange sorting, the first variable is compared with each of the other variables. If the value being compared is smaller, the two are interchanged. This continues through the array. The result is the smallest value in cell 1. The same procedure is followed for cell 2, etc. See Figure 5-2 for large-to-small logic.

5b

Example Programs and Programming Exercises Using Subprograms and Case Structure

General Notes on Chapter 5 Examples

**General Program Example 5—
Payroll Reports**
Problem Description for General Example 5
Program Documentation for General Example 5
Notes on General Example 5

**Mathematical Program Example 5
—Numerical Integration**
Program Description for Mathematical Example 5
Program Documentation for Mathematical Example 5
Notes on Mathematical Example 5

Programming Exercises
Description of Assignment
Mathematics and Statistics
Business and Economics
Science and Engineering
Humanities and Social Sciences
General
Interactive Scientific and Engineering

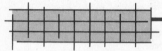

General Notes on Chapter 5 Examples

The example programs illustrate the use of subroutines and function subprograms, COMMON and EQUIVALENCE statements, and the case structure. The program for general example 5, payroll report, is designed for batch execution and file input. It makes use of two function subprograms and a subroutine. It includes the case structure as well as named and blank COMMON, EQUIVALENCE, DIMENSION, and DATA statements. The program for mathematical example 5, numerical integration, is designed for interactive execution and keyboard data input. It uses the same features as the payroll program, except for the case structure and DATA statement. Optional double slashes without a name are used for the blank COMMON declaration. This technique more clearly shows the difference between blank and named COMMON declarations. An additional section, *subroutine and function identification,* has been added to the variables identification block.

The basic logic of the general program has not changed from Chapter 4, so the explanations will focus on new Chapter 5 features. The mathematical problem extends the concept of integration, used in Chapter 4b, to compare the results from three methods.

General Program Example 5—Payroll Reports

The program reads input data from files and produces the same sort of reports as its predecessor in Chapter 4 for gross pay, total deductions, and net pay. The report-printing logic is the same except that several other error conditions are checked, and hence the "notes" section of the payroll report is altered. Retirement and tax computations are more complex and make use of additional input data. Tax is calculated by a function subprogram, and retirement is calculated by a subroutine. The case structure is used in the pension subroutine. A rounding function subprogram is used to adjust all dollar and cents values to the nearest penny.

Problem Description for General Example 5

The program is to read from two files, department names and numbers and employee pay data, and produce two reports: (1) Paycheck Report: Table Values and Error Messages and (2) Employee Paycheck Report. The latter report contains a line for each employee and a line of totals at the end of the report. The employees are grouped by department in the report. In the Employee Paycheck Report, net pay that is negative or over $300 is accompanied by a warning note. Also, errors in input code for union and management employees are to be noted.

The first input file for the program consists of a set of five records with department numbers and names, one pair per record. Input validation for this input consists of visual verification output that echoes the table. The table is printed as part of the Paycheck Report: Table Values and Error Messages. Input data from the second file consists of the payroll period date plus one record for each employee, giving ID number, name, department number where employed, hours worked, wage rate, miscellaneous deductions, number of dependents, and union or management code. During reading of employee input records, error messages reflecting the detection of data-type errors or invalid data are printed immediately on the Paycheck Report: Table Values and Error Messages, and the error record is not processed further for the subsequent Employee Paycheck Report. After all records are read and validated for input errors, a total record count and number of rejected records are printed on the report following the error messages.

Program Documentation for General Example 5

The documentation of program design is given by a pseudocode description (Figure 5-6) and a program flowchart (Figure 5-7). The program listing is shown in Figure 5-8. The pseudocode, flowchart, and program listings are not complete; only those parts of the program documentation that differ from the corresponding program in Chapter 4 are presented. This allows the discussion to focus on the use of subprograms and error handling. Therefore, the pseudocode, flowcharts, and program listings are complete for the subprograms. For the main program, there is no pseudocode or flowchart, but there is a partial program listing. For the parts of the program that are not shown in the listing, refer to Figure 4-19, which is the program listing for the payroll program in Chapter 4b. Test data is documented in Figure 5-9, the corresponding Paycheck Report: Table Values and Error Messages is given in Figure 5-10, and the Employee Paycheck Report is shown in Figure 5-11.

Notes on General Example 5

The variables identification block has been enlarged to include a section to identify any subroutine and function subprograms by name and to provide a brief description (lines 57–61). Note that throughout this entire block, each name must be unique.

Since COMMON, DIMENSION, and DATA statements all control storage (memory) allocation, they are grouped at the beginning, before any executable code, in the storage allocation block (lines 72–76). However, data locations in blank common storage cannot be initialized using a DATA statement. The variables to be initialized are specified as being in named COMMON, and the DATA statement to initialize them is placed in a separate BLOCK DATA subprogram (lines 426–439).

Many of the features of this program are identical to general program example 4. However, the computation block has been altered somewhat to reflect more complex formulas of the number of dependents. While this relationship could have been inserted directly in the program in place of code line 172, it was preferable to code it as a function subprogram (called RATE) so that the specific formula could be isolated from the general program flow. If the formula changes, it is easily identified for

Function rate	Establish storage common with other program units
	Test dependents code
	  IF one dependent, use standard rate;
	  IF more than one dependent
	
	  $\text{RATE} = \left(1 - \dfrac{N}{N + 6}\right)$ * standard rate
	
	  [N = number of dependents]
	RETURN

Subroutine pnsion	Establish storage common with other program units
	Test for legal employee type code
	  If out of bounds, set error note to 2 and set type code to 1 as
	    default option
	  Else continue
	Select case for employee type
	  Case 1 (Union employee)
	    Pension contribution = 6 percent of GRSPAY
	  Case 2 (Management, employee)
	    Pension contribution is 5 percent of $200 base pay plus 7.5
	    percent of pay over base
	RETURN

Function pnyrnd	Round a value to nearest penny RETURN
Block data	Declare named COMMON storage Initialize variables in named COMMON with DATA statement

Figure 5-6 Pseudocode description of subprograms for general program example 5—payroll reports.

changes to be made. Similarly, a subroutine called PNSION has been used to implement the specific procedure for computing pension contributions (line 177). As a matter of style, to differentiate program units, the last comment line of the main program has END OF MAIN PROGRAM in it, and for subprograms, there is an END OF SUBPROGRAM message. This comment line is just before the END statement that is the last statement of the program. The same block structure is used in subprograms as in the main program. For example, there is an identification block at the beginning of each subprogram.

Although the flowchart for the main program is not given, it is almost the same as the flowchart of the payroll program in Chapter 4b. One major difference between the payroll program flowchart in 4b and a flowchart for 5b is a segment which shows

Figure 5-7 Program flowcharts for subprograms for general example 5—payroll reports (numbers next to symbols are line numbers from program listing).

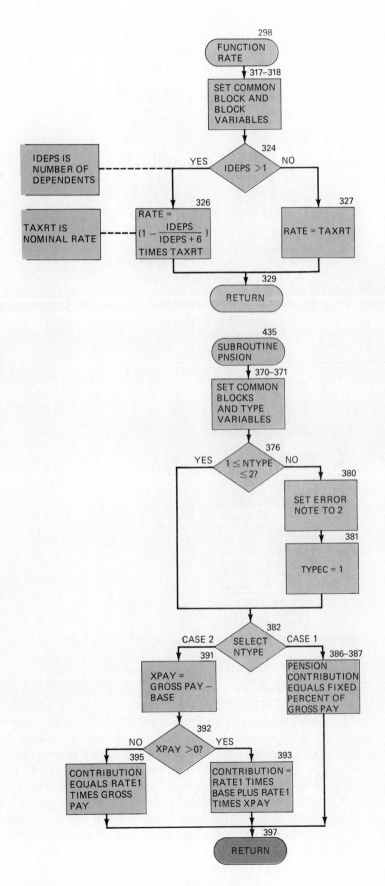

Figure 5-7 concluded

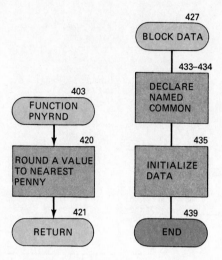

the computation of the elements of the paycheck. The flowchart segment for 5b shows the use of subprograms by the subprogram symbol as shown below.

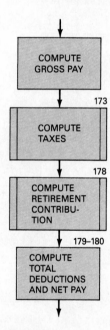

There are some interesting error-handling procedures in the program. The concept of flagging an error or potential error by a note is expanded to include four error notes, including the notation that no errors were detected. The program logic for the error notes begins with an error count (NERRS) for each record that will determine the error notes to be referenced. The error-count storage locations are set to zero in the initialization block (lines 101–104). In line 380 in the subroutine PNSION, the error code is set to 2 if the type-of-employee code is neither 1 nor 2 (the only allowable possibilities). Lines 376–381 illustrate the concept of a default option. Frequently, when an error is detected, it is useful to assign one code or result as the most likely rather than not processing the record. A warning message is printed for

Figure 5-8 Program listing for general program example 5—payroll reports. Missing sections are the same as Figure 4-19.

PROGRAM

```
 1 **********
 2 *                          PROGRAM IDENTIFICATION
 3 **********
 4 *
 5 *     This program computes employee paychecks based
 6 *     upon hours worked, wage rate and various deductions.
 7 *     It prints employee data (File DATA5E) grouped by
 8 *     departments (DATA5D). Variable tax and pension rates
 9 *     are computed. Developed for file input and batch execution.
10 *     Written 7/12/77 by T. Hoffmann  rev. 1/22/82  3/27/87
11 *
12 **********
13 *                          VARIABLES IDENTIFICATION
14 **********
15 *
16 *     DEPTS    - Number of departments (integer)
17 *     RECS     - Number of records read (integer)
18 *     NUM      - Number of valid employee records accepted (integer)
19 *     NOTVLD   - Number of not valid employee records (integer)
20 *     OTIME    - Hours of overtime (excess over 40.0)
21 *     RETIRE   - Retirement contribution by employee
22 *     TAXES    - Taxes due: $
23 *     TOTNET   - Total of net pay amounts
24 *     TOTPAY   - Total gross pay for company: $
25 *     TOTDUC   - Total of all employee deductions
26 *     WKEND    - Date of week payroll ended (MM/DD/YY) (character)
27 *
28 *****                      ARRAY IDENTIFICATION
29 *
30 *     ID       - Employee identification number (integer)
31 *     GRSPAY   - Gross pay: $
32 *     NAME     - Employee names (character)
33 *     NDEP     - Dept. Number where worked (integer)
34 *     DEPT     - List of department numbers (integer)
35 *     DEPTNM   - Corresponding list of department names (character)
36 *     PAYCHK   - Net paycheck amount: $
37 *     PAYDAT   - Payroll input data (hrswrk,wgrate,deduc)
38 *     TDEDUC   - Total of all deductions for an employee
39 *     NERRS    - List of error code notes
40 *     NDEPS    - Number of claimed dependents
41 *     MTYPE    - Union(=1), management(=2) type of employee
42 *
43 *****                      IDENTIFICATION OF CONSTANTS
44 *
45 *     PLIMIT   - Maximum paycheck value to allow = $300.00
46 *     TAXRT    - Base tax rate = 0.15
47 *     MAXEMP   - Maximum number of valid employee records = 14
48 *     PRATU    - Pension rate for union employees = 0.06
49 *     BASE     - Base salary for management pension = 200.00
50 *     PRATM1   - Base pension rate for management = 0.05
51 *     PRATM2   - Pension rate for $ over base = 0.075
52 *
53 *****                      TEMPORARY VARIABLE NAMES
54 *
55 *     MATCH,PAYNET,XPAY,NTYPE
56 *
57 *****                      SUBROUTINE AND FUNCTION IDENTIFICATION
58 *
59 *     RATE     - Calculates proper tax rate
60 *     PNSION   - Computes pension contribution
61 *     PNYRND   - Rounds computations to nearest penny
62 *
63 **********
64 *                          TYPE DECLARATION AND STORAGE ALLOCATION
65 **********
66 *
67 *     Maximum number of valid employee records is 14 (MAXEMP)
68 *     Maximum number of departments is 5
69 *
70       INTEGER DEPT,RECS,DEPTS
71       CHARACTER NAME(15)*12,DEPTNM*4,WKEND*8
72       COMMON /A/ TAXRT
73       COMMON /PENCOM/GRSPAY(15),NERRS(15),PRATU,PRATM1,PRATM2,BASE
```

Figure 5-8 continued

```
 74        DIMENSION DEPT(6),DEPTNM(6),ID(15),NDEP(15),PAYDAT(15,3),
 75      1    TDEDUC(15),PAYCHK(15),NDEPS(15),MTYPE(15)
 76        DATA PLIMIT/300.0/MAXEMP/14/
 77  *
 78  **********
 79  * BLOCK 0000            INITIALIZATION BLOCK
 80  **********
 81  *
 82      OPEN(7,FILE='DATA5D')
 83      OPEN(8,FILE='DATA5E')
 84  *
 85  *                 READ DATE AND PRINT HEADER
 86  *
 87      READ(8,1) WKEND
 88    1 FORMAT(A8)
 89      WRITE(6,3) WKEND
 90    3 FORMAT(' Paycheck Report: Table Values and Error Messages'/
 91      1    20X,'Week Ended ',A8/)
 92  *
 93  *              ZERO ACCUMULATORS AND INITIALIZE COUNTERS
 94  *
 95      TOTPAY = 0.0
 96      TOTNET = 0.0
 97      TOTDUC = 0.0
 98      RECS = 0
 99      NUM = 1
100      DEPTS = 0
101      DO 6 I = 1,MAXEMP
102         NERRS(I) = 0
103    6 CONTINUE
104  *
105  *              READ AND PRINT DEPARTMENT NUMBERS AND NAMES
106  *
107      DO 8 K = 1,6
108         READ(7,7,END=9) DEPT(K),DEPTNM(K)
109    7 FORMAT(I4,A4)
110      DEPTS = DEPTS + 1
111  *
112  *                 TEST TO PREVENT ARRAY OVERFLOW
113  *
114         IF(DEPTS .GT. 5) GOTO 908
115    8 CONTINUE
116    9 WRITE(6,10)
117   10 FORMAT(' Table of Departments'/3X,' Number    Name')
118      WRITE(6,11) (DEPT(K),DEPTNM(K),K=1,DEPTS)
119   11 FORMAT(5X,I4,4X,A4)
120  *
121  *                 PRINT ERROR MESSAGE HEADER
122  *
123      WRITE(6,13)
124   13 FORMAT(///6X,'Error messages during data input'//)
125  *
126  **********
127  * BLOCK 0100         READ EMPLOYEE DATA
128  **********
129  *
130  101 READ(8,102,END=301,ERR=901) ID(NUM),NAME(NUM),
131      1    NDEP(NUM),(PAYDAT(NUM,K),K=1,3),NDEPS(NUM),MTYPE(NUM)
132  102 FORMAT(I5,2X,A12,2X,I4,2X,F4.1,2X,F4.2,2X,F5.2,2X,I2,2X,I1)
133  *
134  *        TEST TO PREVENT ARRAY OVERFLOW. IF ARRAY'S NOT FULL
135  *               GO ON TO CHECK DATA VALIDITY
136  *
137      IF(NUM.GT.MAXEMP) GOTO 906
138      RECS = RECS + 1
139  *
140  *                 VALIDATE PAYROLL DATA
141  *
142      IF(PAYDAT(NUM,1) .LE. 0.0 .OR. PAYDAT(NUM,1) .GT. 60.0) GOTO 910
143      IF(PAYDAT(NUM,2) .LE. 0.0 .OR. PAYDAT(NUM,2) .GT. 10.0) GOTO 910
144      IF(PAYDAT(NUM,3) .LT. 0.0 .OR. PAYDAT(NUM,3) .GT. 65.0) GOTO 910
145  *
146  *        CHECK FOR VALID DEPARTMENT NUMBER IN EMPLOYEE CARD
147  *            WHEN FOUND, PROCESS EMPLOYEE DATA
148  *
149      DO 105 K=1,DEPTS
150         IF(DEPT(K).EQ.NDEP(NUM)) GOTO 201
```

Figure 5-8 continued

```
151 105 CONTINUE
152 *
153 *              ERROR -- NO MATCH FOUND FOR EMPLOYEE DEPT. NUMBER
154 *
155     GOTO 903
156 *
157 **********
158 * BLOCK 0200      COMPUTE GROSS PAY, DEDUCTIONS & NET PAY BLOCK
159 **********
160 *
161 *              COMPUTE PAY, INCLUDING OVERTIME, IF ANY.
162 *
163 201 OTIME = PAYDAT(NUM,1) - 40.0
164     IF(OTIME.GT.0.0) THEN
165         GRSPAY(NUM) = PNYRND((40.0 + 1.5*OTIME)*PAYDAT(NUM,2))
166     ELSE
167         GRSPAY(NUM) = PNYRND(PAYDAT(NUM,1)*PAYDAT(NUM,2))
168     ENDIF
169 *
170 *              COMPUTE TAXES USING RATE FUNCTION
171 *
172     TAXES = PNYRND(GRSPAY(NUM)*RATE(NDEPS(NUM)))
173 *
174 *              COMPUTE RETIREMENT CONTRIBUTION BASED UPON
175 *                      UNION/MANAGEMENT TYPE
176 *
177     CALL PNSION(MTYPE(NUM),RETIRE,NUM)
178     TDEDUC(NUM) = PAYDAT(NUM,3) + TAXES + RETIRE
179     PAYCHK(NUM) = GRSPAY(NUM) - TDEDUC(NUM)
180 *
181 *              INCREMENT TOTALS AND COUNTER
182 *
183     TOTPAY = TOTPAY + GRSPAY(NUM)
184     TOTDUC = TOTDUC + TDEDUC(NUM)
185     TOTNET = TOTNET + PAYCHK(NUM)
186     NUM = NUM + 1
187 *
188 *              GO BACK TO READ ANOTHER DATA RECORD
189 *
190     GOTO 101
191 *
192 **********
193 * BLOCK 0300      PRINT DETAIL BY DEPARTMENT GROUPING
194 **********
195 *
196 *              PRINT SUMMARY OF DATA INPUT MESSAGES
197 *
198 301 NOTVLD = RECS - NUM + 1
199     WRITE(6,302) RECS,NOTVLD
200 302 FORMAT('0',I4,' Records read'/I5,' Records in error')
201 *
202 *              PRINT HEADER/TITLE LINE FOR EMPLOYEE DETAIL REPORT
203 *
204     WRITE(6,303) WKEND
205 303 FORMAT('1',T17,'Employee Paycheck Report'/T19,'Week Ended ',A8/)
206     WRITE(6,304)
207 304 FORMAT(5X,'Employee',5X,'ID',3X,'Dept',3X,'Gross',4X,
208    1     'Total',6X,'Net',4X,'Notes'/7X,'Name',12X,'Name',4X,
209    2     'Pay',3X,'Deductions')
210 *
211 *              FOR EACH DEPARTMENT FIND EACH EMPLOYEE & PRINT DETAIL
212 *
213     DO 310 J=1,DEPTS
214         MATCH = DEPT(J)
215         DO 309 I=1,NUM-1
216             IF(NDEP(I).NE.MATCH) GOTO 309
217     PAYNET = PAYCHK(I)
218 *
219 *              CHECK FOR VALID PAYCHECK AMOUNT
220 *
221     IF(PAYNET.GT.0.0 .AND. PAYNET.LE.PLIMIT) GOTO 305
222     IF(NERRS(I) .NE. 0) THEN
223         NERRS(I) = 3
224     ELSE
225         NERRS(I) = 1
226     ENDIF
227 305 WRITE(6,307) NAME(I),ID(I),DEPTNM(J),
```

Figure 5-8 continued

```
228 1      GRSPAY(I),TDEDUC(I),PAYCHK(I),NERRS(I)
229 307    FORMAT('0',2X,A12,I6,2X,A4,3X,F6.2,3X,F6.2,3X,F6.2,I6)
230 309    CONTINUE
231 310 CONTINUE
232 *
233 **********
234 * BLOCK 0400          PRINT SUMMARY AND TERMINATE
235 **********
236 *
237    WRITE(6,402) TOTPAY,TOTDUC,TOTNET
238 402 FORMAT(//20X,'Totals',3X,F7.2,2F9.2)
239    WRITE(6,403)
240 403 FORMAT(///5X,'Notes'
241 1    /5X,'0 - No errors'
242 2    /5X,'1 - Net pay is out of bounds. Do not issue check.'
243 3    /5X,'2 - Union/management code error. Union assumed.'
244 4    /5X,'3 - Both type 1 and 2 errors.')
245 410 CLOSE (7)
246    CLOSE (8)
247    STOP
248 *
249 **********
250 * BLOCK 0900          ERROR MESSAGE BLOCK
251 **********
252 *
253 901 RECS = RECS + 1
254    WRITE(6,902) RECS
255 902 FORMAT(//' *****',' ERROR IN EMPLOYEE RECORD NUMBER '
256 1    ,I2,' *****')
257    GOTO 918
258 *****
259 *
260 903 WRITE(6,904) RECS
261 904 FORMAT(//' ***** ERROR - DEPT. NO. NOT VALID. RECORD NO. ',I4,
262 1    2X,'*****')
263    GOTO 918
264 *****
265 *
266 906 WRITE(6,907) MAXEMP
267 907 FORMAT(///' ***** ERROR. ATTEMPTED TO READ ',
268 1 'MORE THAN',I3,' VALID DATA RECORDS'/7X,'PROGRAM ABORTED.')
269 *
270 *             CLOSE FILES AND ABORT RUN
271 *
272    GOTO 410
273 *****
274 *
275 908 WRITE(6,909)
276 909 FORMAT (///' ***** ERROR. ATTEMPTED TO READ TOO MANY DEPARTMENT ',
277 1 'NAMES. *****')
278 *
279 *             CLOSE FILES AND ABORT RUN
280 *
281    GOTO 410
282 *****
283 *
284 910 WRITE(6,911) RECS,ID(NUM),NAME(NUM),(PAYDAT(NUM,I),I=1,3),
285 1    NDEPS(NUM),MTYPE(NUM)
286 911 FORMAT('0','***** Data outside validation limits--input ',
287 1 'rejected ***** record',I3/7X,'Data contents ',
288 2    I5,2X,A12,2X,F5.1,2X,F5.2,2X,F6.2,2X,I4,2X,I4)
289 *
290 *             GO BACK AND READ ANOTHER EMPLOYEE RECORD
291 *
292 918 GOTO 101
293 *
294 * END OF MAIN PROGRAM
295 *
296    END
```

Figure 5-8 continued

```
297 *
298       FUNCTION RATE(DEPS)
299 *
300 *********
301 *                        PROGRAM IDENTIFICATION
302 *********
303 *
304 *        Compute proper tax rate based upon number of dependents
305 *
306 *********
307 *                        VARIABLES IDENTIFICATION
308 *********
309 *
310 *        DEPS     = Number of claimed dependents (integer)
311 *        TAXRT    = Base tax rate
312 *
313 *********
314 *                        TYPE DECLARATION AND STORAGE ALLOCATION
315 *********
316 *
317       INTEGER DEPS
318       COMMON /A/ TAXRT
319 *
320 *********
321 * BLOCK 0100              COMPUTATION BLOCK
322 *********
323 *
324       IF(DEPS .GT. 1) THEN
325            RATE = (1.0 - (FLOAT(DEPS)/FLOAT(DEPS+6)))*TAXRT
326       ELSE
327            RATE = TAXRT
328       ENDIF
329       RETURN
330 *
331 * END OF SUBPROGRAM
332 *
333       END
```

follow-up. The test for the existence of code 1 for union or code 2 for management is followed (if the code is neither) by a statement in line 381 to set it to a default option of union. The error code that is set will provide a warning message.

The segment of the main program that tests for the error code set by the subroutine is given in lines 222–226. The logic follows from the fact that the error code (NERRS) is initialized at zero but may have been set to another value by the subroutine PNSION. In the main program, if there is a negative or out-of-limit paycheck, this should set an error code (but doing so would change any error code already set by the subroutine). The way this is handled is to check if there was an error from the subroutine (NERRS is not equal to zero); if so, the code is reset to 3 which defines a double error. Otherwise, the code is set to 1 which defines only a negative or out-of-limit error.

The function subprogram and the subroutine subprogram illustrate the two ways for transferring data between a subprogram and the calling (using) program. The two ways are to define data as being in common storage and to transfer data by means of the parameter list. Note in FUNCTION RATE, the TAXRT base tax rate is in COMMON (line 318), while the number of claimed dependents is transferred by means of the parameter (line 298). For the SUBROUTINE PNSION, there are a number of variables declared as being in named COMMON called PENCOM (line 371). Three variables are transferred with the parameter list: TYPEC, CASH, and NUM. Two of these are results from the subroutine that will be stored in the locations assigned for the results by the calling statement. These are MTYPE (NUM) and RETIRE as shown by line 177. The variable NUM is transferred for use by the subroutine.

Figure 5-8 continued

```
334 *
335       SUBROUTINE PNSION(TYPEC,CASH,NUM)
336 *
337 **********
338 *                    PROGRAM IDENTIFICATION
339 **********
340 *
341 *        Compute pension contribution based upon type of employee.
342 *        union = 1     management = 2     error = other
343 *
344 **********
345 *                    VARIABLES IDENTIFICATION
346 **********
347 *
348 *        TYPEC   = Type of employee code (integer)
349 *        CASH    = Retirement contribution
350 *        NUM     = Employee number (integer)
351 *        PRATU   = Pension rate for union employees
352 *        BASE    = Base salary for management pension
353 *        PRATM1  = Base pension rate for management
354 *        PRATM2  = Pension rate for $ over base
355 *        XPAY    = Pay over base
356 *
357 *****                ARRAY NAMES
358 *
359 *        GRSPAY  = Gross pay: $
360 *        NERRS   = List of error code notes (integer)
361 *
362 **********            FUNCTION IDENTIFICATION
363 *
364 *        PNYRND  = Rounds computations to nearest penny
365 *
366 **********
367 *                    TYPE DECLARATION AND STORAGE ALLOCATION
368 **********
369 *
370       INTEGER TYPEC
371       COMMON /PENCOM/GRSPAY(15),NERRS(15),PRATU,PRATM1,PRATM2,BASE
372 *
373 **********
374 * BLOCK 0100           COMPUTATION BLOCK
375 **********
376       IF(TYPEC.GE.1 .AND. TYPEC.LE.2) GOTO 102
377 *
378 *        CASE ERROR - SET ERROR INDICATOR AND ASSUME TYPEC IS 1
379 *
380       NERRS(NUM) = 2
381       TYPEC = 1
382 102 GOTO (103,104),TYPEC
383 *
384 *        CASE ONE - UNION TYPE EMPLOYEE
385 *
386 103 CASH = PNYRND(PRATU*GRSPAY(NUM))
387       GOTO 106
388 *
389 *        CASE TWO - MANAGEMENT TYPE EMPLOYEE
390 *
391 104 XPAY = GRSPAY(NUM) - BASE
392       IF(XPAY.GT.0.0) THEN
393            CASH = PNYRND(PRATM1*BASE + PRATM2*XPAY)
394       ELSE
395            CASH = PNYRND(PRATM1*GRSPAY(NUM))
396       ENDIF
397 106 RETURN
398 *
399 * END OF SUBPROGRAM
400 *
401       END
```

Figure 5-8 concluded

```
402 *
403       FUNCTION PNYRND(VALUE)
404 *
405 **********
406 *                      PROGRAM IDENTIFICATION
407 **********
408 *
409 * Values are rounded to the nearest penny
410 * Called from main and pnsion
411 *
412 **********
413 *                      VARIABLES IDENTIFICATION
414 **********
415 *
416 * VALUE    = Value of expression to be rounded
417 *
418 **********
419 *
420     PNYRND = FLOAT((INT(100.0*(VALUE + 0.005))))/100.0
421     RETURN
422 *
423 * END OF SUBPROGRAM
424 *
425     END
```

```
426 *
427     BLOCK DATA
428 *
429 **********
430 *                  INITIALIZE COMMON BLOCK DATA
431 **********
432 *
433     COMMON /A/ TAXRT
434     COMMON /PENCOM/GRSPAY(15),NERRS(15),PRATU,PRATM1,PRATM2,BASE
435     DATA TAXRT/0.15/PRATU/0.06/PRATM1/0.05/PRATM2/0.075/BASE/200.0/
436 *
437 * END OF SUBPROGRAM
438 *
439     END
```

In Chapter 3, the problem was discussed of format rounding in business-type reports that show all figures to the nearest cent and contain totals based on footing (adding down columns) and crossfooting (adding across rows). The result in the report footing and crossfooting totals may differ slightly if rounded data is used for one and unrounded data for the other. One solution is to round all data internally in the same form as it is to be printed out (nearest penny) and use the rounded data in all footing and crossfooting. It is cumbersome to write the rounding computations as part of every statement where applicable. An alternative method is to use a rounding function. Such a function, called PNYRND, is part of the pay report program (lines 402–425). Note how it consists of only one assignment statement (line 420), a RETURN statement, and an END statement. The function is used in statements in the main program. One example is line 167:

```
GRSPAY(NUM) = PNYRND(PAYDAT(NUM, 1) * PAYDAT (NUM, 2))
```

See also lines 165 and 172.

Figure 5-9 Annotated
input test data for general
program example 5—payroll
reports.

```
1234FIN
4275ENGR
7269MKTG
7531PROD
8551ACCT


03/19/87
23456   P. HOFFMANN    7531   40.0   3.57   27.95   02   1
15786   RALPH JONES     8551   39.9   6.28   24.68   04   1
36985   J. JOHNSON      7269   22.0   0275   03598   01   1
23457   T. HOFFMANN     1596   40.0   3.57   27.95   03   2    Dept no. not valid
69852   T. NAMAN        4275   10.0   2.67   27.50   09   1    Negative pay
35748   L. SMITH        4275   40.1   9.94   30.68   04   4
W. RONG                 1596.  GEN                             Invalid data
42753   R. M. NELSON    1234   40.0   7.45   57.64   03   2
74365   A. PETERSON     7531   54.0   4.82   54.63   00   0    Error 2 — union/mgt.
62475   F. MORLOCK      4275   37.5   8.24   65.34   02   2    Outside limits
```

Figure 5-9 Annotated input test data for general program example 5—payroll reports.

The program also makes use of a BLOCK DATA subprogram to initialize data in named COMMON. Note that the COMMON statements define the variables in the named COMMON and the DATA statement places values in them. For example, the TAXRT is set at .15. In summary, review the following features of this pay report program:

1. The use of a function and a subroutine to isolate key computations that may need to change
2. The identification list in the main program of all functions and subroutines called by the main program
3. The use of named COMMON (lines 72 and 73)

Figure 5-10 Example of
report with table values and
error messages from payroll
reports program.

```
Paycheck Report: Table Values and Error Messages
                Week Ended 03/19/87
Table of Departments
    Number    Name
     1234     FIN
     4275     ENGR
     7269     MKTG
     7531     PROD
     8551     ACCT



     Error messages during data input



***** ERROR - DEPT. NO. NOT VALID. RECORD NO.      4  *****


***** ERROR IN EMPLOYEE RECORD NUMBER  7 *****

***** Data outside validation limits--input rejected ***** record 10
        Data contents 62475  F. MORLOCK  37.5   8.24   65.34     2       2

   10 Records read
    3 Records in error
```

Figure 5-11 Example of Employee Paycheck Report from payroll reports program.

```
                    Employee Paycheck Report
                    Week Ended 03/19/87

     Employee      ID   Dept   Gross     Total      Net    Notes
       Name              Name    Pay   Deductions

   R. M. NELSON  42753   FIN    298.00   104.79    193.21     0

   T. NAMAN      69852   ENGR    26.70    30.70     -4.00     1

   L. SMITH      35748   ENGR   399.09    90.55    308.54     3

   J. JOHNSON    36985   MKTG    60.50    48.69     11.81     0

   P. HOFFMANN   23456   PROD   142.80    52.59     90.21     0

   A. PETERSON   74365   PROD   294.02   116.37    177.65     2

   RALPH JONES   15786   ACCT   250.57    62.26    188.31     0


                    Totals    1471.68   505.95    965.73


   Notes
   0 - No errors
   1 - Net pay is out of bounds. Do not issue check.
   2 - Union/management code error. Union assumed.
   3 - Both type 1 and 2 errors.
```

4. The style of dimensioning all common arrays in the COMMON declaration and only local arrays in a DIMENSION statement (lines 74 and 75)
5. Use of PNYRND rounding function
6. The use of the case structure in the pension subroutine
7. The use of a default value and warning message as shown in the pension subroutine
8. The use of a BLOCK DATA subprogram to initialize variables in named COMMON using a DATA statement

Mathematical Program Example 5— Numerical Integration

Problem Description for Mathematical Example 5

The program, designed for keyboard input and interactive execution, compares different methods of numerical integration. The basic concept of computing small areas defined by the function to be integrated (as explained in Chapter 4b) is followed, but the area segments are approximated by three different methods and the results compared. The three methods are a simple rectangle method, a trapezoidal method, and Simpson's rule. Each of the three methods is a separate subroutine; the function to be integrated is defined in a function subprogram.

The logic of the three methods of integration differ in the weight assigned to each ordinate. The weights assigned by the trapezoidal method and Simpson's rule compensate, in part, for the irregular shape of the area being integrated.

Rectangle method Each ordinate is assumed to be the left side of a rectangle with the segment width being the base. The last ordinate is not used.

Trapezoidal method   The first and last ordinates are averaged; all other ordinates have a weight of one.

Simpson's rule   The first ordinate has a weight of one, the even-numbered ordinates have a weight of two, and the odd-numbered ordinates have a weight of four. The last ordinate is not used. The sum of the weighted ordinates is divided by 3, and the result is then multiplied by the segment width to give the area for the interval.

As demonstrated by the example output in Figure 5-15, Simpson's rule provides a more correct answer than the other two for integration using a small number of segments. For a larger number of very small segments, the results of the methods are very close.

Program Documentation for Mathematical Example 5

The documentation consists of a pseudocode program description (Figure 5-12), a program flowchart (Figure 5-13), a program listing (Figure 5-14), and sample output (Figure 5-15) from an interactive session.

Notes on Mathematical Example 5

The variables identification block has been augmented with a section listing the three subroutine names and one function name. Note that all names in this block are unique. The storage allocation block contains explicit type statements for all variables and blank and named COMMON statements because these all affect memory (storage) allocation. Following the style suggestions in Chapter 5a, arrays that are common to several program units are dimensioned in a COMMON statement. The named COMMON (called YBLOCK in line 46) is used to group common variables that are logically associated. Note the optional use of double slashes to specify blank COMMON (line 47).

The data input and validation block prints a session heading and then requests two different inputs:

1. Beginning and ending values for interval over which to integrate. Note that the message is very explicit in the following:
   (*a*) Two positive values (line 57–58)
   (*b*) Values separated by spaces or comma (line 59)
2. How many steps to use in the integration procedure. They are specified as
   (*a*) Even number (line 65)
   (*b*) Not more than 1000 (line 65)

There is a validation of the inputs for the specifications described above. If the inputs are incorrect, an error message is output and new input(s) requested. In the validation, note the use of a compound logical expression with a logical OR (line 64). Also, look at the expression (line 70) which checks for even numbers. It uses the modulus intrinsic function. This function gives the remainder from a division by the modulus (2, in this case).

The computation block containing the main program's computation is quite short and explicit. The loop in lines 82–85 sets up the necessary ordinate values in the array ORD, which are then used by the several subroutines. This separation of functions allows easy program modification. The placement of the function to be integrated in a separate function subprogram makes it quite easy to test the efficiency of the several integration techniques on different functions by simply replacing the function-to-be-integrated subprogram with a different one. Note that a change in the

Main program	Declare type for variables
	Establish storage common with other program units
	   WRITE heading for session
	   <u>WRITE</u> input prompt for beginning and ending values
	   READ beginning and ending x values
	   IF data–type error or negative inputs, WRITE error message and go
	     to <u>Termination</u> test for corrected set of inputs
	READ steps
	Test for even number of intervals (steps) or greater than 1000
	   IF not even or greater than 1000, WRITE error message and go to
	     <u>Termination</u> test
	   ELSE continue
	Set initial abscissa to initial x value
	Compute interval size based on beginning and ending value of x and
	     number of intervals in range
	Echo input data and problem factors
	Compute ordinates in range
	Call Subroutines RECT, TRAP, and SIMP beginning and ending x
	   WRITE results of three methods of integration
	<u>Termination</u> test
	   IF reply to 'enter new data' is yes,
	     Go back to <u>WRITE</u> input prompt for new data
	   ELSE STOP

Subroutine rect	Type variables Establish storage common with other program units Set initial sum to value of ordinate zero Add sum of ordinates for second through next to last one to initial sum Area = interval size times sum of all ordinates RETURN
Subroutine trap	Type variables Establish storage common with other program units Set initial sum to average of zeroth and last ordinate Add sum of the rest of the ordinates to initial sum Area = interval size times sum of all ordinates RETURN
Subroutine simp	Type variables Establish storage common with other program units Set SUM1 to sum of zeroth and last ordinate Initialize SUM2 and SUM4 to zero Compute SUM2 as sum of even ordinates Compute SUM4 as sum of odd ordinates Area = (SUM1 + 2 * SUM2 + 4 * SUM4) * (Interval width/3) RETURN
Function anyf(x)	Any function of x may be used here ANYF = $\sin x - \log x + e^x$ RETURN

Figure 5-12 Pseudocode description of mathematical program example 5—numerical integration.

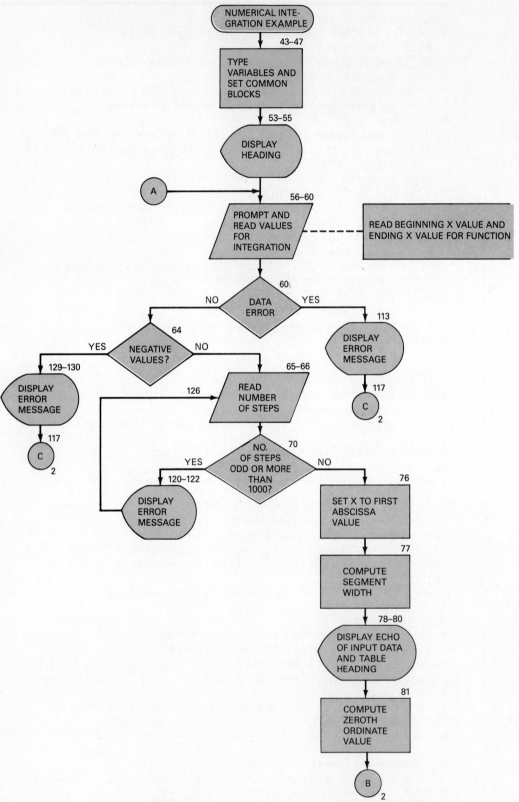

Figure 5-13 Program flowchart for mathematical program example 5—numerical integration. (Numbers next to symbols are line numbers from program listing.)

Figure 5-13 continued

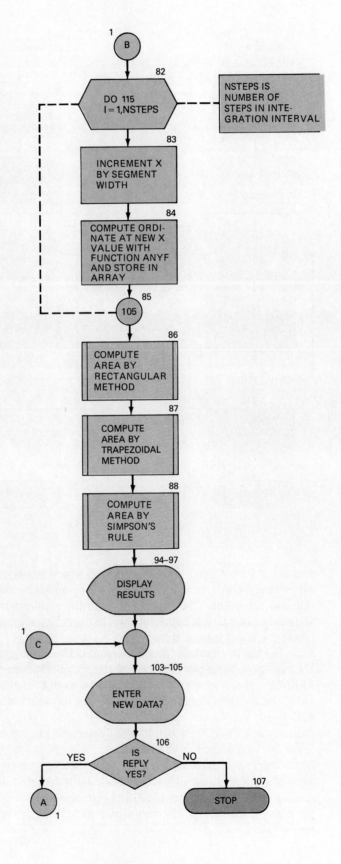

Figure 5-13 continued

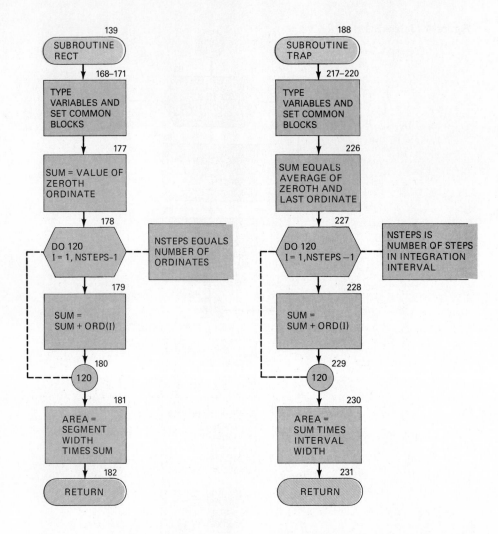

function does not affect line 81 or line 84, which processes the function. Similarly, other integration techniques could easily be added by replacing or substituting a different subroutine. The connection with the main program is through the CALL statement (lines 86–88) which includes in the calling argument list the variable name where the result is to be stored.

For the three subroutines, the layout of the subprograms follows the pattern of the main program except that the first statement of the program unit is the statement identifying it as a subroutine (the same applies to a function) and giving the name.

The variables identification and storage allocation blocks are similar in form to both the main program and the subprograms. As a matter of style, each program unit has a suitable END OF PROGRAM UNIT comment just before the END statement that is the last line of each program unit.

There is a difference between the handling of errors with the interactive application and the payroll batch application. In the batch application, there is use of a default value (with message) to allow processing to continue; in the interactive application, the invalid data record is rejected and new entry of data is requested immediately.

Figure 5-13 concluded

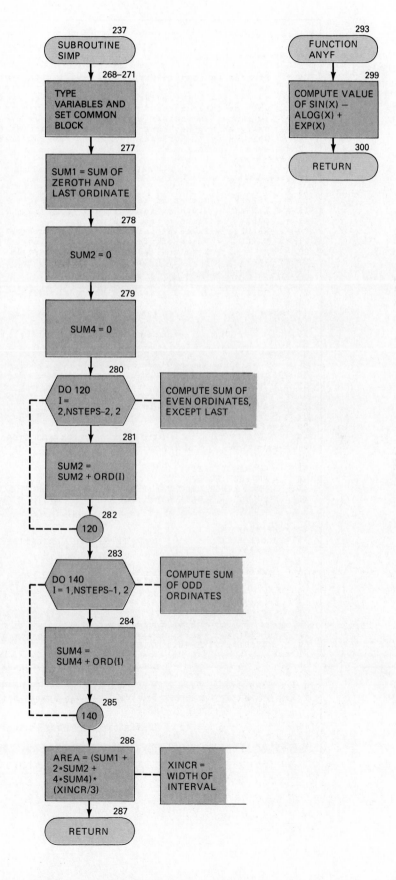

Figure 5-14 Program
listing of mathematical
program example 5—to do
numerical integration using
subprograms for three
methods.

```
 1 *********
 2 *                        PROGRAM IDENTIFICATION
 3 *********
 4 *
 5 *   Program to compare numerical integration techniques --
 6 *   Rectangular, Trapezoidal, and Simpson's rule --
 7 *   by using all three for the same function over
 8 *   various intervals and with different numbers of
 9 *   segments. The number of segments must be even.
10 *   Designed for keyboard input and interactive execution.
11 *   Written by T. Hoffmann  07/11/77  rev. 1/22/82  3/17/87
12 *
13 *********
14 *                        VARIABLES IDENTIFICATION
15 *********
16 *
17 *   NSTEPS  - Number of segments in integration interval
18 *   XINCR   - Width of segment
19 *   ORDZ    - Value of zero'th ordinate
20 *   VALU1   - Value of left boundary of integration interval
21 *   VALU2   - Value of right boundary of integration interval
22 *   X       - X Values (abscissas) of intervals
23 *   RAREA   - Area using rectangular technique
24 *   TAREA   - Area using trapezoidal rule
25 *   SAREA   - Area using Simpson's method
26 *   REPLY   - Y or N answer to query of whether to enter new data
27 *
28 *****                    ARRAY IDENTIFICATION
29 *
30 *        ORD       - Ordinates of the function
31 *
32 *****                    SUBROUTINE AND FUNCTION NAMES
33 *
34 *   RECT    - Computes area using rectangular procedure
35 *   TRAP    - Computes area using trapezoidal procedure
36 *   SIMP    - Computes area using Simpson's rule
37 *   ANYF    - Function to be integrated
38 *
39 *********
40 *                        TYPE DECLARATION AND STORAGE ALLOCATION
41 *********
42 *
43     CHARACTER REPLY*1
44     INTEGER NSTEPS
45     REAL XINCR,ORDZ,VALU1,VALU2,X,RAREA,TAREA,SAREA,ORD
46     COMMON /YBLOCK/ ORD(1000),ORDZ
47     COMMON // NSTEPS,XINCR
48 *
49 *********
50 * BLOCK 0000           DATA INPUT AND VALIDATION BLOCK
51 *********
52 *
53     WRITE(6,3)
54   3 FORMAT(//13X,'COMPARISON OF NUMERICAL INTEGRATION TECHNIQUES'//
55    1    '     INTEGRATION OF SIN(X) - ALOG(X) + EXP(X)'/ )
56   5 WRITE(6,6)
57   6 FORMAT(/1X, 'Between what two positive values ',
58    1    'do you wish to integrate?')
59     PRINT *, 'Separate values by spaces or commas. '
60     READ(5,*,ERR=901) VALU1,VALU2
61 *
62 *                        ALOG IS NOT DEFINED FOR NEGATIVE VALUES
63 *
64     IF (VALU1 .LT. 0.0 .OR. VALU2 .LT. 0.0) GOTO 905
65   7 PRINT *, 'In how many steps(an even number not more than 1000)?'
66     READ(5,*,ERR=903) NSTEPS
67 *
68 *                        NUMBER OF STEPS MUST BE EVEN AND NOT OVER 1000
69 *
70     IF (MOD(NSTEPS,2) .NE. 0 .OR. NSTEPS .GT. 1000) GOTO 903
71 *
```

Figure 5-14 continued

```
 72 *********
 73 * BLOCK 0100          COMPUTATION BLOCK
 74 *********
 75 *
 76 104 X - VALU1
 77     XINCR - (VALU2 - VALU1)/FLOAT(NSTEPS)
 78     WRITE(6,105) VALU1,VALU2,NSTEPS,ABS(XINCR)
 79 105 FORMAT(//1X,'The function''s value from ',F5.2,' to ',F5.2,
 80   1     ' integrated in ',I4,' steps of size ',F5.3)
 81     ORDZ - ANYF(X)
 82     DO 115 I - 1,NSTEPS
 83        X - X + XINCR
 84        ORD(I) - ANYF(X)
 85 115 CONTINUE
 86     CALL RECT(RAREA)
 87     CALL TRAP(TAREA)
 88     CALL SIMP(SAREA)
 89 *
 90 *********
 91 * BLOCK 0200          DETAIL PRINT BLOCK
 92 *********
 93 *
 94     WRITE(6,202) RAREA,TAREA,SAREA
 95 202 FORMAT( 1X,'By the rectangular technique is ',T38,E15.8/
 96   1     1X,'By the trapezoidal rule is ',T38,E15.8/
 97   2     1X,'By Simpson''s method is ',T38,E15.8//)
 98 *
 99 *********
100 * BLOCK 0300          TERMINATION BLOCK
101 *********
102 *
103 301 PRINT *, 'Do you want to enter new data (Y or N)? '
104     READ(5,302,END=399) REPLY
105 302 FORMAT(A)
106     IF( REPLY .EQ. 'Y' .OR. REPLY .EQ. 'y' ) GOTO 5
107 399 STOP
108 *
109 *********
110 * BLOCK 0900          ERROR MESSAGE BLOCK
111 *********
112 *
113 901 PRINT *, 'ERROR IN DATA. PLEASE RE-ENTER.'
114 *
115 *          GO BACK TO CHECK FOR NEW DATA
116 *
117     GOTO 301
118 *****
119 *
120 903 WRITE(6,904)
121 904 FORMAT(/1X,'THE NUMBER OF STEPS MUST BE EVEN AND NOT OVER 1000.'/
122   1     1X,'PLEASE RE-ENTER DATA'/)
123 *
124 *          GO BACK TO RE-READ STEP DATA
125 *
126     GOTO 7
127 *****
128 *
129 905 PRINT *, 'ERROR. VALUES MUST BE POSITIVE FOR THIS FUNCTION.'
130     PRINT *, 'PLEASE RE-ENTER DATA.'
131 *
132 *          GO BACK TO CHECK FOR NEW DATA
133 *
134     GOTO 301
135 *
136 * END OF MAIN PROGRAM
137     END
```

Figure 5-14 continued

```
138 *
139       SUBROUTINE RECT(AREA)
140 *
141 *********
142 *                    PROGRAM IDENTIFICATION
143 *********
144 *
145 *         This subroutine integrates the area under a curve
146 *         using the method of rectangles.  Ordinates of the
147 *         curve must have been previously stored in the
148 *         array ord.
149 *
150 *********
151 *                    VARIABLES IDENTIFICATION
152 *********
153 *
154 *         AREA    = Area under curve
155 *         SUM     = Sum of ordinates of curve
156 *         NSTEPS  = Number of segments in integration interval
157 *         XINCR   = Width of segment
158 *         ORDZ    = Value of the zero'th ordinate
159 *
160 *****                ARRAY IDENTIFICATION
161 *
162 *         ORD     = Ordinates of the function
163 *
164 *********
165 *                    TYPE DECLARATION AND STORAGE ALLOCATION
166 *********
167 *
168       INTEGER NSTEPS
169       REAL AREA,SUM,XINCR,ORDZ,ORD
170       COMMON /YBLOCK/ ORD(1000),ORDZ
171       COMMON // NSTEPS,XINCR
172 *
173 *********
174 * BLOCK 0100          COMPUTATION BLOCK
175 *********
176 *
177       SUM = ORDZ
178       DO 120 I = 1,NSTEPS-1
179          SUM = SUM + ORD(I)
180   120 CONTINUE
181       AREA = SUM*ABS(XINCR)
182       RETURN
183 *
184 * END OF SUBPROGRAM
185 *
186       END
```

In summary, the mathematical program has certain style characteristics that should be noted:

1. The list of subroutine and function names in the main program identifies the purpose of each subroutine and function used by the main program.
2. Arrays in COMMON are dimensioned in the COMMON declaration (lines 46–47).
3. A single FORMAT statement is used to print a multiple-line heading. Note the use of slashes and the indentation of the continuation lines (lines 54–55).
4. Input validation is performed on the beginning and ending values for the integration interval to make sure they are positive.
5. Input validation is performed to make sure the number of steps is even and not greater than 1000. Line 70 uses the MOD intrinsic function. MOD(NSTEPS, 2)

Figure 5-14 continued

```
187 *
188        SUBROUTINE TRAP(AREA)
189 *
190 **********
191 *                    PROGRAM IDENTIFICATION
192 **********
193 *
194 *        This subroutine integrates the area under a curve
195 *        using the method of trapezoids.  Ordinates of the
196 *        curve must have been previously stored in the
197 *        array ord.
198 *
199 **********
200 *                    VARIABLES IDENTIFICATION
201 **********
202 *
203 *        AREA    - Area under curve
204 *        SUM     - Sum of ordinates of curve
205 *        NSTEPS  - Number of segments in integration interval
206 *        XINCR   - Width of segment
207 *        ORDZ    - Value of the zero'th ordinate
208 *
209 *****                ARRAY IDENTIFICATION
210 *
211 *        ORD     - Ordinates of the function
212 *
213 **********
214 *                    TYPE DECLARATION AND STORAGE ALLOCATION
215 **********
216 *
217        INTEGER NSTEPS
218        REAL AREA,SUM,XINCR,ORDZ,ORD
219        COMMON /YBLOCK/ ORD(1000),ORDZ
220        COMMON // NSTEPS,XINCR
221 *
222 **********
223 * BLOCK 0100           COMPUTATION BLOCK
224 **********
225 *
226        SUM = (ORDZ + ORD(NSTEPS))/2.0
227        DO 120 I = 1,NSTEPS-1
228            SUM = SUM + ORD(I)
229    120 CONTINUE
230        AREA = SUM*ABS(XINCR)
231        RETURN
232 *
233 * END OF SUBPROGRAM
234 *
235        END
```

provides the remainder from division by 2. If the remainder is not zero, the input was an odd number.

6. Program termination is programmed by an explicit interactive question as to more input.
7. The block structure of the program follows a structured style:
   (a) Type declaration and storage allocation
   (b) Data input and validation
   (c) Computation
   (d) Detail print
   (e) Termination
   (f) Error message

Figure 5-14 concluded

```
236 *
237       SUBROUTINE SIMP(AREA)
238 *
239 **********
240 *                    PROGRAM IDENTIFICATION
241 **********
242 *
243 *        This subroutine integrates the area under a curve
244 *        using Simpson's rule.  Ordinates of the curve must
245 *        have been previously stored in the array ORD.
246 *
247 **********
248 *                    VARIABLES IDENTIFICATION
249 **********
250 *
251 *        AREA     - Area under curve
252 *        SUM      - Sum of ordinates of curve
253 *        NSTEPS   - Number of segments in integration interval
254 *        XINCR    - Width of segment
255 *        ORDZ     - Value of the zero'th ordinate
256 *        SUM1     - Sum of the first and last ordinate
257 *        SUM2     - Sum of the even numbered ordinates
258 *        SUM4     - Sum of the odd numbered ordinates
259 *
260 *****                ARRAY IDENTIFICATION
261 *
262 *        ORD      - Ordinates of the function
263 *
264 **********
265 *                    TYPE DECLARATION AND STORAGE ALLOCATION
266 **********
267 *
268       INTEGER NSTEPS
269       REAL AREA,SUM,XINCR,ORDZ,ORD
270       COMMON /YBLOCK/ ORD(1000),ORDZ
271       COMMON // NSTEPS,XINCR
272 *
273 **********
274 * BLOCK 0100          COMPUTATION BLOCK
275 **********
276 *
277       SUM1 = ORDZ + ORD(NSTEPS)
278       SUM2 = 0.0
279       SUM4 = 0.0
280       DO 120 I = 2,NSTEPS-2,2
281           SUM2 = SUM2 + ORD(I)
282   120 CONTINUE
283       DO 140 I = 1,NSTEPS-1,2
284           SUM4 = SUM4 + ORD(I)
285   140 CONTINUE
286       AREA = (SUM1 + 2.0*SUM2 + 4.0*SUM4)*ABS(XINCR)/3.0
287       RETURN
288 *
289 * END OF SUBPROGRAM
290 *
291       END
```

```
292 *
293       FUNCTION ANYF(X)
294 *
295 **********
296 *                    ANYF CAN BE EQUATED TO ANY FUNCTION
297 **********
298 *
299       ANYF = SIN(X) - ALOG(X) + EXP(X)
300       RETURN
301 *
302 * END OF SUBPROGRAM
303 *
304       END
```

Figure 5-15 Output from interactive session showing input and output for execution of mathematical program example 5— numerical integration using three methods.

```
          COMPARISON OF NUMERICAL INTEGRATION TECHNIQUES

     INTEGRATION OF SIN(X) - ALOG(X) + EXP(X)

Between what two positive values do you wish to integrate?
Separate values by spaces or commas. 0.2,1.4

In how many steps (an even number not more than 1000)? 20

The function's value from 0.20 to 1.40 integrated in 20 steps of size 0.060
By the rectangular technique is       0.40025964E+01
By the trapezoidal rule is            0.40528364E+01
By Simpson's method is                0.40509639E+01


Do you want to enter new data (Y or N)? Y

Between what two positive values do you wish to integrate?
Separate values by spaces or commas. 0.2 1.4

In how many steps (an even number not more than 1000)? 998


The function's value from 0.20 to 1.40 integrated in 998 steps of size 0.001
By the rectangular technique is       0.40499544E+01
By the trapezoidal rule is            0.40509610E+01
By Simpson's method is                0.40509615E+01

Do you want to enter new data (Y or N)? Y

Between what two positive values do you wish to integrate?
Separate values by spaces or commas. EN D

ERROR IN DATA. PLEASE RE-ENTER.
Do you want to enter new data (Y or N)? Y

Between what two positive values do you wish to integrate?
Separate values by spaces or commas. 1.4,0.2

In how many steps (an even number not more than 1000)? 20


The function's value from 1.40 to 0.20 integrated in 20 steps of size 0.060
By the rectangular technique is       0.41030765E+01
By the trapezoidal rule is            0.40528369E+01
By Simpson's method is                0.40509644E+01

Do you want to enter new data (Y or N)? Y

Between what two positive values do you wish to integrate?
Separate values by spaces or commas. -1,2

ERROR. VALUES MUST BE POSITIVE FOR THIS FUNCTION.
PLEASE RE-ENTER DATA.
Do you want to enter new data (Y or N)? Y

Between what two positive values do you wish to integrate?
Separate values by spaces or commas. 1.4,1.9

In how many steps (an even number not more than 1000)? 31

THE NUMBER OF STEPS MUST BE EVEN AND NOT OVER 1000.
PLEASE RE-ENTER DATA

In how many steps (an even number not more than 1000)? 32

The function's value from 1.40 to 1.90 integrated in 32 steps of size 0.016
By the rectangular technique is       0.28576767E+01
By the trapezoidal rule is            0.28755374E+01
By Simpson's method is                0.28754900E+01


Do you want to enter new data (Y or N)? N
```

Programming Exercises

Description of Assignment

Select one or more problems (or take the problems assigned by your instructor). Write each of the computational procedures in the problem as a function and/or subroutine subprogram. Use the case structure where applicable. Follow the style guidelines and prepare the following.

1. Pseudocode description
2. Program flowchart
3. Program listing
4. List of test data and expected results, testing for both valid and invalid data
5. Output including output from error conditions

Mathematics and Statistics

1. For each of the following sets of data, compute the mean and variance of each subset X and Y and the correlation coefficient of the sets. See Chapter 4 problem 1 for the correlation coefficient formula. The variance for X can be calculated as:

$$\text{Var} = \frac{\Sigma X^2 - [(\Sigma X)]^2/n}{n - 1}$$

Set 1		Set 2	
X	Y	X	Y
34.22	102.43	20	27.1
39.87	100.93	30	28.9
41.85	97.43	40	30.6
43.23	97.81	50	32.3
40.06	98.32	60	33.7
53.29	98.32	70	35.6
53.29	100.07	80	37.2
54.14	97.08		
49.12	91.59		
40.71	94.85		
55.15	94.65		

2. There are many ways to prepare sequences of random numbers; two of these are the inner product or squaring method and the power residue procedure. The inner product method takes a number of digits, say four, squares it, and picks out the central four digits of the product as a random number. The four-digit random number is squared, etc. For example, starting with

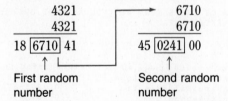

4321 produces the sequence 6710, 0241, etc. The power residue method chooses a starting value, neither even nor ending in a 5, and a special constant multiplier (91 is a good choice to obtain a sequence of four-digit random numbers). Form the product of the starting value and the constant and save the low-order four digits as the random number and the base to use for the next multiplication. For example, a starting value of 1907 and a constant of 91 produces the sequence 3537, 1867, etc.

$$
\begin{array}{ccc}
1907 & & 3537 \\
\underline{91} & & \underline{91} \\
17\,\boxed{3537} & \longrightarrow & 32\,\boxed{1867}
\end{array}
$$

Write a program to generate random numbers by each of these procedures, and compute the average value of each sequence. Use the following values as test cases:

Length of sequence	Initial value	Constant multiplier (method 2 only)
100	4321	91
1000	4321	91
10000	4321	91
500	5023	3219
5000	7023	3219

3. The Newton-Raphson technique can be used effectively to find the real roots of a function by successive approximations. Given a function of x, the following relationship is used:

$$
x_{i+1} = x_i - \frac{f(x_i)}{f'(x_i)}
$$

where $x_i =$ the current estimated value
$x_{i+1} =$ the next estimated value
$f(x_i) =$ the function evaluated at x_i
$f'(x_i) =$ the first derivative of the function evaluated at x_i

An initial estimate x_0 is required as input to the process, and it must terminate when $|x_{i+1} - x_i| <$ some epsilon value. Write a program to compute a root of $f(x) = x^3 - 3x^2 + 5$ to an accuracy of 0.001 or better. Print out the number of iterations and root. Write the program so that it can be easily modified for other functions and epsilons. Use the following initial estimates: 1.0, −1.0, 0.0, 3.0, −30.0.

Business and Economics

4. Various techniques are used to depreciate capital assets; most common are the straight-line, double-declining balance, and sum-of-the-years' digits. Assuming an initial cost C, a salvage value S, and a useful life of N years, the relationships for depreciation D_n in year n are as follows:

Straight line:

$$
D_n = \frac{C - S}{N}
$$

Sum-of-the-years' digits:

$$
D_n = (C - S)\,\frac{N - n + 1}{\text{sum}}
$$

where n is a particular year and

$$
\text{Sum} = \sum_{i=1}^{N} i = \frac{N(N + 1)}{2}
$$

Double-declining balance:

$$D_n = \frac{2}{N}\left(C - \sum_{i=1}^{n-1} D_i\right) \quad \text{until} \quad C - \sum_{i=1}^{n} D_i = S$$

Write a program to depreciate each of the following assets over their useful lives, showing the annual depreciation by each technique.

Asset number	Initial cost	Salvage value	Useful life
1	$ 10,000.00	$ 3,000.00	6 years
2	37,006.00	4,127.37	8
3	6,000.00	327.00	8
4	75,745.00	8,165.00	7
5	365,000.00	27,500.00	10

5. Modify problem 5 of Chapter 4 by making the interest computations as subprograms.

6. Various forecasting techniques can be applied to time series data. Among the simplest of these are exponential smoothing, weighted moving averages, and simple moving averages. These equations are as follows:

Three-period simple moving average:

$$f_{n+1} = \frac{d_n + d_{n-1} + d_{n-2}}{3}$$

where d_i is the ith actual demand and f_j is the forecast for the jth period.

Three-period weighted moving average:

$$f_{n+1} = \frac{3d_n + 2d_{n-1} + d_{n-2}}{6}$$

Exponential smoothing:

$$f_{n+1} = ad_n + (1 - a)f_n$$

where a is a decimal between 0 and 1. (Read in .2 for this problem.) Write a program to compute forecasts by each of these techniques: Start with period 4 and assume f_3 for exponential smoothing equals the mean of the first two values.

Period	Demand series 1	Demand series 2
1	31.8	100
2	33.7	300
3	32.1	450
4	29.3	570
5	33.9	750
6	37.0	820
8	42.5	915
9	36.7	945
10	31.0	975
11	35.8	1000

Science and Engineering

7. Frequently an experiment results in a set of empirical data that arise because of a functional relationship. Fitting a straight line or curve to the data is often done in order to better understand the relationship. The method of least squares, which minimizes the squares of the differences between actual and fitted function values, is the most common mathematical technique used to do this. The general equation for a straight line is

$$y = a + bx$$

From a set of x and y paired observations, the desired coefficients can be computed as:

$$b = \frac{n\Sigma xy - (\Sigma x)(\Sigma y)}{n\Sigma x^2 - (\Sigma x)^2}$$

$$a = \bar{y} - b\bar{x}$$

where $\bar{y}$ and $\bar{x}$ are the means of their respective data sets. Similarly, an equation of the form $y = ax^b$ can be rewritten as

$$\log y = \log a + b \log x$$

Letting $Y = \log y$, $X = \log x$, and $A = \log a$, one can see that this is similar to a straight-line equation as before:

$$Y = A + bX$$

and thus b and a can be derived with the same equations modified for logarithms. The following data was derived from the pull characteristics of an alternating current magnet. Write a program to compute coefficients for both types of equations.

Pounds pull, Y	Ampere-turns, X
3.0	1.5
4.5	2.0
5.5	3.5
6.0	5.0
7.5	6.0
8.5	7.5
8.0	9.0
9.0	10.5
9.5	12.0
10.0	14.0

8. Referring to problem 8 of Chapter 3, make the degree-to-radian conversion of a function.

9. Referring to problem 9 of Chapter 4, place the graphing routine as a subroutine and the function to be plotted as a function subprogram.

Humanities and Social Sciences

10. Modify problem 10 of Chapter 4 so that alternate printouts are available at the user's choice. That is, the user can request only Table 1, only Table 2, both Table 1 and Table 2, a Table of Income versus Politics, or a Table of Income versus Sex.

11. The binomial probability distribution is often applicable to sampling situations. For example, among two candidates for office, there does not appear to be a clear winner. A poll is taken of 900 people and 540 prefer candidate A. How likely is this result if indeed the entire population of voters are evenly split? The equation for this is

$$P\left(\begin{matrix} n \\ x \end{matrix}\right) = \frac{n!}{x!(n-x)!} p^x (1-p)^{n-x}$$

where $p = 0.5$ for this problem.

Write a program to compute the probabilities for the following situations. If n is less than 10, compute factorials by multiplying, that is,

$$n! = 1 \times 2 \times 3 \times \cdots \times n$$

If n is 10 or greater, use Stirling's approximation for factorials:

$$n! = e^{-n}n^n\sqrt{2\pi n}$$

Situation number	Sample size	Yes answers
1	9	5
2	90	50
3	90	54
4	10	5
5	100	52

12. The combined effect of wind and temperature on the human body is quite severe, particularly in cold climates. The relative effect of their combination is referred to as the *windchill factor*. Prepare a windchill chart for Fahrenheit temperatures from -50 to $+10$ degrees (in 10-degree increments) and wind speeds of 5 to 30 miles per hour. The relevant formulas are

$$V_1 = 0.477 \times \text{wind speed}$$
$$V_2 = (10.45 + 10\sqrt{V_1} - V_1)(33.0 - \text{TEMP}_c)$$

$$\text{Windchill TEMP}_c = 33.0 - \frac{V_2}{22.034}$$

Note that the temperatures are Celsius and the table is to be in Fahrenheit. (Use a function subprogram for conversion.)

General

13. Refer to problem 13 of Chapter 4, and replace inline code for computing averages with a function subprogram.

14. Write a program to deal three sets of four poker hands of five cards each. Shuffle the deck between each deal. Write the shuffling procedure as a subroutine, and use either a random number generator available as a system library subprogram or one of the procedures described in problem 2 of this chapter.

15. Reprogram problem 13 of Chapter 2b to make use of the case structure for currency conversion.

Interactive Scientific and Engineering

16. The euclidean distance d between two points in a plane can be computed by the following equation, where the coordinates of one point are x_1 and y_1 and for the other are x_2 and y_2:

$$d = \sqrt{(x_1 - x_2)^2 + (y_1 - y_2)^2}$$

Write a program to compute the distances between each pair of five points, print the table of those distances, and point out which two are furthest apart. Program the distance formula as a function subprogram and write a logical function to test whether the user wants to revise the input data or go on (and return a value of TRUE or FALSE).

17. The temperature-humidity index is a measure of the perceived warmth of air. When the indoor air is heated in the winter, the relative humidity declines. Since humans perceive dry air to be cooler than humid air of the same temperature, the "comfort index" may be improved by increasing the humidity. The index I has been established empirically to be related to the temperature T in degrees Fahrenheit and the relative humidity H in percentages as follows:

$$I = T - (0.55 - 0.0055\,H)(T - 58)$$

Write a program to compute the index for any above-freezing and below-boiling temperature in Fahrenheit or Celsius and any legitimate relative humidity. Write the temperature conversion and index computations as function subprograms.

18. Write a program to compute the number of days between two dates using the usual calendar. Allow for leap years and centuries. (*Note:* There is one day between successive dates.) Check for valid data entry. Compute the time from zero month, day, year to any particular date in a subroutine; create a logical function to determine whether or not (TRUE or FALSE) a given year is a leap year; check the data validity in a subroutine. Put only data input and output in the main program.

Use of Files on External Storage

Files in FORTRAN
Records and Files
Unformatted Input and Output
Storage Media and File-Access Methods
Self-Testing Exercise 6-1

Sequential-Access Processing
READ and WRITE Statements for Sequential Access
File-Positioning Statements
Self-Testing Exercise 6-2

Direct-Access Processing
Self-Testing Exercise 6-3

OPEN, CLOSE, and INQUIRE Statements
Opening and Closing a File
Obtaining Information about a File
Self-Testing Exercise 6-4

Summary

Answers to Self-Testing Exercises

Questions and Problems

The FORTRAN problems and programs in the first five chapters assumed that data would be input from a keyboard or read from a simple sequential file that was created for input purposes. Output from processing has been immediately printed or displayed. These procedures are generally satisfactory for computational problems with relatively little data, but there are situations where files are more complex and the programs manage large amounts of data that are input, processed, and then stored for later use. This chapter will explain how to program the use of files on *external storage* (also called *secondary*, or *auxiliary*, *storage*). Another type of file, called *internal files*, will be explained in Chapter 7.

Files in FORTRAN

As background for the input/output instructions, this section will review records and files and explain external storage file-access methods.

Records and Files

A *data item* is a set of numeric (or alphanumeric) characters treated as a unit for processing. In FORTRAN, each data item is uniquely identified by a variable name. Examples are a pay rate, an identification number, a measurement, etc. A collection of related data items constitutes a *record*. Examples of a record are data items from a research questionnaire, all data items related to the payroll for one employee, or all data describing a chemical process. A collection of records constitutes a *file*. For example, the research questionnaire records make up the research record file, the payroll records make up the payroll file, and the chemical process records compose the chemical process data file. This relationship is shown in Figure 6-1.

Figure 6-1 Relationship of character, item, record, and file.

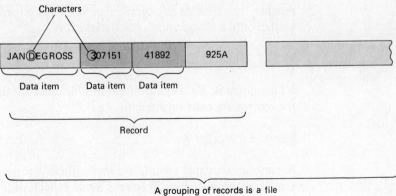

Characters

JAN D E GROSS 307151 41892 925A

Data item   Data item   Data item

Record

A grouping of records is a file

The records in a file are stored on some medium such as diskettes, tape, or disks. Records occupy storage space on the storage medium, and each item within the record takes up part of this space. The storage space (described conceptually in numbers of character storage positions) for an item is the *field* size for the item. For example, −3.758 takes a field of six characters; 3758 requires a field of four characters. The actual physical storage space used is implementation-dependent.

In FORTRAN, any set of input or output records constitute a file, but the term is most commonly used to refer to files on external storage. The user of FORTRAN need not understand the technical characteristics of secondary storage because the language handles file storage in a standard manner rather than requiring the programmer to furnish all of the specifications. However, one storage characteristic that the programmer may specify is formatted versus unformatted representation.

Unformatted Input and Output

Two methods for input and output have been used in previous chapters: list-directed input and output and format-directed input and output. Both list-directed and format-directed input and output require considerable computer processing because at input the external representation of data must be converted to the internal representation suitable for processing. For output the internal representation must be converted to external representation. For example, an input item may be 3765, but the FORMAT statement defines the data as F4.2. On input, the value 3765 must be converted to the internal numeric representation for 37.65. The same holds for formatted output. If the internal representation is the equivalent of 89.56427132 and it is to be output with two digits beyond the decimal point, the data must be processed to output the characters for 89.56. During processing, the numeric data items are stored internally in a fairly compact form; when formatted for input and output, each of the output characters is coded separately. The character coding requires more storage space.

An alternative to formatted output and input is *unformatted output and input*. In unformatted output, data items are output as strings of bits without any output format conversions. In unformatted input, data items are read as strings of binary digits (bits) without any conversion based on FORMAT statements. Because formatting takes extra time and extra storage space, a computer application that processes thousands of records may benefit in reduced processing time and storage space by using unformatted input and output. Also, as shown in the example above, where the internal representation of 89.56427132 is output as 89.56, formatting output that will be used as input for subsequent processing may result in loss of precision.

Unformatted read and write operations are specified by a READ or WRITE command with an input/output unit number but without a FORMAT statement number or asterisk. As an example, if unformatted records containing X, Y, M are to be written onto a file on unit 8, the statement is

```
WRITE(8) X, Y, M
```

A subsequent READ statement from this file must use the unformatted form because the records are not formatted:

```
READ(8) X, Y, M
```

Because unformatted records are more efficient in terms of processing time, they should be considered for all large external FORTRAN files on tape or disk.

Storage Media and File-Access Methods

The two most common external storage media—magnetic tape and disks—differ in their operation. The magnetic tape is read or written in serial fashion from beginning to end. The first record on the tape is read first, the second record is read second, etc. The second record cannot be accessed without reading the first. It operates very much like a reel of magnetic tape or a tape cassette used for home recording.

Records on tape are stored in physical blocks separated by interblock gaps. The gaps allow the tape unit to start and stop between the reading and writing of blocks. The FORTRAN programmer need not be concerned with the physical record on tape because FORTRAN requires only that the programmer define a program record; the compiler arranges physical record storage.

The disk or diskette drive can access any part of the storage by an access arm (or arms) that moves to the set of storage positions (on a track) where a record is stored. These storage positions have a physical location called an *address*. Records on disk storage may be written and read serially, or records may be accessed directly by taking advantage of the direct-access capabilities of the disk drive. The direct-access method requires each record to have an identifier that specifies its location in the file. The identifier is not an actual disk address. The connnection between the record address identifier and a disk address is performed automatically by the operating system.

In files to be read serially, it is common to have some method for noting the end of a set (file) of records. This is frequently accomplished by a special record containing an end-of-file character (or characters), but other methods may be used such as a record counter maintained by the system. As far as the FORTRAN programmer is concerned, the end-of-file record in a sequential file is the next record after the last data record. When records are to be written at the end of a file, the new records must be written after the last existing record but before the end-of-file record.

The file-access methods available in standard FORTRAN are sequential access and direct access. A file must be defined as either one or the other and may be used only in the defined access mode. However, a file on disk storage can be defined as sequential for one use and defined as direct access for a different use, assuming the records are stored so that both methods are feasible.

1. *Sequential access*   Records are read in serial fashion in the same order they were written. All data records in a file must be formatted or unformatted. An end-of-file record may be used to mark the end of the file. Sequential-access files can be implemented on either tape or disk storage. The simple files used in the first five chapters have been sequential files. This was not specified in the simple OPEN statement used to this point because sequential file is the default option for an OPEN statement. The sequential files in the programs of the prior chapters may have used any of the forms of storage—diskette (for a microcomputer) or disk or tape (for a mainframe computer).

2. *Direct access*   This can be implemented only on direct-access storage such as disks. Direct-access input/output statements must be used to write or read, and records may be read or written in any order. Each record must have a unique positive integer identifier, called a *record number*, specified when the record is first written. The records must have the same length and must be all formatted or all unformatted. List-directed input or output cannot be used. End-of-file records are not used.

Sequential files and direct-access files differ in the procedure for changing or updating a single record in the file. In general, to alter the contents of any record in a sequential file, the entire file is read and rewritten, making the required change (delete a record, add a record, or change part of the record). In a direct-access file, the contents of a single record may be altered without rewriting the rest of the file. A complete discussion of file updating procedures is available in data processing references.

Self-Testing Exercise 6-1

1. Classify the following as probably a record or a file.
   (a) Height and weight observations for 100 men from an experiment.
   (b) Height and weight for one man.
   (c) Income, age, children, and occupation for one family.
   (d) Income, age, etc., for all families in a study.

2. True or false.
   (a) A formatted file is generally more efficient for processing.
   (b) Both tape and disk storage can be used for sequential access.
   (c) Tape storage can be used for direct access.
   (d) A record number is required for direct access.
   (e) Secondary storage and auxiliary storage are the same.

3. Complete the table:

Access method	Order records read	File medium	Use of list-directed I/O	Use of end-of-file record
Sequential	Same order as written	Tape, disk, or diskette	Allowed	Yes
Direct				

Sequential-Access Processing

This section will review the simple file READ and WRITE statements used in previous chapters; in addition, it will explain a new specification for use in error handling.

READ and WRITE Statements for Sequential Access

The sequential-access READ and WRITE statements contain the word READ or WRITE followed by a control list enclosed in parentheses. The unit number to be used for disks, diskettes, or tapes is specified first; the next specification is the FORMAT statement number (for formatted input or output). The unit number used in the READ or WRITE statement may be preassigned by the implementation, be specifically assigned by job control instructions with the program, or assigned by an OPEN statement. This chapter will focus on the use of the OPEN statement method. The OPEN statement is generally preferred because it is an explicit method of including the specifications with the program rather than having them done as installation default procedures or by job control instructions.

Example I
Read a record from magnetic tape unit 10 based on the FORMAT statement 700.

```
READ (10, 700) A, B, X
```

This instruction specifies a formatted, sequential-access processing and assumes the records were written using a formatted WRITE statement.

Example 2
Read the three items in list-directed sequential access written using a list-directed output statement.

```
READ (10, *) A, B, X
```

The general form of the READ and WRITE statements is the same as presented in Chapter 3, with square brackets indicating an optional element.

READ (control list) [I/O variables list]
WRITE (control list) [I/O variables list]

The control list presented in earlier chapters consisted only of the unit number for the input/output device, the FORMAT statement label, ERR = statement label, and END = statement label; additional control list specifiers that can be used with files will be presented in this chapter. Five specifications that have not been used in previous chapters and that may be useful for sequential-access files are shown in the box.

Each element in the control list consists of an alphabetic identifier—for example, UNIT or FMT— followed by an equals sign and a specifier that may be a number identifying a unit, a statement label, or a variable name. The alphabetic identifier is optional with the unit number and the FORMAT statement label, but if not used, the unit number, and FORMAT statement label must be first and second in the control list. The style of this text is to specify unit and FORMAT statement label as the first two control specifications without the alphabetic identifiers.

SPECIFIERS FOR SEQUENTIAL-ACCESS CONTROL LIST

[   ] mean optional part of specifier

[UNIT =]   unit number of device
[FMT =]   FORMAT statement label for specific formatting or * for list-directed formatting
ERR =   statement label to which control goes if there is an I/O error
END =   statement label to go to if end-of-file
IOSTAT =   integer variable to hold error code, 0 = no error, negative = end-of-file, and positive = error code.

The following are identical in their effect:

```
READ (5, 700) ALPHA
READ (UNIT = 5, FMT = 700) ALPHA
READ (5, FMT = 700) ALPHA
```

The ERR specification has been explained in Chapter 3; a new specification for use with ERR is IOSTAT. The reasons for the new specification is that, in reading or writing files, there may be a number of reasons for an error condition. The one mentioned in prior chapters was a format specification error. Since there may be several causes of errors, the program must be able to detect the reason in order to take proper action or to give the proper error message. The IOSTAT defines an integer variable to which the program will assign an error code in the event of an error. A zero value means no error, a positive error code identifies different errors, and a negative integer value signifies an end-of-file condition. The positive and negative integer values to be used as codes are defined by the FORTRAN implementor and will usually vary for different compilers.

The IOSTAT specifier is normally used in conjunction with the ERR specifier. An input or output error will send control to the statement number specified by ERR = s. If IOSTAT is also used, the processing statements specified by the transfer on ERR can be executed to analyze the error code of IOSTAT to determine the exact reason for the I/O error. Thus, a combination of ERR and IOSTAT can provide for more information and diagnostic messages than the use of ERR alone. The use of IOSTAT is optional. If no use is made of it, the information available in the case of an error will depend on the operating system.

The END statement has been used in previous chapters to signal the end of input data. This condition has initiated a transfer of control to cause the printing of totals, end-of-program messages, etc. But assume that the new records are to be added to the end of a sequential file. The new records cannot be added unless the file is positioned at the end of the existing records and before the end of file record. Since the END statement detects the end-of-file record, the sequential file can be read to its end and then backspaced one record to be in a position to add new records.

File-Positioning Statements

In a sequential file, reading or writing is done serially. In addition to READ and WRITE commands, three other operations are used: rewind, backspace, and write the end-of-file record.

Rewind means to go back to the beginning of the file. In the case of tape, the tape is rewound. For a disk or diskette, rewind means to position the read-write record pointer at the first record in the file.

Backspace means to go back one record in the sequential file. This essentially means to set the read-write record pointer to one less than the current record.

The ENDFILE specification writes an end-of-file record at the current position. This record is the one that is detected by the END specification. In some cases, the end-of-file record may be written by the operating system without this command being specified.

The file-positioning statements, given in the box, apply to sequential files on tape, disk, or diskette; they do not apply to direct-access files.

FILE-POSITIONING STATEMENTS

BACKSPACE unit	or	BACKSPACE (alist)
ENDFILE unit	or	ENDFILE (alist)
REWIND unit	or	REWIND (alist)

where alist contains:

[UNIT =] unit (UNIT = is optional)
ERR = statement label

BACKSPACE Example

```
    READ (10, 700, ERR = 800) JIM
700 FORMAT (I5)
    BACKSPACE 10
    READ (10, 700, ERR = 800) JON
```

The preceding program segment reads from unit 10 into a variable named JIM. The BACKSPACE and subsequent READ does a re-read of the same value that was read into JIM, placing it into JON. (It is, of course, not efficient to do it this way, since JON = JIM will accomplish the same effects.) The ERR = 800 specification in the READ statement sends control to statement label number 800 if a read error such as a data-type error is present.

ENDFILE Example

```
ENDFILE 8    or    ENDFILE (UNIT = 8)
```

This statement writes an end-of-file record at the end of a sequential file on unit 8.

The rewind instruction positions a file at the beginning. There are occasions where the programmer may wish to read the data more than once (perhaps doing searching or using the data differently each time). It is often a good practice to rewind sequential files on auxiliary storage at the beginning of the program to ensure proper positioning. If the file is already rewound, no action is taken. It is generally a desirable procedure to rewind all sequential files before terminating the program.

Self-Testing Exercise 6-2

1. Write statements to read the variables X, Y, Z from a list-directed input file (use unit 5), and write them onto a magnetic tape (use unit 8) in a list-directed, sequential output method.

2. Rewrite the list-directed statements from problem 1 to write onto a sequential file on a disk (unit 10), using the UNIT and FMT specifiers.

3. Rewind the file written in problem 1 and read the data.

4. Repeat problems 1 and 2 using format-directed input and output and FORMAT statement 700.

5. Backspace the file in problem 1 and then read the data.

6. Would using rewind in place of backspace in problem 5 ever have the same effect? Explain.

Direct-Access Processing

A direct-access file in FORTRAN consists of a set of storage locations; each location is capable of storing one record and each location has an identifying number. The storage locations are numbered from 1 to N (where N is the maximum number of records in the file). If, for example, the direct-access file is to hold a maximum of 100 records, the record locations are numbered 1 to 100. A numbered location can be empty—with no record currently being stored.

1	Storage for 1 record
2	Storage for 1 record
3	Storage for 1 record

n	Storage for 1 record

Storage and retrieval of records is based on the record location numbers. Using the record number, the records can be read or written in any order. For example, in building a file, the records could be written in the order 3, 7, 2, 1, 5, 9, ... Direct-access files are sometimes called *random-access files* (in contrast to serial-access sequential files). When an instruction is given to read or write in a direct-access file, the program must be provided with the record location number where the record is to be stored or from which it is to be read. The record number is stored prior to the READ or WRITE in a storage location with an integer variable name, and this location is identified in the READ or WRITE statement.

The records in a FORTRAN direct-access file must all be the same length. The direct-access records in a file can be formatted or unformatted, but not both types in the same file. List-directed input and output is not allowed. An end-of-file record is not used because it has no purpose.

A direct-access file may be established and defined by job control statements or by OPEN statements (to be explained later in the chapter). The instructions for the direct-access file READ and WRITE are the same as for sequential file READ and WRITE used in prior chapters except for one new control list specification and the omission of the END control specifier.

The ERR and IOSTAT are optional with direct-access files; their use is the same as with sequential files. The REC specifier is required for a direct-access file because the program must have a variable name where the record number of the record storage location to be accessed will be stored. This location is specified by the REC = i control specification. For example,

```
   READ (*, 10) IR, VAL
10 FORMAT (I3, F3.2)
   WRITE (7, REC = IR) VAL
```

The preceding reads two values, IR and VAL, from the keyboard input and then writes VAL in unformatted form onto unit 7 (a direct-access file) at the record location specified by IR.

SPECIFIERS FOR DIRECT-ACCESS CONTROL LIST

[   ] means optional part of specifier

[UNIT =] unit number of direct-access storage device
 [FMT =] FORMAT statement label for formatted input or output
    REC = integer expressions (constant or variable) specifying record number of record storage location to be accessed (this is required)
 IOSTAT = integer variable to hold error code: 0 = no error, positive = type of error code
    ERR = statement number to go to if I/O error

Once an individual record storage location in a direct-access file has been occupied by storing a record there, the location may be referenced by its identifying number to read the record or a new record may be stored there, replacing the existing record. Of course, a record may not be read before it has been written. Backspace and rewind are not meaningful in the context of direct-access processing.

Self-Testing Exercise 6-3

1. Read 12 records with the variables ID, NAME, and PAY in a format of (I2, A10, F6.2). Write NAME and PAY unformatted onto a direct-access file (unit 10) using ID as the record number. Use IOSTAT and ERR, but the statements referenced need not be written.

2. Read record number 5 from the file created in exercise 1.

3. Read every other record from the file in exercise 1, and print them with labels.

OPEN, CLOSE, and INQUIRE Statements

This section will review the basic OPEN and CLOSE statements, explain additional features for these statements, and describe the INQUIRE statement. The OPEN and CLOSE statements are provided in FORTRAN to specify files, associate files with devices, disconnect files, etc. The OPEN statement used in prior chapters referred only to sequential files; direct-access files require an additional specification. The INQUIRE statement allows the program to obtain characteristics and status of a file. The effects of these statements are often dependent on the specific FORTRAN compiler. Hence, they should be used only after reading the appropriate implementor reference manual(s). Because of the implementor-dependent status and advanced nature of the instructions, the discussion will survey the capabilities of the OPEN, CLOSE, and INQUIRE statements but will not describe them in detail.

Opening and Closing a File

The OPEN statement is used to associate (connect) an existing file to an input/output unit or create a new file on a unit. If an option is not specified, the compiler selects the most common or default option. The CLOSE statement terminates the connection. When a specifier is a character string (for example, OLD), it can be a character constant enclosed in single-quote marks or a character variable having that value. For example, the following are equivalent: STATUS = 'OLD' or STATUS = STS1, where STS1 is a character variable with the value 'OLD'.

The FILE = 'file name' specifies a name in the form required by the implementation. For example, a microcomputer file designation includes a drive letter (A, B, C, etc.) with a colon, a name with one to eight characters, and an optional extension of up to three characters (an illustration is A:MYFILE.GBD).

Comparing specifications used in prior chapters for simple sequential files with the specifications in the box, note that the prior chapters have relied on several default options as follows:

STATUS = 'UNKNOWN' which means the file could be NEW or OLD or SCRATCH
ACCESS = 'SEQUENTIAL'
FORM = 'FORMATTED'
BLANK = 'NULL'

> **OPEN STATEMENT**
>
> OPEN(olist)
>
> The olist is a list of specifiers for features of the file, unit number always being required, others being optional except record length, which is required for a direct-access file:
>
> | [UNIT =] | unit number (UNIT = is optional; if omitted, unit number must be first) |
> |---|---|
> | IOSTAT = | integer variable for input/output status |
> | FILE = | name of the file (character string); if absent, implementor-dependent |
> | ERR = | statement label for transfer if error |
> | STATUS = | 'OLD', 'NEW', 'SCRATCH', or 'UNKNOWN'; UNKNOWN is default. |
> | ACCESS = | 'SEQUENTIAL' or 'DIRECT'; SEQUENTIAL is default option |
> | FORM = | 'FORMATTED' or 'UNFORMATTED'; default is FORMATTED for sequential file and UNFORMATTED for direct-access file |
> | RECL = | record length for a direct-access file (required) |
> | BLANK = | 'NULL' or 'ZERO' to specify handling of blanks; NULL is default |

A direct-access file requires at least two explicit specifications not required with a sequential file:

ACCESS = 'DIRECT'
RECL = record length

The record length for a direct-access file is defined according to the FORTRAN implementation manual; normally, it will be the number of bytes for each record. All direct-access records in the file are of this same length.

A new direct-access unformatted file on unit 12 might be opened by

```
OPEN (12, IOSTAT = INDIK, ERR = 600, FILE = 'SAMPLE',
    STATUS = 'NEW', ACCESS = 'DIRECT', RECL = 200)
```

where the specifications indicate that the file is named SAMPLE, it is a new file, it is direct-access, and the length of each record is 200 characters. If an error is encountered in opening the file, control transfers to statement 600 and the variable INDIK receives an error code. Since FORM = is not specified in this example, it is assumed to be unformatted (because that is the default for a direct-access file). It is better programming style with a direct-access file to specify FORM explicitly to provide better documentation.

Two file specifications not described before are STATUS and BLANK. The status of a file can be NEW in order to set up a new file, OLD in order to access an old file, SCRATCH to define a temporary file that will not be saved at the end of the processing session, and UNKNOWN to let the file be any of the above. UNKNOWN is the default option. Although UNKNOWN will allow the greatest flexibility, the other specifications are used as appropriate to provide better documentation for the program.

The BLANK specification serves the same purpose as a BZ or BN in a FORMAT statement (Chapter 7). It refers to how to interpret embedded blanks and trailing blanks (leading blanks are ignored in all cases). The default option is NULL, which is to ignore all blanks unless the field is all blanks in which case it is assigned a value of zero. To illustrate the difference, assume an input data field of I5 with the value 4bbbb where (b = blank space).

BLANK = 'NULL' will interpret this value as 4.
BLANK = 'ZERO' will interpret this value as 40000.

CLOSE STATEMENT

CLOSE(clist)

where the clist is a list of specifiers, unit number being the only one required:

[UNIT =]   unit number (UNIT = is optional)
  IOSTAT = input/output status specifier variable
     ERR = statement label
  STATUS = 'KEEP' or 'DELETE'; KEEP is default option

As seen in the box, there are three specifications not previously used with CLOSE: IOSTAT, ERR, and STATUS. IOSTAT and ERR perform the same function as with the OPEN statement. The STATUS specification is used to *delete* or *keep* a file. The default is KEEP. If a file on unit 8 is to be released for other use (it will no longer be available), the CLOSE might read:

```
CLOSE (8, STATUS = 'DELETE')
```

Obtaining Information about a File

All the specifiers for an existing file are stored with the file, and thus information about the properties of a file can be obtained by using the INQUIRE statement. An INQUIRE statement can be executed before or after a file is opened or after it is closed. The output from the requests reflect the current properties of the file.

To make use of an INQUIRE statement, a variable of the appropriate type must be assigned to each specifier to be used. When INQUIRE is executed, the value for each of the specifications in the statement will be stored as the value of the variable to which it assigned. The program can then use the value assigned to the variable.

Example 1
The statement INQUIRE (FILE = 'STUDENT', NEXTREC = RECNUMBR) puts the integer value of the location of the next record (NEXTREC) of a direct-access file (called STUDENT) into a variable called RECNUMBR.

Example 2
The statement INQUIRE (FILE = 'STUDENT', OPENED = OPENST) will check to see if the file called STUDENT is open; if yes, it sets the value of the logical variable OPENST to .TRUE.; if not, it sets it to .FALSE. This also means OPENST must be defined as a logical variable. The value of OPENST may be used in a statement. If the file is to be opened only if it is not already open, the statement might read:

```
IF (.NOT. OPENST) THEN
    OPEN (4, FILE = 'STUDENT', ERR = 901)
ELSE . . . .
```

Example 3
```
INQUIRE (UNIT = 16, FORM = FRM, RECL = LENGTH)
```

INQUIRE STATEMENT

There are two forms of the INQUIRE statement: file and unit. The form of the file inquiry is

INQUIRE(FILE = file name and other specifiers)

This returns specifications for the named file. The form of the unit inquiry is

INQUIRE([UNIT =] unit number, and other specifiers)

The list of specifiers is used by the programmer to assign a variable name to store the value of each specifier included in the list.

Specifier	Assignment	Values returned or result
IOSTAT	Integer variable	0, negative, or positive
ERR	Statement label	Transfer if error
EXIST	Logical variable	True (exists) or false (does not exist)
OPENED	Logical variable	True (opened) or false (not open)
NUMBER	Integer variable	Number of unit connected to file
NAMED	Logical variable	True (named) or false (no name)
NAME	Character variable	Name of file
ACCESS	Character variable	SEQUENTIAL or DIRECT
DIRECT	Character variable	YES, NO, or UNKNOWN
FORM	Character variable	FORMATTED, UNFORMATTED, or UNKNOWN
FORMATTED	Character variable	YES, NO, or UNKNOWN
UNFORMATTED	Character variable	YES, NO, or UNKNOWN
RECL	Integer variable	Record length of records in file
NEXTREC	Integer variable	Number of next record in direct-access file
BLANK	Character variable	NULL or ZERO (zero blank control)

After execution, FRM will contain the characters FORMATTED, UNFORMATTED, or UNKNOWN, and LENGTH will contain the length of the records in the file connected to unit 16. The variable FRM must be declared as CHARACTER.

Self-Testing Exercise 6-4

1. Write the statements to open and to write a record containing PAYNO and PAYRTE onto a new direct-access file called PAY on unit 8. The record number is IRNO, the error routine label is 900, and the record length is 250. The record is formatted.

2. Inquire what the next record number is after the one just written in question 1.

3. Write the statements to open a formatted sequential file on unit 9 and to write a record composed of COURSE and GRADES. Backspace and read the record just written and print it. Close the file. The name of the file is STUDNT.

Summary

FORTRAN programs do not need auxiliary storage if input is processed as entered and the results are then displayed or printed. The need for files on external storage arises when input items are to be stored for later use or data items are to be used repeatedly by the same program or different programs or the data items exceed the storage space available for arrays. Under these conditions, storing the data records as a file on external storage is a desirable approach.

A record in FORTRAN consists of a set of data items that is read or written by a READ or WRITE statement. All records of a given type (same data items) constitute a file. The file may be sequential access or direct access. The common storage media of tape, disk, and diskette support sequential access; direct access requires a direct-access device such as a disk or diskette.

In the simplest case of sequential access, reading or writing from the file is the same as for keyboard or printer except for a different unit number. It is possible to add additional specifications by the control list. The file may be positioned (rewound or backspaced) by file-positioning statements.

A direct-access file consists conceptually of a numbered set of fixed-length storage locations numbered from 1 to N. The file may be predefined by the operating system, defined by job control statements, or defined by an OPEN statement. Direct-access READ and WRITE statements require a record number specification in the control list. Other specifications may be included.

The 1977 FORTRAN standard provides additional, very flexible facilities for specifying files, connecting files to devices, disconnecting files, inquiring about the status of a file, etc. These will be useful in situations requiring extensive file handling. Their use frequently requires information from the implementor manual for the compiler being employed.

Answers to Self-Testing Exercises

Exercise 6-1

1. (a) File   (b) Record   (c) Record   (d) File

2. (a) False   (b) True   (c) False   (d) True   (e) True

3.

Access method	Order records read	File medium	Use of list-directed I/O	Use of end-of-file record
Sequential	Same order as written	Tape, disk, or, diskette	Allowed	Yes
Direct	Random order	Disk or diskette	Not allowed	No

Exercise 6-2

1. ```
READ (5, *)X, Y, Z
WRITE (8, *)X, Y, Z
```

2. ```
READ (5, * )X, Y, Z
WRITE (UNIT = 10, FMT = *)X, Y, Z
```

3. ```
REWIND 8
READ (8, *)X, Y, Z
```

4. ```
(1)     READ(5, 700)X, Y, Z
        WRITE (8, FMT = 700)X, Y, Z
    700 FORMAT (3F10.2)
```

```
(2)        READ (5, 700)X, Y, Z
           WRITE (10, 700)X, Y, Z
       700 FORMAT (3F10.2)
```

5.
```
BACKSPACE 8
READ (8, * )X, Y, Z
```

6. Yes, it would be the same, if there were only one record in the file. If there were two or more physical records, rewind would position to read the first, while backspace would position to read the prior record.

Exercise 6-3

1.
```
       DO 100 J = 1, 12
           READ (5, 20, ERR = 30, IOSTAT = ENCODE) ID, NAME, PAY
        20     FORMAT (I2, A10, F6.2)
           WRITE (10, REC = ID, ERR = 40, IOSTAT = ERCODE) NAME, PAY
       100 CONTINUE
```

2.
```
       READ (10, REC = 5) NAME, PAY
```

3.
```
       DO 10 I = 1, 10, 2
           READ (10, REC = I) N, P
           PRINT 30, I, N, P or WRITE (6, 30) I, N, P
        30     FORMAT (' ID = 'I2,' NAME = ',A10,' PAY = ',F6.2)
       10 CONTINUE
```

Exercise 6-4

1.
```
OPEN  (8,  ERR=900,  FILE='PAY',  STATUS='NEW',  ACCESS=
       'DIRECT', RECL=250, FORM='FORMATTED')
WRITE (8, 700, REC = IRNO, ERR = 900) PAYNO, PAYRTE
```

2.
```
INQUIRE (UNIT = 8, NEXTREC = INEXT)
```

where record number of next record will be placed in INEXT.

3.
```
OPEN (9, ERR=900, FILE='STUDNT', FORM='FORMATTED',
       STATUS='NEW', ACCESS='SEQUENTIAL')
```

Note that FORM and ACCESS specifications are not required because these specifications are default options, but it is better to be explicit.

```
    WRITE (9, 700, ERR = 900) COURSE, GRADES
700 FORMAT (2F10.2)
    BACKSPACE 9
    READ (9, 700, ERR = 900) COURSE, GRADES
    WRITE (6, *) COURSE, GRADES
    CLOSE (9)
```

Questions and Problems

1. Define the following terms:
   (a) Character
   (b) Data item
   (c) Direct-access storage
   (d) End-of-file record
   (e) Field
   (f) File
   (g) Record
   (h) Sequential-access storage

2. Differentiate between (a) use of tapes and disks for FORTRAN files and (b) formatted and unformatted records and the impact on FORTRAN file use.

3. A researcher has 1000 sets of data that will be processed by a number of different programs over a period of 7 months. The data consists of sets of research observations (call them X's) with observations in each set (X_1 through X_9). Each set of observations has an integer number from 1 to 1000 that identifies the set. The data is now on index cards with each set on a separate card.
   (a) Write statements to create a sequential file on device 10 (say a tape).
   (b) Write statements to read half of the data, rewind, and read the first 500 sets of observations again.

4. Assume a file as in problem 3.
   (a) Create a direct-access file. Use the number of each set (1 to 1000) as the direct-access file record number.
   (b) Read the sets of data randomly using record numbers equal to the numbers created by a sampling function. Call the function ISAMPL(SEED), where SEED has already been defined.

5. Assume a file as in problem 4, but create an unformatted file and then read the second 10 records.

6. Assume a file as in problem 3 but use list-directed data (separated by commas) on input. Read the data, create a file, rewind, and then read the first five records.

Example Programs and Programming Exercises Using External Files

General Notes on Chapter 6 Examples

General Program Example 6—Payroll Reports
Problem Description for General Example 6
Program Documentation for General Example 6
Notes on General Example 6

Mathematical Program Example 6—Processing and Filing Research Data
Problem Description for Mathematical Example 6
Program Documentation for Mathematical Example 6

Random Number Generation Using a Computer
Flowcharting Use of Files
Notes on Mathematical Example 6

Programming Exercises
Description of Assignment
Mathematics and Statistics
Business and Economics
Science and Engineering
Humanities and Social Sciences
General
Interactive Scientific and Engineering

The example programs illustrate typical use of external files. The program for general example 6, payroll reports, uses an external sequential-access file to hold reference data items which are matched with variable data read from a previously prepared input file; the program for mathematical example 6, research measurements, uses both a direct-access and a sequential-access file. The second program example illustrates features not used in the first, so that both should be reviewed.

General Notes on Chapter 6 Examples

External data files are used in several ways. In one sense, these files are just a different form of an array. If the array must be saved between runs of the program, its contents can be written to a file and read in the next time the program is run. Such a run may simply extract data from the file, update it, or perform a combination of these procedures. Another reason for a file is that storing all data to be available for use by the program creates an array that is too large for the main memory, and thus the data sets, which for a small problem would have been stored in an array, are written as records on an external file.

General Program Example 6—Payroll Reports

The program produces the same reports as its predecessor in Chapter 5. The report-printing logic and the computational procedures are identical to those in Chapter 5. The difference is that only the variable data (departments to be included in these reports and the hours worked by each employee) are read from a previously prepared sequential-access file. The reference data items on each employee are kept on an external sequential-access file.

In other words, the program illustrates three uses for files: retention of reference data, input file (presorted in sequence), and semivariable data file that changes infrequently. The reference file (also called *master file*) is a sequential-access file sequenced on the employee identification numbers (Figure 6-4). To avoid having to search the file from the beginning each time an employee data record is read, the input data records (Figure 6-4) are sorted in order based on the ID numbers.

Problem Description for General Example 6

The program is to read employee pay data and produce two reports: (1) Paycheck Report: Table Values and Error Messages and (2) Employee Paycheck Report. The Employee Paycheck Report is to contain a line for each employee and a total line at the end of the report. The employees are to be grouped by department in the report. In the Employee Paycheck Report, net pay that is negative or over $300 is accompanied by a warning note. Also, errors in input code for union/management are noted.

The first input to the program consists of a file with five records containing department numbers and names, one pair per record. Input validation for this data consists of an output table that echoes the values for visual verification. The input data file consists of a date record plus one input record for each employee, giving ID number, department where worked, and hours worked. These are arranged in ascending order on employee ID number. Errors detected on input are noted immediately with a suitable message. Following the reading of each employee record, one or more records are read from the reference file until reference data concerning the particular employee is found, or until it is established that the matching record is missing or a data error is present. When a matching record is found, it is retained in an array for use in computation and output. The reference file records consist of employee ID number, name, department number, pay rate, miscellaneous deductions, number of dependents, and type of employee (union/management). After all employee input records have been read, a total record count and count of rejected records are printed.

Program Documentation for General Example 6

Since there are very few differences between this program and general example 5, only a portion of the flowchart (Figure 6-5) and two blocks with code segments that are changed will be shown here (Figures 6-2 and 6-3). No pseudocode is given. New test data is documented in Figure 6-4. The Paycheck Report: Table Values and Error Messages is shown in Figure 6-6. The Employee Paycheck Report, identical to Figure 5-10, is not shown here.

Notes on General Example 6

Two differences between this program and general example 5 are in block 000 where files are opened and block 100 where the employee data records are read. See lines 115–118 in Figure 4-19 for the method used in Chapters 4 and 5. In the reading of input (Figure 6-2), general example 6 uses three files instead of two. The more permanent information about an employee is stored on one file; the variable information for each pay period is on a second file. As with the earlier programs, the list of department names and numbers are also on a separate file. The three files from which data records are read in the example were written by other programs not shown here.

Three additional error messages have been added in block 900 (Figure 6-3) to reflect possible file errors. Data-type errors and invalid input data errors print on the Table Values and Error Messages (Figure 6-6); errors that cause the program to be terminated are not shown in the sample output. Since each employee number is supposed to be on the reference file and both the reference file and data inputs have been sorted in ascending order, an error is indicated if a higher ID number is found in the reference file than on the current input record. Also an error occurs if the reference file comes to an end without finding the ID number for the current input record. If the error were an improper sort or a data-entry error rather than a missing employee record, more elaborate coding could be done to repeat the search of the file. For the sake of simplicity, the example program makes an abnormal stop after printing a suitable message and attempts no recovery or diagnostic procedure.

Figure 6-2 Part of program blocks 000 and 100 as changed from general program example 5 to general program example 6 for payroll reports program.

```
  1 **********
  2 *                        PROGRAM IDENTIFICATION
  3 **********
  4 *
  5 *    This program computes employee paychecks based upon
  6 *    hours worked, wage rate and various deductions. It prints
  7 *    employee data grouped by departments. Variable tax and pension
  8 *    rates are computed. Permanent employee records are kept on a
  9 *    file (DATA6E) while variable data is maintained on a separate
 10 *    file (DATA6V) and department data is on yet another file
 11 *    (DATA6D). Employee files are presorted on ascending employee
 12 *    numbers. Developed for file input and batch execution.
 13 *    Written 7/12/77 by T. Hoffmann  rev. 1/22/82  3/27/87 4/9/87
 14 *
 15 **********
    — — — — — — — — — — — — — — — — — — — — — — — — — — — — — — —
 84 **********
 85 * BLOCK 0000          INITIALIZATION BLOCK
 86 **********
 87 *
 88     OPEN(4,FILE='DATA6V',ACCESS='SEQUENTIAL')
 89     OPEN(7,FILE='DATA6D',ACCESS='SEQUENTIAL')
 90     OPEN(8,FILE='DATA6E',ACCESS='SEQUENTIAL')
 91 *
    — — — — — — — — — — — — — — — — — — — — — — — — — — — — — — —
132 *
133 **********
134 * BLOCK 0100          READ EMPLOYEE DATA
135 **********
136 *
137 101 READ(4,102,END=301,ERR=901) IDNUM,NDEPT,HOURS
138 102 FORMAT(I5,2X,I4,2X,F4.1)
139 103 READ(8,104,END=920,ERR=930) ID(NUM),NAME(NUM),
140   1   NDEP(NUM),PAYDAT(NUM,2),PAYDAT(NUM,3),NDEPS(NUM),MTYPE(NUM)
141 104 FORMAT(I5,2X,A12,2X,I4,2X,F4.2,2X,F5.2,2X,I2,2X,I1)
142     IF(ID(NUM) .LT. IDNUM) GOTO 103
143     IF(ID(NUM) .GT. IDNUM) GOTO 940
144     PAYDAT(NUM,1) = HOURS
145 *
146 *        TEST TO PREVENT ARRAY OVERFLOW. IF ARRAY'S NOT FULL
147 *              GO ON TO CHECK DATA VALIDITY
148 *
149     IF(NUM.GT.MAXEMP) GOTO 906
150     RECS = RECS + 1
151 *
```

Note that this program with sequential-access files requires very little change to use three files instead of the two used in Chapter 5. The coding of file use in this program uses simple procedures and relies in some cases on the error-handling facilities of the operating system. For example, several READ and WRITE statements do not have ERR specifications; they rely upon the READ and WRITE error diagnosis and messages from the operating system.

Mathematical Program Example 6— Processing and Filing Research Data

This example illustrates the use of both a sequential file and a direct-access file. It also illustrates interactive terminal input and outut, the use of a function for obtaining random numbers, the use of a subroutine for correction procedures, and the use of a log file for accumulating raw data and "backing up" analysis data. The problem has been deliberately kept simple to focus on these features.

Figure 6-3 Program block 900 as changed from general program example 5 to general program example 6 for payroll reports program.

```
266 **********
267 * BLOCK 0900              ERROR MESSAGE BLOCK
268 **********
269 *
270 901 RECS = RECS + 1
271     WRITE(6,902) RECS
272 902 FORMAT(//' *****',' ERROR IN EMPLOYEE RECORD NUMBER '
273    1    ,I2,' *****')
274     GOTO 918
275 *****

310 *****
311 *
312 920 WRITE(6,921) RECS
313 921 FORMAT(//5X, 'ATTEMPTED TO READ PAST END OF PERMANENT ',
314    1    'EMPLOYEE RECORD FILE.'/10X,I4,' RECORDS READ.')
315     WRITE(6,922)
316 922 FORMAT(10X,'RUN ABORTED.')
317 *
318 *              CLOSE FILES AND ABORT RUN
319 *
320     GOTO 410
321 *****
322 *
323 930 WRITE(6,931)
324 931 FORMAT(//5X,'UNREADABLE DATA ON PERMANENT EMPLOYEE RECORD FILE')
325     WRITE(6,922)
326 *
327 *              CLOSE FILES AND ABORT RUN
328 *
329       GOTO 410
330 *****
331 *
332 940 WRITE(6,941)IDNUM,NDEPT,HOURS
333 941 FORMAT(//5X,'EMPLOYEE DATA RECORD OUT OF ORDER OR MISSING FROM',
334    1 ' PERMANENT EMPLOYEE RECORD FILE.'/10X,2I5,F5.1,' IS DATA.')
335     WRITE(6,922)
336 *
337 *              CLOSE FILES AND ABORT RUN
338 *
339     GOTO 410
340 *
341 * END OF MAIN PROGRAM
```

Problem Description for Mathematical Example 6

A researcher takes temperature and humidity measurements from 12 sites selected randomly each day from 132 possible measurement locations. This will be done every day for 365 days. The data-recording procedure is the following:

1. Take measurements from 12 randomly selected locations (see step 4).
2. Add the measurements to the cumulative analysis record for each of the 12 sites. Use a random-access file with records numbered from 1 to 132, so that record numbers correspond to site numbers; for example, the cumulative record for site 18 will be record number 18.
3. Add the 12 measurements to a log file of measurements. This sequential file is essentially a cumulative file of all measurements taken. It is a backup file of raw data in case there is a problem with the cumulative analysis file. It also provides raw data for further analysis at the end of the experiment.
4. Make random selection of the 12 sites from which to obtain measurements the following day.

Figure 6-4 Test data on the three external files for general program example 6. See also Figure 5-10.

```
INPUT DATA FILE (DATA6V)
- - - - - - - - - - - - - - - - - - - - - - - - - - - - - - - - - - - - - -
04/10/87
15786    8551    39.9
23456    7531    40.0
23457    1596    40.0
35748    4275    40.1
36985    7269    22.0
42753    1234    40.0
45914    4275    3&.5
62475    4275    37.5
69852    4275    10.0
74365    7531    54.0

- - - - - - - - - - - - - - - - - - - - - - - - - - - - - - - - - - - - - -


DATA RECORDS ON MASTER FILE (DATA6E)
- - - - - - - - - - - - - - - - - - - - - - - - - - - - - - - - - - - - - -

15786    RALPH JONES     8551    6.28    24.68    04   1
19834    JOHN SMITH      2467    3.57    30.93    02   2
23456    P. HOFFMANN     7531    3.57    27.95    02   1
23457    T. HOFFMANN     1596    3.57    27.95    03   2
35748    L. SMITH        4275    9.94    30.68    04   4
36985    J. JOHNSON      7269    0275    03598    01   1
40865    OSCAR JAMES     7531    4.57    44.74    04   2
42753    R. M. NELSON    1234    7.45    57.64    03   2
54309    B. GRUENZEL     1596    4.85    707.9    02   1
62475    F. MORLOCK      4275    8.24    65.34    02   2
69852    T. NAMAN        4275    2.67    27.50    09   1
74365    A. PETERSON     7531    4.82    54.63    00   0

- - - - - - - - - - - - - - - - - - - - - - - - - - - - - - - - - - - - - -


DEPARTMENT NUMBER AND NAME FILE (DATA6D)
- - - - - - - - - - - - - - - - - - - - - - - - - - - - - - - - - - - - - -

1234FIN
4275ENGR
7269MKTG
7531PROD
8551ACCT

- - - - - - - - - - - - - - - - - - - - - - - - - - - - - - - - - - - - - -
```

The researcher sends the 12 data collection records to the computer through a terminal and receives back a report at the terminal consisting of four parts:

1. List of input data entered
2. List of cumulative analysis results for the 12 sites affected by the input data
3. Randomly selected list of 12 sites for measurement the next day
4. Random start seed for use the next day

The FORTRAN program processes data entered from a terminal and maintains the files at a computer center. This requires the program to do the following:

1. Establish an unformatted sequential file to act as the log file. This file will be opened each day and read until end of file, and will add records. Note that this may be a tape or a disk file used sequentially.
2. The unformatted direct-access analysis file is opened, and using the site number on the input as a record number, the analysis record to be processed is read. The input is used to update the analysis record, and the updated result for the analysis record is printed. After all 12 inputs are processed and printed, the analysis file is closed.

Figure 6-5 Flowchart showing part of file processing in block 100 of general program example 6 and associated error messages in block 900.

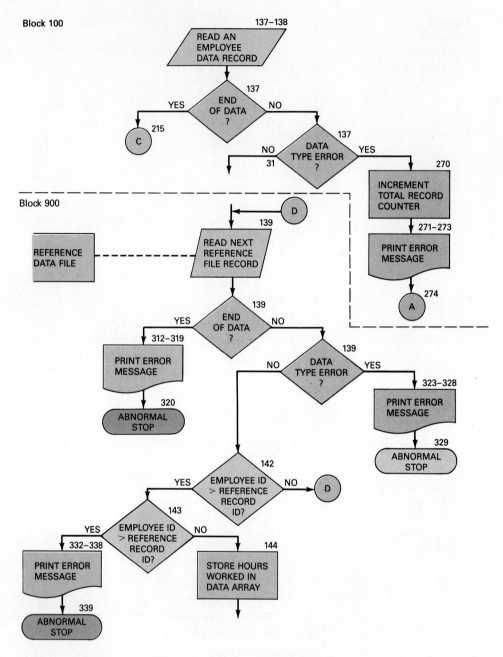

3. The 12 sites are selected using a random number generator. The researcher enters a seed from the previous day. The terminal prints the 12 measurement sites as well as the random seed for the next day.

The data inputs, external file record contents, and outputs are as follows.

Data Inputs at Terminal
Date DDMMYY (characters for day, month, and year)
Measurements for 12 sites: site number, Fahrenheit temperature, humidity in percent
Seed for random selection of sites for next measurement

Figure 6-6 Paycheck
Report: Table Values and
Error Messages—for general
example 6 program using
external storage.

```
Paycheck Report: Table Values and Error Messages
                Week Ended 04/10/87

Table of Departments
   Number    Name
    1234     FIN
    4275     ENGR
    7269     MKTG
    7531     PROD
    8551     ACCT



    Error messages during data input



***** ERROR - DEPT. NO. NOT VALID. RECORD NO.     3 *****


***** ERROR IN EMPLOYEE RECORD NUMBER  7 *****

***** Data outside validation limits--input rejected ***** record 8

     Data contents 62475 F. MORLOCK   37.5 8.24 65.34   2    2

  10 Records read
   3 Records in error
```

Record Contents

Sequential log file: date, site, temperature, and humidity in each record
Direct-access file for cumulative analysis: site (record number), number of observations to date, average temperature, and average humidity

Outputs at Terminal

Various messages to prompt input, verify data validation, and make corrections
List of cumulative analysis for sites being processed
List of sites for next measurements
Seed for next use of random number generator
List of input data

Program Documentation for Mathematical Example 6

The documentation consists of a pseudocode program description (Figure 6-7), a program flowchart (Figure 6-8), a program listing (Figure 6-9), and a sample of results from processing a set of data (Figure 6-10). Note the three parts of the program—the main program, the correction subroutine, and the function to generate a random number.

Random Number Generation Using a Computer

When obtaining random numbers, it should not be possible to predict the next random number from the current random number, so true random numbers must be generated by some completely random process. When using a computer, numbers that appear to be random are generated by a deterministic process; if repeated, the computations yield the same sequence of numbers. For this reason, random numbers generated by computer are termed *pseudorandom numbers*. Overall, these numbers

Main Program
```
OPEN log file (sequential access)
OPEN data file (direct access)
Position log file at its end
Input date of data readings from terminal
PRINT prompt of data to terminal
READ set of sites, temperatures, and humidities; store in arrays
PRINT input set (item number, sites, temperature, humidity)
PRINT'ANY CHANGES OR CORRECTIONS'
READ answer
If answer is Y (yes), then CALL data correction subroutine
PRINT report headings to terminal
For set of entries in arrays
   WRITE entry group to log file
   READ corresponding cumulative record from data file
   Compute new averages or establish initial values
   WRITE revised record to cumulative record data file
   PRINT revised record
End of loop
Prompt and READ random number input seed
PRINT header
Compute 12 unique site numbers (1 ≤ site ≤ 132)
PRINT sites
PRINT new seed
REWIND log file
CLOSE data cumulative record file
END
```

Subroutine Corect
```
Prompt and READ item number to be changed from terminal (on end-
       of-file, RETURN)
READ new site, temperature, humidity from terminal
Go back to Prompt
END
```

Function random
```
Initialize variables
Compute large random digit number
Compute high-order digits with MOD function
Compute low-order digits by subtraction of high-order digits
Scale random digits to between 0 and 1 (or bias interval)
RETURN
```

Figure 6-7 Pseudocode description of logic for mathematical program example 6—processing and filing research data with interactive input and output.

exhibit the characteristics of random numbers even though they are generated by a completely determined process.

If a random number computational process on a computer begins with the same initial value, it produces the same set of random numbers. This is very useful because a researcher may wish to repeat the same sequence of random numbers. However, in successive use of random numbers, it is important that the random number sequence

Figure 6-8 Program flowchart of mathematical program example 6—processing and filing research data with interactive input and output.

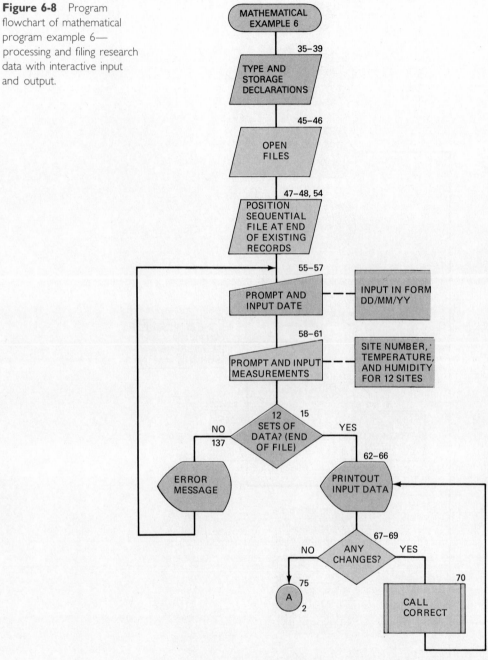

continue rather than start over so that the random numbers used tomorrow do not repeat the random numbers used today. To continue the random number sequence, we carry forward from one session to the next a seed value that starts the random number computational process. For example, the seed at the end of one day can be saved and used as the seed at the beginning of the next day. (There are other possibilities for introducing randomness each day, but these are beyond the scope of this discussion.)

Random numbers typically are a string of digits in the range of values from 0 to 1 (decimal fractions) or in integer form. In the sample problem, the random numbers

Figure 6-8   continued

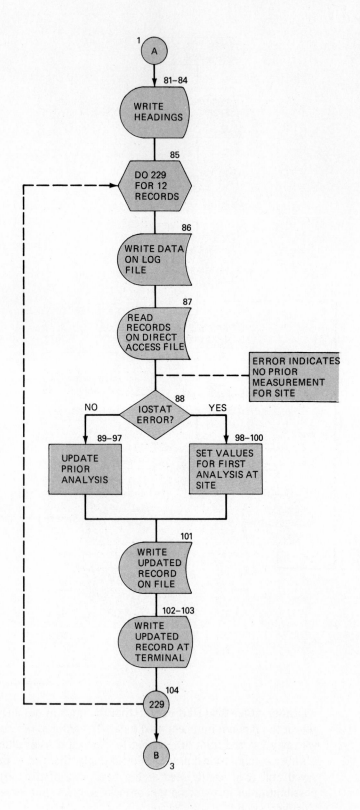

Figure 6-8 continued

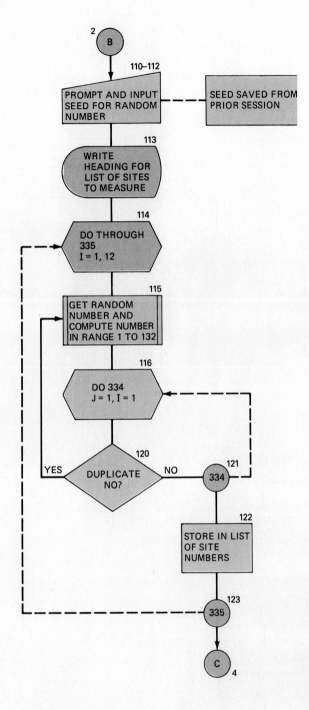

are in the range from 0 to 1. The user of the random number must process it to achieve a number within the desired range. For example, in the sample program (line 115), the program takes the integer value after multiplying the random number by 132 to yield a value between 0 and 131, and then adds 1 to provide a random number in the range 1–132.

In any set of random numbers, the same number can appear more than once. For example, if one is doing a random selection of numbers between 1 and 132, it is

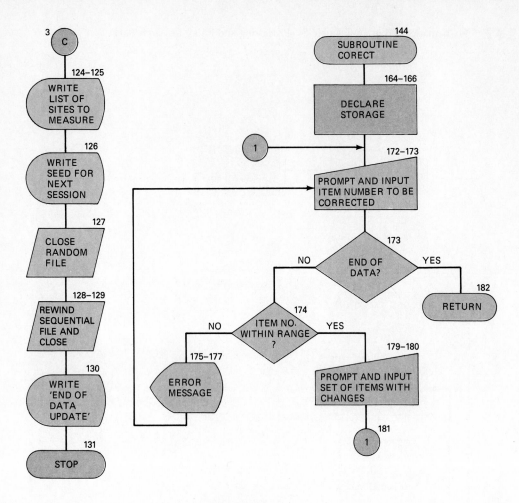

3
C

124-125
WRITE LIST OF SITES TO MEASURE

126
WRITE SEED FOR NEXT SESSION

127
CLOSE RANDOM FILE

128-129
REWIND SEQUENTIAL FILE AND CLOSE

130
WRITE 'END OF DATA UPDATE'

131
STOP

144
SUBROUTINE CORECT

164-166
DECLARE STORAGE

1

172-173
PROMPT AND INPUT ITEM NUMBER TO BE CORRECTED

173
END OF DATA? —NO / YES—

182
RETURN

174
ITEM NO. WITHIN RANGE ? —NO / YES—

175-177
ERROR MESSAGE

179-180
PROMPT AND INPUT SET OF ITEMS WITH CHANGES

181
1

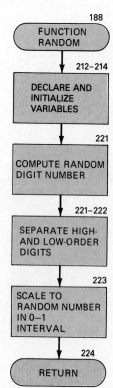

188
FUNCTION RANDOM

212-214
DECLARE AND INITIALIZE VARIABLES

221
COMPUTE RANDOM DIGIT NUMBER

221-222
SEPARATE HIGH- AND LOW-ORDER DIGITS

223
SCALE TO RANDOM NUMBER IN 0-1 INTERVAL

224
RETURN

Figure 6-8 concluded

Figure 6-9 Program listing for mathematical program example 6—processing and filing research data with interactive input and output.

```
 1  **********
 2  *                          PROGRAM IDENTIFICATION
 3  **********
 4  *
 5  *     RESRCH maintains a direct access file of average temps
 6  *     and humidities at 132 sites. For further analysis at the
 7  *     completion of an experiment, a sequential log file is
 8  *     maintained.  Sites for random sampling are generated.
 9  *     Written by T. R. Hoffmann 01/29/82  rev. 4/6/87
10  *
11  **********
12  *                          VARIABLES IDENTIFICATION
13  **********
14  *
15  *     ANS      = Response to interactive inquiry
16  *     DATE     = Date of update
17  *     HUMID    = Average humidity
18  *     IOS      = I/O Status: 0 = no error or EOF
19  *     MEASUR   = New temp. And humidity (array)
20  *     NSITE    = New site candidate
21  *     OBS      = Cumulative number of observations
22  *     SEED     = Seed for random number generator
23  *     SITE     = List of sites (array)
24  *     TEMP     = Average temperature
25  *
26  **********              SUBROUTINE AND FUNCTION IDENTIFICATION
27  *
28  *     CORECT   = Corrects input data
29  *     RANDOM   = Random number generator
30  *
31  **********
32  *                          TYPE DECLARATION AND STORAGE ALLOCATION
33  **********
34  *
35        CHARACTER DATE*8,ANS*1
36        INTEGER SITE(12),NSITE,IOS
37        REAL MEASUR(12,2),HUMID,OBS,SEED,TEMP
38        COMMON /IN/SITE,MEASUR
39        COMMON /RAN/SEED
40  *
41  **********
42  * BLOCK 0000            INITIALIZE FILES
43  **********
44  *
45        OPEN(7,FORM='UNFORMATTED',FILE='DATA6L',ACCESS='SEQUENTIAL')
46        OPEN(21,ACCESS='DIRECT',RECL=19,FILE='DATA6C',FORM='UNFORMATTED')
47        DO 2 I= 1,4380
48      2 READ(7,END=101)
49  *
50  **********
51  * BLOCK 0100            READ INPUT DATA
52  **********
53  *
54  101 BACKSPACE 7
55        PRINT *, 'For what date are the following readings (DD/MM/YY)?'
56        READ(5,103) DATE
57  103 FORMAT (A)
58        WRITE(6,104)
59  104 FORMAT(1X,'What are the 12 sites, temperatures, and humidities?'/)
60        DO 112 I = 1,12
61  112 READ(5,*,END=901) SITE(I),MEASUR(I,1),MEASUR(I,2)
62  113 WRITE(6,114)
63  114 FORMAT(1X,'Item',3X,'Site',2X,'Temp.',4X,'Humidity')
64        DO 115 I = 1,12
65  115 WRITE(6,117) I,SITE(I),MEASUR(I,1),MEASUR(I,2)
66  117 FORMAT(1X,I4,3X,I4,F7.1,F9.1)
67        WRITE(6,*) 'Any changes or corrections (Y/N)? '
68        READ (5,103) ANS
69        IF (ANS .EQ. 'Y' .OR. ANS .EQ. 'y') THEN
70            CALL CORECT
71  *
72  *                        GO BACK AND PRINT CORRECTED DATA INPUTS
73  *
74            GOTO 113
75        ENDIF
```

Figure 6-9 continued

```
76 *
77 **********
78 * BLOCK 0200              COMPUTE AVERAGES, UPDATE FILES, AND PRINT
79 **********
80 *
81      WRITE(6,221) DATE
82 221 FORMAT(///1X,'Cumulative analysis for sites measured on',1X,
83   1    A8//1X,'Site',4x,'Number of',6x,'Average',5x,'Average'/
84   2    8X,'Observations',2X,'Temperature',3X,'Humidity'//)
85      DO 229 I = 1,12
86          WRITE(7) SITE(I),MEASUR(I,1),MEASUR(I,2)
87          READ(21,REC = SITE(I),IOSTAT=IOS) OBS,TEMP,HUMID
88          IF(IOS .EQ. 0) THEN
89              TEMP = TEMP*OBS + MEASUR(I,1)
90              HUMID = HUMID*OBS + MEASUR(I,2)
91              OBS = OBS + 1.0
92              TEMP = TEMP/OBS
93              HUMID = HUMID/OBS
94          ELSE
95 *                       FIRST TIME PROCESSING
96 *
97              OBS = 1.0
98              TEMP = MEASUR(I,1)
99              HUMID = MEASUR(I,2)
100         ENDIF
101         WRITE(21,REC = SITE(I)) OBS,TEMP,HUMID
102         WRITE(6,228) SITE(I),OBS,TEMP,HUMID
103 228     FORMAT(1X,I3,6X,F5.0,8X,F7.1,5X,F7.1)
104 229 CONTINUE
105 *
106 **********
107 * BLOCK 0300              GENERATE FUTURE SITE SAMPLE
108 **********
109 *
110     PRINT *,
111     PRINT *, 'What is the seed for the next random selection? '
112     READ(5,*) SEED
113     WRITE(6,*) 'Sites for next set of observations'
114     DO 335 I = 1,12
115 333     NSITE = INT(RANDOM(0.0)*132.0) + 1
116         DO 334 J = 1,I-1
117 *
118 *       CHECK FOR UNIQUENESS - IF ALREADY SELECTED, CHOOSE ANOTHER
119 *
120             IF(NSITE .EQ. SITE(J)) GOTO 333
121 334     CONTINUE
122         SITE(I) = NSITE
123 335 CONTINUE
124     WRITE(6,337) (SITE(I),I=1,12)
125 337 FORMAT(1X,6(I5,2X))
126     WRITE(6,*) 'New seed is ',INT(SEED)
127     CLOSE(21)
128     REWIND 7
129     CLOSE(7)
130     WRITE(6,*) 'End of data update'
131     STOP
132 *
133 **********
134 * BLOCK 0900              ERROR MESSAGE BLOCK
135 **********
136 *
137 901 WRITE(6,*)'ERROR - INSUFFICIENT DATA. RE-ENTER FROM BEGINNING.'
138     GOTO 101
139 *
140 * END OF MAIN PROGRAM
141 *
142     END
```

Figure 6-9 continued

```
143  *
144         SUBROUTINE CORECT
145  *
146  *********
147  *                    PROGRAM IDENTIFICATION
148  *********
149  *
150  *                    CORRECT OR CHANGE INPUT DATA
151  *
152  *********
153  *                    VARIABLES IDENTIFICATION
154  *********
155  *
156  *        ITEM    = Item number of set to be changed
157  *        MEASUR  = New temperature and humidity (array)
158  *        SITE    = List of sites (array)
159  *
160  *********
161  *                    TYPE DECLARATION AND STORAGE ALLOCATION
162  *********
163  *
164         REAL MEASUR(12,2)
165         INTEGER SITE(12),ITEM
166         COMMON /IN/ SITE,MEASUR
167  *
168  *********
169  * BLOCK 0100          CORRECT A DATA SET
170  *********
171  *
172         WRITE(6,*) 'Which item number do you want to change? '
173  103 READ(5,*,END=111) ITEM
174         IF(ITEM .LT. 1 .OR. ITEM .GE. 12) THEN
175            WRITE(6,*)'ERROR -- ITEM NUMBER MUST BE BETWEEN 1 AND 12.'
176            WRITE(6,*) 'RE-ENTER ITEM NUMBER.'
177            GOTO 103
178         ENDIF
179         WRITE(6,*) 'To what site, temperature, and humidity? '
180         READ(5,*) SITE(ITEM),MEASUR(ITEM,1),MEASUR(ITEM,2)
181         GOTO 103
182  111 RETURN
183  *
184  * END OF SUBPROGRAM
185  *
186         END
```

possible that 10 will appear twice, simply because of the random character of the sampling. This is the concept of *sampling with replacement*. What is desired in this particular case is sampling without replacement, so that a number will not be repeated within the sample once it has been chosen. This must be handled by the program. Each value is tested to determine if the number has already been obtained. This simple comparison is coded in the sample program in lines 116–121.

A random number can be obtained in two ways. One way is to write a random number function, as was done in this particular case. The second way is to use an external function, which is normally available from the computer center where one is running problems. Specifications must be obtained from the computer center to use such a function. It is not necessary to understand the details of random number computations to understand this problem. For more information, see the description of the procedure in programming exercise 2 of Chapter 5.

Figure 6-9 concluded

```
187 *
188       FUNCTION RANDOM(DUM)
189 *
190 **********
191 *                    PROGRAM IDENTIFICATION
192 **********
193 *
194 *       Random number generator. Called from main program
195 *
196 **********
197 *                    VARIABLES IDENTIFICATION
198 **********
199 *
200 *       B         = Constant multiplier = 3213.0
201 *       C         = High order digits of product
202 *       SEED      = Low order digits of product
203 *       F         = Constant scale factor = 1.0E7
204 *       S         = Constant scale factor = 10000.0
205 *       DUM       = Dummy argument or bias factor
206 *       R         = Random digits
207 *
208 **********
209 *              TYPE DECLARATION AND STORAGE ALLOCATION
210 **********
211 *
212       REAL B,C,F,S,R,SEED,DUM
213       COMMON /RAN/SEED
214       DATA S/10000./F/1.0E7/B/3213.0/C/1230000./
215 *
216 **********
217 * BLOCK 0100          GENERATE RANDOM NUMBER
218 **********
219 *
220       R = AMOD((AMOD(B*C,F) + AMOD(B*SEED,F)),F)
221       SEED = AMOD(R,S)
222       C = R - SEED
223       RANDOM = R/F + DUM
224       RETURN
225 *
226 * END OF SUBPROGRAM
227 *
228       END
```

Flowcharting Use of Files

The flowcharting of the file processing example with direct-access and sequential files uses both general and device-specific symbols. There are two general file symbols.

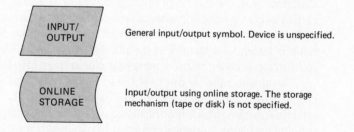

INPUT/OUTPUT — General input/output symbol. Device is unspecified.

ONLINE STORAGE — Input/output using online storage. The storage mechanism (tape or disk) is not specified.

The first general symbol can be used instead of the three more specific symbols. The online file storage symbol can be used if the storage device or medium is

Figure 6-10 Output from interactive execution of mathematical program example 6—processing and filing research data with interactive input and output.

```
For what date are the following readings (DD/MM/YY)? 02/09/88

What are the 12 sites, temperatures, and humidities?
21,60,73
28,44,24
35,5,37
51,70,55
56,48,77
63,73,45
64,47,23
74,49,75
77,40,85
96,83,22
107,75,48
83,60,35

Item   Site   Temp.   Humidity
  1      21    60.0     73.0
  2      28    44.0     24.0
  3      35     5.0     37.0
  4      51    70.0     55.0
  5      56    48.0     77.0
  6      63    73.0     45.0
  7      64    47.0     23.0
  8      74    49.0     75.0
  9      77    40.0     85.0
 10      96    83.0     22.0
 11     107    75.0     48.0
 12      83    60.0     35.0
Any changes or corrections (Y/N)? n
```

```
Cumulative analysis for sites measured on 02/09/88

Site    Number of      Average        Average
        Observations   Temperature    Humidity


 21        7.            59.9          72.7
 28       36.            45.1          20.2
 35        7.             4.4          32.7
 51       20.            68.0          56.7
 56       20.            44.6          76.3
 63       22.            71.6          43.9
 64       37.            45.9          14.4
 74       28.            48.4          80.4
 77       11.            39.4          88.1
 96       37.            80.8          17.3
107       10.            74.7          47.4
 83        1.            60.0          35.0
```

```
What is the seed for the next random selection? 4567

Sites for next set of observations
    88     10    127     25    105     29
    58      1    114      4    130    102
New seed is          8171
End of data update
```

unspecified. If it were known that magnetic tape or magnetic disk were being used for file storage, specific device symbols can be drawn:

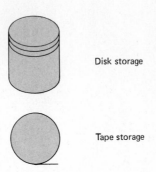

Disk storage

Tape storage

In the sample problem flowchart, the programmer specifies online storage. For the random-access file, this must be disk storage; for the sequential file, it can be either form of storage. Therefore, we chose to flowchart both files at the more general online storage symbol. General input/output preparation operations, such as opening and closing files, were diagrammed with the most general input/output symbol because these involve both operating system and device directory operations.

The flowcharting of input/output from the terminal could have always been done with a pair of symbols—the first for displaying the prompting message for entering input and the second for input from the terminal. If prompting is followed by input, we have used only one symbol and have included the prompt as part of the input symbol, as shown below:

Notes on Mathematical Example 6

Input is in list-directed input so that the user at the terminal does not need to spend time formatting and ensuring that the data appears in the correct columns (lines 61 and 112). Errors detected through input validation are immediately displayed at the terminal, and correct input is requested.

The program has a number of interesting features and uses relative to files and interactive terminal input/output.

1. The files to be used are opened. The sequential file on unit 7 is declared to be unformatted (line 45), and the file on unit 21 is declared to be direct and have a record length of 19 units, which allows for expansion (line 46). The ACCESS = 'SEQUENTIAL' specification is not necessary because it is the default, but adding it provides useful documentation. The same is true with respect to the direct-access file; it is by default unformatted, but FORM = 'UNFORMATTED' is included as an explicit specification. All other specifications are default. The

direct-access record length depends on the design of the computer being used (in this case, in characters) and thus the specific manual must be consulted.

2. The file names are associated with unit numbers (7 and 21) through the OPEN statements in lines 45–46. Units 5 and 6 do not require definition if they are default units for terminal input and output.

3. Since data items are to be added to the previous contents of the sequential file, the file must be positioned at this point. Lines 47 and 48 read until END; then the file is positioned by a BACKSPACE for addition of a new record. The OPEN statement may, in many systems, position the sequential file at the end, just before the end-of-file record. The coding used here does not depend on that; it can handle the file being positioned at the beginning, the end, or elsewhere.

4. The prompting question for input of the date specifies the desired form since data could be in different forms (line 55).

5. The addressing of records in the direct-access file uses an item of input data (the site number). It is specified in the REC = clause in the READ and WRITE statements (line 87).

6. The program asks for 12 sets of measurements. If the records end before 12 sets are received (ended by a terminal RETURN without data), the END condition is processed (line 61) and the program prints an error message and asks for re-entry of data from the beginning (line 137). The request for complete re-entry is reasonable for a small amount of input; if there were a large amount of input, some correction might be attempted.

7. The program prints the input data and specifically requests verification that there are no errors (line 67). Perhaps more validation could also be programmed, but a request for visual validation is a good control procedure. Note that file alteration does not occur until after data validation.

8. Error correction is an error-prone activity. In the example, prompting of error correction inputs is handled by a separate subroutine (CORECT) that is called if errors are identified (line 70). In CORECT, the line number to be changed is requested, and the item number is validated as being within the range of 12 input items. The corrected set of data is then entered. Note that after the return from CORECT, control goes back to print the set of inputs with corrections (line 74).

9. The logic of the program is to read the previous analysis data on a site from the direct-access file, to add the current measurements, and to increment the count of measurements. The difficulty is with the first measurement for a site (a first-time-through situation). Until the first measurements are recorded, the record contents are undefined. In the sample program, this is handled by an IOSTAT specification in the READ statement (line 87). If the program attempts to read where no data has been stored, IOS is set to a nonzero value. IOS is tested in line 88 and control is transferred appropriately. If there is no error, the record is updated; if an error is present, the three lines of code (lines 98–100) establish the initial contents using the first measurement. The program then continues with the analysis printout and writing of the updated (or initial) data on the direct-access file (lines 101 and 102).

10. The program uses a seed saved from the previous time to start the random number generator. The first time the program is used, an initial seed is specified. A prime number is generally used for this purpose, because a prime number will generate a higher quality random number series.

11. The file READ and WRITE statements (lines 48, 86, 87, and 101) could have included an ERR = specification. In this case, the decision was made to rely on

the operating system error messages rather than the FORTRAN error codes. The END specification does not apply to direct-access files (lines 87 and 101).

12. The sequential log file (file 7) is rewound (line 128). The explicit statement makes it clear the file is rewound so processing will be correct at the next use. The CLOSE statement also implies keep (save) the file (the default option).

Programming Exercises

Description of Assignment

Select one or more problems (or take the problems assigned by your instructor). Write each of the programs in such a manner as to make use of an external file. Follow the style guidelines and prepare the following:

1. Pseudocode description
2. Program flowchart
3. Program listing
4. List of test data and expected results, providing validity checks
5. Output including error detection

Mathematics and Statistics

1. Sometimes data sets may be quite large and hence they are stored on external files. Modify the program for problem 1 of Chapter 5 to read the data sets from a file, each record of which contains a number pair.

2. When forming the product of two matrices, it may be desirable to store the product in the location of one of the original matrices. An easy way to accomplish this is to form the product a vector at a time on a file and then to read the completed product back into the location of one of the original matrices. (For small matrices an array could be used, but that would not be practical for large matrices because of storage limitations.) Write a program that accomplishes this procedure. Print out the final matrix. As demonstration data use the following two pairs of matrices and form A $\times$ B and B $\times$ A (if defined).

A

2	7	11	
3	9	-3	
4	-1	4	
-6	3	8	

B

1	5	7	11
-2	9	-3	4
6	5	-2	1
0	6	9	2

2

17	4	1	8	15
23	5	7	14	16
4	6	13	20	22
10	12	19	21	3
11	18	25	2	9

2	3	9	-10	-4
-5	1	7	8	-11
-12	-6	0	6	12
11	-8	-7	-1	5
4	10	-9	-3	-2

3. Random number generators can be tested in a variety of ways to ensure that they are not biased. One way is the χ^2 (chi-square) test for uniform distribution of the numbers. In theory, if N random numbers distributed between 0 and 1 are generated and divided into n classes of equal size, there should be N/n values in each class. For example, if 20 classes were established, they would be as follows:

Class number	Interval boundaries
1	0.00–0.04999 . . .
2	0.05–0.09999 . . .
3	0.10–0.14999 . . .
.	.
.	.
.	.
20	0.95–0.99999 . . .

Assuming 2000 numbers were used, they should be distributed with 100 values in each class. The conformance of actual (A_i for the ith class) to theoretical can be tested by computation of the following:

$$X^2 = \sum_{i=1}^{n} \frac{[A_i - (N/n)]^2}{N/n} = \sum_{i=1}^{20} \frac{(A_i - 100)^2}{100} \quad \text{for the example}$$

This value can be compared to the appropriate χ^2 value for $n - 1$ degrees of freedom and a 5 or 10 percent significance level. If X^2 is greater than the appropriate χ^2 value, the random number generator is faulty.

Write a program to test three random number generators: the midsquare method described in problem 2 in Chapter 5, the power residue method shown as part of mathematical example 6, and the function provided as a system or local library function. Write the program so that the number of values generated is from 100 to 10,000 and the number of cells from 10 to 30. The program should contain the capability of printing the computed X^2 and χ^2 values for 5 and 10 percent significance levels. Prepare a file containing a table of χ^2 values that might be needed, and read the appropriate values from it.

Business and Economics

4. Write a program designed to maintain the personnel data file of general example 6. It should be capable of correcting data errors (such as the incorrect union/management codes), deleting entire records, or adding new records in their appropriate place. A report should accompany each such update run that tells what alterations were made and accounts for the input data read, records changed, and new and old file sizes (in numbers of records).

5. Refer to problem 6 in Chapter 4. Write the program so that the portfolio is maintained as a direct-access file and only the transactions are from a keyboard. Program it in such a way that both a summary report of the transactions and a final position statement are printed.

6. Do problem 5 above using a sequential file.

Science and Engineering

7. A common utility package available at each computer installation is an external file sorting program. The sorting program, frequently used by many other programs, is called a *system utility*. Various techniques exist for sorting; one of these is the following. Assume first that two strings of presorted data exist and that they are to be merged into one long, sorted string. This can be accomplished by comparing just two records at a time as illustrated in Figure 6-11. If there were two such pairs of strings

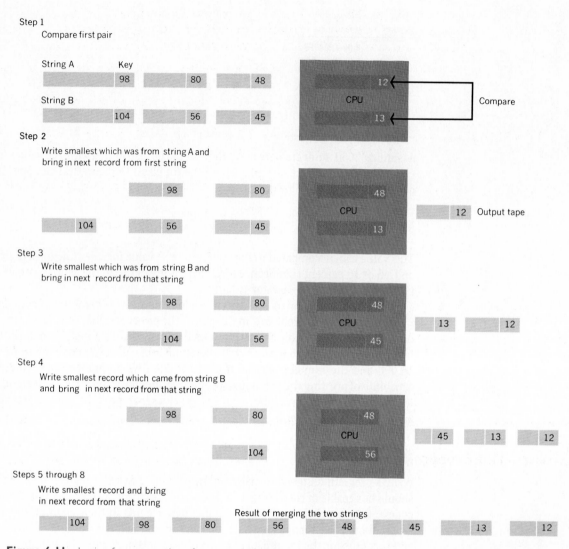

Figure 6-11 Logic of merge sorting of presorted strings.

initially, each pair could be merged into a long string and then those long strings could be merged into a final sorted string. The initial strings can be established by taking a relatively small set of records and sorting them internally by a method such as the bubble sort described in problem 7 in Chapter 4. Write a program that will take a file of unsorted four-digit numbers and sort it as described above. For sample data use either 80 randomly generated numbers or numbers taken from a phone directory. Internally sort groups of 10 numbers to generate the initial strings. Print out the initial unsorted data and the final sorted data.

8. Editing of data files is a common task, and many installations have text editors. As a very rudimentary form of text editing, write a program that will operate upon your

program file from Chapter 5 and separate all comment lines from the rest of the program. Print out three listings: full program, comments only, and balance of program. Use external files so this can be accomplished in only one run.

9. External files are often established when data sets are expected to become very large. Write a program that can take as input hourly temperatures and add them to a data file on a daily basis. The program should also prepare periodic summary reports on daily maximum, minimum, and average temperatures.

   In addition, it should print out the cumulative number of heating or cooling degree days for the period. These are defined as

$$\bar{t} = \text{mean temperature} = \frac{\text{maximum temperature} - \text{minimum temperature}}{2}$$

Degree day (cooling) $= t - 65$

Degree day (heating) $= 65 - t$ (Fahrenheit temperatures used here)

Humanities and Social Sciences

10. Since the number of respondents to a survey is initially unknown and responses may come in over time, it is often useful to store the data on an external file. Create the file and reprogram problem 10 of Chapter 5 to read response data from such a file.

11. Concordances are usually not done on short texts such as given in problem 11 of Chapter 4. In fact the volume of data may be quite large. Create a text file, and reprogram that problem to read the source text from an external file one line at a time.

12. A study is to be made of the eating habits of a target population. Create two programs: one that will add, correct, and maintain the data file and another that will summarize its contents. The file contains a record for each meal eaten by an individual. The record simply indicates whether or not something from each of the following food groups was eaten at a particular meal:

   Dairy products
   Cereals
   Fruit
   Meat
   Vegetables

   The survey data should indicate the percentage, for each major meal, of each category that was consumed. The summary should be for all subjects or, alternatively, for a selected subject.

General

13. Student grades are a function of homework scores and grades on quizzes and a final exam. Write a program that creates, corrects, and adds to a file of student grades. Consider each of the following columns of data to be update information for the file that must be handled by separate runs of the program.

Name	HW1	Q1	Q2	F
Anderson, Alan	95	67	70	74
Brown, Stewart	95	87	70	80
Carr, David	100	60	80	70
Daly, William	60	65	65	68
Erickson, Jane	45	79	90	87
Gruenzel, Lorna	90	93	87	95
Kohler, Wayne	95	82	80	78
Nelson, Joyce	75	73	75	84
Ray, Ruth	100	85	65	87
Taylor, Alice	50	73	60	75

In addition, the following corrections had to be made after the original grade was recorded.

Name	Action
Carr, David	HW1 from 100 to 90
Kohler, Wayne	Q1 from 82 to 87
Ray, Ruth	Q2 from 65 to 73

14. External data files are often maintained because new data is being added over an extended period of time. Write a program that will create and maintain a file of batting statistics for a baseball team. Include times at bat, runs batted in, and hits. Print out updated totals with each change of a record. Employ a direct-access file, and use each player's number as an index to the player's record.

15. A personalized dictionary of words or names can be quite useful. In the age of personal computers, such files are quite common. Write a program that will create, correct, and maintain such a file. It should be capable of adding or deleting definitions and, of course, searching for words already in it and printing out the definition. As minimum test data select 15 FORTRAN words or commands from this text and create your own definition of them.

Interactive Scientific and Engineering

16. In many research projects a subset of a large data base may be wanted in order to investigate a particular group of interest. Consider a situation in which a large research data base (file 1) contains records of fixed length (63 characters), each of which has mixed numeric and alphabetic data in six fields. The fifth field (characters 61 and 62) contains a two-digit identifying number. All the records are arranged in ascending order based on this number. There may be multiple records containing the same ID number, but they will be together in the file. On another file (file 2) there is a set of ID numbers, also arranged in ascending order. Write a program which will read the ID numbers from file 2, select only those records from file 1 with matching ID numbers, and write the selected records to a third file (file 3). Print a message if no matching records are found in file 1 for an ID number in file 2. (*Note:* Watch for ID numbers in file 2 greater than the largest one in file 1.)

17. For a matrix of real numbers, assume that there is insufficient memory to store the entire matrix, and therefore it will exist as an external file with only memory space for the program and a partial set of the rows or columns. Further assume that the file contains a header record with the dimensions of the matrix followed by the matrix values in row-by-row order. Find the largest element in each row and the smallest of

these largest elements for the entire set of rows and its position. Also find the smallest element in each column in the matrix and the largest of these smallest elements and its position. To test the program you may use the following specifications and matrix:

$$
\begin{vmatrix}
7 & 4 & & \\
1 & 11 & 21 & 8 \\
10 & 20 & 7 & 9 \\
19 & 6 & 16 & 18 \\
5 & 15 & 17 & 27 \\
14 & 24 & 26 & 4 \\
23 & 25 & 3 & 13 \\
28 & 2 & 12 & 22
\end{vmatrix}
$$

18. Referring to problem 2 in this chapter, assume that the matrices are stored as direct-access files and that there is not enough memory to read in an entire row or column. Write the product of the two matrices to a third direct-access file. Design the program for interactive use. Assume the matrices are large, and so do not print out the result. For this exercise, use the data from problem 2.

Additional Features

Additional Data Types
Double-Precision Type
Complex Type
Type Declaration for Other Data Types
Additional Intrinsic Functions for Other Data Types
Nonstandard Type Specifications
Self-Testing Exercise 7-1

Additional Character String Instructions
Defining and Manipulating a Character String or Substring
Intrinsic Functions for Character Data
Self-Testing Exercise 7-2

Advanced FORMAT Features
Additional FORMAT Edit Descriptors
FORMAT specifications in Input/Output Statement or Character Storage
Self-Testing Exercise 7-3

Additional Statements and Features
PARAMETER Statement
Constant Expression in Dimensions
Logical Equivalence or Nonequivalence
Main PROGRAM Statement
Self-Testing Exercise 7-4

Additional Subprogram Features
SAVE Variables for Subprograms

Alternate Entry to Subprogram and Alternate Return Points for the Calling Program
Variable Dimensions
Subprogram and Intrinsic Function Names in an Argument List
Self-Testing Exercise 7-5

Internal Files

Statements and Features Not Recommended
PAUSE Statement
Assigned GOTO
Statement Function

Order of Statements

Additional Topics in Understanding and Using FORTRAN
FORTRAN Standards and Changes in the Language
Supercomputers and FORTRAN
FORTRAN Source Code Management

Summary

Answers to Self-Testing Exercises

Questions and Problems

This chapter explains elements of FORTRAN not previously described—additional data types and character string processing, additional FORMAT specifiers, some additional statements and features having relatively little use, additional instructions for subprograms, and handling of internal files. Some statements are also summarized that should be avoided because they impair clear, well-understood programming. The chapter concludes with notes on changes to FORTRAN, use in supercomputers, and source code management.

Additional Data Types

The concept of data type was presented in Chapter 2a, where the difference between integer and real types was explained and the first letter convention (I–N for integer-type data) was described. In addition to integer and real types, the character and logical types were explained. The type statements to declare INTEGER, REAL, CHARACTER, or LOGICAL were introduced and used in problems.

Two additional types of data are allowed in FORTRAN. This section will explain the added types, their representation, and the way a variable is specified as being one of these types. The additional data types are double precision and complex. These additional types are not part of subset FORTRAN.

Double-Precision Type

Precision in computing was explained in Chapter 2a. Implementations of FORTRAN differ in the precision they provide for integer and real data items. The differences are based on the architecture of the computers used plus design decisions by the developers of the translators. The precision can vary significantly between computers, with very high precision being provided by large scientific computers and supercomputers.

Double-precision real data type and double-precision intrinsic functions are provided in FORTRAN to allow the programmer to specify greater precision (approximately double) than is normally used for single-precision processing and storage. Double-precision real variables require more storage space, and double-precision processing usually takes longer, so single precision is used except where greater precision is required.

Some useful intrinsic functions for double-precision processing are the following:

Intrinsic function	Meaning
DBLE	Converts any integer, real, or real part of complex argument to double precision
SNGLE	Converts double precision to single precision (usually by truncation, but some implementations will round instead of truncate)
DPROD	Multiplies two real variables (two arguments) and returns result as double-precision type

363

Complex Type

Complex type variables and constants are required for arithmetic and operations that use complex arithmetic. Complex data items are represented by an ordered pair of real data items: one representing the real part and one the imaginary part of a complex number. A complex data constant is written as an ordered pair inside parentheses; for example, (3.5,4.1) where 3.5 is the real part and 4.1 is the imaginary part.

The intrinsic functions for complex quantities perform operations on the two parts: the real part and the imaginary part.

Intrinsic function	Meaning
CMPLX	Conversion to complex. If one argument is specified, it becomes the real part of the complex result and the imaginary part is set to zero. If two arguments are given, the second is converted to the imaginary part.
AIMAG	Result is conversion of imaginary part to a real variable.
CONJG	Result is the complex conjugate.

Type Declaration for Other Data Types

As explained earlier, integer and real data types may be defined by the first-letter convention, but that convention may be overridden by a type declaration. Character data and logical data must be declared as CHARACTER or LOGICAL in a type declaration. The additional data types (DOUBLE PRECISION and COMPLEX) may use any symbolic name (up to six characters) with any first letter. The name chosen for these data types is designated as referring to a given type by a type declaration. The type declaration must appear before the first use of any variable it defines. We recommend that it be placed in the type declaration and storage allocation block at the beginning of the program in which it is used.

> **TYPE DECLARATION FOR TYPES OTHER THAN CHARACTER**
>
> type $v_1, v_2, \ldots, v_n$
>
> where type may be
>
> INTEGER
> REAL
> DOUBLE PRECISION
> COMPLEX
> LOGICAL
>
> v_1 refers to a variable name, array name, array declarator, or function name to be defined as of the stated type.

Note that the type declaration can be used for a single variable, an array, or a function name. The array can be dimensioned as part of the type statement. Some examples illustrate these type declarations.

COMPLEX ALPHA makes ALPHA refer to a complex type variable.

DOUBLE PRECISION X,Y,Z makes X, Y, and Z the names of double-precision variables.

DOUBLE PRECISION GOOD (100) declares the array GOOD to be double precision and size 100.

The FORTRAN language has an implicit type for integer and real variables based on the first letter of the variable name (I–N for integer variables, A–H and O–Z for real variables). It is possible to alter the first-letter convention by making all variables with a given first letter a declared type. In other words, not only may the integer and real first-letter convention be altered, but first-letter typing may be defined for other types. This is done with the IMPLICIT declaration. It must appear before any other specification statements. Explicit type declaration overrides IMPLICIT.

Be careful when declaring variable names integer. It should probably not be used except for some fairly global change such as making all variables in a program of integer type.

IMPLICIT DECLARATION

IMPLICIT type $(C_1, C_2, \ldots, C_n)$

makes any variable name starting with the letter C_i of the declared type.

IMPLICIT type $(C_m - C_n)$

makes all variables names beginning with C_m to C_n (alphabetic order) of the declared type.

If type is CHARACTER, it defines a one-character length unless a length is specified as part of the IMPLICIT declaration or by individual CHARACTER declarations.

Examples
```
IMPLICIT INTEGER (A, B), REAL (L-N)
COMPLEX ABLE, BAKER
IMPLICIT CHARACTER*6 (O-R)
IMPLICIT INTEGER (A-Z)
```

The first statement defines variables with names starting with A or B as integer and variable names starting with L, M, or N as real. If the second statement follows the first in the program, variable names ABLE and BAKER refer to complex variables even though they begin with A and B, because the explicit type declaration overrides the preceding IMPLICIT declaration. The next statement defines all variable names beginning with the letters O–R as referencing character variables of a six-character length. The last statement defines all variable names to be of integer type.

Additional Intrinsic Functions for Other Data Types

There are intrinsic functions to handle arithmetic involving the double-precision and complex data types. The generic name or the specific name may be used. In general, the specific name is the same one used for real variables but with a D prefixing double-precision functions and a C prefixing complex functions (where complex functions make sense). For example, the SQRT real function is DSQRT for double precision and CSQRT for complex data types. The complete list of functions is given on the inside of the front cover.

Nonstandard Type Specifications

Because of the internal storage constraints of personal computers, some nonstandard type specifications are frequently added to personal computer FORTRAN to allow the programmer to specify the storage to be used as numbers of 8-bit bytes. The following nonstandard specifications illustrate these instructions for Microsoft FORTRAN and IBM's Personal Computer Professional FORTRAN for integer, real, and logical data.

Specification	Bytes	Represents	Comments
INTEGER * 2	2	32,768†	Saves storage
INTEGER * 4 (default)	4	2,147,483,648†	Same as INTEGER
REAL * 4 (default)	4	About 8 decimal digits†	Same as REAL
REAL * 8	8	About 16 decimal digits†	Same as double precision
REAL * n	n	Variable	Allows variable precision
LOGICAL * 1	1	True or false	Uses 1 byte instead of 4

† Up to.

Self-Testing Exercise 7-1

1. Declare variable CVAR as a complex type.

2. If CVAR is a complex variable, what does this mean in terms of storage?

3. Declare ALPHA, M, and Y as double-precision variables.

4. If ALPHA is declared as a double-precision variable, what does this mean in terms of (*a*) storage required and (*b*) precision (explain)?

5. Assuming X is defined as the type specified, write statements to store the constant value in X.

Type	Constant to be stored
(*a*) COMPLEX	Real value of 4 and imaginary value of 2.1
(*b*) DOUBLE PRECISION	91.05676500007842
(*c*) DOUBLE PRECISION	1.0

6. Take the square root of a double-precision variable DRATE. Store the result in DX.

7. Make all variables in a program real variables except INTRST, which is to be integer.

Additional Character String Instructions

It may be useful to summarize handling of character data. The string of characters is assigned a variable name. Variable names assigned to character strings do not have any special first letter. A variable name is explicitly defined as character type by a CHARACTER type declaration. The CHARACTER type declaration can be used for individual variable names, for character arrays, and for functions that are to be declared as character type. Variables declared to be CHARACTER can be any length because the length is specified by the type statement. Also, variables declared to be CHARACTER can be initialized in a DATA statement.

Defining and Manipulating a Character String or Substring

In addition to instructions for processing strings of characters stored as character variables, FORTRAN provides instructions to process substrings. A character substring is a continuous portion of a character string. It has a name and may be assigned values and referenced. The substring name is followed by the character position identification for the first and last characters to be included, separated by a colon. For example, the characters stored in positions 8 to 10 of character variable ALPHA are assigned a substring name BETA by the following:

```
BETA = ALPHA (8:10)
```

Integer expressions can also be used to specify the limits of the substring. For example,

```
BETA = ALPHA (3 * JIX:20)
```

where the beginning of the substring is the integer value of 3 * JIX and the end is 20.

Character strings or substrings can be combined by the concatenation operator //. For example, if A, B, and X are defined as character type variables of length 3, 3, and 6 and A and B contain 'NOW' and 'bIS', the statement

```
X = A//B
```

will produce a string X with the value 'NOW IS'. Note there is a space in the combined result because 'IS' is stored as a three-character variable in the form bIS (leading blank). As explained in Chapter 3a, the stored representation for strings with insufficient characters to fill the storage positions assigned for the variable are stored at the right and blank spaces fill the unused positions at the left. Character constants may be used. For example,

```
X = 'NOW'//B
```

will also yield a stored value in the character variable X of 'NOW IS'.

Intrinsic Functions for Character Data

In processing character strings, it is often necessary to find the length of a string and the position where a substring begins. Two functions are provided to locate the position and length of character data. Also, since many applications of character processing involve sorting and positioning of data, two instructions are available to identify the position in the collating sequence. The collating sequence determines the order in which character data items will be sorted (A before B, etc.).

Intrinsic function	Argument	Result
LEN (c)	Character variable name	Length of the character string stored in the character variable
INDEX (c_1,c_2)	Character variable, expression, or constant for string c_1 and substring c_2	Integer giving starting position of first occurrence of substring in string

The n characters in the processor collating sequence of the computer being used are numbered from 0 to n − 1. For example, if G is 39, R will be 50.

CHAR (ie)	Integer or integer expression	The character in the integer position of collating sequence
ICHAR (c)	A character variable containing one character	An integer identifying position in the collating sequence of the character defined by the argument

Examples

Assume (for illustration purposes) collating sequence with A = 65, B = 66, etc.

IDL = ICHAR (UNKNON) will yield a value of 71 for IDL if UNKNON stores 'G'.
IDN = CHAR (NCARA) will provide a value of 'F' if NCARA contains 70.
ISTR = INDEX (STR1, STR2) will provide a value of 3 for ISTR if STR1 contains
    AWFUL and STR2 contains FU.

The following instructions will edit a text stored in a variable ATEXT and change an occurrence of 'centre' to 'center'.

```
TOFIX = INDEX (ATEXT, 'centre')
ATEXT (TOFIX:TOFIX + 5) = 'center'
```

There are four intrinsic functions for comparing standard lexical relationships of two character strings.

Intrinsic function	Result returns value of true if
LGE (a_1,a_2)	The character string a_1 is equal to or follows a_2 in the collating sequence.
LGT (a_1,a_2)	The character string a_1 follows a_2 in the collating sequence.
LLE (a_1,a_2)	The character string a_1 is equal to or precedes a_2 in the collating sequence.
LLT (a_1,a_2)	The character string a_1 precedes a_2 in the collating sequence.

The collating sequence in all cases is defined as the ASCII, *A*merican National *S*tandard *C*ode for *I*nformation *I*nterchange, which includes a standard collating sequence. Programs using these functions will therefore produce identical results without regard to the collating sequence designed into the computer being used. As an example of the lexical intrinsic functions, assume two character strings named NAME1 and NAME2 containing JENNIFER and CLARK. The instruction

```
IF (LGT (NAME1, NAME2)) GOTO 200
```

will transfer control to statement 200 because JENNIFER follows CLARK in the standard collating sequence. The importance of the LGE, etc., functions is apparent in comparisons with special characters. Is 'AB$' less than or greater than 'ABC'? When using standard .GT., etc., functions, it depends on the collating sequence built into the computer. The Lxx comparison functions are based on an agreed-upon standard (ASCII); thus, for all compilers, the results will be that 'AB$' is less than 'ABC'.

    The ASCII collating sequence is given in Appendix B. Refer to it and note a few significant features:

Codes 000 through 031 are used for control (with some exceptions).
Codes for uppercase letters are lower in collating sequence than lowercase letters.
Non-English letters used in German, French, Scandinavian, etc., are higher in the
    collating sequence than the lowercase letters.
Graphics characters are coded from 176 to 223.
Greek letters are coded from 224 to 238.

The appendix gives the entire set of 256 ASCII codes. The printing or visual display of the characters depends on the graphics capabilities of the printer or visual display unit being used.

Self-Testing Exercise 7-2

1. Define a substring MISS (call it STR1) out of MISSISSIPPI that is stored in STATEM.

2. If I = 1, concatenate MISS in STR1 with STR2 containing OURI.

3. Compare a character variable LNAME with the constant CLARK. If equal, go to 600.

4. Define a substring ABREV as characters 1 to 3 of LNAME.

5. Concatenate the contents of ABREV and the constant 'ABC' to form a variable called CBREV.

6. Initialize a character variable FNAME with the characters AARON using DATA.

7. An 11-character field MISSISSIPPI is to be printed using a specification of A6. What will be printed?

8. Find the length in characters of a heading (HEAD) to be centered. Store it in HEADLN.

Advanced FORMAT Features

The basic FORMAT features were explained in Chapter 3. However, the additional data types explained in this chapter require special FORMAT edit descriptors. Also, there are additional FORMAT descriptors that are not commonly used, but they may be useful in special situations. It is also possible to be more flexible in FORMAT specification use by storing and referencing them as character variables or character arrays or by writing them in the input or output statement.

Additional FORMAT Edit Descriptors

Before presenting the added edit descriptors, it may be helpful to review the basic edit descriptors already explained (w = field length in characters, d = number of positions to right of decimal, n = integer constant, and h = Hollerith character).

Descriptor	Meaning
Iw	Integer input/output
Fw.d	Real input/output
Ew.d	Exponent form of real input/output
Aw	Character input/output
Lw	Logical field containing T (or .TRUE.) or F (or .FALSE.)
'h . . .'	Apostrophe form of character output
/	Terminate record
Tc	Tabulate to position c for next output or input
nX	Skip over n positions

These basic edit descriptors are all included in subset FORTRAN except for Tc. Of the additional edit descriptors, only BN, BZ, and nP are included in subset FORTRAN.

A useful alternative to F or E when data values have a wide range is:

Gw.d	Same as F editing for input. Compiler chooses E or F editing for output based on data values.

The FORMAT edit descriptors for the double-precision and complex data types are:

Data type	Descriptor	Meaning
Double precision	Dw.d	To define input or output editing for double-precision data. The output will be similar to F format, but a larger number of digits may be available for use.
Complex		Complex data (in two parts) is read by two F, E, D, or G edit descriptors.

There are also added FORMAT edit descriptors to alter the normal editing for input or output.

For Input

BN	BN specifies that blank characters (leading, embedded, and trailing blanks) are to be ignored. This is the default case in 1977 FORTRAN. However, a field of all blanks is given a zero value.
BZ	BZ specifies nonleading blank characters are interpreted as zeros. This was often the default case in earlier versions of FORTRAN.

Note: A specification of BN or BZ applies to input editing specifications that follow it in the FORMAT statement. When the use of the FORMAT statement is completed, editing by other FORMAT statements returns to the default specifications.

The two specifications may be valuable in reading data items prepared for some older FORTRAN versions that may have relied upon BZ as a default condition. The BN explicit or default specification removes the requirement in prior versions that all integer data be right-justified within an input field. More than one BZ and BN may appear in the same FORMAT statement. For example, a specification of a BZ in a FORMAT list may be followed later in the same FORMAT statement by a BN to restore the normal interpretation for the remaining editing within the statement.

As an example of BN and BZ edit specifications, assume integer data items called JCOUNT are defined as being in columns 1–5. Using three inputs to illustrate, the data will be interpreted by an I5 specification and BZ or BN as follows:

Input	Data					Interpreted by I5 and BZ as	Interpreted by I5 and BN as
1			3	7		370	37
2		1		2		1020	12
3				1	3	13	13

For Input and/or Output

nP	Scale factor. Used with F, E, D, and G fields. The scale factor is an integer constant or an integer constant signed with a minus. The scale factor of n on an input field without an exponent or on an F field for output increases the size of the number by 10^n. On input with an exponent, there is no effect; on output, the decimal point is shifted n places and the exponent adjusted accordingly so that the value is unchanged. Once the scale factor is written, it applies to all succeeding real field descriptors in the FORMAT statement. If normal scaling is to be reinstated, a zero scale factor is written.

	The scale factor is most commonly used with an E field to shift the decimal point in the output. For example, if E17.8 causes an answer to be printed out as 0.34769334E +05, then 2PE17.8 will cause an output of 34.76933425E + 03.
TLc	The next character is input or output c positions backward from (to the left of) the current position. Essentially, this is a backward positioning.
TRc	The next character is input or output c positions forward (to the right) from the current position—a forward positioning.
Ew.dEc	Used for an exponent form in which the exponent may be more than three digits. The c represents an integer that specifies the number of digits in the exponent. For example, a FORMAT of E22.12E5 allows a 12-digit fraction and a 5-digit exponent. An edited output might be $-0.371945673256E + 19050$.
:(colon)	Terminates format control if there are no more items in the input/output list.

For Output

SP	Print + for positive data for all subsequent data.
SS	Do not print + for positive data (the most common default conditions).
S	Restore + convention used by compiler.
Iw.m	m defines minimum number of digits for integer output. Leading zeros may be necessary. For example, at least a three-digit output may be desired even if result is less than three digits. The specification I5.3, if data item is 7456, will print as 7456; but if data item is 2, it will print three digits or 002.

FORMAT Specifications in Input/Output Statement or Character Storage

The FORMAT specification is normally included in a separate FORMAT statement, but 1977 full FORTRAN allows the FORMAT specification to be placed in a READ or WRITE statement. This can be done in two ways:

1. A character constant containing the characters in the FORMAT specifications is used in a READ or WRITE statement in place of the FORMAT statement label reference.
2. A character string describing the FORMAT specifications is stored as a character variable or a character array. The name of the character string is placed in a WRITE or READ statement in place of the FORMAT statement label reference.

In the character constant approach, the FORMAT specifications (including the parentheses) that normally follow the word FORMAT in a FORMAT statement are placed in a READ or WRITE statement in place of the FORMAT statement reference. This means that the character constant can follow the input/output unit specification without using FMT =, or it can appear elsewhere in the list of specifications by using FMT = constant. The following are equivalent:

```
      WRITE (6, 700)A, B, C
700 FORMAT (3F10.2)

      WRITE (6, '(3F10.2)')A, B, C
      WRITE (6, FMT = '(3F10.2)')A, B, C
```

If character output is to be included in the format constant, each part of the specification before and after the characters must be enclosed by apostrophes.

```
WRITE (6, '(' 'ANSWERS' ' 3F10.2)')A, B, C
```

In some situations, it is useful to use the second method and store format specifications in a character variable or character array. This allows the program to alter the format specifications themselves as a function of program computations. As an example, suppose the array IFORM contains the following character string (including the parentheses)

```
('1', T9,6F7.2)
```

and each character is stored in a separate cell in IFORM, that is, IFORM(6) = T and IFORM(14) =). It would then be possible to do the following:

```
IF  (LINE .EQ.1) THEN
    IFORM (3) = '1'
ELSE
    IFORM (3) = '0'
ENDIF
WRITE (6, IFORM) list
```

IFORM would be used as the format specification, and if LINE (a counter) equals 1, the page would be set to the top before printing by the '1' in the format. Otherwise, double spacing would occur since IFORM would contain

```
('0',T9,6F7.2)
```

Variable horizontal positioning could be achieved by altering IFORM(7), which is the digit following T.

Self-Testing Exercise 7-3

1. Write FORMAT statements to print the variables X, Y, Z under each of the following specifications:
   (a) Make output as normal decimal form or as exponent form, depending on the size of output (eight significant digits).
   (b) The variable X is complex-type data (field size of 12 with 6 fractional digits for each part of X); field size of 10 with 2 fractional digits for Y and Z.
   (c) The output of Y is double precision (16 significant digits).
   (d) The output of Z is a logical field (field size of 5).
   (e) The plus sign is to be printed for X (field size of 10 with 2 fractional digits) but not for output of Y or Z.

2. Write FORMAT statements for input of A and B when blank characters should be treated as zeros.

3. Print the value for X but make it exponent form with an exponent that can be six digits.

4. Summarize the edit descriptors that are included in subset FORTRAN (and therefore will be generally available on all sizes of computers). Make a separate list of specifiers included only in full FORTRAN.

5. Define an 80-character array called FARRAY that will be used to hold a FORMAT specification. Write an output statement to write X and Y using FORMAT specification in FARRAY.

6. Write the following READ and FORMAT statements as one statement.

```
READ (5, 100)X,Y,J
    100 FORMAT (2F10.0, I6)
```

Additional Statements and Features

There are a number of additional, useful features that will be described in this section.

PARAMETER Statement

The PARAMETER statement is used in full 1977 FORTRAN to give a constant a symbolic name. The form of the PARAMETER statement and an example are

PARAMETER (name = constant, . . .)

PARAMETER(FIVE=5.0,RATE=4.3,HEADING='PAYROLL REPORT')

The constant name and its value must be of the same type. The constant name can be used in any statement to refer to the constant, for example, IF (X.GT.FIVE). . . . But the value of the name cannot be altered by an assignment statement; that is, a symbolic constant name cannot appear to the left of the equals sign. The statement FIVE = FIVE + 1.0 is not allowed. This statement may be useful in defining a constant such as π that may appear in several formulas and should not be altered. It cannot be used in array bounds.

Constant Expression in Dimensions

A dimension feature of full 1977 FORTRAN allows integer constant expressions (expressions using constants and +, −, *, and operators) and also exponentiation in dimensions. For example, 5 + 30 and 10* *2 are allowed as dimensions.

Logical Equivalence or Nonequivalence

Two additional logical operators are available in 1977 FORTRAN:

.EQV.   Logical equivalence (expression is true if both expressions connected by .EQV. have same truth value—both are true or both are false)
.NEQV.   Logical nonequivalence (opposite of .EQV.)

The precedence of EQV and NEQV is the lowest logical operator (performed last). For example,

```
IF (A .GT. B .EQV. C .LT. D) GOTO 301
or  IF ((A.GT.B) .EQV. (C.LT.D)) GOTO 301
```

In this example, for the IF to be true so that control goes to statement 301, the variable A must be greater than B and C must be less than D (both comparisons are true) or A is not greater than B and C is less than D (both comparisons are false).

Main PROGRAM Statement

FORTRAN does not need or require a main program to have a name, but it does allow it. Some operating systems make use of the name, so that it may be required by some computer centers. In fact, many compilers will assign a name such as MAIN to an unnamed routine. Explicit naming is performed by a PROGRAM statement, which is the first statement of the main program. It consists of the word PROGRAM followed by the symbolic name. For example, a program to be called DAVIS will use the statement PROGRAM DAVIS.

Self-Testing Exercise 7-4

1. Write a statement to define SIXTY as always referring to the constant 60.0.

2. A statement in a FORTRAN program reads:

```
IF (A .EQ. 100.0 .EQV. A .EQ. 1.0) GOTO 301
```

For what values of A will the program transfer to statement 301?

Additional Subprogram Features

As explained in Chapter 5, subprograms are a useful and versatile feature of FORTRAN. The fundamental features of subprograms were presented in that chapter; this section describes additional features. In general, these features receive less use than the basic features described in Chapter 5.

SAVE Variables for Subprograms

It was noted in Chapter 5 that variables in a subprogram that are not in blank COMMON or in the argument list are lost when control is returned to the calling program. It is possible to save all data from the subprogram by the SAVE statement.

SAVE STATEMENT	
SAVE	Save all variables in the subprogram
SAVE variable or array names or named COMMON block name (written within slashes)	Save named items, for example: SAVE X, Y,/NBLOCK/
The SAVE statement is placed in the subprogram as the last statement in the type declaration and storage allocation block.	

Alternate Entry to Subprogram and Alternate Return Points for the Calling Program

The ENTRY statement (in full FORTRAN but not subset) allows a call to a function subprogram or subroutine subprogram to begin at a point other than the beginning.

In essence, ENTRY defines a subprogram within a subprogram. There may be more than one such entry point in a subprogram. At each alternate entry point, the statement is written as ENTRY *en* or ENTRY *en* (dummy argument list), where *en* is the name assigned to the entry point. The call to the alternate entry point uses the name (and appropriate argument list) for the entry point. Program execution begins at the entry and proceeds until a RETURN or END statement is encountered.

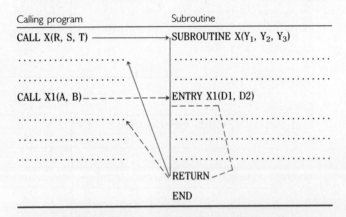

In Chapter 5, the subroutine return was always to the statement following the CALL statement. In 1977 full FORTRAN, alternate return points in the calling program can be programmed. The statement labels in the calling program which represent alternate return points are coded in the argument list of the CALL statement, each statement number being preceded by an asterisk. For example,

```
CALL SUBX (X, Y, *101, *210, *215)
```

This statement specifies that the return for RETURN 1 in the subroutine is statement 101, the return point for RETURN 2 is 210, and the return point for RETURN 3 is statement 215. Note that the RETURN statements in the subroutine that are to be associated with the alternate returns must be assigned a number, with RETURN 1 associated with the first return point in the calling list, etc. If a RETURN statement is not numbered, the alternate return points do not apply, and return is to the statement following the CALL statement. (See example on page 376.)

The subroutine is written so that the numbered RETURN statements will be executed only if the return is to be to the alternate return associated with that statement. This approach might be useful for cases in which the results of processing by the subroutine should be followed by alternate calling program processing. In general, however, it is considered better programming practice to have one exit and one return point for a subroutine and to make the selection of alternate processing in the calling program based on data values that are passed via the parameter list.

Variable Dimensions

DIMENSION has been previously defined as requiring an integer constant or integer constant expression to define the maximum dimension requirements of an array. The main program must always completely specify the size of its array in order for storage to be allocated. However, a subprogram using the same array as the main program does not cause extra storage to be allocated, and thus subprogram array specifications can be variable and depend on the array defined by the main program. The array

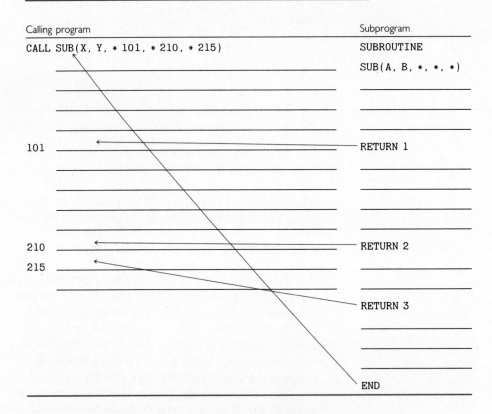

specifications in the subprogram (for an array that is defined by the main program) define a dummy array. The dummy array in the subprogram and the array in the main program are associated when the subprogram is called by the main program. In previous chapters, the size of the dummy array in the subprogram and the size of the array in the main program have been assumed to be the same. But what if they are not? Suppose the subprogram array is size 100 and the other is size 50? This can be handled by making the dummy array equal to the maximum size and sending the actual size to the subprogram as an argument in the calling statement. This works only for one-dimensional arrays. Another approach that works with all arrays is the use of variable dimensions within the array specifications in the subprograms.

There are two forms of variable dimensions in subprograms:

1. *Assumed size array*   The array size (or upper boundary if lower and upper boundary are used) is specified by an asterisk. This means that the subprogram

array will be defined at execution as equal in size to the calling program array. If the calling statement contains an array name with a subscript (instead of simply the array name), this is interpreted as defining the subprogram array as the size of the remaining part of the calling array.

2. *Adjustable array* The array size is specified by an integer variable. The variable must be given a value before subprogram execution by including a value in the calling arguments.

These methods allow subprograms to be more general and to be specified fully at execution. The following examples illustrate the features.

1. Assumed size array declarations in subprograms:

```
DIMENSION A ( * )
DIMENSION BETA ( 10 , * )
```

The dimension of the array A and the second dimension of the matrix BETA will be defined as equal to the array size in the calling program.

2. Adjustable array declarations in subprograms:

Subprogram
```
SUBROUTINE SAMP ( I , XDATA )
DIMENSION XDATA ( I )
```

Main program
```
DIMENSION ZDATA ( 100 )
CALL SAMP ( 100 , ZDATA )
```

where ZDATA will be equated to XDATA and XDATA will be specified as size 100 during execution.

Subprogram and Intrinsic Function Names in an Argument List

There may be programs in which an intrinsic function name, an external function name (that is, the name of function subprogram that is not intrinsic), or a subroutine needs to be used in an actual argument list of a function or subroutine call. The difficulty is that because of their similar form, the compiler cannot distinguish between variable names and functions or subroutine names. In order to specify that an intrinsic function name in an actual argument list is to be interpreted as the name of an intrinsic function, the program must contain an INTRINSIC statement. An EXTERNAL statement is used in the same way for names of external procedures (functions or subroutines). The form is the word INTRINSIC or EXTERNAL followed by the name to be declared. As an example, a CALL statement may wish to specify which function (SIN or COS) the subroutine is to use (in place of a function called TRIG). The name SIN or COS is therefore part of the actual argument list. This requires an INTRINSIC statement in the main program to declare SIN and COS as intrinsic function names.

Self-Testing Exercise 7-5

1. Write a subroutine subprogram called XD0 having dummy variables X, Y, and I (with values of 0, 1, 2) with entry points at XD01 and XD02. Provide for alternate returns

following XD01 and XD02. Code assignment statements for XD0, XD01, and XD02, setting X = Y* *2 + 1.0 for XD0, X = Y**2 + 2.0 for XD01, and X = Y**2 + 3.0 for XD02. Based on the value of 1, a call to XD0 will execute the first, second, or third of these statement (value of I is 0 for first, 1 for second, and 2 for third).

2. Code a call to XD0 with alternate return to 150 and 160 and actual variables A, B, and J.

3. Code a call to XD01 with actual variables A and B.

4. Save variables A, B, and J used locally in subroutine XD0NE.

5. Write subroutine statements for an array ABX with variable dimension JIX. Show the main program statements required (array X in actual argument). Transfer dimension through common storage.

Internal Files

There are instances in which records need to be read before the format and other characteristics are known. FORTRAN facilitates this process by providing a method for storing the data and examining it as though it were being read from an external file. This capability is provided through internal files. These are not really files in the sense of the external files discussed in Chapter 6; rather, these are character variables or arrays that are "written" to or "read" from with formatted WRITE or READ statements using a character variable name as unit specifier.

As an example of creating an internal file, consider a program segment:

```
INTEGER A, B
CHARACTER*12 C
A = 17
B = 269
WRITE (UNIT = C, FMT = 15)A, B
15 FORMAT (2I5)
```

Instead of writing to an input or output device, the statement writes to the character variable C. After executing this code, the 12 character positions of variable C contain

bbb17bb269bb

where b stands for blank. Note that UNIT = and FMT = are optional in the WRITE statement. What has been accomplished is the conversion of the number 17 stored in A to the characters 1 and 7 in C. Using a field of five positions (based on a FORMAT of I5), the values are right-adjusted and blanks are filled within each field. Any undefined characters in C (the two rightmost positions in the example) are filled with blanks.

As a visual aid, the character variable or array sometimes can be thought of as a line or set of lines that are being printed (WRITE) or input (READ). The external file statements OPEN, CLOSE, and INQUIRE are not allowed for internal files. After each READ or WRITE, the internal file is repositioned at its first location, and thus REWIND, BACKSPACE, and ENDFILE are also prohibited. In addition, list-directed I/O is forbidden.

As an example of the way internal files may be used, consider a problem in which an external file consists of sets or blocks of 72-character records. Each block consists of a header record followed by a variable number of detail records. As each READ is performed, there is no way to know in advance whether the record being read is a header or detail type. Assume that the header record contains a zero in position 1 and the rest of the record is alphabetic (for example, department names), while detail records contain a 1 in position 1 and mixed numeric or alphabetic data in the balance of the record (for example, employee numbers, names, hours worked). Since a different format is needed to read these different types of records, there is a problem: Until the record has been read, there is no way to know which format to use to read it. To solve this, define an internal file and read each record into it as characters. After reading a record into the internal file, test the first position for record type and then read from the internal file into the appropriate variable location as follows:

```
      INTEGER EMPNO
      CHARACTER COL1 * 1, BUFF * 71, DEPTNM * 15, EMPNM * 20
      READ (5, 16, END = 101, ERR = 901) COL1, BUFF
   16 FORMAT (A1, A)
      IF (COL1 .EQ. '1') THEN
          READ (UNIT = BUFF, FMT = 17, END = 801, ERR = 904)
     +         DEPTNM
      ELSE
          READ (UNIT = BUFF, FMT = 18, END = 803, ERR = 909)
     1    EMPNM, EMPNO, HRSWK
      ENDIF
      CONTINUE
   17 FORMAT (8X, A15)
   18 FORMAT (A20, I5, F4.1)
```

Another illustration of an application for internal files is to print out a real array with blanks in all locations having missing or zero values. Use of an F or G conversion will cause zeros to appear in the printout. To overcome this, an internal file can be created as a character array and blanks inserted whenever data characters are missing. This example illustrates the way in which the character array is treated as both an internal file and a normal character array. A simple program and its output are shown in Figure 7-1.

Statements and Features Not Recommended

There are some FORTRAN features that are part of the language, but experience has shown them to be error-prone or inconsistent with a disciplined, clear programming style. The arithmetic IF [IF (condition) s_1, s_2, s_3] was explained in Chapter 2 with the recommendation that it not be used. Other features that generally should be avoided are the PAUSE statement, the assigned GOTO, and the statement function.

PAUSE Statement

The PAUSE and PAUSE n statements are the same as the STOP and STOP n statements in that they cause the program to halt. In the case of PAUSE or PAUSE n, the halt is to

Figure 7-1 Simple program and its output to illustrate internal files.

```
 1  **********
 2  *                      PROGRAM IDENTIFICATION
 3  **********
 4  *
 5  *         Illustration of the use of internal files
 6  *         Written by T. Hoffmann 02/08/82 rev. 4/17/87
 7  *
 8  **********
 9  *                      VARIABLE IDENTIFICATION
10  **********
11  *
12  *         MATRIX  - Array containing missing values
13  *         ROW     - Row of character values
14  *
15  **********
16  *                      TYPE DECLARATION AND STORAGE BLOCK
17  **********
18  *
19        REAL MATRIX(3,3)
20        CHARACTER*10 ROW(3)
21  *
22  **********
23  * BLOCK 0000           INITIALIZE REAL ARRAY
24  **********
25  *
26        DO 4 I=1,3
27           DO 3 J=1,3
28              MATRIX(I,J)=0.0
29     3        CONTINUE
30     4     CONTINUE
31        MATRIX(1,1) = 7.57
32        MATRIX(1,3) = 12.23
33        MATRIX(2,2) = 17.74
34        MATRIX(3,1) = 10.98
35        MATRIX(3,2) = 0.67
36  *
37  **********
38  * BLOCK 0100           CONVERT REAL ARRAY TO CHARACTER ARRAY
39  **********
40  *
41        DO 119 I = 1,3
42           WRITE(UNIT=ROW,FMT=110) (MATRIX(I,J),J=1,3)
43    110     FORMAT(F10.2)
44  *
45  *   SET ZEROS (MISSING DATA) IN REAL TO BLANKS IN CHARACTER ARRAY
46  *
47           DO 115 J = 1,3
48              IF(MATRIX(I,J) .LE. 0.0) ROW(J) = ' '
49    115     CONTINUE
50           WRITE(6,118) (ROW(J),J=1,3)
51    118     FORMAT(3A10)
52    119 CONTINUE
53  *
54  **********
55  * BLOCK 0200           NORMAL TERMINATION BLOCK
56  **********
57  *
58        STOP
59        END
```

OUTPUT

```
      7.57              12.23
                 17.74
     10.98        .67
```

be temporary; pressing RUN on the computer console or ENTER on a terminal or PC allows the program to continue. PAUSE was useful in computing situations where results at a given point were to be examined before proceeding with the program. It is generally inconsistent with present mainframe computer center operations and will usually be treated the same as a STOP. It may still be useful for personal computer FORTRAN programs.

Assigned GOTO

Since the assigned GOTO is part of the language, it will be explained, but good programming practice suggests that it should not be used. The reason for advising against its use is that it makes the logic of a program difficult to follow. The assigned GOTO feature is essentially a variable GOTO. There are two statements: the ASSIGN and the assigned GOTO. The ASSIGN statement assigns an integer statement label to an integer variable.

ASSIGN s TO i

where s = a statement label
 i = an integer variable

Example

```
ASSIGN 23 TO KIX
```

The assigned GOTO list contains statement labels to which the program may go and specifies the variable that contains the value for the transfer of control. Both ASSIGN and GOTO must be in the same program unit.

GOTO i $(s_1, s_2, \ldots, s_n)$

where s_i = statement labels to which control may transfer; list is optional
 i = integer variable containing the value of one of the statement labels to which control is to be transferred

As an example, suppose that the program might transfer to statements 13, 21, or 45 and that a variable KIX would specify which of these statements would be used. Then the pair of statements to transfer control to 21 would be

```
ASSIGN 21 TO KIX
GOTO KIX (13, 21, 45)
```

The ASSIGN statement can also be used to assign a FORMAT statement label to an integer variable, which is used as the format reference in an input or output statement. For example, if there are three possible FORMAT statements labeled with statement numbers 360, 370, and 380 that can be selected by an output statement, the selection of 370 can be programmed by the ASSIGN statement as follows:

```
ASSIGN 370 TO IFMAT
WRITE (6, IFMAT)A, B, JIX
```

Statement Function

If the same one-statement computation appears several times in a program, FORTRAN allows a statement function to be defined in the program itself instead of using a separate function subprogram. The statement function is used in a program in the same manner as an intrinsic function. The statement function is defined by writing a statement in which the name chosen for the function is set equal to an expression that uses the dummy variables in it. The list of dummy arguments are separated by commas and enclosed in parentheses. The name is formed in the same way as a variable name (begins with I–N for integer, etc.). This statement only defines the function; it is not executed. The definition statement must precede its first use as a function.

In order to use the function that has been defined, the name of the function is written in an expression with the actual variable names to be employed written in place of the dummy variables. The actual variables are listed in the same order and have the same type as the dummy variables. The program will make the computation defined by the function using the values of the actual variables in the argument list. The resulting value will be put into the statement being executed as the value of the function. For example:

Defining statement: `DESCF (B, A, C) = (B**2 - 4.0 * A * C)`
Using the function: `X = BETA + DESCF (ALPHA, Y, Z)`

The effect of the function is the insertion of the function into the statement using the calling variables in place of the dummy variables. In the example, this means that the statement to be executed will perform the following computation:

```
X = BETA + (ALPHA**2 - 4.0 * Y * Z)
```

If it is appropriate to use this feature, confusion can be avoided by placing the statement function definition in a separate block preceding any executable statements.

Order of Statements

The order of program statements is as follows:

1. PROGRAM (if used), FUNCTION, SUBROUTINE, or BLOCK DATA (In the block structure style in the text, this statement is the first in the program preceding the identification block.)
2. IMPLICIT
3. Type statements
4. PARAMETER
5. Other specifications (DIMENSION, COMMON, EQUIVALENCE, EXTERNAL, INTRINSIC)
6. DATA

In the type declaration and storage allocation block

7. Statement function definition statement (if used, place in separate block)
8. Executable statements

Comments may appear anywhere in the program. FORMAT statements may appear anywhere after the first group of statements listed above (PROGRAM, FUNCTION, etc.), but as a matter of style, we have chosen to place them immediately after the first input or output statement in which they are used.

Additional Topics in Understanding and Using FORTRAN

Three additional topics are included to enhance understanding and effective use of FORTRAN. The first two provide added background for programming in FORTRAN—the continuing work on FORTRAN standards and the use of FORTRAN as the language of choice in supercomputers. The third topic on FORTRAN source code management describes how the source code for very large FORTRAN programs can be managed using a combination of FORTRAN features and system utilities.

FORTRAN Standards and Changes in the Language

One of the advantages of FORTRAN as a programming language is that there is a widely accepted standard version, FORTRAN 77. This makes FORTRAN programs very portable; a user can be confident that a FORTRAN program written in standard FORTRAN 77 can be compiled and executed on another computer with another FORTRAN 77 compiler and the results will be the same. If there are differences, they will be understood and explainable (such as those due to different precision explained earlier in the chapter). This is one reason the text has emphasized adherence to the standards and the avoidance of nonstandard features that may be offered.

There are situations, however, when nonstandard features may be very useful. Programmers may wish to use them but should include notes in the documentation so that each nonstandard feature can be identified if the program is to be moved to a compiler that does not accept the feature. Another useful consequence of nonstandard features is that their successful use may suggest enhancements for the standard language.

The general rules for American National Standards is that they are voluntary and periodically are to be reviewed and revised. Therefore, FORTRAN will not remain the same; there will be a new revised standard. On the basis of past standards, the revision will add useful features and drop some little used or error-prone features. There will be an effort to avoid major incompatibility of the new and old standard versions.

In 1987, there was a standards committee recommendation for a minor revision of FORTRAN. The proposals were mainly for the addition of array-processing instructions, abstract specification of number representation, derived data types, and modular definitions. These would be useful enhancements to the language.

The array processing would provide instructions to perform arithmetic functions on arrays such as multiplying one matrix by another.

The abstract specification of number representation would leave the decision on single or double precision to the compiler.

The derived data types would prevent improper use of data items, such as adding data items that should not be summed.

Modular definitions would allow a programmer to link the common elements of subroutines or other objects.

Should these recommendations be adopted, they will not affect anything presented in the text; rather they will be added features. Even if adopted, the new features will not be available for some time. On the other hand, the recommendations for changes in FORTRAN 77 may not be adopted as proposed. Some industry representatives are concerned that the language will become too large for microcomputers, while others desire more features not included.

Supercomputers and FORTRAN

The supercomputers are interesting with respect to FORTRAN because it is the primary language for programming problems for them, and they present unique problems in writing FORTRAN that use their capabilities.

"Supercomputer" is an imprecise term but refers to the very fast computers used primarily in engineering and scientific computation. They are used for weather forecasting, oil exploration analysis, analysis of intelligence data, design of physical equipment such as power plants, etc.

Supercomputer computing can be divided into two broad categories based on how the computer is designed to work: vector machines and parallel machines.

Vector machines are designed for efficient array processing. One machine-language instruction will add (multiply, etc.) one array to a second array and store the result in a third array. In a standard computer, this would require 5 to 10 instructions. The addition of array-processing instructions to standard FORTRAN would make more effective use of this capability.

Parallel machines have a number of individual processing units which work on different parts of the program simultaneously (in parallel). Rather than waiting to perform an operation until the preceding operation is complete, the two can be performed at the same time. There are a number of situations in large computational jobs in which significant improvement in processing time can be achieved by parallel processing. Instructions might be added to standard FORTRAN to specify subroutines that can be performed in parallel.

The FORTRAN compilers for the supercomputers often attempt to take advantage of the capabilities of the supercomputer design by analyzing the program for array-processing and parallel-processing opportunities. In many cases, however, the programmer writing FORTRAN for a supercomputer will need to assist the compiler to assemble an efficient program by providing appropriate specifications. The supercomputer vendors provide manuals to assist in writing FORTRAN that will be efficiently processed.

FORTRAN Source Code Management

Large FORTRAN programs often exceed 10,000 source statements and contain many subroutines and function subprograms. Programs of this magnitude are usually written by a number of programmers. Also, a program may be only a small part of a larger set of interrelated programs that share common data structures and/or file definitions. The management of a project with a number of programmers is improved through the use of FORTRAN source code management techniques. This section will explain how some FORTRAN features can be combined with system utilities to manage large programs.

A program library is a collection of programs, subroutines, functions, and reusable code modules that are logically related and can be combined. A program for execution is composed of a subset of the members of the library. Several different programs may share code modules from the library.

As an example to illustrate the concept of source code management, assume a program library contains the following five parts: two programs, two subroutines, and one reusable module (a COMMON block).

```
PROGRAM ONE
PROGRAM TWO
SUBROUTINE GETINP
SUBROUTINE CHKINP
COMMON /IDATA/ . . .
```

Assume also that PROGRAM ONE and PROGRAM TWO use the two subroutines to read input data and to do input validation. The two subroutines in turn make use of the same common block to hold the input data.

To illustrate common practice in source code management, the following instructions might make use of the source code described above. It uses a format that is available on several source code management systems; different systems will use alternative statements for including code modules, but the principle is the same. In the code, the *CALL statement instructs the source code management system to insert the named source code module at that point. Note that the common block COMMON /IDATA/ . . ., must be inserted in the main program (PROGRAM ONE), while the two subroutines are added at the end of the main program.

```
      PROGRAM ONE
*CALL IDATA
*
*         The *CALL statement tells the source code
*         management utility to get the library module
*         IDATA and insert it at this point.
*
*         Use subroutine to read data.
*
          CALL GETINP
*
*         See if input is valid using subroutine.
*
          CALL CHKINP
*
*         Compute results with unique routine not part of
*            library.
*
          CALL COMPUT
          STOP
          END
*CALL GETINP
*CALL CHKINP
```

The output from these instructions to the source program utility will be a valid FORTRAN source program with the common block inserted and the two subroutines added to the program. The value of this can be seen in the fact that PROGRAM TWO can be written to make use of the same modules (except for a unique computation module). If we eliminate the comment lines, the specifications for preparing the second program will be as follows:

```
    PROGRAM TWO
*CALL IDATA
    CALL GETINP
    CALL CHKINP
    CALL TWOCOD (unique computation routine for PROGRAM
        TWO)
    STOP
    END
*CALL GETINP
*CALL CHKINP
```

There are several advantages. Different modules can be assigned to different programmers. The modules that are used by more than one program can be written and debugged carefully once; thereafter, they can be used with confidence and do not need extensive testing. Isolating functions into modules, which are assembled into programs makes it possible to perform any maintenance that affects several programs on the single module, and the programs can then be reassembled and compiled.

Summary

Items explained in the chapter include additional data types, character string processing, and advanced format features. Also summarized but not explained in detail were advanced features and features of limited use.

Two additional data types—complex and double precision—were explained. The type statement is used to declare explicitly variables of these types. The first-letter conventions for integer and real can be changed by an IMPLICIT statement.

Useful features for manipulation of character strings were explained. Putting together or concatenation of character strings is performed with a concatenation operator. Strings can also be compared.

A number of additional format edit descriptors were presented in the chapter. In addition, a method in FORTRAN for referencing the list of format descriptors stored as character data was explained. This stored character data reference approach allows flexible formatting and input of format editing lists as variable data.

Additional statements and features presented were the PARAMETER statement for naming a constant, logical equivalence, and the main PROGRAM statement.

Some additional features for subprograms were summarized. These provide for saving of subprogram variables, using intrinsic function and external procedure names in an actual argument list, alternate entry to subprograms, alternate return points, and variable dimensions for a subprogram.

There are situations in which it is desirable to be able to read data into an internal file or buffer for examination or processing and to read from the buffer using formatting based on the data. This is performed by internal file procedures.

The PAUSE, assigned GOTO, and the statement functions were explained. Since these are error-prone, they generally should not be used.

Three additional topics were discussed in order to enhance understanding and effective use of FORTRAN. They were FORTRAN standards, FORTRAN and supercomputers, and FORTRAN source code management.

Answers to Self-Testing Exercises

Exercise 7-1

1. COMPLEX CVAR

2. It requires twice as much storage because each complex variable has two parts.

3. DOUBLE PRECISION ALPHA, M, Y

4. The computer uses a double storage area for a double-precision variable. The precision is the number of significant digits that are represented; for double-precision variables, this is approximately double the precision of a single-precision variable.

5. (a) X = (4.0, 2.1)
   (b) X = 91.05676500007842D+00 or
       X = 9.105676500007842D+01
   (c) X = 1.0D+00

6. DX = DSQRT (DRATE)

7. IMPLICIT REAL (A—Z)
   INTEGER INTRST
   Explicit typing overrides the implicit typing.

Exercise 7-2

1. TEMP = INDEX (STATEM, 'MISS')
   STR1 = STATEM (TEMP:TEMP + 4)

2. IF (I .EQ. 1) X = STR1//STR2

3. IF (LNAME .EQ. 'CLARK') GOTO 600

4. ABREV = LNAME (1:3)

5. CBREV = ABREV//'ABC'

6. DATA FNAME /'AARON'/

7. MISSIS

8. HEADLN = LEN (HEAD)

Exercise 7-3

1. (a) FORMAT (3G16.8)
   (b) FORMAT (2F12.6, 2F10.2)
       (The complex data item requires two FORMAT specifications for the real and imaginary parts.)
   (c) FORMAT (F10.2, D23.16, F10.2)
   (d) FORMAT (2F10.2, L5)
   (e) FORMAT (SPF10.2, S2F10.2)

2. FORMAT (BZ, F10.2, F10.2, BN). BN is used to restore the blanks convention explicitly.

3. FORMAT (E19.8E6)

4. See the list of 1977 ANS standard FORTRAN statements (following the index).

In subset FORTRAN	Only in full FORTRAN
Iw	Tc
Fw.d	Gw.d
Ew.d	Dw.d
Aw	Complex
'h . . .'	TLc
nHh . . .	TRc
/	Ew.dEe
nX	Gw.dEe
Lw	SP
BN	SS
BZ	S
nP	Iw.m

5.
```
CHARACTER FARRAY (80)
WRITE (6, FARRAY)X, Y
```

6.
```
READ (5, FMT = '(2F10.0, I6)')X, Y,J
```

Exercise 7-4

1.
```
PARAMETER (SIXTY = 60.0)
```

2. Both expression can never be true. If A = 100, it cannot also equal 1.0. However, both expressions can be false and control goes to 301. Thus, control goes to 301 as long as A is neither 100 nor 1.0.

Exercise 7-5

1.
```
      SUBROUTINE XD0 (X, Y, I, *, *)
      GOTO (50, 100, 200), I + 1
      GOTO 250
50    X = Y**2 + 1.0
      RETURN
      ENTRY XD01 (X, Y)
100   X = Y**2 + 2.0
      RETURN 1
      ENTRY XD02 (X, Y)
200   X = Y**2 + 3.0
      RETURN 2
250   PRINT *, 'ERROR WITH I', I
      END
```

2.
```
CALL XD0 (A, B, J, * 150, * 160)
```

3.
```
CALL XD01 (A, B)
```

4.
```
SAVE A, B, J
```

```
5.  SUBROUTINE EXAMPL (ABX)
    COMMON JIX
    DIMENSION ABX (JIX)
    _____

    _____
    Main program
    _____

    COMMON JIX
    JIX = . . .
    CALL EXAMPL (X)
```

Questions and Problems

1. The programmer got confused. To fix the program, declare all integer variables in a program to be real and all real variables to be integer.

2. Code declaration and input/output to:
   (a) Read a double-precision variable and print it.
   (b) Read a complex variable and print it.

3. Write a program segment to define the day names, SUNDAY, etc., for the first week in October 1988 and to compare a character input data item (say MONDAY) to find out which day it is.

4. Write FORMAT statements to read and/or write to produce stated results.

Data on input	Output
(a) 45 13	45.13
(b) 0.1765E.15	17.65E. + 13
(c) 347.0	+347.
(d) 78	0078
(e) .TRUE.	T

5. Explain the usefulness of
   (a) PARAMETER
   (b) PROGRAM
   (c) IMPLICIT
   (d) Logical equivalence
   (e) Alternate entry for subprograms and return for subroutines
   (f) SAVE statement
   (g) ASSIGN statement (with FORMAT statements)

Example Programs and Programming Exercises Using Additional Features

General Program Example 7— Manhattan Island
Problem Description for General Example 7
Program Documentation for General Example 7
Notes on General Example 7

Mathematical Program Example 7— Simulation of Sales, Supply, and Inventory of Perishable Product
Problem Description for Mathematical Example 7
Program Documentation for Mathematical Example 7
Notes on Mathematical Example 7

Programming Exercises
Description of Assignment
Mathematics and Statistics
Business and Economics
Science and Engineering
Humanities and Social Sciences
General
Interactive Scientific and Engineering

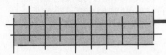

The example programs illustrate the use of some of the additional data types and other FORTRAN features which may sometimes be useful or necessary.

General Program Example 7—Manhattan Island

This program uses double-precision computations in order to accurately find the value of an amount of money compounded over a long period of time. Depending upon the computer on which it is run, this may make a noticeable difference in the accuracy of the result.

Problem Description for General Example 7

The program is to compute the amount to which the original $24 paid for Manhattan Island in 1626 would have grown by a given year, assuming various interest rates. It is to compare the results obtained by both single- and double-precision computations. Input consists of a year and an interest rate.

Program Documentation for General Example 7

Full documentation is not given because of the simple nature of the program. The program listing is given in Figure 7-2. The sample input data has not been shown because it is printed as part of the output listing (Figure 7-3).

Notes on General Example 7

The program provides a comparison of the precision achieved by a commercial computer and a supercomputer, both for single precision and double precision. There are several interesting features illustrated in this simple program:

1. All variables are explicitly typed, as explained earlier. The explicit typing specifies the variable as REAL, INTEGER, or DOUBLE PRECISION (lines 29–31).
2. The intrinsic function DBLE is used in line 39 to obtain a double-precision equivalent of a single-precision variable.
3. Double-precision constants are used (line 59). Note that 0.4D + 1 is equivalent to 4.0D + 0; either can be used.
4. The exponent on line 59 need not be double precision to achieve a double-precision result.
5. The format edit descriptor P is used in the second and third lines of the FORMAT statement to print the decimal fraction percentage in the common format of a number greater than 1. The 2P is used to modify the F5.1 edit descriptor. In order

Figure 7-2 Program listing for general program example 7—Manhattan Island.

```
  1  **********
  2  *                      PROGRAM IDENTIFICATION
  3  **********
  4  *
  5  *         Manhattan island program calculates the amount to which
  6  *         the $24.00 invested in 1626 to purchase Manhattan Island
  7  *         would have grown by a given year, assuming some interest
  8  *         rate and compounding quarterly.
  9  *         Both single and double precision computations are made.
 10  *         Written by T. Hoffmann 08/08/1977 rev. 6/01/87
 11  *
 12  **********
 13  *                      VARIABLE IDENTIFICATION
 14  **********
 15  *
 16  *         YEAR    - Year to which to compound
 17  *         IRATE   - Interest rate
 18  *         DIRATE  - Interest rate (double precision)
 19  *         NYEARS  - Number of years to compound
 20  *         AMOUNT  - Compound amount
 21  *         AMTDBL  - Compound amount (double precision)
 22  *         DOLLAR  - Amount paid for Island - $24.00
 23  *         DBLDOL  - Dollar expressed in double precision
 24  *
 25  **********
 26  *                      TYPE DECLARATION AND STORAGE ALLOCATION
 27  **********
 28  *
 29        REAL IRATE,NYEARS,DOLLAR,AMOUNT
 30        INTEGER YEAR
 31        DOUBLE PRECISION DIRATE,AMTDBL,DBLDOL
 32        CHARACTER REPLY*1
 33        DATA DOLLAR/24.0/
 34  *
 35  **********
 36  * BLOCK 0000           INITIALIZATION BLOCK
 37  **********
 38  *
 39        DBLDOL - DBLE(DOLLAR)
 40        WRITE(6,'(6X,''Manhattan Island Interest Problem'')')
 41  *
 42  **********
 43  * BLOCK 0100           INPUT AND COMPUTATION
 44  **********
 45  *
 46  101 PRINT *, 'To what year do you want to compound? '
 47        READ *, YEAR
 48        IF(YEAR .LE. 1626) THEN
 49            PRINT *, 'Since the island was acquired in 1626 the year'
 50            PRINT *, 'must be greater than that. Please enter again, '
 51            GOTO 101
 52        ENDIF
 53        PRINT *, 'At what interest rate? '
 54        READ *, IRATE
 55        IF (IRATE .GT. 1.0) IRATE - IRATE/100.0
 56        NYEARS - FLOAT(YEAR-1626)
 57        DIRATE - DBLE(IRATE)
 58        AMOUNT - DOLLAR*(1.0 + IRATE/4.0)**(4.0*NYEARS)
 59        AMTDBL - DBLDOL*(1.0D+0 + DIRATE/0.4D+1)**(4.0*NYEARS)
 60  *
 61  **********
 62  * BLOCK 0200           OUTPUT BLOCK
 63  **********
 64  *
 65        WRITE(6,202) DOLLAR,YEAR,IRATE,AMOUNT,AMTDBL
 66  202 FORMAT(//5X,'$',F6.2,' INVESTED IN 1626, COMPOUNDED QUARTERLY',
 67      1    'THROUGH',I5,', AND'/5X,'AT A RATE OF',
 68      2    2PF5.1,' PERCENT, WOULD AMOUNT TO'/
 69      3    1X,'$',0PE20.14,' OR, MORE PRECISELY, $',D30.24/)
 70  *
 71  *                      ANOTHER PROBLEM?
 72  *
 73        PRINT *, 'Do you want to compute again? '
 74        READ(5,'(A)') REPLY
 75  *
 76  *                      IF YES, THEN GO BACK
 77  *
 78        IF(REPLY .EQ. 'Y' .OR. REPLY .EQ. 'y') GOTO 101
 79        STOP
 80        END
```

Figure 7-3 Output using two different computers for Manhattan Island problem with double-precision processing.

```
Output from IBM personal computer PC/AT
-----------------------------------------------------------------
      Manhattan Island Interest Problem
To what year do you want to compound? 1976
At what interest rate? 6


    $ 24.00 invested in 1626, compounded quarterly through 1976, and
      at a rate of  6.0 percent, would amount to
$0.27081342976000E+11 or, more precisely,
$0.2708134250148986050500000D+11

Do you want to compute again? y
To what year do you want to compound? 1988
At what interest rate? 10


    $ 24.00 invested in 1626, compounded quarterly through 1988, and
      at a rate of 10.0 percent, would amount to
$0.80978284061393E+17 or, more precisely,
$0.8097828178107244800000000D+17

Do you want to compute again? n
-----------------------------------------------------------------
Output from Cray-2 supercomputer
-----------------------------------------------------------------

      Manhattan Island Interest Problem
  To what year do you want to compound?
1976
  At what interest rate?
.06


    $ 24.00 invested in 1626, compounded quarterly through 1976, and
      at a rate of  6.0 percent, would amount to
$0.27081355025278E+11 or, more precisely,
$0.27081355025255497814707307D+11

  Do you want to compute again?
y
  To what year do you want to compound?
1988
  At what interest rate?
10


    $ 24.00 invested in 1626, compounded quarterly through 1988, and
      at a rate of 10.0 percent, would amount to
$0.80978239164876E+17 or, more precisely,
$0.80978239165018335680012D+17

  Do you want to compute again?
n
```

to restore the multiplier to normal for the rest of the values printed out, 0P is inserted before the next descriptor in the list.

6. A character string is used in place of a FORMAT statement in the READ statement in line 74.

The program does some simple validation of inputs. The year that is entered is checked (lines 48–50) to make sure it is greater than 1626, when Manhattan Island was acquired. A useful approach to handling ambiguous input format is illustrated. The user is not told whether to enter the interest rate as a percentage or as a decimal. (In the case of 6 percent, should it be entered as 6 or .06?) The program could have been very explicit, but there could still have been misunderstandings; as an alternative, the program checks (line 55) whether the interest rate value is greater than 1.0; if it is, the value is assumed to be a percent and is therefore divided by 100.0 to obtain the decimal value needed in the computation. That means the program will not work correctly for an interest percentage input less than or equal to 1.0, but such a low interest rate is unrealistic.

Two sets of results from two different computers are given in Figure 7-3. These are the Cray-2 supercomputer and the IBM PC-AT personal computer using IBM's Professional FORTRAN. The results from double precision compared to single precision do not differ as much for the Cray-2 as for the PC-AT. The difference between the double- and single-precision results on the same computer for the 6 percent interest rate (where the value of Manhattan is over $27 billion) is:

Cray-2 $ .023
IBM PC-AT   474.51

The amount of difference between single and double precision reflects the precision built into the computer designs. The Cray computer was designed for high-precision, scientific processing; the IBM computer was designed as a general-purpose computer without a need for high precision in most situations. In the double-precision result, the IBM computer does not have results beyond 18 digits, so the remaining digits are zeros.

There is a difference in the results obtained with the two computers at double precision for the 6 percent rate of $12,523.77 (lower for IBM PC-AT). Given the $27 billion amount, this is a very small difference but does show that some differences are due to underlying computer architecture and computational procedures. They are not overcome by double precision. On the other hand, it is not meaningful to print out as many digits as shown. In a problem with the result in billions, showing results beyond the millions is not meaningful.

One other minor difference that may sometimes appear is illustrated in the two outputs. The normal procedure is for a list-directed output to begin with a line feed to move the paper to the next line to be printed. The instruction uses position 1, so this is left blank on output. After the line is printed, there is no line feed because the next line to be printed will have its own line feed that will also return to the beginning of the line. If there is a READ following the printout or display, will the input be on the same line following after the output or will it be on a separate line? The IBM PC-AT Professional FORTRAN does not return to a new line for the input; the Cray-2 FORTRAN starts the input on a new line.

Mathematical Program Example 7—Simulation of Sales, Supply, and Inventory of Perishable Product

The example illustrates an important use of computers in simulating a system. The general concept of simulation of a system in which phenomena are not governed by certainty is very useful. Among the many examples of such systems are customers in a grocery, bank, or airline ticket queue; weather phenomena and hydraulic or airfoil flow situations.

This program shows the use of the following features introduced in Chapter 7a:

DOUBLE PRECISION type variables and the use of double-precision intrinsic functions SNGL and DMOD

The writing of detail output to a file while summary data items are written to the terminal

An array dimension specified as a range

The use of a character constant to define a format within a WRITE statement (with and without the use of the FMT designator)

The H edit specifier

The PARAMETER statement

Alternate entry point to a subroutine

Logical variables were introduced in Chapter 3 but have had little use. This program employs logical variables and a logical function.

Problem Description for Mathematical Example 7

The problem is to simulate the conduct of a business in which customers arrive randomly to obtain perishable goods. The goods last only one day, but they may, under management decision, be carried over for sale the next day but not beyond. A bakery selling fresh baked goods might present this type of system behavior. The amount each customer orders is also uncertain, as is the supply of goods obtained for sale. The simulation is termed a *stochastic* simulation because the program simulates random events. In other words, there is uncertainty. Although the number of customers, the amount of product ordered by each, and the supply of goods are uncertain, they can be described by statistical distributions which specify the long-term percentages for each probable number of customers, each order quantity, and each supply amount. The user of the simulation enters the percentages, and the simulation program generates the three distributions and obtains data by sampling from them.

In the system described by the example problem, customers arrive at a service facility to obtain a perishable product according to a discrete distribution, that is, one in which the number of customers is an integer (there cannot be half a customer). Customers demand a quantity which is variable and discrete (they do not order half a unit). The available supply of product each day is also a discrete variable. The basic logical flow of supply and demand is modified by two alternatives for system behavior that can be chosen by the person who is running the simulation:

1. Disposition of product left at the end of the day. It may or may not, depending on the user's choice, be carried over to the next day but not to a third day.
2. Effect of unfilled orders. If customers do not have their orders filled the same day, the user can specify either no penalty or a stockout penalty. The penalty is a reduction in the next day's customer arrivals equal to the unsatisfied customers for the day. This is certainly a reasonable assumption if customers can go to another place (such as another bakery).

The results of a simulation run on the computer are statistics on the behavior of the system in terms of customer service level (percentage of customers provided with their orders), service level for units ordered (percentage of demand satisfied), average product left at end of day, and average daily shortage (unfilled demand). Review the output in Figure 7-6, which provides these results. By changing values for the distribution of customers, distribution of demand by customers (percentage demanding 4, 5, 6, etc., units), and distribution of supply, the effect of changing conditions may be examined. If customers change their ordering habits, what is the effect? If facilities are expanded to increase the supply, what is the effect? What is the effect of a policy of carrying over product to the next day? If there is no competition, so there is no stockout penalty, how will the system work compared to one with a stockout penalty? These and other questions can be examined through the simulation.

Program Documentation for Mathematical Example 7

The program documentation is simplified in order to concentrate on the interesting characteristics of the program and use of features from the chapter rather than the detailed logic. The flowchart (Figure 7-4) shows the major flow of logic. The program listing is given in Figure 7-5 and example outputs in Figure 7-6. The interactive inputs are shown as part of the listing of the outputs.

Notes on Mathematical Example 7

This program is interesting for three reasons: the illustration of computer simulation, the use of features described in the chapter, and the use of logical variables and logical functions (which has not been done to any extent in earlier chapters). In considering these three major features of the program, note the following:

1. The frequency distributions for each of the three variables (supply, customers, and demand by customers) are read as a set of pairs of numbers. The input is managed by a subroutine named READER (called in lines 132, 135, and 138). The same subroutine is used for all three distributions; the parameter list in the CALL specifies 1, 2, or 3 to indicate which distribution is being read. Each pair of numbers read by subroutine READER (described in lines 303–392) are interpreted as one quantity and its associated probability expressed as a decimal. They appear in ascending order based on quantity. For example, if the demand for a quantity of 3 has a probability of 50 percent, the inputs are 3, .5; if a quantity of 4 has a probability of 20 percent and quantity of 5 a probability of 30 percent, the next two input pairs will be 4, .2 and 5, .3. The probabilities must add up to 1.0. If the quantity is constant and does not vary, the probability for the quantity is given as 1.0. The set of input data items is terminated by an input of a ' − 1,0' pair. Review the printout of interactive input of frequency distributions in Figure 7-6. The inputs illustrate a frequency distribution with several inputs, a quantity that has a probability of 1.0, and the use of − 1,0 to indicate the end of the inputs for each distribution.

2. The theoretical means and cumulative distributions for each of the three variables are formed (lines 139–150). Sampling is accomplished by generating a random number between zero and one in the function RANDOM (lines 420–459). The random number is compared to the cumulative probabilities in the function SAMPLE (lines 254–301) to determine the appropriate quantity. The demand may be modified to reflect a shortage penalty. The quantity available is modified if carryover of day-old stock is allowed. The process is repeated for as many days as the user has specified.

3. If the detail file option is selected, detail results for each day are written to a file (lines 96–105). If the detail file is opened, it is closed upon termination (lines 82, 247). Detail data items can subsequently be examined with an editor or printed separately after an examination of the summary statistics which are written to the terminal or screen. This procedure of first checking the summary statistics avoids creation of many pages of unnecessary output.

4. Logical variables have been established (line 61) and used as switches to be tested to control the logic flow (lines 171, 194, 202, 247). Their initial values are set to .FALSE. (lines 73–75), and they are reset to .TRUE. depending on user input (lines 91, 95, 100).

5. A logical function subprogram called YES (lines 461–488) is used in several places (lines 91, 95, 99, 246) to test user responses. The function uses a logical

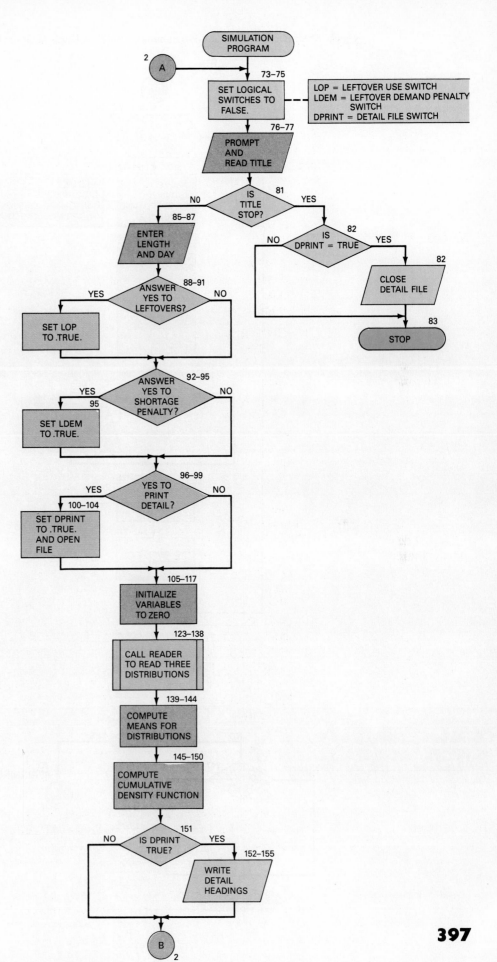

Figure 7-4 Flowchart for mathematical program example 7—simulation.

Figure 7-4 continued

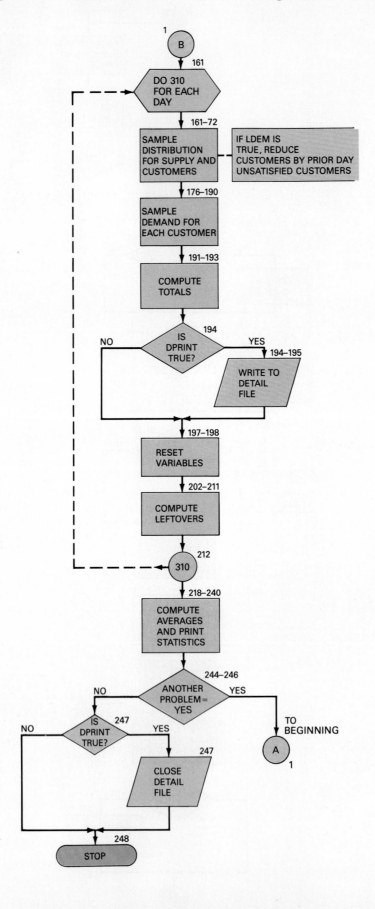

Figure 7-4 concluded

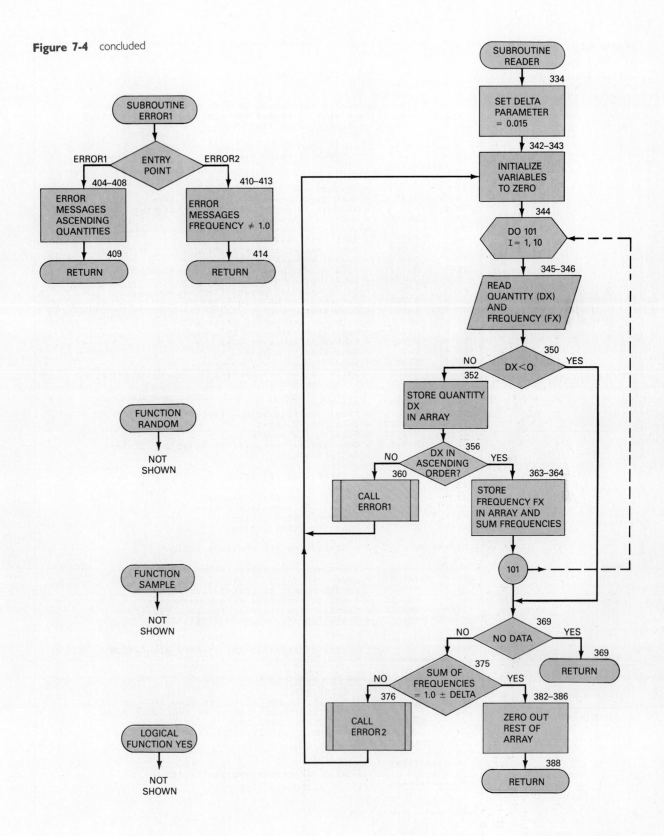

Figure 7-5 Program listing for mathematical program example 7—simulation.

```
 1 **********
 2 *                    PROGRAM IDENTIFICATION
 3 **********
 4 *
 5 *    Simple inventory simulation program. Detail data may be
 6 *    written to a file. Designed for interactive input.
 7 *    Written by T. Hoffmann  11/17/86
 8 *
 9 **********
10 *                    VARIABLE IDENTIFICATION
11 **********
12 *
13 *    ALEFT   - Average left over
14 *    ALFT    - Left overs available for next day
15 *    ANS     - Answers to input questions (character)
16 *    AVAIL   - Average units each day
17 *    CD      - Counter of days
18 *    DAY     - Number of days to simulate
19 *    DCUST   - Daily number of customers
20 *    DEM     - Demand by each customer
21 *    DETAIL  - File on which to print detailed output (character)
22 *    DPRINT  - Detail print switch (logical)
23 *    DUSC    - Daily count of unsatisfied customers
24 *    FIFO    - Leftovers to be sold first
25 *    LDEM    - Lost demand switch (logical)
26 *    LOP     - Leftover use switch (logical)
27 *    NCUST   - Number of customers in a day
28 *    NSTOUT  - Number of stockout days
29 *    SUP     - Sample daily supply
30 *    TDEM    - Total demand
31 *    TITLE   - Title of run (character)
32 *    TOTC    - Total customers
33 *    TOTDEM  - Total demand
34 *    TOTSUP  - Total supply
35 *    TUSC    - Total unsatisfied customers
36 *    TUSHRT  - Total units short
37 *    TUXCES  - Total units excess
38 *    UNSAT   - Unsatisfied customers previous day (integer)
39 *    XS      - Daily excess
40 *
41 *****                ARRAY IDENTIFICATION
42 *
43 *    AMEAN   - Mean of each distribution
44 *    CDF     - Cumulative density function
45 *    FD      - Frequency distribution
46 *    XD      - Quantity distribution
47 *
48 *****                SUBROUTINE AND FUNCTION NAMES
49 *
50 *    ERROR1  - Print error messages (subroutine)
51 *    ERROR2  - Alternate entry to error1
52 *    RANDOM  - Random number generator (function)
53 *    READER  - Reads distribution data (subroutine)
54 *    SAMPLE  - Samples from the distributions (function)
55 *    YES     - Test of query response (logical)
56 *
57 **********
58 *                    TYPE DECLARATION AND STORAGE ALLOCATION
59 **********
60 *
61    LOGICAL LOP,DPRINT,LDEM,YES
62    INTEGER UNSAT,NCUST,NSTOUT
63    REAL ALEFT,ALST,AVAIL,CD,DAY,DCOST,DEM,DUSC,FIFO,SUP,TDEM,TOTC,
64   1    TOTDEM,TOTSUP,TUSC,TUSHRT,TUXCES,XS,AMEAN,CDF,FD,XD
65    CHARACTER ANS*1,TITLE*40,DETAIL*12
66    COMMON XD(3,0:10),FD(3,10),CDF(3,10)
67    DIMENSION AMEAN(3)
68 *
69 **********
70 * BLOCK 0100         READ PARAMETERS AND INITIALIZE
71 **********
72 *
73    101 LOP = .FALSE.
74        LDEM = .FALSE.
```

Figure 7-5 continued

```
75          DPRINT = .FALSE.
76          WRITE(6,'(1X,''Title? '')')
77          READ(5,'(A)') TITLE
78 *
79 *                    PROGRAM TERMINATES IF TITLE IS "STOP"
80 *
81          IF(TITLE .EQ. 'STOP' .OR. TITLE .EQ. 'stop') THEN
82              IF(DPRINT) CLOSE(7)
83              STOP
84          ENDIF
85          WRITE(6,104)
86      104 FORMAT(1X,'Simulation length? ')
87          READ(5,*) DAY
88          WRITE(6,105)
89      105 FORMAT(1X,'Save leftovers(Y/N)? ')
90          READ(5,'(A)') ANS
91          IF(YES(ANS)) LOP = .TRUE.
92          WRITE(6,106)
93      106 FORMAT(1X,'Shortage penalty(Y/N)? ')
94          READ(5,'(A)') ANS
95          IF(YES(ANS)) LDEM = .TRUE.
96          WRITE(6,107)
97      107 FORMAT(1X,'Print everything(Y/N)? ')
98          READ(5,'(A)') ANS
99          IF(YES(ANS)) THEN
100             DPRINT = .TRUE.
101             PRINT *, 'On which file should the detail be printed?
102             READ(5,'(A)') DETAIL
103             OPEN(7,FILE =DETAIL,ACCESS='SEQUENTIAL')
104             WRITE(7,'(A)') TITLE
105         ENDIF
106         ALFT = 0.0
107         XS = 0.0
108         TOTC = 0.0
109         TOTDEM = 0.0
110         TOTSUP = 0.0
111         UNSAT=0
112         TUXCES = 0.0
113         TUSHRT = 0.0
114         AVAIL = 0.0
115         DUSC=0.0
116         NSTOUT=0
117         TUSC=0
118 *
119 **********
120 * BLOCK 0200           READ DISTRIBUTIONS AND SET ARRAYS
121 **********
122 *
123         WRITE(6,201)
124     201 FORMAT(1X,'Enter each of the following distributions as '
125        1    ,'"Quantity,Probability",'/1X,'one pair per line, ',
126        2    'in ascending order based upon "Quantity".'/1X,
127        3    'Terminate each set with a "-1,0" entry pair.'/1X,
128        4    'If only "-1,0" is entered, data from the previous run',
129        5    ' will be reused.'/)
130         WRITE(6,202)
131     202 FORMAT(1X,'What is the supply distribution?'/)
132         CALL READER(1)
133         WRITE(6,203)
134     203 FORMAT(1X,'What is the customer distribution?'/)
135         CALL READER(2)
136         WRITE(6,204)
137     204 FORMAT(1X,'What is the demand/cust. distribution?'/)
138         CALL READER(3)
139         DO 206 I = 1,3
140             AMEAN(I) = 0.0
141             DO 207 J = 1,10
142                 AMEAN(I) = XD(I,J)*FD(I,J) + AMEAN(I)
143     207     CONTINUE
144     206 CONTINUE
145         DO 208 I = 1,3
146             CDF(I,1)=FD(I,1)
147             DO 215 J = 2,10
148                 CDF(I,J) = CDF(I,J - 1) + FD(I,J)
```

Figure 7-5 continued

```
149 215      CONTINUE
150 208 CONTINUE
151      IF(DPRINT) WRITE(7,209)
152      WRITE(6,209)
153 209 FORMAT(51X,6('*'),'Service',7('*')/3X,
154    1 'Day',4X,'Customers',3X,'Demand',3X,'Supply',' Available',
155    1 4X,'Excess',3X,'Unsatisfied'/52X,'Units',4X,'Customers'/)
156 *
157 **********
158 * BLOCK 0300          SAMPLE DISTRIBUTIONS & GENERATE EVENTS
159 **********
160 *
161      DO 310 CD = 1.0,DAY
162          SUP = SAMPLE(1)
163          AVAIL=AVAIL + SUP
164 *
165 *                DETERMINE NUMBER OF CUSTOMERS THIS DAY
166 *
167          NCUST = SAMPLE(2)
168 *
169 *                ASSIGN APPROPRIATE SHORTAGE PENALTY
170 *
171          IF(LDEM) NCUST=NCUST-UNSAT
172          DEM=0.0
173 *
174 *                DETERMINE DEMAND FOR EACH CUSTOMER
175 *
176          DO 313 K=1,NCUST
177              DEM = DEM + SAMPLE(3)
178              IF(DEM .LE. AVAIL) GOTO 313
179              TUSC=TUSC+1.0
180              DUSC=DUSC+1.0
181 313      CONTINUE
182          FIFO=DEM-ALFT
183          XS=SUP-FIFO
184          IF(XS .LT. 0.0) THEN
185              TUSHRT = TUSHRT + XS
186              NSTOUT=NSTOUT+1
187          ELSE
188              TUXCES = TUXCES + XS
189          ENDIF
190          DCUST = FLOAT(NCUST)
191          TOTC = TOTC + DCUST
192          TOTDEM = TOTDEM + DEM
193          TOTSUP = TOTSUP + SUP
194          IF(DPRINT) WRITE(7,322) CD,DCUST,DEM,SUP,AVAIL,XS,DUSC
195 322      FORMAT(1X,F5.0,6F10.0)
196 330      AVAIL = 0.0
197          UNSAT = INT(DUSC)
198          DUSC=0.0
199 *
200 *                COMPUTE LEFT OVERS FOR TOMORROW
201 *
202          IF(.NOT.(.NOT. LOP .OR. XS .LT. 0.0)) THEN
203              IF(FIFO .GE. 0.0) THEN
204                  ALFT = XS
205              ELSE
206                  ALFT = SUP
207              ENDIF
208          ELSE
209              ALFT = 0.0
210          ENDIF
211          AVAIL = ALFT
212 310 CONTINUE
213 *
214 **********
215 * BLOCK 0400          COMPUTE AVERAGES AND PRINT THEM
216 **********
217 *
218      WRITE(6,443)
219 443 FORMAT(1X,'Totals')
220      WRITE(6,442) DAY,TOTC,TOTDEM,TOTSUP,TUXCES+TUSHRT,TUSC
221 442 FORMAT(1X,F5.0,3F10.0,12X,2F10.0/)
222      WRITE(6,*) NSTOUT,' Stockout days'
```

Figure 7-5 continued

```
223        WRITE(6,402) (TOTDEM+TUSHRT)/TOTDEM
224    402 FORMAT(' Service level (per unit)',F11.6)
225        WRITE(6,403) (TOTC-TUSC)/TOTC
226    403 FORMAT(' Service level (customers)',F10.6)
227        WRITE(6,404) TUXCES/DAY
228    404 FORMAT(' Average excess',F12.6)
229        WRITE(6,405) -TUSHRT/DAY
230    405 FORMAT(' Average shortage',F10.6)
231        WRITE(6,410)
232    410 FORMAT(/' Averages',8X,'Theoretical',4X,'Sample')
233        WRITE(6,406) AMEAN(2),TOTC/DAY
234    406 FORMAT(' Customers ',5X,2F12.6)
235        WRITE(6,407) AMEAN(3),TOTDEM/TOTC
236    407 FORMAT(' Dem./Cust.',5X,2F12.6)
237        WRITE(6,408) AMEAN(2)*AMEAN(3),TOTDEM/DAY
238    408 FORMAT(' Demand/Day',5X,2F12.6)
239        WRITE(6,409) AMEAN(1),TOTSUP/DAY
240    409 FORMAT(' Supply/Day',5X,2F12.6///)
241 *
242 *                          ANOTHER PROBLEM?
243 *
244        PRINT *, 'Do you want to do another problem? '
245        READ(5,'(A)') ANS
246        IF(YES(ANS)) GOTO 101
247        IF(DPRINT) CLOSE(7)
248        STOP
249 *
250 * END OF MAIN PROGRAM
251 *
252        END
253 *
254        FUNCTION SAMPLE(NTYPE)
255 *
256 *********
257 *                       PROGRAM IDENTIFICATION
258 *********
259 *
260 *       This subroutine samples from the cumulative
261 *       distributions of each type.
262 *
263 *********
264 *                       VARIABLE IDENTIFICATION
265 *********
266 *
267 *       NTYPE    = Row index of array
268 *       RNO      = Random number for sampling
269 *
270 *****               ARRAY IDENTIFICATION
271 *
272 *       CDF      = Cumulative density function
273 *       FD       = Frequency distribution
274 *       XD       = Quantity distribution
275 *
276 *****               SUBROUTINE AND FUNCTION NAMES
277 *
278 *       RANDOM   = Random number generator
279 *
280 *********
281 *                 TYPE DECLARATION AND STORAGE ALLOCATION
282 *********
283 *
284        INTEGER NTYPE
285        REAL RNO,CDF,FD,XD
286        COMMON XD(3,0:10),FD(3,10),CDF(3,10)
287 *
288 *********
289 * BLOCK 0100              SAMPLING BLOCK
290 *********
291 *
292        RNO = RANDOM(0.0)
293        DO 102 I = 1,10
294            IF(RNO .LE. CDF(NTYPE,I)) GOTO 103
295    102 CONTINUE
296    103 SAMPLE = XD(NTYPE,I)
```

Figure 7-5 continued

```
297        RETURN
298 *
299 *    END OF FUNCTION SAMPLE
300 *
301        END
302 *
303        SUBROUTINE READER(INDEXI)
304 *
305 **********
306 *                         PROGRAM IDENTIFICATION
307 **********
308 *
309 *        Data is read into the appropriate array
310 *
311 **********
312 *                         VARIABLE IDENTIFICATION
313 **********
314 *
315 *        DELTA    - Round off error allowance
316 *        DX       - Quantity
317 *        FX       - Frequency
318 *        INDEXI   - Array index 1
319 *        INDEXJ   - Array index 2
320 *        SUMF     - Sum of frequencies
321 *
322 *****                    ARRAY IDENTIFICATION
323 *
324 *        CDF      - Cumulative density function
325 *        FD       - Frequency distribution
326 *        XD       - Quantity distribution
327 *
328 **********
329 *                    TYPE DECLARATION AND STORAGE ALLOCATION
330 **********
331 *
332        INTEGER INDEXI,INDEXJ
333        REAL DX,FX,SUMF,CDF,FD,XD
334        PARAMETER (DELTA - 0.015)
335        COMMON XD(3,0:10),FD(3,10),CDF(3,10)
336 *
337 **********
338 * BLOCK 0100           DATA ENTRY AND COMPUTATION BLOCK
339 **********
340 *
341        XD(INDEXI,0) - 0.0
342   100 SUMF - 0.0
343        INDEXJ - 0
344        DO 101 I - 1,10
345            WRITE(6,'(1X,''?'')')
346            READ(5,*) DX,FX
347 *
348 *                    NEGATIVE VALUE SIGNALS END OF INPUT
349 *
350        IF(DX .LT. 0.0) GOTO 102
351        INDEXJ-INDEXJ+1
352        XD(INDEXI,INDEXJ)-DX
353 *
354 *                    DATA MUST BE IN ASCENDING ORDER
355 *
356        IF(DX .LT. XD(INDEXI,INDEXJ-1)) THEN
357 *
358 *                    PRINT ERROR MESSAGE AND RE-ENTER DATA
359 *
360            CALL ERROR1
361            GOTO 100
362        ENDIF
363        FD(INDEXI,INDEXJ)-FX
364        SUMF - SUMF + FX
365   101 CONTINUE
366 *
367 *                    ZERO VALUE SIGNALS NO NEW DATA WAS ENTERED
368 *
369   102 IF(INDEXJ .EQ. 0) RETURN
370 *
```

Figure 7-5 continued

```
371 *          IF SUM OF PROBABILITIES NOT EQUAL TO APPROXIMATELY ONE,
372 *          THEN THERE HAS BEEN A DATA ERROR SO PRINT MESSAGE
373 *          AND GO BACK TO RE-ENTER DATA
374 *
375      IF(SUMF .GT. 1.0 + DELTA .OR. SUMF .LT. 1.0 - DELTA) THEN
376          CALL ERROR2
377          GOTO 100
378      ELSE
379 *
380 *                        ZERO OUT REST OF ARRAY
381 *
382          INDEXJ=INDEXJ+1
383          DO 106 K=INDEXJ,10
384              XD(INDEXI,K)=0.0
385              FD(INDEXI,K)=0.0
386  106      CONTINUE
387      ENDIF
388      RETURN
389 *
390 * END OF SUBROUTINE READER
391 *
392      END
393 *
394      SUBROUTINE ERROR1
395 *
396 **********
397 *                        PROGRAM IDENTIFICATION
398 **********
399 *
400 *        Data input error messages are printed
401 *
402 **********
403 *
404      WRITE(6,'(1X,''Values must be in ascending order.'')')
405      WRITE(6,2)
406      WRITE(6,4)
407    2 FORMAT(//' Error in data entry.')
408    4 FORMAT(' Re-enter this entire data set.'/)
409      RETURN
410      ENTRY ERROR2
411      WRITE(6,FMT='(1X,26HFrequencies must total one)')
412      WRITE(6,2)
413      WRITE(6,4)
414      RETURN
415 *
416 * END OF SUBROUTINE ERROR1
417 *
418      END
419 *
420      FUNCTION RANDOM(DUM)
421 *
422 **********
423 *                        PROGRAM IDENTIFICATION
424 **********
425 *
426 *        Random number generator
427 *        Called from SAMPLE
428 *
429 **********
430 *                        VARIABLE IDENTIFICATION
431 **********
432 *
433 *        B      - Constant multiplier - 3213.0
434 *        C      - High order digits of product
435 *        D      - Low order digits of product
436 *        S4     - Constant scale factor - 1.0D+4
437 *        S7     - Constant scale factor - 1.0D+7
438 *        DUM    - Dummy argument or bias factor
439 *        R      - Random digits
440 *
441 **********
442 *                        TYPE DECLARATION AND STORAGE ALLOCATION
443 **********
444 *
```

Figure 7-5 concluded

```
445       REAL DUM
446       DOUBLE PRECISION B,C,D,R,S4,S7
447       DATA B/3213.0D+0/C/123.0D+4/D/4567.0D+0/S4/1.0D+4/S7/1.0D+7/
448 *
449 *                 GENERATE RANDOM NUMBER
450 *
451       R = DMOD((DMOD(B*C,S7) + DMOD(B*D,S7)),S7)
452       D = DMOD(R,S4)
453       C = R - D
454       RANDOM = SNGL(R/S7) + DUM
455       RETURN
456 *
457 * END OF FUNCTION RANDOM
458 *
459       END
460 *
461       LOGICAL FUNCTION YES(ANS)
462 *
463 **********
464 *                 PROGRAM IDENTIFICATION
465 **********
466 *
467 *       Test query reply for 'yes' response. Return 'True' if
468 *       response is Y or y; return 'False' for any other.
469 *
470 **********
471 *                 VARIABLE IDENTIFICATION
472 **********
473 *
474 *       ANS      = Response being tested (character)
475 *
476 **********
477 *
478       CHARACTER ANS*1
479       YES = ((ANS .EQ. 'Y') .OR. (ANS .EQ. 'y'))
480       RETURN
481 *
482 * END OF LOGICAL FUNCTION YES
483 *
484       END
```

expression to test whether the user response is "Y" or "y"; if it is, the function is set to a value for true; if not, it is set to a value for false. A typical test of this function value is written IF (YES(ANS)). . . .

6. The specification of both beginning subscript and ending subscript is illustrated in the program. The array XD is dimensioned as 3 by 0:10 (line 335). In other words, there are three types of distributions with 11 entries (columns) with the column subscript referenced as 0 through 10 rather than the normal 1 through 11. Setting the numbering of a subscript to start with a zeroth entry overcomes the difficulty in testing the first value read in when testing for increasing values (lines 356). In other words, the current value being read (subscript J) is tested to see if it is larger than the previous entry (J − 1). Defining a zeroth entry which is set to zero by line 341 and using it for comparing the first set of data is one way of handling the first comparison; it can also be programmed in other ways.

7. The use of a character constant in a WRITE statement is illustrated in lines 76, 104, 345, 404, and 411. Note that when the format itself includes apostrophe fields, double apostrophes must be used around the character string to show that they are not delimiters. This should be contrasted with line 411 in which the character string is defined with an H edit descriptor and hence the extra apostrophes are not needed. The use of the FMT = specifier (line 411) is not required but may be included for clarity of style.

Figure 7-6 Sample output from simulation program.

```
Title? Sample run with detail output

Simulation length? 10

Save leftovers(Y/N)? n

Shortage penalty(Y/N)? y

Print everything(Y/N)? y

On which file should the detail be printed? TRIAL

Enter each of the following distributions as "Quantity,Probability",
one pair per line, in ascending order based upon "Quantity".
Terminate each set with a "-1,0" entry pair.
If only "-1,0" is entered, data from the previous run will be reused.

What is the supply distribution?

?16,1

?-1,0

What is the customer distribution?

?4,1

?-1,0

What is the demand/cust. distribution?

?4,.5

?5,.4

?6,1

?-1,0

Frequencies must total one


Error in data entry.
Re-enter this entire data set.

?4,.5

?5,.4

?6,.1

?-1,0
                                              ******Service*******
  Day    Customers   Demand   Supply Available  Excess    Unsatisfied
                                                 Units     Customers

Totals
  10.       35.       164.       160.            -4.          6.

               6 Stockout days
Service level (per unit)   0.920732
Service level (customers)  0.828571
Average excess    0.900000
Average shortage  1.300000

Averages            Theoretical      Sample
Customers            4.000000       3.500000
Dem./Cust.           4.600000       4.685714
Demand/Day          18.400000      16.400000
Supply/Day          16.000000      16.000000



Do you want to do another problem? n
```

Figure 7-6 concluded

OUTPUT

```
Sample run with detail output
                                          ******Service*******
  Day    Customers    Demand    Supply  Available   Excess   Unsatisfied
                                                     Units    Customers

   1.        4.         19.       16.       16.       -3.        1.
   2.        3.         17.       16.       16.       -1.        1.
   3.        3.         14.       16.       16.        2.        0.
   4.        4.         19.       16.       16.       -3.        1.
   5.        3.         13.       16.       16.        3.        0.
   6.        4.         18.       16.       16.       -2.        1.
   7.        3.         14.       16.       16.        2.        0.
   8.        4.         17.       16.       16.       -1.        1.
   9.        3.         14.       16.       16.        2.        0.
  10.        4.         19.       16.       16.       -3.        1.
```

8. The DOUBLE PRECISION type declaration (line 446) is used in the function RANDOM to improve the accuracy of the generation process. The double-precision intrinsic modulus function DMOD is used. Refer to Chapter 6b and exercise 2 in Chapter 5b for more explanation of the procedure. Since the value of the random number itself need only be single precision, the result of the computation is made single precision by use of the SNGL intrinsic function (line 454).

9. The PARAMETER declaration (line 334) is used to set the value for a variable called DELTA. Since decimal fractions often cannot be represented exactly in the finite word size of the computer, testing for the sum of the probabilities to be exactly 1 (a real number which can be expressed exactly) may not yield a correct result. To allow for this possibility, the test at line 375 checks for the sum to be approximately 1, that is, 1.0 plus or minus DELTA. The appropriate value for DELTA is a function of the expected sizes of the probabilities. If one of them might be very close to zero, then DELTA must be set quite small. But if DELTA is too small, then an "error" might be identified which is simply the result of the precision of the internal representation. For this problem, values less than 0.1 are not anticipated and hence DELTA is set at 0.015.

10. Two entries are provided to the subroutine ERROR1 (lines 394–418). The normal entry is at the beginning, and a second entry is in the middle of the routine (line 410). The two entries allow the same or similar logic and FORMAT statements to be grouped together.

11. An interesting programming issue is illustrated by the test for termination of the program in lines 81–83. The user is asked to input the title of the simulation (simulation identification), but if the use of the program is to be ended, the user enters "STOP" or "stop." The uppercase and lowercase alternatives are tested, but what about the case of "Stop"? This potential problem was discovered in reading the program; it was not changed, but it could easily be remedied by adding a third comparison. Another design decision might be whether to allow the user to enter "S" or "s" instead of the full word. This is frequently allowed in software.

Programming Exercises

Description of Assignment

Select one or more problems (or take the problems assigned by your instructor). Write each of the programs so as to use features described in this chapter. Follow the style guidelines and prepare the following:

1. Pseudocode description
2. Program flowchart
3. Program listing
4. List of test data and expected results, including test for both valid and invalid data
5. Output including testing for error conditions

Mathematics and Statistics

1. Refer to problem 1 in Chapter 4. Make use of at least the FORMAT specifications in the READ statements.
2. Refer to problem 2 in Chapter 4. Make use of at least the character functions and FORMAT specification in character storage to print the output in the usual equilateral triangle shape.
3. Refer to problem 3 in Chapter 5. Make use of at least the statement function.

Business and Economics

4. Refer to problem 4 in Chapter 6. Make use of at least the LOGICAL type statements and logical variables.
5. Refer to problem 5 in Chapter 4. Make use of at least the P format edit descriptor and the PNYRND function subprogram of general example 6 as a statement function.
6. Refer to problem 6 in Chapter 5. Make use of at least the statement function.

Science and Engineering

7. Refer to problem 7 in Chapter 4. Make use of at least the LOGICAL type statement.
8. Refer to problem 9 in Chapter 5. Make use of at least the PARAMETER statement and the statement function.
9. Refer to problem 9 in Chapter 6. Make use of FORMAT specifications in input/ output statements or in character storage.

Humanities and Social Sciences

10. Refer to problem 11 in Chapter 4. Make use of at least the index function and character substrings.
11. Refer to problem 11 in Chapter 5. Make use of at least the DOUBLE PRECISION type statement and corresponding double-precision intrinsic functions and the statement function.
12. Refer to problem 12 in Chapter 6. Make use of at least the LOGICAL and IMPLICIT statements.

General

13. Refer to problem 13 in Chapter 6. Make use of at least the LOGICAL and IMPLICIT statements.
14. Refer to problem 14 in Chapter 5. Make use of at least the IMPLICIT statement.
15. Refer to problem 15 in Chapter 6. Make use of at least the IMPLICIT statement, alternate entry feature, and SAVE statement.

Interactive Scientific and Engineering

16. Refer to problem 17 in Chapter 5. Eliminate all FORMAT statements and list-directed output. Use the PARAMETER statement and statement functions.
17. Refer to problem 18 in Chapter 2. Make use of IMPLICIT DOUBLE PRECISION, and use double-precision functions and output formats.
18. Refer to problem 3 in Chapter 6. Compare just the power residue methods in both single- and double-precision computations. Use a single subroutine with multiple-entry points, use the PARAMETER statement, and name the program.

APPENDIX

Differences between Versions of FORTRAN

Differences between 1977 Standard FORTRAN and 1966 Standard FORTRAN

Full 1977 FORTRAN Features Not Included in 1977 Subset FORTRAN

Common Supplemental Instructions to 1977 Standard FORTRAN

Microcomputer Versions of FORTRAN 77

FORTRAN was first implemented in April 1957. The language developed rapidly with new features and revisions to previous features. The 1966 American National Standard FORTRAN was a landmark in the development of the FORTRAN language because the language was codified into a standard version. During the period 1966 to 1977, many implementors of FORTRAN made enhancements to the language. Among the most significant developments were WATFOR and WATFIV, student-oriented FORTRAN compilers developed by the University of Waterloo in Ontario, Canada, for use on IBM 360 and 370 computers. A student-oriented FORTRAN comparable to WATFIV, called MNF, was also developed at the University of Minnesota for use on large-scale Control Data computers. Another interesting development was WATFIV-S, a special version of WATFIV containing instructions for use in structured programming. The 1977 FORTRAN can be viewed as an enhancement of the 1966 standard FORTRAN, including most of the added features in WATFOR, WATFIV, MNF, and other compilers. The 1977 standard has a simplified version called subset FORTRAN.

After the introduction of the 1977 FORTRAN standard, there were various organizations such as the U.S. Department of Defense which proposed supplements to the standard. The supplements are added features; they do not alter the standard. Some of these supplemental features that are frequently implemented in FORTRAN compilers are END DO, DO WHILE, INCLUDE, and bit manipulation. As explained in Chapter 7a, the American National Standards Institute reviews standards periodically. In 1987, it proposed some supplemental instructions. It also proposed a review of all instructions and features in the future.

Microcomputer versions of FORTRAN generally adhere to the FORTRAN 77 standard. Some implement the subset FORTRAN plus some of the features of full FORTRAN; others implement all features. Although standard, the microcomputer versions may have a few nonstandard instructions to take advantage (or overcome disadvantages) of the microcomputer environment.

This appendix on differences among versions of FORTRAN has four sections:

1. Differences between 1977 standard FORTRAN and 1966 standard FORTRAN. The purpose of this section is to aid a programmer in using or modifying old FORTRAN programs.
2. Full 1977 FORTRAN features not included in 1977 subset FORTRAN. This section is to identify features that should not be used if the lowest level of compatibility is to be achieved.
3. Common supplemental instructions to 1977 standard FORTRAN. This section explains a few commonly implemented supplemental instructions, including END DO, DO WHILE, INCLUDE, and bit manipulation.
4. Microcomputer versions of FORTRAN 77. Although they adhere to the 1977 standard, there are usually some supplementary features that reflect the micro-computer environment.

Differences between 1977 Standard FORTRAN and 1966 Standard FORTRAN

The 1977 American National Standard FORTRAN specifications are used in this text. The 1977 standard was generally compatible with the 1966 standard, but there were a few conflicts. Also, many new features were added. These differences and additions are listed in relationship to the text chapters.

Text chapter	Feature in 1977 FORTRAN	Conflict	New feature
1	List-directed input/output		X
2	Use of generic intrinsic function names		X
	Generic names MAX and MIN		X
	Block IF(IF . . . THEN . . . ELSE . . . ENDIF)		X
	Mixed-mode expressions allowed		X
3	READ fs, list and PRINT fs, list		X
	Apostrophe edit descriptor		X
	T edit descriptor		X
	END for end of data and ERR for data error		X
	The + or − required before exponent in E field	X	X
	Dropping of implied method for handling character (Hollerith) data	X	
	Dropping of Hollerith constant using H statement	X	
	CHARACTER data type		X
	Expression in output list		X
4	Use of any integer arithmetic expression for subscript (limited to $i \pm k$, $k * i$, and $k * i \pm k$ in 1966 FORTRAN)		X
	Upper and lower bounds for dimensions		X
	DO loop control variable can be integer or real variable (instead of only integer variables)		X
	DO loop parameters may be negative, real variable, or integer or real expression (instead of only an integer or integer variable)		X
	If DO loop termination parameter value is greater than initial value, loop will not be executed (undefined previously)		X
	Comma in DO statement after statement number allowed but optional, for example, DO s [,]i = m_1, m_2, m_3		X
	Transfer of control into range of a DO statement not allowed	X	
5	Comma optional before control variable in computed GOTO, for example, GOTO(s_1,s_2)[,]i		X
	Any integer expression allowed as index for computed GOTO		X
6	OPEN, CLOSE, and INQUIRE statements		X
	UNIT = and FMT = control specifiers		X
7	Additional intrinsic functions—ACOS, ANINT, ASIN, CHAR, COSH, DACOS, DASIN, DCOSH, DDIM, DNINT, DPROD, DSINH, DTAN, DTANH, ICHAR, IDNINT, INDEX, LEN, LOG, LOG10, NINT, SINH, and TAN		X
	IMPLICIT declaration		X
	Dropping of reading into Hollerith format descriptor	X	
	Concatenation operator		X
	Substrings		X
	Lexical relationship functions—LGE, LGT, LLE, and LLT		X
	Additional format, edit specifications BN, BZ, Ew.dEe, Iw.m, Gw.dEe, TRc, TLc, S, SP, SS, and :		X
	FORMAT specifications in character storage		X
	FORMAT in input/output statement		X
	PARAMETER statement		X

Text chapter	Feature in 1977 FORTRAN	Conflict	New feature
7	Logical equivalence (EQV and NEQV)		X
	PROGRAM statement		X
	SAVE statement		X
	Alternate entry and alternate return points for subroutines		X
	Variable dimensions		X
	INTRINSIC statement		X

Full 1977 FORTRAN Features Not Included in 1977 Subset FORTRAN

The differences between the full FORTRAN and subset FORTRAN are arranged by book chapter.

Chapter	Feature not included in subset
1	List-directed input and output
2	Generic function name
	CLOSE statement
	OPEN (except for use with ACCESS = DIRECT and RECL = record length)
3	ERR specifier
	READ *fs*, list and PRINT *fs*, list
	Tc format edit descriptor
	Expressions in output list
4	More than three subscripts (full FORTRAN allows seven subscripts)
	Array element reference or function reference in subscript
	Upper and lower bounds for array declarator
	DO loop control variable can be real variable
	DO parameters can be integer or real expressions
	Implied DO loops in DATA statement (also, DATA statement must follow specification statement but precede executable statements in subset)
	Real variables allowed in implied DO loop as control and parameters
5	Index expression of a computed GOTO may be an integer expression
	BLOCK DATA subprogram
6	Formatted direct-access records
	INQUIRE statement
7	Double-precision and complex types
	Double-precision and complex expressions and intrinsic functions
	LEN, CHAR, and INDEX functions
	Unequal length for character variables
	Asterisk length specifier for character functions
	Character functions
	Substring
	Concatenation operator
	FORMAT edit descriptors—Iw.m, Dw.d, Gw.d, Gw.dEe, Ew.dEe, Tc, TLc, TRc, S, SP, and SS
	Format scan terminator (colon)
	UNIT = and FMT = control specifiers
	Use of character variables or array elements as FORMAT specification
	PARAMETER statement
	SAVE statement without a list
	ENTRY statement
	Alternate return from subroutine

Common Supplemental Instructions to 1977 Standard FORTRAN

The FORTRAN standard does not preclude supplemental instructions. Even when the supplemental instructions are proposed by influential organizations, they should be used with care, because they may not be implemented in all compilers or may be implemented in different ways. An example of an important organization setting up supplementary instructions is the Department of Defense supplement to FORTRAN 77. A few of the commonly implemented supplementary features are described here in order to provide the user with some insight into their purpose and form.

Many implementations of FORTRAN now allow mixed use of uppercase and lowercase in source statements. They are interpreted the same. In the case of Hollerith (character) constants, uppercase and lowercase are still significant.

The following statements are frequently provided as supplementary statements to standard FORTRAN 77:

END DO	Provides an explicit statement to mark the end of a DO loop. In the style of this text, the CONTINUE statement is used for this purpose.
DO WHILE (condition)	A loop instruction which specifies repeated execution of the loop as long as the loop condition is not satisfied. For example, the statement at the beginning of the loop might read:
	DO WHILE (I .LT. 1.0)
	The loop will be repeated as long as (while) the value of I is less than 1.0.
INCLUDE 'filename'	This is a compiler-directing instruction. It directs the compiler to include source code from a file. It is useful in copying source code modules into a program.

Bit manipulation instructions allow a FORTRAN programmer to code very detailed machine-level operations on individual bits or strings of bits. These capabilities should probably only be used when there are strong storage or performance reasons because they are prone to error and misunderstanding. They are not compatible with the understandable, machine-independent nature of FORTRAN programs. Why then are such capabilities provided? The answer is primarily in situations in which the individual bits or bit patterns are used in the control of processing. As an example, if a program has a large number of program control switches that can be set and need to be tested, each switch can be an individual logical variable, and testing them will require a large number of instructions. By using each bit as a switch, the entire set of switches can be tested as a switch pattern with one instruction.

There are instructions to set, clear, change, and test a bit; instructions to do bit arithmetic; and instructions to shift and rotate bit strings. In dealing with bit strings, the bits are numbered from the right starting with 0. For example, the fourth bit from the right is bit number 3. In the following, the bit position within a string of bits designated by i is indicated by an integer expression p. An integer variable, constant, or expression is denoted by iek. Binary constants are written using either octal or hexadecimal notation. A hexadecimal constant uses a Z and the octal an O. Therefore, a constant for a bit pattern of '00111111' could be written in hexadecimal as Z'3F'.

Set, Clear, or Change a Bit and Test Value of Bit

IBSET (i, p)	The pth bit of string i is set to value 1.
IBCLR (i, p)	The pth bit of string 1 is set to value 0.
IBCHNG (i, p)	Reverse value of pth bit in string i.
BTEST (i, p)	Logical function. True if pth bit of i is 1.

Bit Arithmetic Using OR and AND Complement Operations

IOR (iek$_1$, iek$_2$)	The two integer expressions are combined using inclusive OR logic (1 + 1 = 1)
IEOR (iek$_1$, iek$_2$)	Exclusive OR logic (1 + 1 = 0)
AND (iek$_1$, iek$_2$)	Also I (iek$_1$, iek$_2$). Logical AND function
NOT (iek)	Logical complement (0 = 1; 1 = 0)

Shift Bit Strings Right or Left or Rotation

ISHFT (iek$_1$, iek$_2$)	Also ISHL. Shift bits in iek by iek positions to the right or left (depending on positive or negative value of iek). Bits pushed out are lost; zeros enter to fill positions vacated by the shift.
ISHA (iek$_1$, iek$_2$)	Shift as above but exclude sign bit from shift
ISHFTC (iek$_1$, iek$_2$)	Also ISHC. Shift in circular fashion with bits pushed out entering at opposite end of string.

Microcomputer Versions of FORTRAN 77

FORTRAN has been implemented on microcomputers, primarily on the IBM Personal Computer and microcomputers that are compatible with it. The first widely used implementation was by Microsoft Corporation; hence this was referred to as Microsoft FORTRAN, or MS FORTRAN. Microsoft Corporation has been involved in many subsequent implementations as well. There have been improved and enhanced implementations of microcomputer FORTRAN along with improved and enhanced microcomputers. The microcomputer implementation of FORTRAN used during preparation of the revision of the text was IBM's Professional FORTRAN, which requires a math coprocessor chip (with a model PC-AT or compatible).

The implementations of FORTRAN on microcomputers can be either subset FORTRAN 77 with some full features or full FORTRAN 77. The difference between the two implementations will generally depend on the use of a math coprocessor chip. The coprocessor chip is an add-on board for the microcomputer that contains processing logic for mathematical functions. It performs processing using a very high precision "temporary real" data type. The result is converted after receipt from the coprocessor to the data type specified by the program. In addition to mathematical functions, it computes common trigonometric, hyperbolic, inverse hyperbolic, logarithmic, and exponential functions using a single machine-level instruction for each function. The math coprocessor chip significantly increases the speed of execution for FORTRAN; it also allows the addition of features that otherwise might make the compiler very large and the compiled program unwieldy. In other words, a serious user of FORTRAN should consider a math coprocessor chip in order to use the most complete implementations of FORTRAN and to achieve improved performance.

The FORTRAN compiler and compiled program make use of the operating system. This appendix will assume the dominant MS-DOS operating system. The Microsoft FORTRAN included a number of metacommands to direct compilation. The metacommands are on a separate line and begin with a $. An example of a compiler metacommand is $INCLUDE:<file name>. This instructs the compiler to include a stored routine in the program being compiled. An example of a runtime command is $DEBUG, which turns on runtime checking for arithmetic overflow, division by zero, and other debugging tests. These metacommands are not part of all implementations.

Although Microsoft's earliest implementation of FORTRAN was subset FORTRAN with some added features of full FORTRAN, one full feature was list-directed input and output. This feature is consistent with interactive input/output and keyboard entry of data by users. In 1987, Microsoft released its first full FORTRAN 77 for IBM PC-compatible microcomputers. All implementations of FORTRAN on microcomputers tend to have the following extensions to the standard:

User-defined names can be greater than six characters (but the characters beyond six, in some implementations, may not be significant). For IBM's Professional FORTRAN, global variable names can have up to eight significant characters.

Tab characters are allowed in the source statement. In fact, a tab character in the first six columns during entry of the source program causes the next character to be placed in column 7 and blanks inserted appropriately. This reduces the effort to space to column 7 for beginning the statement.

FORTRAN source statements can be entered in either uppercase or lowercase letters. They are interpreted the same. However, in the case of Hollerith output, lowercase or uppercase is significant. The $ may be allowed in a name (in some implementations).

The advancement to the next record (associated with the completion of a READ or WRITE) may be different for different implementations. A feature of Microsoft FORTRAN is the use of a backslash to indicate suppression of the advancement in order to allow input on the same line as output message requesting it.

The implementations provide an optional length specifier, for example, REAL $*$ 4, and the additional data types LOGICAL $*$ 1 and INTEGER $*$ 2.

Storage in microcomputer FORTRAN is treated as static. Unlike mainframes which may treat subprogram storage as dynamic and release the storage used by a subprogram after its use, microcomputer FORTRAN dedicates storage to each subprogram. The use of the SAVE command to save the data from a subprogram execution is usually not necessary in a microcomputer (but may be used for compatibility even though it may have no effect).

Hexadecimal constants may be used in some implementations (such as IBM's Professional FORTRAN) in a DATA statement. A numeric hexadecimal constant uses a Z. For example, Z'4A1' is a hexadecimal numeric constant. A hexadecimal character constant uses a pair of hexadecimal characters for each character. If used as a hexadecimal character constant, Z'44' will be interpreted as the character D. The hexadecimal 44 is equivalent to the decimal 68, which is the ASCII decimal code for the character D.

There are, generally, debugging options available, such as the Microsoft $DEBUG command or the insertion of lines in IBM's Professional FORTRAN with a D in column 1 (which specifies the statement is a DEBUG statement and should be executed only in debug mode specified by a compiler command [/D]).

In addition to the above, there may be other extensions of the standard FORTRAN in a microcomputer implementation. Using IBM's Professional FORTRAN as an example, there are DOS time and date functions, an INCLUDE statement, and bit manipulation instructions (described in the previous section). The time and date instructions are useful in setting the time and date on the microcomputer. Each of the variables involved must be declared as INTEGER * 2. There is a function to get and a function to set:

GETTIM (ihour, iminute, isecond, ihundredsecond)
SETTIM (ihour, iminute, isecond, ihundredsecond)
GETDAT (iyear, imonth, iday)
SETDAT (iyear, imonth, iday)

This discussion should alert the reader to the possibilities in a microcomputer implementation; the implementation manual should be read for specific features.

ASCII Standard
Character Codes

American Standard Codes for Information Interchange (ASCII) are used for the interchange of information among computers with different internal coding schemes. They are also the dominant coding standard for microcomputers (including word processing). The FORTRAN language assumes a collating sequence based on the ASCII codes. Also, there are instructions to identify the position of a character in the collating sequence that are based on ASCII.

ASCII can be considered an 8-bit code with a 7-bit subset. Frequently, the 7-bit subset is the one referenced when coding in FORTRAN. The standard FORTRAN character set consists of only 49 characters:

ASCII value	Character	ASCII value	Character	ASCII value	Character	ASCII value	Character
000	(null)	032	(space)	064	@	096	`
001	☺	033	!	065	A	097	a
002	●	034	''	066	B	098	b
003	♥	035	#	067	C	099	c
004	♦	036	$	068	D	100	d
005	♣	037	%	069	E	101	e
006	♠	038	&	070	F	102	f
007	(Beep)	039	'	071	G	103	g
008	■	040	(	072	H	104	h
009	(Tab)	041	)	073	I	105	i
010	(Line feed)	042	*	074	J	106	j
011	(Home)	043	+	075	K	107	k
012	(Form feed)	044	,	076	L	108	l
013	(Carriage return)	045	-	077	M	109	m
014	♫	046	.	078	N	110	n
015	☼	047	/	079	O	111	o
016	▶	048	0	080	P	112	p
017	◀	049	1	081	Q	113	q
018	↕	050	2	082	R	114	r
019	‼	051	3	083	S	115	s
020	π	052	4	084	T	116	t
021	§	053	5	085	U	117	u
022	▬	054	6	086	V	118	v
023	↨	055	7	087	W	119	w
024	↑	056	8	088	X	120	x
025	↓	057	9	089	Y	121	y
026	→	058	:	090	Z	122	z
027	←	059	;	091	[	123	{
028	(Cursor right)	060	<	092	\	124	¦
029	(Cursor left)	061	=	093	]	125	}
030	(Cursor up)	062	>	094	∧	126	~
031	(Cursor down)	063	?	095	—	127	⌂

26 uppercase letters of English alphabet
10 digits from 0 to 9
13 special characters:

=, +, −, *, /

(,), comma, ., $, ', :

blank

However, there is a tendency to extend the FORTRAN character set to include lowercase letters. Also, most implementations of FORTRAN will allow the use of any ASCII character in a character variable or Hollerith constant. Therefore, a printout for a Swedish user can contain the characters that are unique to the Swedish language.

The 7-bit code provides for 128 different characters (including 31 control characters); the other 128 characters in the full 256-character ASCII code are alphabetic characters unique to non-English languages (such as è, é, ä, and ü) graphics characters, and mathematical symbols (including Greek letters used in mathematics). The full table is given in this appendix with the commonly referenced subset other than control characters marked in color.

ASCII value	Character	ASCII value	Character	ASCII value	Character	ASCII value	Character
128	Ç	160	á	192	∟	224	α
129	ü	161	í	193	┴	225	β
130	é	162	ó	194	┬	226	Γ
131	â	163	ú	195	├	227	π
132	ä	164	ñ	196	─	228	Σ
133	à	165	Ñ	197	+	229	σ
134	å	166	ª	198	╞	230	μ
135	ç	167	º	199	╟	231	τ
136	ê	168	¿	200	╚	232	Φ
137	ë	169	⌐	201	╔	233	Θ
138	è	170	¬	202	╩	234	Ω
139	ï	171	½	203	╦	235	δ
140	î	172	¼	204	╠	236	∞
141	ì	173	¡	205	═	237	Ø
142	Ä	174	≪	206	╬	238	∈
143	Å	175	≫	207	╧	239	∩
144	É	176	░	208	╨	240	≡
145	æ	177	▒	209	╤	241	±
146	Æ	178	▓	210	╥	242	≥
147	ô	179	│	211	╙	243	≤
148	ö	180	┤	212	╘	244	⌠
149	ò	181	╡	213	╒	245	⌡
150	û	182	╢	214	╓	246	÷
151	ù	183	╖	215	╫	247	≈
152	ÿ	184	╕	216	╪	248	°
153	Ö	185	╣	217	┘	249	•
154	Ü	186	║	218	┌	250	·
155	¢	187	╗	219	█	251	√
156	£	188	╝	220	▄	252	ⁿ
157	¥	189	╜	221	▌	253	²
158	Pt	190	╛	222	▐	254	■
159	ƒ	191	┐	223	▀	255	(Blank 'FF')

Index

A edit descriptor, 142–149, 156–158
Access methods, 323–324
ACCESS specifier, 329–330
Accuracy, 97–99
Add to previous sum, 93
Address for direct access, 323, 328
Adjustable size array, 375–376
Alphabetic control identifier, 325–326
Alternate entry and return, 374–375
American National Standard (ANS), 2–3
American Standard Code for Information Interchange, 12, 420–421
AND operator, 78–80
Apostrophe edit descriptor, 153–154
Application program, 5
Arguments:
    function, 266
    subroutine, 271–273
Arithmetic:
    in FORTRAN, 37–39
    mixed-type, 67–70
    in subscript, 204–206
Arithmetic assignment statement, 37–39
Arithmetic IF statement, 88
Arrays, 201–202
    adjustable size, 375–376
    assumed size, 376
ASCII, 12, 420
Assembly system, 7
ASSIGN statement, 381
Assigned GOTO statement, 381
Assignment statement:
    arithmetic, 37–39
    character, 367
    logical, 74
Assumed size array, 376

BACKSPACE statement, 326–327
Batch execution, 13
Batch processing, 13, 17–20
Binary file, 322
Bit manipulation, 414–416
Bits, 6–7
Blank COMMON, 275–276
Blank spaces, 40–41
BLANK specifier, 329–330
Blanks, 146–147
Block, program, 48–49
BLOCK DATA subprogram, 276–277
Block IF statement, 74–83, 120
Block numbering, 85, 110
Blocks, program (see Modules)
BN and BZ edit descriptors, 370

Boundary value testing, 96–97
Bubble sort, 255

CALL statement, 271–273
Case structure, 279–281
CHAR intrinsic function, 367–368
Character data, 156–158
Character expressions, 366–368
Character intrinsic functions, 367–368
Character substring, 367–368
CHARACTER type declaration, 71–73
Characters in record, 321
CLOSE file statement, 93–94, 329–331
Codes, 12, 420–421
Collating sequence, 367–368
Colon (:) edit descriptor, 371
Combinatorial formula, 130
Comment line, 25, 48
COMMON:
    blank, 275–276
    named, 276–277
COMMON statement, 274–277
Comparison for equality, 78–79, 120
Compiler, 5–6, 26–27
Compiling and executing a program, 13, 26–27
Complex data, 364
COMPLEX type declaration, 364
Compound interest formulas, 132
Computed GOTO statement, 279–281
Concatenation, 366–367
Connectors in flowchart, 230
Constants, 28–32
    identification block, 49
    naming of, 49
Continuation line, 25
CONTINUE statement, 210–212
Control list:
    for direct access, 327–328
    for sequential access, 324–326
Control structure for multiple cases, 94–95, 118
Control variable in DO loop, 210–211, 217
Conversion between real and integer, 68–69
Correcting files, 16
Correlation coefficient equation, 253
Curve fitting formula, 317
Cylindrical tube, properties, 199

D edit descriptor, 370
Data error, 160
Data items in record, 321
DATA statement, 221–222
Data types, 70–74, 363–366

423

$DEBUG, 417
Debugging, 97, 164–165, 176–181
Delayed selection, 88
DELETE specifier, 331
Depreciation formulas, 315–316
DIMENSION statement, 204–206
    constant expression, 373
    upper and lower bounds, 204–205
    variable, 375–376
Direct-access files, 322–323, 327–329
DIRECT file specifier, 330, 332
Disk file, 323
Displacement of piston, 199
DO loop, 10–11
DO statement, 209–217
    in DATA statement, 221–222
    in input/output, 219–221
    style guidelines, 223
DO WHILE pattern, 10–11
DO WHILE statement, 415
Double precision, 98–99, 363–364
    type declaration, 363–364
Dummy arguments, 266–268

E edit descriptor, 142–149, 369, 371
E (exponent) form for constants, 30–32
Echo check, 55
Economic order quantity formula, 60, 130, 198
Efficiency in FORTRAN coding, 216–217
ELSE statement, 75–83
ELSEIF statement, 80–83
END control specifier, 159, 173–174, 325
END DO, 415
End of data, programming for, 159–160
End-of-file records, 322–327
END statement, 39–40
    in subprogram, 267–268, 273
ENDFILE statement, 326–327
ENDIF statement, 76–83
Entering program, 12, 24–26
ENTRY statement, 374–375
Equality comparison, 78–79, 120
EQUIVALENCE declaration, 278
EQV operator, 373
ERR control specifier, 160, 173–174, 325–328
Executing program, 13, 26–27
EXIST specifier, 332
Explicit method of declaring character variables, 156–157
Explicit-type declaration, 70–74
Exponent notation, 30–31
Exponential smoothing formula, 316
Exponents, allowable types, 70
Expressions:
    arithmetic, 37–39
    character, 366–368
    logical, 76–80
    in output list, 164
EXTERNAL statement, 377
External subprograms, 263–265

F edit descriptor, 142–149
FALSE, 73–74, 88
Field, 322
Field size for output, 142–145, 157
File, 6
    in FORTRAN, 321–333
File-positioning statements, 326–327
FILE specifier, 330, 332
First-time-through logic, 92–93, 121, 128
Flowchart, 22–24, 54–55
Flowcharting:
    DO loop, 212
    files and interactive input/output, 352, 354
FMT control specifier, 325, 328
Forecasting formulas, 316
FORM specifier, 330, 332
Format-directed input/output, 137–166
FORMAT for internal files, 378
FORMAT specifications:
    A edit descriptor, 158
    edit descriptors, 142–149, 369–372
    in input/output statement, 371–372
    repetition, 149–150
    reuse, 161–163
FORMAT statement, 141–155
FORMATTED specifier, 330, 332
FORTRAN:
    development of, 2–3
    how to study, 3–4
    Microsoft, 3
    versions, 2–3
Function subprogram, 265–270
Functional modules, 9–10

G edit descriptor, 369
Gamma function equation, 253
GOTO:
    assigned GOTO, 381
    computed GOTO, 278–281
    GOTO statement, 85
    pseudocode for, 112
    style of use, 111–112, 128

H edit descriptor, 154
Hardware, 4–5
Headings on output, 152–154
Heat flow in insulated pipe, 198–199
Hexadecimal, 417
High-level language, 7
Hollerith data, 152–154
    (See also Character data)
Hollerith format specifications, 152–154
Horizontal positioning of output, 150, 181–182, 371

I edit descriptor, 142–149, 369
ICHAR function, 367–368
IF block, 74–83, 120

IF loop, 90–92, 128
IF statement:
   arithmetic, 88
   block, 74–83
   logical, 86–88
   nested block, 80–83
IF. . . ELSE coding pattern, 74–83
Immediate processing, 13
IMPLICIT declaration, 365
Implied DO loop:
   in DATA statement, 221–222
   in input/output, 219–221
INCLUDE, 415, 417
$INCLUDE, 417
INDEX function, 367–368
Initialization block, 49
Initialization for first time through, 93
Initialization module, 9
Input, format editing, 146–148
Input data validation, 89, 121, 128
INQUIRE statement, 330, 332
Integer division, 67–68
Integer-type data, 29, 67–72
INTEGER type declaration, 71–72
Interactive input, 128
Interactive processing, 12–13
Interblock gap, 323
Internal files, 378–380
International Standards Organization (ISO), 2
Intrinsic functions, 65–66, 367–368, 416, 418,
     inside front cover
   for type conversion, 68–69
INTRINSIC statement, 377
IOSTAT control specifier, 325–328, 355
ISO (International Standards Organization), 2
Iterations in DO loop, 210–211, 217

Job control instructions, 14, 26–27

KEEP specifier, 331
Keyboard entry of program, 24–26
Keyboard input, 36–37

L edit descriptor, 369
Language:
   high-level, 7
   machine-level, 6–7
Last-time-through logic, 92–93
Layouts, input and output, 172–174
Learning curve formula, 132
LEN function, 367
Lexical functions, 368
Library subprograms, 264–265
Line numbers, 47–48
List-directed input and output, 33–36
List-directed WRITE statement, 34–37, 138–141

Log-on, 14
Logical assignment statement, 74

Logical data, 73–74
Logical equivalence, 373
Logical expressions, 76–80
Logical IF statement, 86–88
Logical operators, 78–80, 373
Logical structures in program, 10–12
LOGICAL type declaration, 73–74
Logical variables, 73–74
Loop (see Repetition structure)
Low-level language, 7
Lower bound in subscript, 205–206
Lowercase in FORTRAN, 12, 49–50

M77, 412
Machine-level language, 6–7
Magnetic tape, 323
Matrices, 201–202
Merge sorting, 357–358
Metacommands, 416–417
Microcomputer, 3, 5, 416–418
Microsoft FORTRAN, 3, 416
Missing data, 150–152
Mixed-type arithmetic, 67–70
MNF, 412
Modular design, 9–10
Modules, program, 9–10
Moving average formula, 316
MS-DOS, 416
Multiple cases, programming for, 94–95

Named COMMON, 276–277
NAMED specifier, 332
NEQV operator, 373
Nesting, 11, 80–83, 212
NEW file specifier, 330
Newton-Raphson technique, 315
NEXTREC specifier, 332
1966 Standard FORTRAN, 413–414
NOT operator, 78–80
NULL specifier, 330, 332
NUMBER specifier, 332

Object program, 7, 26–27
OLD file specifier, 330
OPEN file statement, 329–330
OPEN statement, 93–94, 131
OPENED specifier, 332
Operating system, 6, 14, 26–27
Operations symbols, 38
Operators:
   arithmetic, 38
   concatenation, 366–367
   logical, 78–80, 373
   relational, 76–77
Order of statements, 382
Output, format editing, 143–146
Overflow, 143

P edit descriptor, 370, 391
PARAMETER statement, 373
Parameters in DO loop, 210–211
Parenthesis rule, 38–39
Pascal's triangle, 253
PAUSE statement, 380–381
PDL (program design language), 21–22, 51–54
Pendulum period formula, 132
Personal computer, 3, 5, 416–418
Physical blocks, 323
Physical records, 160–163
Planning program, 20–23
Planning program logic, 51–55, 92–93, 114, 118–119
Plus sign (+) in format, 181–182
Portability of program, 7, 9
Positional editing, 150, 371
Precedence:
    of arithmetic operators, 38–39
    of logical operators, 78, 373
Precision, 97–99, 128
Prime numbers, 256
PRINT statement:
    format-directed, 138–141
    list-directed, 34–37
Probability equations, 246, 317
Professional FORTRAN, 416
Program, 5
Program design language (PDL), 21–22, 51–54
Program identification block, 49
Program library, 384
Program modules, 21
Program planning, 20–23
PROGRAM statement, 374
Program switch, 88
Programming, structured, 10–12
Programming discipline, 8–12
Programming style, 48–50, 58, 80–81, 85, 99–101, 165–166, 223
Projectile formula, 131
Prompt character, 17
Prompting of interactive input, 36–37
Pseudocode, 21, 51–54
Pseudorandom numbers, 314–315, 343–351, 356–357

Quality assurance, 95–97
Quality control program, 164–165

Random access (see Direct-access files)
Random number generation, 314–315, 343–352, 356–357
READ internal files, 378–380
READ statement:
    format-directed, 138–141
    list-directed, 33–34
    unformatted, 322
Real-type data, 29, 67–72

REAL type declaration, 71–72
REC specifier, 328
RECL specifier, 330
Record, 160–161, 321–322
Record number for direct access, 323
Records, 138
Relational expressions, 76–77
Relational operators, 76–77
Repetition structure, 10–11, 90–92, 209–210
RETURN statement, 267–268, 273, 375
REWIND statement, 326–327
Rounding, 163–164, 182, 299
Routine, 5

S edit descriptor, 371
SAVE statement, 374
Scale factor, 370, 391
SCRATCH specifier, 330
Selection structure, 10–11, 75–76
Sequence structure, 10
Sequential file access, 323–324
SEQUENTIAL file specifier, 330
Signs in format editing, 142–143, 160–161, 181–182, 371
Simpson's rule, 245
Sine function formula, 129
Slash (/) in format, 160–161
Software, 4–5
Sorting:
    bubble method, 255
    merge, 357–358
Source code management, 384–386
Source program, 7, 26–27
SP edit descriptor, 371
Special characters, 30
SS edit descriptor, 371
Standard deviation formula, 129
Standard FORTRAN of 1966, 413–414
Statement function, 382
Statement label (number), 47–48, 83–85
Statistical routines, 264–265
STATUS specifier, 330
Stirling's formula (factorial), 130, 318
STOP statement, 39–40
Storage, 5
Structure, planning of, 20–21
Structured programming, 10–12
Style in programming, 48–50, 58, 80–81, 85, 99–101, 120, 165–166, 223
Subprogram names as arguments, 376–377
Subprograms, 262–270, 374–377
Subroutines, 270–273, 374–377
Subscripted variables, 201–207
Subscripts, 203–206
Subset FORTRAN, differences in, 414
Substring, 367–368
Supercomputers, 3, 384
Symbolic assembly language, 7
Symbolic variable names, 30, 55

T edit descriptor, 150, 371
Terminal input, 36–37
Terminal statement in DO loop, 210, 217
Termination of input data, 111–112, 127
Test data, 96
Testing, 164–165, 176–181
Testing of programs, 95–97
Text editor, 13–16
TL and TR edit descriptors, 371
Trigonometric functions, 66–67
TRUE, 73–74, 88
Truncation in integer processing, 68–70
Type conversion, 68–69
Type declaration, 70–74, 363–366
  and storage allocation block, 72, 112–113
Type statement, 70–74

Unformatted input/output, 322
UNFORMATTED specifier, 330
Unit designation, 138–141, 325, 328, 330
UNIT specifier, 328, 330–331
UNKNOWN specifier, 332
Upper bound in subscript, 205–206
Uppercase in FORTRAN, 12, 49–58

Validation of input data, 55, 89, 121, 128
Variable, 28
  logical, 73–74

Variable dimensions, 375–376
Variable identification block, 48–49
Variables:
  character, 156–157
  naming of, 29–30
  subscripted, 201–207
Variance formula, 314
VDU input, 36–37
Vertical spacing control, 154–155, 181–182
Visual validation, 55

Waterloo, University of (Ontario, Canada), 3, 412
WATFOR/WATFIV/WATFIV-S, 412
Wind-chill chart, 318
Word processing, 15
WRITE internal files, 378–380
WRITE statement:
  format-directed, 138–141
  list-directed, 138–141, 34–37
  unformatted, 322

X edit specifier, 150

Zero from blanks on input, 330, 332
ZERO specifier, 330, 332

427

List of 1977 American National Standard FORTRAN Statements and Specifications

Symbols Used in List of Statements

Shaded	Not included in 1977 Subset of standard FORTRAN	s	Statement label
A	Name of an array	st	Statement
d	Places to right of decimal in FORMAT	u	Unit designator (integer constant or variable) for I/O statement
e	Expression		
f	Subprogram name or statement function name	v	Variable name (either real or integer)
fs	FORMAT statement label	vk	Variable or constant (either real or integer)
i	Integer variable	vek	Variable or expression or constant (either real or integer)
ie	Integer variable or integer expression		
ik	Integer variable or integer constant	w	Field width in FORMAT statement
iek	Integer variable, integer expression, or integer constant	x	Dummy arguments in subprogram declaration
k	Constant of any type	[ ]	Optional item in statement
n	An integer number of five or less digits or a character constant		

Executable Statements

Reference in text	Description of statement	Form	Example
	ASSIGNMENT		
	Assignment operators	$v = e$	
	operators		
	+ addition		
	− subtraction or negation		
	* multiplication		
	/ division		
	** exponentiation		
	// concatenation		
	where e =		
37–39, 67–70	arithmetic expression		X = 5.0 + Y*Z**2
367	character string		NME = 'NAME'
367–368	character substring		STRNG = SUB1 // SUB2
73–74	logical variable		SWITCH = .TRUE.
381	Assignment of statement label	ASSIGN s TO i	ASSIGN 210 TO ILABEL
	TRANSFER OF CONTROL		
85	Unconditional GOTO	GOTO s (or GO TO s)	GOTO 910
278–281	Computed GOTO	GOTO $(s_1,s_2, \ldots ,s_n)$[,]i	GOTO(210, 260, 320) , INDX
		GOTO $(s_1,s_2, \ldots ,s_n)$ [,]ie	GOTO(210, 260, 320), I + (3 * J)
381	Assigned GOTO	GOTO i$(s_1,s_2, \ldots ,s_n)$	GOTO ILABEL(320, 415, 210)
88	Arithmetic IF	IF (e) s_1, s_2, s_3 (s_1 if e is negative, s_2 if zero, s_3 if positive)	IF(SIN(X) + 0.3) 250, 350, 210
86–88	Logical IF	IF (e) st where e is a relational expression or logical expression	IF (A .EQ. 0.0) B = B + 1.0
76–77		Relational operators:	IF (SWITCH) STOP
		.LT. Less than	
		.LE. Less than or equal to	
		.EQ. Equal to	IF(X .GT. Y) GOTO 350
		.NE. Not equal to	IF(X .LE. Y) Z = Z + 1.0
		.GT. Greater than	
		.GE. Greater than or equal to	
78–80		Logical operators:	
		.NOT. Logical negation	
		.AND. Logical conjunction	
		.OR. Logical inclusive disjunction	IF(X.GT.Y.AND.Y.LT.17.0) GOTO 260
		.EQV. Logical equivalence	
		.NEQV. Logical nonequivalence	
373		IF (e) THEN	IF (IVAR .GE. JVAR)THEN
		statement block	J2 = J2 + 1
			K2 = J2**2
74–83	Block IF	ELSE	ELSE
		statement block	KIX = JIX / 2
		ENDIF (or END IF)	ENDIF

Page	Description	Syntax	Example

80–83	Nested block IF		IF (IVAR .GE. JVAR)THEN
			  J2 = J + 1
			  KJ = J2**2
			ELSE
			  KIX = JIX / 2
			  IF (KIX .EQ. 0)THEN
			    PRINT *, KJ
			  ELSE
			    PRINT *, J2
			  ENDIF
			ENDIF

80–83	Nested IF tests	ELSEIF (e) THEN
		(or ELSE IF)
			IF (X .LT. 3.5)THEN
			  KTR = KTR + 1
			  Y = SIN(B)
			ELSEIF (X .GT. 4.7)THEN
			  NTR = NTR + 1
			  Y = COS(B)
			ELSE
			  Y = TAN(B)
			ENDIF

39–40	Stop with no restart	STOP[n]	STOP or STOP 3 or STOP 'ERROR'
380–381	Pause with restart	PAUSE [n]	PAUSE or PAUSE 2
39–40, 267–268	End of program unit	END	END

LOOP

Page	Description	Syntax	Example
209–217	Establishing loop parameters, subset full	DO s[,]i = ik_1, ik_2, [ik_3] DO s[,]v_1 = vek_1, vek_2, [vek_3]	DO 210 I = 1, N3 DO 210 X = .01, 3.0*Y, .05
210–212	Define end of DO loop	s CONTINUE	210 CONTINUE

INPUT AND OUTPUT

Page	Description	Syntax	Example
33–34	Read, list-directed and predefined unit	READ*[,list]	READ *, X, I
140–141	Read, list-directed	READ (u,*)[list]	READ (5, *)X, I
138–141	Read, format-directed	READ (u,fs)[list]	READ (5, 160)X, E
139–140	Read format-directed and predefined unit	READ fs[,list]	READ 160, X, I
159–160, 324–328	Read, with control list specifiers For full list, see Chapter 6	READ (u,fs, control specifiers)[list] Examples are END = s and ERR = s	READ (5, 160, END = 510, ERR = 920)
322	Read, unformatted (from files on external storage)	READ(u)[list]	READ (10)X, I
34–37	Write, list-directed and predefined unit	PRINT*[,list]	PRINT *, X, I, 'TOTAL'
140–141	Write, list-directed	WRITE(u,*)[list]	WRITE (6, *) X, I, 'TOTAL'
138–141	Write, format-directed	WRITE (u,fs)[list]	WRITE (6, 210)X, X**2, 3, 14
139–140	Write, format-directed and predefined unit	PRINT fs[,list]	PRINT 210, X, I
324–328	Write, with control list specifiers For full list, see Chapter 6	WRITE (u,fs, control specifiers)[list]	WRITE (7, 210, REC = 12)X, I
164	List (for any WRITE) may include constants and expressions	WRITE (u,fs)vek_1, vek_2 . . . vek_n	WRITE (6, 210)X, X**2, 3, 14.4
322	Write, unformatted (to files on external storage)	WRITE (u)[list]	WRITE (10)X, I
93–94, 131, 326–331	Files on external (auxiliary) storage (see text for details)	REWIND, BACKSPACE, ENDFILE, OPEN, CLOSE, and INQUIRE	REWIND 7 ENDFILE 8

Format Specifications

Both subset and full FORTRAN

Reference in text	Specification symbol	Form	Specifies
142–149	F	Fw.d	Real data
142–148	E	Ew.d	Data in exponent form
142–148	I	Iw	Integer data
156–159	A	Aw	Character data, specified field width
156–159	A	A	Character data, field width based on data
150	X	wX	Skipping of field
160–161	/	///.../	Skip to next unit record, or skip over n − 1 unit records
154	H	nH ···	Hollerith character (n = number of characters following H)
153–154	' '	'characters'	Hollerith
142–143	L	Lw	Logical data
370	B	BN	Blanks on input ignored
370	B	BZ	Blanks are input as zero
370	P	nP	Scaling (nP precedes F, E, D, or G specification)

Full FORTRAN only

Reference in text	Specification symbol	Form	Specifies
369	E	Ew.dEe	Exponent of e digits
369	I	Iw.m	Integer data with at least m field length
369	G	Gw.d	Either E or F edit depending on data
369	G	Gw.dEe	Exponent of e digits
370	D	Dw.d	Double-precision data
150	T	Tc	Tabulate to column c
371	T	TLc	Tabulate backward c position from current position
371	T	TRc	Tabulate forward c positions from current position
371	S	S,SP,SS	SP = print +, SS = do not print +, S return to compiler option
371	: (colon)		Terminates FORMAT control if no more data items in list

Control Characters for Vertical Spacing (pages 181–182)

Character in position 1 of output	Vertical spacing before output
Blank	One line (single space)
0 (zero)	Two lines (double space)
1	To first line of next page
+	No advance

Nonexecutable Specifications or Declarations

Reference in text	Description of specifications or declaration	Form	Example
141–155	FORMAT of data record	fs FORMAT (specifications) (see specifications list)	210 FORMAT(F10.0, 2X, 'TOTAL')x
371–372	In input/output statement	'(specifications)'	WRITE(6,'(F10.0, I6, "NONE")')X, IX
221–222	Initialization of data	DATA $v_1,v_2,\ldots/c_1,c_2\ldots/$ $k * c$ represents k values of c Implied DO loop in DATA statement	DATA X, Y, Z, A / 1.0, 3.5, 2*0.0 / DATA (G(I), I = 1, 10) / 10 * 0.0 /
204–206	Dimension of maximum size of array	DIMENSION $A_1(k_1)$, $A_2(k_1,k_2)$, $A_3(k_1,k_2,k_3)$, $\ldots$ Limited to three dimensions in Subset and seven in full FORTRAN	DIMENSION A(100), B(5, 15, 3)
204–205	Upper and lower bound for a dimension	DIMENSION $A(k:k_1)$, $A(k_1:k_1:k_2:k_2)$, $\ldots$	DIMENSION D(3:12)
373	Constant expression in dimension	DIMENSION $A(k \pm$ or $* *k)$	DIMENSION B(3+2, 5**2)
275–276	Define data names in blank common storage	COMMON [//] v_1,v_2, $A(k)$, $\ldots$ For $A(k)$ k is dimension	COMMON A, B, I or COMMON // A, B, I COMMON A(100), B, I
276–277	Define data names in named COMMON storage	COMMON / name / $v_1,v_2\ldots$	COMMON / ABLOCK / X, M, W
278	Define different variables to use same storage	EQUIVALENCE $(v_1,v_2,\ldots)$, $(v_3 v_4 \ldots)\ldots$	EQUIVALENCE (C, D), (I, N)
70–74, 363–366	Define type of data	type $v_1,v_2\ldots v_n$ v can be in form $A(k)$ INTEGER REAL COMPLEX LOGICAL DOUBLE PRECISION	INTEGER G, ZED, ALPHA (5,6) REAL IX, JON(50) COMPLEX C, DX(5) LOGICAL SWITCH DOUBLE PRECISION A, X, YR(10)
72–73	Define type and length of character variables	CHARACTER name*length, name*length CHARACTER[*length,]name, name$_2$,$\ldots$	CHARACTER BETA*5, GRW*7 CHARACTER *10, LNAME, ALPHA
365	Define first letter as type	IMPLICT type $(a_1,a_2,\ldots a_n)$ or $(a_m - a_n)$	IMPLICIT INTEGER (A, B, R – T)
373	Equate constant and name	PARAMETER (name = constant)	PARAMETER (FIVE = 5.0)
374	Main program (optional)	PROGRAM name	PROGRAM XAMPLE

Subprogram Specifications or Declarations

Reference in text	Description of specification or declaration	Form	Example
382	Statement function declaration	$f(x_1,x_2,\ldots,x_n) = e$	CALC (A, B) = A**2 + SIN(B) / 4.0
265–270	Function subprogram	[type] FUNCTION f($x_1,x_2, \ldots,x_n$)	FUNCTION EOQ(S, C1, C2, CP)
270–273	Subroutine without arguments	SUBROUTINE f	SUBROUTINE X
270–273	Subroutine with arguments	SUBROUTINE f($x_1,x_2, \ldots x_n$)	SUBROUTINE X(A, I, M)
374–375	Subroutine with alternate returns	SUBROUTINE f($x_1,x_2, \ldots,*, *, \ldots$)	SUBROUTINE XED(X, I, *, *, *)
375–376	Variable dimensions for dummy arrays in subprogram:		
376	Assumed size equal to calling program array	In subprogram DIMENSION $A_1(*)$, $A_2(k_1,*)$	DIMENSION ALPH(*), BETA(10,*)
375–376	Adjustable array equal to value of integer variable in calling list or in COMMON	In subprogram SUBROUTINE f($A_1,A_2,i \ldots$) DIMENSION $A_1(i)$, $A_2(i,i)$	SUBROUTINE BEST (D, KX, MB, L, IX) DIMENSION D(MB), KX(L, IX)
		In calling program CALL f($(A_1,A_2,i \ldots)$	CALL BEST (G, MX, 10, 5, 7)
276–277	Block data subprogram	BLOCK DATA [name]	BLOCK DATA A1
374–375	Optional entry point into subprogram	ENTRY f$[(x_1,x_2,\ldots,x_n)]$	ENTRY N1(X, ALPHA)
374	Save data from subprogram	SAVE or SAVE list	SAVE X, L, M
377	Define external function names to be used as arguments	EXTERNAL list of routine names	EXTERNAL MYFUN, YOURFN
377	Define intrinsic function names to be used as arguments	INTRINSIC list of intrinsic functions	INTRINSIC SIN, COS

Statements to Use Subprograms and to Return to Using Program

Reference in text	Description of statement	Form	Example
265–270	Transfer to function	Use function in statement	X = MYFNCT(Y, M) + 3.175
270–273	Transfer to subroutine, no argument	CALL subroutine	CALL DOIT
270–273	Transfer to subroutine with argument list	CALL subroutine (argument list)	CALL DONT(X, I, J)
374–375	Transfer to subroutine with alternate returns	CALL subroutine (argument list with *s for each alternate return statement number)	CALL STAT(A, Y, *210, *340)
267–268	Return to calling program	RETURN	RETURN
374–375	Alternate returns n = 1, 2,...,n	RETURN n	RETURN 2
374–375	Transfer to subroutine with alternate entry	CALL entry name (argument list)	CALL ALT3(GEORGE)